BUDGET RECIPES

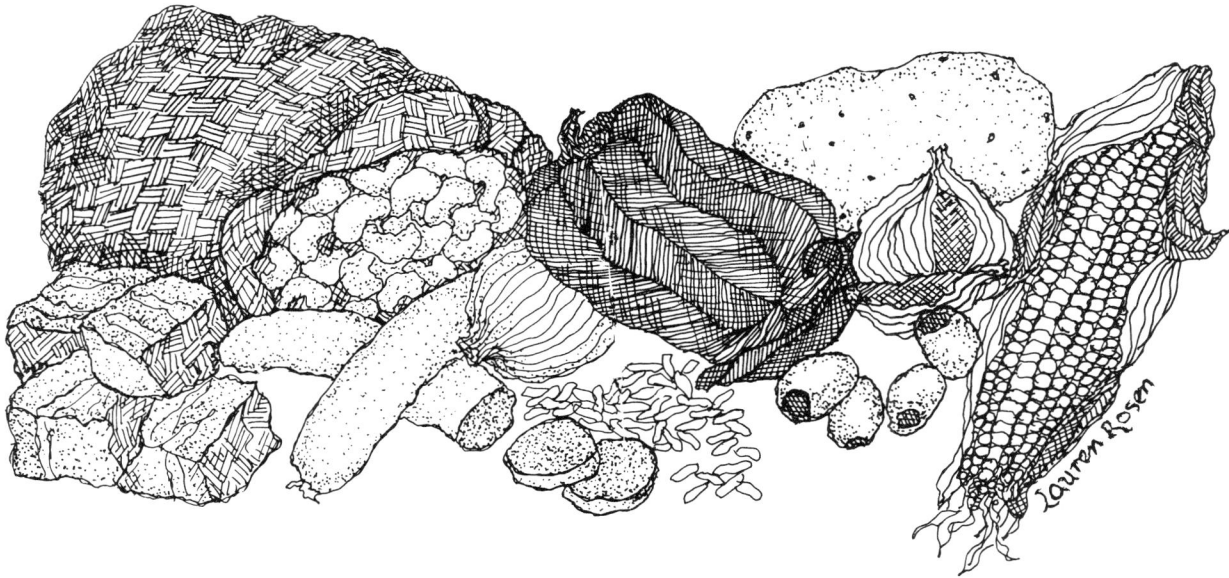

BUDGET RECIPES

Compiled and edited by

JACQUELINE HERITEAU

WINCHESTER PRESS

Cover photograph by Betty and Bill Pell.
Cover dishes are a delicious gourmet casserole made with
chicken, *Blanquette of Chicken* and *Mock Ambrosia*.

Recipes reprinted by permission of Hawthorn Books, Inc.
from *How to Grow It and Cook It* by Jacqueline Heriteau,
copyright © 1970 by Jacqueline Heriteau; and from
Oriental Cooking the Fast Wok Way by Jacqueline Heriteau,
copyright © 1971 by Jacqueline Heriteau.
All rights reserved.

Library of Congress Cataloging in Publication Data

Heriteau, Jacqueline.
    Budget recipes.

    Includes index.
    1. Cookery. I. Title
TX652.H44   641.5′52   76-5498
ISBN 0-87691-220-X

Book design by M. F. Gazze Nimeck

Published by Winchester Press
205 East 42nd Street, New York 10017

Printed in the United States of America

Contents

Introduction

Good Eating and Sound Nutrition—On a Budget   1

SECTION ONE · MEAT, FOWL, AND FISH

Beef and Ground Beef	17
Veal, Lamb, and Mutton	30
Pork	39
Poultry	46
Variety Meats	60
Fish	69

SECTION TWO · VEGETABLES, SALADS, AND DRESSINGS

Vegetables	83
Vegetable Recipes That Make One-Dish Dinners	92
Dressings, Salads	100

SECTION THREE · BEANS, RICE, AND PASTAS

Dried Beans and Vegetables	115
Rice and Cornmeal	120
Pasta	124

SECTION FOUR · SOUPS, EGGS, CHEESE, SANDWICHES, AND SNACKS

Soups and Soup Dinners	133
Omelets, Soufflés, and Egg Dishes	140
Cheese Dishes, Sandwiches, and Snacks	149

SECTION FIVE · BAKED GOODS

Breads and Quick Breads   159
Cakes and Pies   172

SECTION SIX · BUDGET DESSERTS

Chilled Desserts, Sauces, and Fruits   181
Yogurt, Puddings, and Cooked Desserts   187

SECTION SEVEN · PARTY COOKING

Party Appetizers, Exotic Main Dishes, Desserts   195
Drinks, Hot and Cold   216

Index   223

Acknowledgments

It would be remiss to go to print with this book without acknowledging Charlotte Adams' contribution to it. Charlotte, one of America's best-known authors on cooking topics, created the budget concept carried out here, and supervised and edited the original presentation of most of the recipes included. My thanks to my publishers, Hawthorn Books, Inc., and Grosset & Dunlap, for permission to use here recipes from my books, *The How To Grow and Cook It Book of Vegetables, Herbs, Fruits, and Nuts* (Hawthorn), the *Take-It-Along Cookbook* (Hawthorn), and *The Best of Electric Crock Cooking* (Grosset & Dunlap).

Introduction: How To Save Money On Food

The best and happiest way to save money on the food budget is to become a great cook. A great cook is the person who can take any—well, almost any—cut of meat and turn it into something to dream by. Great cooks aren't born great—they're self-made. Notice the flavors of foods when you eat out, especially in good restaurants. Taste—and improve—the flavors of foods as you cook them. Trust your instincts rather than the recipes you cook by. They are the roadmaps to a good end product. The person who makes it perfect is the person who interprets the recipes.

Whatever foods your budget can afford, there are great dishes to be made from those ingredients. Baked beans isn't the same as fresh asparagus, but in its own way a dish of baked beans is just as good, and served on the right occasion, even more welcome. The recipes here are meant to work wonders with simple ingredients. Add your thought, your care, your own particular taste to them, and you'll serve meals everyone will be glad to come home to.

BUDGET RECIPES

Good Eating and
Sound Nutrition—On a Budget

To eat well on little is the purpose of many homemakers today, when soaring food costs blow the budget every few months. You can do it, but you should not be willing to cut the budget at the cost of sound nutrition. Budget trimming begins with an understanding of sound nutrition. It isn't how much you eat that trims the budget, but how you eat. And it isn't how much the food costs that makes a sound diet, but rather what's in it. Knowledge is the key to sound eating—and to a system for marketing that will keep food costs in bounds.

Without becoming a nutritionist you can improve your knowledge of the nutritional contents of the meals you serve by studying product labels.

Understanding Food Labels

The Food and Drug Administration's new regulations on food labeling help you to make wise food selections. The information on the labels at the very least makes you aware of some of the nutrients necessary for good health. If the food producers wish to have nutrition information on the label, they must list values for protein, two minerals, and five vitamins. Amounts of twelve additional vitamins and minerals, type of fat (polyunsaturated or saturated), and amount of cholesterol and sodium content may be given but is not required. (The information on type of fat and cholesterol and sodium content would be useful mainly for people who are modifying their diet on the advice of a physician, and would not help the average consumer in making food choices.)

In order to benefit from the nutrition information on the labels you must first have an understanding of some basic nutrition facts.

All foods are combinations of nutrients. They contain protein, carbohydrate, fat, vitamins, minerals, and water. Foods have energy value (calories). Each person needs different amounts of these nutrients depending on age, size, sex, and amount of daily activity (see Chart I below). An office worker needs less of certain nutrients than a construction worker. A man of 25 needs more of some nutrients than a man of 60. The Recommended Daily Allowances (RDA) are the amounts of nutrients judged to be adequate for maintaining good nutrition in healthy people. These take into account individual differences for various age and sex groups.

Calories Used in Daily Activity

CALORIES USED PER DAY FOR
EACH POUND OF WEIGHT

DAILY ACTIVITY	MEN	WOMEN
Studying	16	15
Editing	16	15
Typing	18	19
Playing a musical instrument	18	19
Bookkeeping	18	19
Selling	20	21
Painting	20	21
Serving table	20	21
Farming	23	25
Housecleaning	23	25
House painting	23	25
Moving furniture	36	36
Road building	36	36
Stone working	36	36

On the labels you will see nutrients listed as a percentage of the U.S. Recommended Daily Allowance. For most nutrients, these U.S. Recommended Daily Allowances are the highest RDA for any sex-age category. The allowances will be higher than is needed by many family members, especially the very young and old. Keep this in mind when you read the labels. It is not necessary for everyone to eat foods totaling 100 percent of the daily allowances.

On the labels you will also see the amount of calories in a serving of food. From this you can determine if a food is a high energy food—one that contains many calories per serving. You can also compare the amount of carbohydrate, fat, and protein in different

foods from the information on the label. These comparisons should be made between similar foods. For example, different types of cheeses should be compared rather than comparing cheese with green beans. On the basis of nutrient comparison, you might decide that Cheddar cheese is a better nutritional buy than cream cheese, since it contains more protein and less fat. However, to compare cheese and green beans would mean less. While they are both good foods, they are not both good sources of the same nutrients and so would not usually be substituted for one another. One food can be substituted for another if both contain the same nutrient.

The Basic Food Groups

Nutritionists speak about four basic food groups. You may remember the Basic Seven from your school days. The four food groups are a simplification of this idea. Foods are grouped together because they contain the same nutrients. Milk and milk products such as cheese and ice cream make up one group. They are good sources of protein, Vitamin A, riboflavin (a B vitamin), and the mineral, food calcium.

Another food group is meat, poultry, eggs, and dry legumes (peas and beans). They provide protein, Vitamin A, thiamin, riboflavin and niacin (B vitamins), and the mineral, iron.

The vegetable and fruit group is not a good source of protein but is a good source of Vitamin A and Vitamin C, and fair sources of B vitamins and the mineral iron.

The last group, bread and cereals, are good sources of protein but the protein is not the same kind as the protein in animal foods and legumes. Bread and cereal protein is not by itself enough to maintain good health and growth. If you eat some animal protein such as eggs or milk along with the bread and cereals, the value of their protein would be improved. Cereals are good sources of B vitamins and the minerals, calcium and iron.

Foods Grouped by Major Nutritional Content

FOODS HIGH IN PROTEINS

Milk
Skim milk
Buttermilk
Evaporated milk
Condensed milk
Cheese
Eggs
Liver
Kidney
Meats (all types)

Poultry
Fish
Soybeans
Nuts
Peanut butter
Beans (dried)
Lentils (dried)
Peas (dried)
Cereals
Whole grain flour

FOODS HIGH IN FATS

Chocolate
Ice cream
Cream
Whole milk
Sour cream
Butter
Margarine
Meat fats

Pork products
Liver
Egg yolks
Vegetable oil
Custard and pie fillings
Cheese
Fatty meats

FOODS HIGH IN CARBOHYDRATES

Sugar
Candy
Chocolate
Syrups
Jellies
Jams
Preserves
Honey
Flour
Spaghetti
Cereals

Breads
Rolls
Macaroni
Noodles
Cakes
Pies
Crackers
Rice
Cornstarch
Beans

Peas
Lentils
Fruits (all types)
Sodas

FOODS HIGH IN VITAMIN A

Yellow vegetables
Green vegetables
Sweet potatoes
Carrots
Corn
Broccoli
Spinach
Peas
Tomatoes

Whole milk
Yellow cheese
Butter
Margarine
Liver
Apricots
Peaches
Cantaloupe

FOODS HIGH IN VITAMIN C

Oranges
Lemons
Limes
Grapefruits
Strawberries
Pineapples
Tomatoes

Cabbage
Potatoes, white
Sweet potatoes
Green peppers
Red peppers
Leafy greens

People in North America get about 75 percent of their calories from these four essential food groups. These groups can be your guide in comparing the nutrient content of foods within the same group as you choose from each food group to make up your day's menus. However, if you were to choose a food simply for its protein content, for example, you might be making a poor choice. It is not always necessary or even desirable to choose the food with the most protein. There are occasions when a food lower in protein is the better choice because it is rich in another nutrient or lower in calories, or because you have served ample protein at other meals that day.

It is important to realize that you must not avoid certain foods because they appear to be low in certain nutrients or even have no values for nutrients on their labels. They may have small amounts of a nutrient, too small to be listed on the label, but these small amounts may add to the total of the day's intake and help to round out meals. There are some nutrients which are needed by the body in very small amounts. These nutrients are not all covered by labeling regulations, but are important for good health. Using a wide variety of foods in your meals will help to ensure good nutrition for your family by providing these nutrients as well as other substances that are not yet considered essential to health but may soon be.

A government publication "Nutritive Value of Foods HG-72" has the nutrient content for over 600 common foods and also the RDA for all age-sex categories. This can be a useful guide for you and is available free of charge from:

Office of Communication
U.S. Department of Agriculture
Washington, D.C. 20250

The Wednesday System
of Marketing

Wednesday is the day most of the super-markets place ads in local papers announcing their weekend specials. Sale prices are usually in effect through Saturday, and often represent big savings over the regular costs. If you shop the sales regularly, you can save from 15 to 25 percent on your yearly food bill. For a family of four, that might mean as much as $650 a year.

Here's how to work the Wednesday System. First, sit down with the Wednesday food ads, pencil, and paper, and a little time to think. You're going to plan a whole week's menus based on the sale prices you find in the paper. You don't have to work it out down to the last gumdrop—just make a general eating plan designed to take advantage of what's cheap and plentiful that week. If beef roasts are on sale, for example, buy a big one and plan to use the leftovers for at least one other meal. If you have a freezer, or even a freezing compartment in your refrigerator, you can buy and store larger quantities when a good sale comes along. Consistently practiced, this will push your yearly savings up even more.

As you make your menu plan, remember the transportation problem. A good rule of thumb is: never go more than 5 miles out of your way without figuring extra costs. It's silly, in other words, to drive 15 miles to get a 20¢ bargain because you'll end up spending more than you save. But if a sale saves you $10, it's probably worth the drive. Generally speaking, do your planning around the stores in your neighborhood, buying the best of what each one has on sale. It's wise to shop steadily at a few places, so the personnel there get to know you. Having a friend behind the meat counter can add up to savings, too. He'll advise you on the best buys.

When should you shop? Most people shop on Saturday. That means there's more stock and more variety in the stores on Saturday than just about any other time. It also means there are a lot more people in the stores. Saturday morning grocery shopping is only for the professional or the brave and patient amateur. It'll take you twice as long on Saturday, and you'll be elbowed twice as often. If you can take it, you might come up with unusual buys or products that are otherwise hard to get. If such gambles aren't worth the fight to you, shop Thursday or Friday at an off-hour like lunch or dinner time. If you work, look for stores with late hours and go in the evening to avoid the Saturday crunch.

Suppose you get to the store and they're all out of the turkeys that were advertised at such a fantastic price. In many areas, stores must give you either a rain check on the advertised item or a comparable product at a comparable price. If you ask them, most stores will do this for you even where they aren't compelled by law. When you don't see an advertised special, ask for it. If you're told the stock is gone, ask for a rain check. It's a bit of a bother, of course, but only a bit, and you help other consumers as well as yourself by getting the stores to live up to their promises.

In order to really know a fantastic sale price when you see one, you have to know what the regular price is. Sometimes this information is printed in the Wednesday ads, but more often it isn't. Some sales aren't sales at all, as in the case of a California chain that advertised canned tomatoes at three for $1 when the normal price was 33¢ a can. On the other hand, some sales are such good deals that you wonder how a store can make any money. In these instances, it probably won't. A grocer will often sell one or two items at a loss to himself, hoping to draw customers who will buy other products as well. These are the sales the Wednesday System user learns to spot.

Making Your Market List

The first step in making a market list is to plan the menu or menus for which you wish to buy food. Look up the recipes for each of the dishes you plan to cook and write down all the ingredients especially needed for their preparation. Next, check all the staple foods required (milk, flour, sugar, salt, etc.) to be certain that you have a good supply of each of them.

One way to get ahead on the staple supply is to have a pad (preferably hung on the kitchen wall) upon which you write down a list of staples which you find, as you cook, are running out. This gives you a start on the market list.

Now put together the list on your kitchen wall and the one you've made for the menu or menus you've planned. Here's how to do it to save yourself time and money.

Make a habit of writing your final shopping list as nearly as possible in divisions which fit the sections of your market. If you know your market well (which you should take time to do), this is quite easy.

You might divide your list into these sections:

Meat
Eggs, butter or margarine, milk, cheese
Fresh fruits and vegetables
Canned goods
Frozen products
Dried foods (rice, pastas, beans, etc.)
Cereals
Baked goods and baking mixes
Coffee and tea
Staples (flour, salt, sugar, oils, vinegar, baking powder, etc.)
Seasonings—including herbs and spices, condiments like catsup, chocolate, cocoa, etc.
Nonfood items (paper products, mops, brushes, scouring cloths and powders, etc.)

If you're not quite sure how much of certain foods you should buy, here is a list which will help you with some foods.

MEATS, POULTRY, AND FISH

Without bone (chopped beef, liver, sausage, veal cutlet, etc.) ⅓ to ½ pound per person
With moderate amount of bone (steak, roasts, chops) ½ to ¾ pound per person

With much bone (neck, breast spareribs, short ribs) 1 pound per person
Broiler-fryers ¼ to ½ bird per person
Roasters ¾ to 1 pound per person
Stewing chickens ½ pound per person
Duck 1 to 1¼ pounds per person
Turkey ¾ to 1 pound per person
Solid meat fish (salmon, halibut, etc.) ¼ to ⅓ pound per person
Fish with bones in (trout, mackerel, blue, etc.) ½ pound per person

DAIRY FOODS

Eggs 1 per person per day
Butter or margarine Buy a week's supply at a time—not more
Milk Children—1 quart a day
        Adults—1 pint a day
Cheese Buy ½ to 1 pound at a time, depending upon frequency of use

FRESH VEGETABLES

Leafy ⅓ to ½ pound per person
In shell (peas, limas) ½ pound per person
Stalk types (broccoli, asparagus) ⅓ to ½ pound per person
Root types (beets, carrots, turnips, potatoes) ¼ to ⅓ pound per person
Corn 1 to 3 ears per person
Eggplant (medium) Serves 3 to 4
Tomatoes ⅓ pound or 1 medium one per person

FRUITS

Quantities of fruit to buy are fairly obvious—half a grapefruit, cantaloupe, etc., per person, an apple or banana per person, etc. The amount to buy at one time varies greatly with eating habits, so the decision on quantity rests largely on knowledge of your family's likes and dislikes.

FROZEN VEGETABLES

One package serves 2 big appetites, 3 average, or 4 birdlike.

CANS	CUPS	SERVINGS
8-ounce	1	1 to 2
10-ounce	1¼	3
16 to 17-ounce	2	3 to 4
1 pound, 4-ounce	2½	4 to 5
1 pound, 13-ounce	3½	6 to 7

How Much Should Your Budget Be?

In 1975, government figures showed that the average share of disposable income (after deducting taxes) spent on food was about 17 percent. This figure may surprise you if you can remember back to the days when it was considered quite proper to spend as much as 33 percent of your disposable income on food. Of course, the better off a family is, the smaller the percentage of income spent on food, so one cannot say that any one percent is The Right One.

So, in starting to make your own food budget you might begin by taking 17 percent of your disposable income as the amount you will probably spend to feed the family. You can then continue to use that planned figure to contrast with the figure of what you actually spend.

After deciding on what you plan to spend you should keep track, in a notebook reserved for the purpose, of precisely what you *do* spend each week. You may continue this for a few weeks or you may prefer to have records for several months before you decide what exact budget you will settle on.

How does your record of what you've actually spent compare with what you planned to spend? Once you allow yourself to become conscious of the budget facts of life, your consciousness of what you spend, backed by your desire to spend less, will almost automatically start trimming the budget.

Remember that a food budget includes only *food* purchases. It does *not* include paper towels, plastic wrap, cleaning necessities, garbage bags, and many other things you probably buy in the same store. It does, however, include meals eaten away from home.

If you're serious about reducing the amount you spend on food, it is essential for you to do some comparative shopping. For instance, compare the costs of any one food in canned, fresh, frozen, or dried form. These costs vary a good deal, and you can save money by taking time in the market to compare them.

Compare "house" and national brands. Many supermarket chains offer their own private label foods. Lots of times they are far cheaper than their nationally advertised equivalents. You will, of course, have to try them out to be sure you and your family like them. Food wasted because nobody will eat it is no bargain!

The "large economy size" can be a real bargain *if* you can store it and *if* you can use the food fast enough so that it stays fresh. For example, a gallon container of milk may cost less than four one-quart containers.

By and large "convenience" foods are likely to cost more than if you made them from scratch in your own kitchen—and yours will probably taste better. On the other hand, remember that at certain times of year a convenience food like frozen peas may cost considerably less than the fresh equivalent. However, if you are very busy or work, the added cost of convenience goods may be worth the time you save.

Keep track of special sales. You can really save money this way. They are likely to occur on weekends and to be advertised in the newspapers or on flyers sent to you in the mail.

It's a good idea to listen to local radio programs which give you information on foods in plentiful supply at the moment. They are likely to be of peak quality and more reasonably priced than usual. If these are locally grown perishable foods, buy them in amounts which can be used up before they start to wilt and fade. Or, plan to freeze.

When you buy meat take into consideration the amount of lean meat, bone, gristle, and fat in the cut you choose. For example, ground beef and short ribs may cost the same amount per pound but the former will give twice as many servings as the latter. On the other hand, lamb neck and shoulder are likely to cost far less, despite the bone in proportion to the meat, than chops or a leg.

Though chicken and turkey have a large proportion of bone to meat they are often bargains compared to other meats. When you buy chicken remember that buying a chicken in parts costs more than buying a whole one. So we suggest that you learn to cut up a chicken yourself; a small household cleaver is a big help in such work.

"Variety" meats (liver, kidneys, sweetbreads, tongue, etc.) are likely to give high nutritional value for the money you spend on them. (See Variety Meats.)

Eggs, dried beans and peas, and peanut butter are all relatively inexpensive substitutes for meat. In buying eggs, remember that, by the dozen, large eggs cost more than small ones. By weight, this is not always the case, so sometimes the larger ones are a better buy.

Buy bread for its weight and food value rather than for the size of the loaf. Read the label to see whether the loaf contains whole grain, is enriched, and contains milk. That's the kind you want to buy.

Home-delivered milk usually costs more than milk bought at the store. Nonfat dry milk and evaporated milk cost less per quart when reconstituted than whole milk and supply comparable amounts of calcium and protein. A glass of whole fluid milk usually costs three times as much as a glass of reconstituted nonfat dry milk. Some manufacturers add Vitamin A to their dry milk. Check the label before buying. Whenever possible, choose the type of pack or the grade of a canned product which is appropriate to the way you're going to use it. For instance, canned tomatoes of lower market grade are perfectly good for stews or sauces.

Buy packaged cereals by weight, rather than by the size of the package. An ounce of cereal from an 18-ounce box, for instance, could cost about 2¢. The cost per ounce of the same brand bought in a pack of 1-ounce boxes would be about three times as much.

Learn to cook well. The most reasonably priced stew *can* be more of a treat than filet of beef *if* it is cooked and seasoned properly.

Last of all, when you're shopping, however carefully you've planned, if something you meant to buy is too expensive, *don't buy it.* Be flexible enough and knowledgeable enough to know what you can substitute for it without changing the nutritional values involved.

An excellent aid to food budgeting which offers you economy, low, medium, and liberal food plans is: *Family Food Budgeting for Good Meals and Nutrition,* Home and Garden Bulletin #94, for sale through the Superintendent of Documents, U.S. Government Printing Office, Washington, D.C. 20402.

Fruits and Vegetables for Freezing and Canning

Fruits and vegetables are available prepackaged and frozen, of course, but you must pay for the work done for you. Freezing your own freshly picked produce can save you money and ensure better quality, too. For super savings, start planning now to have a vegetable garden next spring. As for quality, nobody will ever confuse corn picked in your garden and frozen within the hour with store-bought frozen corn.

Group buying can make canning and freezing profitable if you don't have a garden. In the Northeast and some areas in the Southwest, cut-rate food markets operate just outside urban areas. Here food is sold by the crate, box, or bushel.

Some local farmers invite the public to pick their fruits and vegetables. Because you gather the produce yourself, it is the best possible buy for canning or freezing since it will be at its best as well as low in price. A trip during the harvesting season of your favorite fruits and vegetables usually yields as much canning and freezing material as you can use.

Choosing Vegetables for Canning and Freezing

When they are picked young, vegetables are at their best. The flavor in processed foods depends on processing shortly after picking. If you have had a garden, you can tell at a glance when vegetables are fresh. Crisp means fresh; peas, cucumbers, and tomatoes look plump when really fresh and have a sheen. Snap a bean; it will break easily if fresh. Fresh cucumbers, summer squash, and zucchini are shiny and have skins that break under pressure from a fingernail. Old tomatoes have soft spots and a faintly wrinkled look. Avoid tomatoes green on the underside.

Vegetables with leaves—carrots, beets, kale, spinach—are fresh when the leaves are crisp and the stems brittle. Small carrots and beets are best for processing.

Broccoli, Brussels sprouts, and cabbage are good when buds are curled tightly and held close by crisp stems.

Pumpkins and winter squash seem to hold their flavor and texture for many weeks after harvesting, so you needn't be as fussy about when they were picked.

Buy asparagus for processing from local growers as opposed to imported. Buy as soon as the prices begin to come down. The first harvests of spears seem to be the most tender. Choose medium-size spears with a good color and closed tips.

Prepare vegetables to be frozen as if you were going to cook them. Peel the items you would normally peel, slice or trim, and wash. Except for highly acid ones, such as tomatoes and peppers, blanch vegetables or parboil (see table below) for a few minutes to stop the conversion of natural sweetness to starchiness. Drain and chill in ice water. Pack prepared vegetables into plastic freezer containers, plastic bags, glass freezer jars, or aluminum foil. For vegetables frozen in sauce, you can buy boilable bags that go unopened from freezer to pan.

Many products come packaged in little aluminum trays or pans; these can be transferred into your freezer. First wrap them in freezer paper and seal with masking tape. Be sure to write the date of freezing on the tape.

Fruits, because they lose their shape and sweetness, should be blanched (see table) and packed either in sugar or a sugar-and-water solution (see table below). Frozen fruits could never be mistaken for fresh ones, but they are quite good in their own right and indistinguishable when cooked. A few individual berries can be frozen separately for garnish without sugar. Use about ⅔ cup dry sugar for each quart of fruit. If you plan to eat rather than cook your fruit, use the syrup pack—it preserves their appearance. To avoid discoloration of the fruit, stir in a small amount of pure ascorbic acid powder (Vitamin C) just before you pour the syrup over the fruit. You can make syrup with plain water or, if you have it, with fruit juice. To make a sugar syrup, add the sugar to just-boiling water, stir until the sugar is dissolved, then chill.

A 20 percent syrup is a light syrup, 30 percent medium, 40 percent medium-heavy, 50 percent heavy, 60 percent an extra-heavy syrup. As a rule of thumb, use the sweeter syrups for very acid fruits, or fruits that are rather tasteless. If calorie-counting concerns you, use the lightest syrup.

Meats, Poultry, and Fish for Freezing

The best meat bargains for freezing are generally found at wholesalers. (See the yellow pages of the telephone directory for wholesale

Sugar Syrups for Freezing Fruit

TYPE OF SYRUP	AMOUNT OF SUGAR	AMOUNT OF WATER	YIELD IN SYRUP
20 percent	1 cup	4 cups	5 cups
30 percent	2 cups	4 cups	5⅓ cups
40 percent	3 cups	4 cups	5½ cups
50 percent	4¾ cups	4 cups	6½ cups
60 percent	7 cups	4 cups	7¾ cups

Blanching Chart for Fruit

FRUITS	PREPARATION	TYPE OF PACK
Apples	Peel, core, slice. Put in solution to prevent darkening. Drain and blanch 2 minutes in boiling water or slice directly into chilled syrup.	40% Syrup
Apricots	Wash, cut in halves, pit.	40 or 50% Syrup
Berries, except Strawberries	Pick over, wash, drain well.	30 or 40% Syrup, or in dry sugar, or pack without sugar
Cherries, Sour	Wash, drain, and pit.	50 or 60% Syrup or dry sugar
Cherries, Sweet	Wash, drain, pit, or leave whole.	30 or 40% Syrup
Cranberries	Pick over, wash, drain.	50 or 60% Syrup, or in dry sugar, or pack without sugar
Figs	Wash, remove stems, leave whole, halve, or slice.	30 or 40% Syrup
Peaches Nectarines	Wash, peel, pit. Cut in sections or slices. Put in solution to prevent darkening.	30 or 40% Syrup, or dry sugar with ascorbic acid
Pineapple	Peel, remove core and eyes, slice or dice.	40 or 50% Syrup
Plums and Prunes	Wash, halve, and pit.	Dry sugar or 40 or 50% Syrup
Rhubarb	Wash, trim, cut in 1-inch pieces.	50 or 60% Syrup
Strawberries	Wash, hull, slice, or leave whole.	Dry sugar or 40 or 50% Syrup

Blanching Chart for Vegetables*

VEGETABLES	PREPARATION	BLANCH	TYPE OF PACK
Asparagus	Wash, cut in desired length.	2 to 4 Minutes	Without liquid
Beans, Lima	Shell, wash, sort.	2 to 3 Minutes	Without liquid
Beans, Green or Wax	Wash, cut in 1½ inch pieces, or leave whole.	3 to 4 Minutes	Without liquid
Broccoli	Cut off large leaves and tough stalks. Wash, split lengthwise, no thicker than 1 inch.	3 to 5 Minutes	Without liquid
Brussels Sprouts	Cut off old leaves, leave whole.	4 Minutes	Without liquid
Carrots	Wash, peel. Cut in slices or dice.	3 Minutes	Without liquid
Corn, Sweet, Whole Grain	Husk, silk, cut out bad spots. Wash. Blanch, cut from cob.	5 to 7 Minutes	Without liquid
Greens, All Kinds	Wash well. Discard old leaves and tough stems.	2 to 3 Minutes	Without liquid
Peas	Shell, sort, wash.	1 Minute	Without liquid
Peas, Blackeye	Shell, sort, wash.	2 Minutes	Without liquid
Peppers, Green	Wash. Cut in half or strips. Remove stem and seed.	—	Without liquid

* Other vegetables of similar size can be blanched for the same period of time.

dispensers of meat and fish.) Smaller cities may be without a wholesale meat district, but somewhere within a radius of 50 to 100 miles there will be a center that dispenses meat to the area. Once established with a wholesaler, you can buy for a group at prices that make freezing profitable. Wholesalers consider an order for $100 or more as a wholesale order, though you may buy moderate quantities of each of several types of meat and poultry.

Choosing Meats for Freezing

If you are buying from local markets offering steaks, chops, ground meat, and filets on sale, examine your bargains to be sure they are bargains. Meats packaged with cardboard on the bottom sometimes hide bones or lots of fat. If the sale is going to last several days, sample the quality of the meat at a dinner. Then if you are satisfied that it really is a bargain, buy in quantity. Meat must be repackaged for freezing as soon as you get it home, and freeze immediately.

Meat with a network of thin, fat lines across the grain is usually tender; these fatty veins melt when cooked. Meats without a marble may be firmer. (This is not true of filet of beef.) Avoid chops that have little tenderloins and a lot of gristle and fat at the tip.

Ground beef is on sale often and ground top or bottom round is valuable. Butchers add a quantity of fat to ground meat. If you are planning to use the meat for hamburgers or ground beef steaks, look for consistency of red in the meat; a lot of pink means a lot of fat.

Roasts, chickens, and turkeys offered at good prices are worth freezing. These are often frozen before they are offered, and sometimes butchers will sell them still frozen to consumers. When you are planning to freeze the meat on sale, ask if frozen meats are available before you buy the counter items. Always repackage frozen meats.

If you're lucky enough to have a hunter friend or relative, consider freezer space for their offerings and package these as you would meat purchased from the store.

The important things to remember when freezing raw meat and fish are: Wrap or package tightly; don't overhandle; freeze as fast as possible. Some suppliers will pre-package and quick-freeze meats for you, particularly if you buy a large quantity like a side of beef. There is usually a charge but it will save you time and you can be sure the job was properly done. Meat from the supermarket in clear plastic trays or wrappings can be frozen, but unpack and rewrap in heavy freezer paper.

Freeze meat in pieces as large as you can easily use. Roasts keep longer than chops, and chops longer than ground meat. You can cook meat with or without thawing, although it's sometimes hard to tell when a frozen piece is done. When you do thaw, thaw slowly in the refrigerator rather than at room temperature. If you're in a hurry, thaw the tightly wrapped package under cold running water.

Cooked meat can be frozen. Cut meat into serving-size cubes or thin slices and freeze quickly. Before freezing stew leftovers, remove potatoes or carrots and plan to cook fresh potatoes or carrots to serve with the thawed, heated stew.

Freezing Baked Goods

Breads, cakes, and especially pies, keep very well in the freezer. In most cases, freezing the unbaked dough works well too. This is especially true of "ice-box cookies" and pie crust. You can whip up a homemade pie almost instantly if you have an unbaked crust waiting in the freezer. When you freeze a whole pie, it usually turns out better if frozen unbaked. Since even a baked pie has to be thawed in the oven for half an hour, it's better to count on baking your pies just before serving.

Whether you bake your own bread or buy it, freezing can save you time, and often money. Lots of freezer space might allow you to make weekly or monthly trips to a day-old bread store to load up on products reduced in price but usually not in quality. Or you can freeze your own loaves (still warm from the oven for maximum freshness). Muffins, biscuits, and sweet rolls also freeze well. As with all frozen foods, baked goods should be wrapped or packed and sealed as tightly as possible.

Freezing Milk and Eggs

Fresh milk cannot be effectively kept in the freezer, and cheese keeps long enough for most uses without freezing. But butter and whipped cream can be bought on sale and frozen in quantity. Your own whipped topping, sweetened and flavored, will probably be just as convenient as ready-made ones. Remember to let whipped cream thaw a little before serving.

Whole eggs and egg yolks can be frozen if mixed with either sugar or salt. Freezing is practical if the eggs are used as part of a recipe—for example, in sauces or in cakes. Just allow for the sugar or salt when adding the thawed eggs. Egg whites freeze very well with no additions. Leftover egg whites freeze well, too.

Tips for Better Freezing

Be sure your freezer is cold enough. Food should be stored at 0 degrees Fahrenheit. ("Freezing" temperature for water is 32°.) Buy a freezer thermometer if you don't have one and check the temperature; if your freezer stays much colder than 0°, you can turn it down a bit and save on your electric bill. Keep the freezer itself in a cool place, away from sunshine.

Don't freeze too much at a time. Foods expand as they freeze and should not be tightly packed together when you first put them in the freezer. Heavily loaded freezers may freeze new packages slowly and throw flavor off a little. Most freezers should be loaded with about 2 to 3 pounds of food per cubic foot of capacity. Allow 24 hours between major additions to your freezer. Place new foods to be frozen on the freezer floor if that's where freezing coils are located—or, if you have one, in the flash-freeze compartment.

Prepare foods carefully. Most foods keep well if properly packaged. Almost no food can be taken out of the grocery bag and popped into the freezer. Improper wrapping can actually cost you money since you have to pay for the energy to keep the spoiled item cold, and ultimately you're forced to throw it away.

Use commonsense hygiene procedures when freezing food. Make sure your hands, cutting surfaces, and utensils are clean. Shop for quality. Choose only the best fruits, vegetables, and meats for your freezer. Low quality will only be emphasized by processing and storing. Discard damaged fruits and vegetables, and leave any suspicious-looking meats in the store. When you buy prefrozen foods, be sure they are solidly frozen, clean, and the packages are intact. Don't buy frozen foods from a dirty or disorganized freezer cabinet.

Keep cool in a crisis. If your freezer goes off, for whatever reason, there's a lot you can do to save your frozen foods. Keep the freezer door closed. If you leave it alone, a fully loaded, well-insulated freezer should keep everything frozen for about two days. That's enough time to take care of common household emergencies like a power failure. Thawed or partly thawed foods can be safely refrozen if they still have some ice crystals. Usually, any food that's safe to eat is safe to refreeze, but appearance and taste often suffer in thawed and refrozen foods. Adding "dry ice" (CO_2) to your freezer will keep foods frozen even longer, if power stays off longer than two days.

A Word About Canning, Preserving, and Jellying

These are not difficult procedures, particularly if undertaken in small batches. However, they are exacting procedures, in that proper processing is the only way to ensure no spoilage will occur during storage times. Canning, preserving, and jellying are sound economy measures. If you think you'd like to investigate this area of penny-saving, send for the Home and

Storage Time for Frozen Foods

FRUITS

Apples, baked	8
Apple juice concentrate	12
Cherries	12
Cranberry sauce	12
Grape juice concentrate	12
Orange juice concentrate	12
Peaches	12
Raspberries	12
Strawberries	12

VEGETABLES

Asparagus	8
Beans, baked	6
Beans, green	8
Cauliflower	8
Corn	8
Peas	8
Potatoes, french fried	2
Spinach	8
Sweet potatoes, cooked	6

MEATS

Beef, ground	3
Beef, roast	12
Beef, roast, cooked	6
Beef, steak	12
Lamb, ground	3
Lamb, leg	12
Pork, chops	4
Pork, cured	2
Pork, roasts	8

POULTRY

Chicken, cut up	9
Chicken, fried	4
Chicken, whole	12
Chicken livers	3
Turkey, cut up	6
Turkey, whole	12

FISH

Clams, shelled	3
Crabmeat	3 to 6
Fish, cooked	3
Fish filets	3 to 6
Salmon steaks	2
Shrimp	12
Striped bass, cleaned	3

BAKED GOODS

Bread, sweet	3 to 6
Bread, yeast	3 to 6
Baking powder biscuits	3
Cakes:	
Angel and sponge	1
Baked, general	4
Unbaked, general	2
Cookies, baked	6
Cookies, unbaked	6
Pastry	1 to 2
Pies, fruit, baked	2
Pies, fruit, unbaked	4 to 6

MAIN DISHES

Chicken or turkey dinners with gravy	12
Chicken or turkey pies	12
Creamed dishes	12
Fish dishes	3 to 5
Hash	6
Meat dinners	3
Meat loaf	6
Soups	6
Stews	6

MILK AND EGGS

Eggs, whole (with ½ tablespoon sugar or ½ teaspoon salt per cup)	9
Eggs, whites	9
Eggs, yolks (with 1 tablespoon sugar or ½ teaspoon salt per cup)	9
Butter, salted	6
Butter, sweet	12
Whipped cream, sweetened	3

SANDWICHES OR FILLINGS	2 weeks
DESSERTS, FROZEN	1

Garden Bulletin No. 8, Superintendent of Documents, U.S. Government Printing Office, Washington, D.C. 20402.

Pressure Cooking, Crockery Cooking, and Microwave Cooking

In recent years, several new pieces of cooking equipment, and some old ones, have become money-savers. The newish electric crockery cookers—called slow cookers—save electricity, and work wonders with the tougher cuts of meat. Pressure cookers, which are fast cookers, save cooking fuel costs, and do wonders with the cooking of fresh vegetables. Neither of these pieces of equipment is particularly costly.

Microwave ovens, which are fast cookers, are expensive—just as regular ovens are expensive. They save on fuel costs—will cook a big turkey in an hour—and are developing a following.

Each of these three pieces of equipment, with its particular ability to do particular foods to perfection at savings in energy costs, is worth considering if you are planning an all-out attack on the cost of food for your family.

SECTION ONE · MEAT,
FOWL, AND FISH

Beef and Ground Beef

Meat (we're distinguishing between fowl and meat) is a staple of the Western meal, and one of its most costly ingredients. Certainly, when costs at the supermarket counter are tallied up, meat for the week is apt to weight the cost scales heavily. You don't have to spend all that much money on meat unless you want to.

One way to cut meat costs is to offer smaller portions of meat. You may have a meat-and-potatoes family—if you do, you'll find it hard to wean them away from servings of half a pound of meat per person. But you should try. For one thing, meats are heavy in calories, unless you are dealing in very lean meats, and these often are expensive. Also, if you fill up less on meat, the more room you'll have for soup, for hearty salads, for lots of vegetables—and variety in a meal brings to it a liberal helping of the many different kinds of nutrients the body needs. Meals made up exclusively of meat and potatoes aren't as nourishing as meals made up of lots of smaller servings of different types of foods.

Another way to cut costs and bring variety to meals is to combine meat with stretchers. The Chinese do this magnificently, and I've included some Oriental dishes of this sort throughout the chapters. Stretchers aren't always or necessarily soybean products or bread crumbs. Celery and potatoes are good stretchers. So are eggs used in an omelet as wrappers for meat leftovers. Meat salads combine bits of meat and stretchers, but the stretchers in this case are greens and vegetables.

Yet another way to trim the meat budget is to learn to cook lesser cuts and variety meats, such as kidneys, brains, and hearts.

Beef

Of all cooked meats, beef is the most popular; it lends itself best to leftover dishes.

How far can you stretch a roast? It depends on the size of the roast, the size of the family, and how much that family likes to eat. Usually a boneless, 3-pound roast will serve 3 people for 3 days. This allows about 5 ounces of meat per person per day, an adequate but not generous standard. More of the roast will be eaten on the first day, when it is served in all its glory, less on subsequent "stretched" days. The meat might turn up the second day in a main dish like roast beef crêpes and the third day as a substantial side dish like beef fried rice.

If you have a chance for a bargain on a good roast, even if your family is small, go ahead and buy it. Cooked meat will keep at least 4 days and there are enough ways to change it so nobody will get tired of it. If your roast turns out to be tough, it must be shredded or ground to make it tender enough for most dishes. Roast Beef Hash is probably better made with tougher meats, since hashing is an insulting thing to do to really fine roast beef.

A word about cooking the roast. If you have a cut that seems first-rate, the best way to cook it is to brown it quickly in the oven, reduce the heat, and cook about 20 minutes per pound. To brown, preheat the oven to 450°. Place the roast on a rack above a shallow roasting pan and brown about 20 minutes. Then reduce the heat to 375° and continue cooking. If you get a cut that can only be pot roasted, the meat can still be used in our recipes, though it won't be as juicy as rare roast beef. However you cook meat, it's always a good idea to work with a meat thermometer.

Consider the Lesser Beef Cuts

There are lots of wonderful dishes to be made with the less glamorous beef cuts—and the recipes in this book will give you a beginning way of using them. If the cuts called for in the recipes don't appear often on your supermarket shelves, substitute. The table of beef cuts on page 19 will give you a notion of which cuts might be used interchangeably in recipes.

Beef Recipes

CARBONADE FLAMANDE

Beef cooked in beer, a Flemish staple. To make the herb bouquet for this dish, tie a few sprigs each of parsley and thyme, or ½ teaspoon dried thyme with a bay leaf, into a small cheesecloth bag.

2 pounds rump of beef, cut into ½-inch cubes
¼ cup vegetable oil
2 pounds yellow onions, sliced
Salt and pepper
3 medium cloves garlic, crushed
3 large carrots, cut into rounds
⅔ cup beef stock
1 12-ounce bottle (or can) beer
1 tablespoon brown sugar
1 herb bouquet
2 tablespoons cornstarch
2 tablespoons vinegar

In a Dutch oven, brown beef cubes fast on all sides in the oil. Remove meat as it browns. Put in onions, adding more oil if necessary. Reduce heat and brown lightly (about 10 minutes), stirring occasionally. Season with salt and pepper and stir in garlic. Remove onions from the Dutch oven. Put in half of the beef, season with salt and pepper, and cover with half of the onions and carrots. Add remaining beef cubes and cover with remaining onions and carrots. Pour stock over. Add beer. Stir in brown sugar. Poke the herb bouquet down into the beef slices. Cover the pot and simmer 2½ hours, or until meat is very tender. Mix cornstarch with vinegar. Pour liquid from Dutch oven into a skillet, discard herb bouquet, and remove fat. Stir in cornstarch mixture and simmer 5 minutes, stirring. Correct seasoning and pour gravy back over meat. *Serves 6.*

BOILED BEEF WITH SAUERKRAUT

This is a good recipe for short ribs, flanken, shin beef, plate beef, brisket (not corned beef), or any cut designated as braised beef.

3 pounds braising beef, bone in
1 16-ounce can sauerkraut
1 28-ounce can peeled tomatoes (reserve juice)
1 tablespoon sugar
1 teaspoon salt
⅛ teaspoon pepper

Put meat, sauerkraut with its liquid, tomatoes, and sugar into a large kettle. Bring to a boil over medium heat and reduce to a slow

Basic Beef Cuts

DESCRIPTION	COOKING METHOD
Beef Chuck	Braise or broil
Cross-Rib Pot Roast (Boston or English cut; thick rib roast; bread and butter cut)	Braise
Short Ribs (barbecue, English short, braising, kosher, or flanken short ribs)	Braise
Beef Chuck, Blade Portion	Braise or broil
Blade Roasts (top or under)	Braise
Blade Roasts (7-bone pot roast)	Braise
Beef Chuck Eye Roast (boneless chuck roll or filet, inside chuck roll)	Braise
Mock Tenderloin (chuck eye, filet, or tender; Scotch or Jewish tender; medallion pot roast)	Braise or stew
Top Blade Roast	Braise
Beef Chuck, Neck Pot Roast	Braise, stew, or grind
Beef Brisket, Point Half	Braise or stew
Edge Cut, Half Point	Braise or stew
Beef Brisket, Flat Half	Braise or stew
Beef Brisket, Middle Cut (choicest cut)	Braise or stew
Beef Plate, Short Ribs	Braise or stew
Short Ribs and Spareribs	Braise or stew
Beef Plate Rolled (Yankee pot roast)	Braise or stew
Fore Shank and Hind Shank	Braise or stew
Beef Rib, Rolled Cap Pot Roast	Braise
Beef Rib, Back Ribs (riblets, finger ribs)	Braise or stew
Beef Rib, Short Ribs	Braise or stew
Round Roast	Braise (roast top quality first cuts near rump)
Bottom Round Roast	Braise (roast top quality first cuts near rump)
Eye Round Roast	Braise, roast if very fine quality
Heel of Round (Pike's Peak, Diamond, Denver, or Horseshoe roast)	Braise or stew
Tip Roast (sirloin tip, veiny, face, knuckle)	Braise
Beef Chuck, Shoulder Steak (London broil; clod steak, arm steak)	Broil, sauté, braise
Beef Chuck, Under Blade Steak (book, butler, lifter, petite, or top chuck steak)	Broil, sauté, braise
Beef Plate, Skirt Steak (diaphragm, London broils, London grill steak)	Broil, sauté, braise
Beef Flanksteak	Broil, sauté, braise

simmer. Cover and cook for 2 to 3 hours, or until the meat is completely tender but not falling off the bone. As the meat is cooking, check the liquid level from time to time and add tomato juice when the liquid level falls.

About 30 minutes before the beef is done, taste for seasoning and add salt and pepper if needed. *Serves 3 or 4.*

BEEF IN RED WINE

Serve over mashed potatoes or cooked noodles.

2 pounds lean stewing beef, cut in 1½-inch
    cubes
⅓ cup flour
2 tablespoons fat
1 onion, sliced
1 clove garlic, minced
1 teaspoon salt
Freshly ground black pepper to taste
1 cup red table wine
1 10-ounce can consommé

Dredge beef in flour. Heat a Dutch oven or a large heavy kettle; add fat and brown beef cubes. Add remaining ingredients, cover, and simmer about 2 hours. If the sauce is too thin, simmer with cover off until reduced. *Serves 5 or 6.*

BEEF AND CORN CASSEROLE, JAMAICA-STYLE

2 pounds beef chuck, cut into 1-inch cubes
Salt and freshly ground pepper to taste
1 large onion, finely chopped
1 clove garlic, crushed
1 tablespoon Worcestershire sauce
1 teaspoon hot pepper sauce
1 tablespoon white vinegar
Margarine or vegetable oil
3 cups kernel corn (canned, fresh, or frozen)
Sauce for Beef and Corn Casserole

Combine beef, salt and pepper to taste, onion, garlic, Worcestershire sauce, hot pepper sauce, and vinegar in a large bowl. Cover lightly and allow to stand at room temperature for 2 hours or for 4 hours refrigerated. Rub the inside of a casserole lightly with margarine or vegetable oil. Layer the beef and corn in the casserole, with a little marinade between each layer. Pour Sauce for Beef and Corn Casserole over the casserole and bake, covered, in a 350° oven 2 hours, or until meat is tender. *Serves 6.*

SAUCE FOR BEEF AND CORN CASSEROLE

3 tablespoons margarine
3 tablespoons all-purpose flour
3 cups beef bouillon
Salt and freshly ground pepper to taste
2 tablespoons tomato catsup

Heat margarine in a small, heavy saucepan. When it melts, stir in flour and cook, stirring with a wooden spoon until flour has colored to a golden brown. Gradually stir in beef bouillon, season to taste with salt and pepper, and add catsup. Cook, stirring, until sauce is smooth.

BROILED FLANK STEAK

Have the butcher score the steak crosswise. Cooked properly, this is as good as a much more expensive steak. It must not be over-cooked. It is great if marinated about 2 hours before cooking. Before serving, slice this on a wide diagonal into pieces about ¼ inch thick.

1 tablespoon oil
1 shallot, finely chopped, or 1 slice onion
Salt and freshly ground pepper to taste
1 clove garlic, crushed
2½ pounds flank steak

Combine oil, shallot, salt, pepper, and garlic. Rub this mixture over both sides of the steak, and let stand at room temperature as long as possible before cooking. Broil 5 minutes on each side. *Serves 6.*

SWISS STEAK BRAISED

¼ cup flour
1 teaspoon salt
¼ teaspoon freshly ground pepper
1½ pounds round steak, ¾ inch thick
2 tablespoons oil
1 8-ounce can tomato sauce
½ cup water

Combine flour with salt and pepper and pound into steak with the edge of a heavy saucer. Heat oil in a large skillet and brown steak on both sides about 10 minutes. Reduce to simmer and add sauce and water. Cover and cook for about 1 hour, or until meat is tender. *Serves 6.*

LONDON BROIL

If the butcher will give you the first cut of the piece of top round, cook it this way; serve cut on the diagonal in thin slices.

1 1-inch top-of-round steak
2 tablespoons oil
1 clove garlic, crushed (optional)
1 teaspoon oregano (optional)
1 teaspoon salt
⅛ teaspoon pepper

Set the meat on a plate. Combine the rest of the ingredients and spread on both sides of the steak. Let stand at room temperature for a few hours, turning occasionally. Broil on high, 6 to 10 minutes on each side. *Serves 4.*

BEEF WITH HAM LEFTOVERS

Paper-thin slices of round beef, rather like scallopini of veal, are economical and, stuffed, make wonderful dishes like this. The ham here gives the beef a very special flavor. You can make a similar dish using ground beef—see *Ground Beef and Ham Rolls.*

6 thin slices beef
6 thin slices cooked ham
½ cup cooked rice
1 cup minced celery
1 scallion, finely chopped
Salt and pepper to taste
3 tablespoons margarine or butter
1 tablespoon cooking brandy
1 teaspoon dried sage

Flatten beef on a cutting board and place a slice of ham on top of each piece. Mix rice, celery, scallion, salt, and pepper; spoon this mixture on top of the ham. Roll up each slice and fix with toothpicks. Brown on all sides in sizzling margarine or butter. Combine brandy

and sage. Reduce heat and add to pan, mixing well with margarine. Simmer about 30 minutes, turning often. *Serves 6.*

PEPPERS AND STEAK

2 tablespoons oil
1 pound chuck or flank steak, sliced very thin
1 cup chopped onion
1 cup chopped green pepper
Salt to taste
4 tablespoons soy sauce
3 cups cooked rice

Heat oil in a heavy skillet until a drop of water sizzles violently when dropped in the pan. Add sliced steak and cook rapidly, stirring all the while until all pieces are browned. Remove and set aside. Reduce heat and add chopped onion and green pepper, salt, and soy sauce. Cover and cook for about 10 minutes, or until pepper is barely tender. Stir in the cooked meat and continue cooking until meat is hot throughout. This mixture can be served over cooked rice or you can stir the rice in at the last minute for a one-dish meal. *Serves 4 or 5.*

RUMP OF BEEF ROASTED IN FOIL

1 3-pound piece of beef chuck steak
1 package dehydrated onion soup mix
½ cup dry red wine, or bouillon

Place beef on a large piece of heavy-duty foil. Bend foil up around meat. Sprinkle soup mix over and pour in wine. Fold foil firmly around meat, sealing well. Place in a baking pan and roast in 350° oven about 2½ hours. Slice meat and serve with the sauce poured over. *Serves 6 to 8.*

CHARLENE'S CHUCK ROAST

1 2-pound chuck roast, 1½ to 2 inches thick
Salt and pepper to taste
1 clove garlic, finely minced
¼ cup red wine

1 teaspoon cornstarch dissolved in 2
    tablespoons water

Preheat oven to 425°. Make several deep (1-inch) cuts in the center of the muscle parts of the roast. Sprinkle the top of the roast liberally with salt, pepper, and minced garlic. Line a baking pan with foil and put in the meat, folding up the sides of the foil to hold the juice around the meat. Pour on about half the red wine, just enough to fill up the cuts in the meat. Bake in hot oven 20 minutes or longer, depending on how well done you like your meat. A few minutes before the roast is done, baste it once with the remainder of the wine. Remove roast from oven and cool 5 to 10 minutes before slicing. While meat is cooling, put baking pan on top of stove, bring to a simmer, and add cornstarch and water mixture a little at a time, stirring and scraping up pan juices, until gravy is thickened. If you find too little juice in the pan, dilute with some water. *Serves 4 or 5.*

BEEF BERNE

If this is not refrigerated before baking, bake for 20 to 30 minutes. Serve with chilled, canned sliced baby tomatoes, a big tray of celery, olives, carrot sticks, and scallions, and brown-and-serve hard rolls.

1 pound beef round slices, ¼ inch thick
½ teaspoon salt
Freshly ground black pepper to taste
3 tablespoons vegetable oil
½ cup chopped onion
2 cups green pepper strips
½ teaspoon dried basil
3 cups soft bread crumbs
1 10-ounce can cream of mushroom soup
5 ounces water
2 cups shredded Swiss cheese

Cut round steaks into ½-inch strips. Season with salt and pepper. Lightly brown in vegetable oil in a large skillet. Add chopped onion and sauté just until tender. Add green pepper and basil and cook 5 minutes longer. In a buttered 1½-quart casserole, alternate 2 layers

each of meat mixture and 2 cups of bread crumbs. Pour soup and water over top. Sprinkle cheese over the top, top with remaining bread crumbs. Refrigerate until baking time. Bake in a 340° oven 35 to 40 minutes. *Serves 6.*

BRAISED BEEF

This is a good basic beef stew. Dress it up with mushrooms and some dry red wine or serve it in its natural and simple form with a generous sprinkling of chopped parsley. Serve it with noodles, rice, or Orzo and you have a truly royal meal for a less than royal allowance.

3 pounds stew beef in 1½-inch cubes
1 tablespoon oil
2 large onions
1 clove garlic
1 tablespoon coarse or plain salt
Salt and pepper to taste
¼ cup beef bouillon or water
Finely chopped parsley

Preheat oven to 325°. In a Dutch oven or a big kettle, brown beef in oil, turning often. Peel onions and chop fine, crush garlic with 1 tablespoon salt. Add the onions, garlic, and a dusting of black pepper to the meat and mix well. Add the bouillon or water, scrape up the pan juices, cover, and cook in the oven 1½ to 2½ hours, or until firm but tender. Skim off the fat. Correct the seasoning with additional salt and pepper if needed. Serve sprinkled with finely chopped parsley. *Serves 6.*

OXTAILS IN WINE SAUCE

Supermarkets sometimes offer oxtails at a very good price. They make good soup or can be served as a main course. This way is nice with rice or noodles.

3 pounds oxtails, cut in 1-inch pieces (2 tails)
2 tablespoons fat
1 medium onion, minced
2 tablespoons tomato paste
1 teaspoon dry mustard

1 teaspoon salt
1 teaspoon seasoned salt
Dash freshly ground black pepper
Dash cayenne pepper
1 cup dry red wine
1 cup bouillon
1 6-ounce can mushroom stems and pieces,
    drained,
    or 1 cup celery soup
2 tablespoons arrowroot (omit if using celery
    soup)

Heat a Dutch oven. Add fat and brown oxtails on all sides. Add onion and cook until just
transparent. Add remaining ingredients except
arrowroot, close cover securely, and cook 2 to
3 hours. Remove oxtails and keep warm. Skim
surface fat from sauce. Add 2 tablespoons arrowroot to the sauce and cook without the
cover, stirring until sauce is of the desired consistency. Combine sauce and oxtails and serve.
Serves 5 or 6.

COLD BEEF IN REMOULADE SAUCE

This is an easy way to use up cold cooked beef
of any sort.

3 to 4 cups or 6 to 8 slices cold beef
1 cup mayonnaise
1 tablespoon drained, finely chopped
    cucumber pickle
1 tablespoon drained, chopped capers
2 teaspoons French mustard
1 teaspoon finely chopped parsley
½ teaspoon chopped fresh tarragon
½ teaspoon chervil
½ teaspoon anchovy paste

Combine all ingredients but the beef. Serve
the beef marinated in Rémoulade Sauce or
serve the sauce on the side. *Serves 6 to 8.*

GERMAN BEEF ROULADE

Another way of serving leftover slices of roast
beef, but party-style.

6 slices roast beef
6 teaspoons mustard

2 pickled cucumbers, diced
1 cup thinly sliced carrots
Salt and pepper to taste
1 large bay leaf
1 cup beef broth
1 glass dry sherry
1 cup mushrooms, in pieces
1 tablespoon oil
2 tablespoons all-purpose flour

Spread each slice of roast beef with 1 teaspoon mustard, and sprinkle with some diced
cucumber and a few rounds of carrot, salt, and
pepper. Roll up each slice and skewer with 1
or 2 toothpicks. In a kettle, place bay leaf,
broth, and sherry, and the roulades. Simmer
for 1 to 2 hours, well covered, or until tender.
Sauté mushrooms in oil and add to pot. Use a
few tablespoons of the liquid to blend the
flour, and pour into pot. Bring to a boil until
sauce is thickened. *Serves 3 or 4.*

Ground Beef

Ground beef remains one of the best of all
meat bargains if only because it includes absolutely no waste. Nourishing, an excellent
source of vitamins and proteins, it can be used
as the basis for a remarkable number of dishes.

However, be sure you are getting bargains
in ground beef. Now that the Uniform Retail
Meat Identity Standards Code is in effect, the
words "ground beef" must appear on the label
of each package if the meat is indeed ground
beef. Containers carrying this label must have
in them pure beef ground only from meat attached to the bones, and no odd lots of other
meats can be included. If the beef is from a
chuck cut, the round, or the sirloin, the label
will say so.

Furthermore, in addition to the words
"ground beef," the label must describe the
lean-to-fat ratio. For instance, "No less than 75
percent lean," or "No more than 25 percent
fat." The new standards specify that ground
beef must not contain less than 70 percent
lean. The lean-to-fat ratio must be reflected in

the price—the higher the content in fat, the lower the price per pound of meat.

The amount of fat in ground meat should govern the use to which you put it. Lean ground beef that is 75 to 80 percent lean is recommended for sauce mixtures, such as spaghetti. Ground beef with a higher content of lean—80 to 85 percent—is excellent for meat loaves, meatballs, and casseroles. Ground beef that is 85 to 90 percent lean should be used for hamburgers and low-calorie dishes.

The color of the ground meat in the package can be confusing. The bright red of ground meat comes from exposure to air. Packages that are bright red on the outside and a darker red inside have usually been wrapped fairly recently. If the interior of the package is exposed to the air in the refrigerator, it will probably turn bright red.

Ground beef stretched by the addition of soy products sometimes is offered as "textured vegetable protein, extended ground beef." The product is wholesome and nourishing. Labels must clearly state the percentages of lean meat, moisture, and soy extender. Read labels carefully and compare the price with that of pure ground beef to ascertain whether you are getting a bargain. You may prefer to add your own soy extender for further savings. Soy-extended meat products are used the same way as regular ground beef. They take a somewhat shorter cooking time, and may seem to stick to the skillet more readily than ground beef that has not been extended.

Ground Beef Recipes

MEATBALLS AND CELERY "NOODLES"

A thinning concept, where strips of celery are used instead of calorie-laden noodles.

1½ pounds lean ground beef
1 onion, finely chopped
1 clove garlic, minced
1 teaspoon salt

¼ teaspoon Tabasco sauce
12 ounces drained canned tomatoes
2 bunches celery
2 cups chicken broth or bouillon

Combine ground beef, chopped onion, garlic, salt, and Tabasco. Roll into 1½-inch meatballs and brown under a broiler, turning until all sides are colored. Continue broiling until meatballs are done through. Heat drained tomatoes in a skillet and add cooked meatballs. Trim celery ribs. With a sharp knife, cut each rib into long slivers along its lengthwise grain. Bring chicken broth to a boil in a large pan and add celery slivers. Cook 10 minutes, or until celery is tender. Drain and arrange the "noodles" on a platter. Top with meatballs and sauce. Serves 3.

MEATBALL STEW

1 pound ground beef
1 egg
½ cup soft bread crumbs
1 tablespoon chopped parsley
2 teaspoons salt
2 tablespoons vegetable oil
1 large onion, chopped
1 clove garlic, minced
1 small eggplant (4 cups), pared and diced
1 16-ounce can whole tomatoes
1 teaspoon sugar
1 teaspoon oregano

Combine ground beef with egg, bread crumbs, parsley, and 1 teaspoon of the salt until well blended; shape into small balls. Brown in oil, then set aside and keep warm. Add onion and garlic to the pan; sauté just until soft; add eggplant and meatballs. Combine tomatoes with 1 teaspoon salt, sugar, and oregano; pour over meatballs and eggplant and cover. Simmer, stirring often, 30 minutes, or until eggplant is tender. Serves 4.

GROUND BEEF AND HAM ROLLS

1 pound ground beef
1 egg

¼ cup bread crumbs
¼ cup milk
1 teaspoon grated orange rind
1 teaspoon salt
⅛ teaspoon pepper
8 thin slices boiled ham
¼ cup orange juice
¼ cup light corn syrup
¼ cup brown sugar, firmly packed
1 teaspoon lemon juice
1 teaspoon dry mustard

Combine ground beef with the egg, bread crumbs, milk, orange rind, salt, and pepper. Shape into 8 sausagelike rolls. Roll sausages in ham slices and place, seam side down, in a greased shallow baking dish. Blend orange juice with corn syrup, brown sugar, lemon juice, and mustard; pour over the rolls. Bake at 375° for 45 minutes. *Serves 4.*

CHILI CON CARNE FROM SCRATCH

Chili con carne is popular, and especially economical if you have a slow-cooking electric crockery pot to make it in, and start with dried instead of canned beans. You can make it on the stove top, too, using canned beans.

3 pounds ground chuck
3 large onions, chopped
1 bell pepper, chopped
2 cloves garlic, minced
½ teaspoon dried oregano
¼ teaspoon cumin seed
2 6-ounce cans tomato paste
1 quart water
Salt and freshly ground pepper
3 tablespoons chili powder
2 15 to 17-ounce cans kidney beans

Brown the chuck in a Dutch oven. Add onions, pepper, garlic, oregano, cumin seed, and tomato paste. Stir mixture thoroughly and add water. Stir again. Add salt and pepper, liberally, and chili powder. Cover and simmer about 1½ hours. Add kidney beans and continue to simmer for another ½ hour. Taste the chili and add salt, pepper, or chili powder to suit your taste. *Serves 6 to 8.*

SKILLET HOPPING JOHN

A good way to handle the mixed ground meats.

2 tablespoons bacon fat
1 pound ground meats, mixed
1 medium-size onion, chopped
½ cup beef bouillon
1 cup chopped celery
2 cups black-eyed peas
1 teaspoon salt
1 teaspoon basil
½ teaspoon thyme
1 bay leaf
Few drops red pepper seasoning
½ cup cooked rice
1 cup tomato juice

Heat bacon fat in a skillet. Shape meat loaf mixture into a patty and brown 5 minutes on each side, then break up into chunks; push to one side. Add onion to pan and sauté until soft. Stir in beef bouillon, celery, black-eyed peas, and seasonings. Heat to boiling, cover, and simmer 30 minutes. Stir in rice and tomato juice; cover again. Simmer 10 minutes more, or until rice is heated. Remove bay leaf before serving. *Serves 8.*

NO-BAKE EASY MEAT LOAF

This is also delicious as a spread on crackers for an inexpensive canapé. The meat may be beef, pork, chicken, lamb, or whatever else you have on hand.

1½ cups ground leftover cooked beef,
    lightly packed
1 cup (about ¼ pound) shredded Cheddar
    cheese, lightly packed
1 small onion, grated
1 green pepper, chopped
⅓ cup melted margarine or butter
Salt and freshly ground pepper to taste

Lightly combine meat, cheese, onion, and green pepper. Add margarine or butter, salt, and pepper and mix again. Line a loaf pan with a double thickness of plastic wrap, leaving enough wrap extending over the sides to cover the mixture tightly once you have firmly and evenly packed it into the pan. Refrigerate overnight. Slice to serve. *Serves 4.*

CHOPPED BEEF LOAF

2 pounds lean ground beef
2 slices bread, torn in small bits
1 small package or jar chipped beef
    (about 2½ ounces), minced
2 eggs
¼ cup milk
3 tablespoons mustard relish
Salt and freshly ground pepper to taste

Combine ground beef, bread, and chipped beef; mix with a light touch. Add eggs, milk, mustard relish, salt, and pepper. Add salt sparingly as chipped beef is salty. Mix again. Shape into a loaf and bake in a 350° oven 1¼ hours. *Serves 6.*

PLAIN MEAT LOAF

Spinach noodles with butter and grated Parmesan, Brussels sprouts, crusty bread, and fruit for dessert are great with this meat loaf.

1 large onion, chopped
1 tablespoon margarine or butter
¾ pound ground beef
¾ pound ground pork
1 teaspoon curry powder (optional)
1 egg
½ teaspoon thyme
1½ cups soft bread crumbs
Salt and pepper to taste
2 strips bacon (optional)

In a large skillet, sauté onion in margarine or butter until golden brown. Mix with all other ingredients except bacon, using wet hands and a light touch. Pack lightly into a greased loaf pan. Bake in 375° oven for 1 hour. *Serves 4 to 6.*

FANCY MEAT LOAF

With this, scalloped potatoes, green peas, cloverleaf rolls, and apple pie for dessert make a great meal.

¼ pound mushrooms, chopped
1 medium onion, chopped
2 tablespoons margarine or butter
¼ cup red wine
2 slices white bread, coarsely broken
1 pound ground beef
1 teaspoon salt
½ teaspoon pepper
½ teaspoon paprika
1 egg, slightly beaten

Sauté mushrooms and onion in margarine or butter until tender but not brown. Stir in wine and bring to a boil. Place bread in a large mixing bowl. Pour wine mixture over and mix well to moisten bread. Add ground beef, salt, pepper, and paprika. Add egg and mix until all ingredients are thoroughly blended. Place in a greased loaf pan or shape into a loaf and place in a shallow baking dish. Bake in 375° oven 45 minutes, or until meat loaf is browned. *Serves 4.*

SKILLET MEAT LOAF

Radishes, scallions, carrot sticks and cucumber sticks mixed with sour cream and freshly ground pepper, and French fried potatoes are nice with this. For dessert try thin pancakes rolled around currant jelly and sprinkled with powdered sugar.

1 pound ground beef
2 tablespoons chopped green pepper
¼ cup chopped onion
3 tablespoons chopped celery
2 cups cornflakes
1 egg, slightly beaten
1 teaspoon salt
1 teaspoon tomato catsup
1 teaspoon Worcestershire sauce
¼ teaspoon prepared mustard
1 tablespoon peanut oil

Combine all the ingredients except the oil; mix thoroughly. Heat oil in an 8-inch skillet. Pack meat mixture in firmly. Cover and cook over low heat about 30 minutes, or until nicely browned on the bottom. Turn out onto a hot platter and serve at once. *Serves 4.*

PIZZA MEAT LOAF

Try this with creamed sunchokes (Jerusalem artichokes), frenched green beans, and Swedish Flatbrod—chocolate pudding for dessert.

6 ounces mozzarella cheese
6 slices stale white bread
½ cup milk
1 small onion, chopped
1 teaspoon margarine or butter
1½ pounds chopped chuck
1 6-ounce can chopped mushrooms
1 tablespoon chopped parsley
Dash oregano
Salt and pepper to taste
1 clove garlic, crushed
1 8-ounce can tomato sauce
¼ teaspoon oregano

Cut half the cheese into slices and reserve. Chop remainder of cheese into large chunks. Soak bread in milk. Sauté the onion in butter until golden. Put the chopped cheese, bread, onion, meat, mushrooms, parsley, seasonings, half the crushed garlic and ⅓ the tomato sauce into a large bowl and mix by hand. Shape into a loaf and place in a shallow pan. Bake in 375° oven 45 minutes. Meantime, add remaining garlic and the oregano to ½ the remaining tomato sauce. After 45 minutes, pour this over the loaf, put the slices of cheese on top and pour the remaining sauce over all. Return to the oven for 15 minutes, or until the cheese has melted. *Serves 4 to 6.*

APPLESAUCE MEAT LOAF

A good way to change the meat loaf pace—and use up scraps of leftover applesauce.

1½ pounds ground beef
¾ cup quick or old-fashioned oats, uncooked
1½ teaspoons salt
¼ teaspoon pepper
¾ cup canned sweetened applesauce
1 egg, beaten
2 slices Cheddar cheese

Combine thoroughly in a large bowl all ingredients except cheese. Pack firmly into an 8½ × 4½ × 2½-inch loaf pan. Bake in 350° oven about 1 hour. Meantime, cut cheese slices in half, making triangles. Place triangles on top of the finished loaf and let stand 5 minutes before slicing. *Serves 6.*

PICKLE MEAT LOAF

Like most meat loaves this one is very good cold. If you wish to serve it that way—for a picnic perhaps—cool it completely, then wrap and chill. Hot or cold, garnish with additional pickles and pimiento, if desired. Serve catsup or mustard on the side.

1 cup milk
3 slices white bread, crumbled
1½ pounds ground beef round
½ cup chopped dill pickles
⅓ cup chopped onion
1 egg
1 teaspoon salt
¼ teaspoon garlic powder
¼ teaspoon pepper
1 teaspoon Worcestershire sauce
3 whole medium dill pickles
2 canned pimientos

Combine milk and bread in a large bowl and let stand a few minutes. Add ground beef, chopped pickles, onion, egg, and seasonings. Mix well and shape half the mixture into a 12-inch loaf in a shallow baking pan. Place the whole pickles down the center of the loaf. Top with pieces of pimiento and cover with remaining meat mixture. Bake in 350° oven 50 minutes. *Serves 6.*

BEEF LOAF WELLINGTON

1½ pounds ground chuck
2 egg yolks
¼ cup minced parsley
2 tablespoons soft bread crumbs
1½ teaspoons lemon juice
1½ teaspoons salt
Freshly ground pepper to taste
1 medium onion, chopped fine
Pastry (see below)

Combine thoroughly all ingredients except pastry; mix with a light touch. Shape into a loaf and place on a shallow baking pan. Bake in 350° oven 5 minutes. Remove from oven and turn heat up to 450°. Cover the entire meat loaf with pastry dough rolled out very thin. Moisten the edges of the dough with water to make them stick together. Bake in 450° oven 15 minutes, or until golden brown. *Serves 6.*

PASTRY: PLAIN

2½ cups sifted flour
1 teaspoon salt
⅔ cup shortening
Ice water

Sift flour and salt together. Cut in shortening with a pastry blender or 2 knives. Add just enough ice water to make the ingredients hold together. Chill thoroughly. Roll out to fit the meat loaf.

PASTRY: RICH

2 cups sifted flour
1 teaspoon salt
1 cup shortening
Ice water

Lard makes the shortest crust. Use part lard and part butter if you feel rich. Sift flour and salt together. Cut in shortening with a pastry blender or 2 knives. Add just enough ice water to make the ingredients hold together. Chill thoroughly. Roll out to fit the meat loaf.

PARTY MEAT LOAF

This can be eaten hot or cold. For a change of pace, use ground liver instead, making sure all veins are removed (do not blender, use a meat grinder).

1 pound ground beef or liver
1 cup diced onion
1 cup mixed vegetables
1 cup small canned mushrooms

3 or 4 slices stale bread soaked in ½ cup milk
*   or half-and-half*
1 cup ground nuts (salted)
½ cup currants
½ cup chopped green olives
1 tablespoon finely diced pimiento in oil
1 tablespoon soy sauce
2 eggs, well beaten
Salt and pepper to taste (optional)

Mix thoroughly all ingredients except eggs in a deep bowl with your hands. Add the 2 well-beaten eggs. Taste, and add salt and pepper if necessary. Bake 1½ hours in deep, narrow pan in 250° oven. To serve, turn out upside down onto a platter and slice ½ inch thick. *Serves 6 to 8.*

STUFFED PEPPERS

These can be made ahead of time and frozen.

10 large bell peppers
1 pound ground beef
2 onions, chopped
1 16-ounce can peeled tomatoes (reserve
*   liquid)*
1½ teaspoons salt
½ teaspoon pepper
3 tablespoons rice grains (uncooked)
1 egg
1 tablespoon honey
1 tablespoon lemon juice
¼ cup seedless raisins

Cut out the stem of each pepper and carefully clean out seeds and ribs. Set aside. Brown ground beef slowly in a large saucepan. When meat has begun to render its fat, add chopped onions. When meat is brown and onions transparent, drain off excess fat. Add tomatoes, reserving most of the liquid, and salt and pepper. Simmer uncovered for 30 minutes. In a bowl, mix rice, egg, and tomato liquid. Stir in cooked beef. Stuff peppers with this mixture and return to saucepan with tomato sauce. Cover and simmer again for 1½ hours, add honey, lemon juice, and raisins, and cook another ½ hour, or until peppers are very tender. *Serves 5 to 7.*

CRÊPES MAROTH

A gourmet trick to play with beef leftovers.

1 cup milk
¾ cup water
2 tablespoons butter
4 eggs
2 cups flour
1 to 2 tablespoons oil

Mix together all ingredients except the oil in a blender container and blend until smooth. Or beat thoroughly with a fork. This should be done a few hours in advance if possible. Chill the batter until you're ready to make the crêpes. To cook, put a small amount of oil in the bottom of a flat, 6-inch frying pan. The idea is just to grease the pan, not to have any appreciable amount of oil standing in it. Heat the oil until almost smoking. Add about 2 tablespoons batter, swirling the pan so that the batter spreads out to cover it. Lift edges of crêpe with a fork to check browning. As soon as one side is browned, lift the crêpe with a spatula and flip it over. Cook for 1 minute more. The second side will still be mostly white, but this will be the inside of the crêpe. Pile finished crêpes on top of each other on a large plate. (NOTE: You can store cooked crêpes in the refrigerator, too. Just make sure the sauce you use is hot enough to warm them when you serve them.)

ROAST BEEF STUFFING
AND SAUCE

1 small onion, finely chopped
¼ pound mushrooms, finely chopped
  (optional)
2 tablespoons butter
4 tablespoons flour
2 cups beef bouillon
12 thin slices leftover beef

Sauté the onion and mushrooms in the butter. Let the pan cool, then add flour and stir it into a paste. Cook the paste slowly until flour turns brown. (Do not burn.) Add bouillon and cook slowly, stirring, until thickened. Pour half the sauce into a separate pan and set aside. With the heat on, add beef shreds to half the sauce, warm for a minute or so, and remove from heat. Put some of the beef mixture on each crêpe, roll it up, and top with some of the plain sauce. Serve immediately. Makes about 12 crêpes. *Serves 4.*

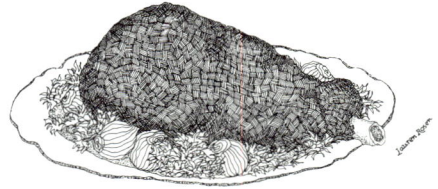

Veal, Lamb, and Mutton

Veal and lamb recipes are very often interchangeable. Each meat has a rather special flavor of its own, but they are not dissimilar. Of the two, lamb is generally the better buy, but occasionally inexpensive veal appears in the supermarkets, and should be snatched up if only to vary the menu.

Veal

Veal is, of course, a young beef. The best veal meat is almost white, but the better buys usually tend toward pink, the color of beef. The meat is tender and very fine-grained. It cooks quickly, and is often used in breaded sautéed recipes and Italian cuisine. Veal for sautéing is expensive. However, stew veal, from the shoulder, breast of veal, and ground veal are good buys, so recipes have been included for them. When you run across a good buy in veal, try a lamb recipe using a comparable cut—you'll find that it is very good.

VEAL STEW

3 tablespoons olive oil
2 pounds stew veal in 1-inch cubes
4 onions, finely chopped
2 cloves garlic, crushed
4 tomatoes, peeled, seeded, and chopped,
    or drained canned tomatoes
¼ cup strained lemon juice
¼ teaspoon salt
Freshly ground black pepper to taste
1½ to 2 cups chicken bouillon

Heat oil in a Dutch oven and sauté veal until browned. Add onions and garlic and sauté another 10 minutes. Add tomatoes, lemon juice, salt, and pepper and simmer 5 minutes. Add chicken bouillon and bring to a boil. Reduce heat and simmer 2 to 3 hours. Add more broth if the dish dries out. *Serves 4.*

VEAL PAPRIKA

2 pounds boned veal shoulder or round, in
    1-inch cubes

2 tablespoons bacon fat
½ cup minced onion
1 medium clove garlic, peeled and minced
1 teaspoon salt
⅛ teaspoon pepper
1 tablespoon paprika plus extra for garnish
2 tablespoons all-purpose flour
1 cup chicken bouillon
¾ cup sour cream

In the bottom of a Dutch oven over medium-high heat, sauté veal cubes in bacon fat until meat is brown on all sides. Add onion and garlic and sauté, stirring, for another 2 or 3 minutes. Remove from heat and add salt, pepper, 1 tablespoon paprika, and flour. Toss thoroughly, then pour in chicken bouillon. Stir until sauce is smooth. Cover, and simmer 1½ to 2 hours, or until meat is tender. Lift meat into a warm serving bowl. If sauce seems thin, simmer on high heat in a small skillet until thickened, then remove from heat and stir in sour cream. Reheat just enough to warm the cream, but don't boil. Pour it over meat and garnish with a dash of paprika. *Serves 4 to 6.*

BREAST OF VEAL, STUFFED

2½ pounds boned veal breast
¼ cup margarine or butter
6 tablespoons minced onion
2 cups fresh bread crumbs
1 teaspoon salt
⅛ teaspoon pepper
1½ teaspoons ground sage
¾ cup minced parsley
3 tablespoons oil
¼ cup hot chicken bouillon
1 bay leaf
1 small onion stuck with 3 cloves
¼ teaspoon ground thyme

If the veal has cartilage, trim it off, and lay the meat flat on a cutting board. Score one side with long slashes. Turn. In a skillet over medium heat, melt margarine or butter and sauté onion until transparent. Add bread crumbs, salt, pepper, sage, and parsley, and toss contents of the skillet until well com-

bined. Spread over the unscored side of the veal, leaving ¼ inch free at the edges. Roll up and secure the meat with toothpicks. Add oil to the skillet and brown the roll on all sides. Place in an ovenproof casserole. Add chicken bouillon to the skillet, scrape up the pan juices, and add to the Dutch oven with bay leaf, onion stuck with cloves, and thyme. Cover and bake at 350° 2 to 3 hours. Remove onion and bay leaf before serving. *Serves 4 to 6.*

VEAL LOAF IN ASPIC

1 veal knuckle, cut into pieces
1 pound lean veal from the shoulder
1 medium onion stuck with 4 whole cloves
1 bay leaf
½ teaspoon ground thyme
Large sprig parsley
2 teaspoons salt
6 peppercorns
Water to cover
½ teaspoon pepper
2 hard-boiled eggs, sliced in rounds
6 sprigs fresh parsley
2 tablespoons minced parsley

In a large kettle, place knuckle pieces and veal with the onion stuck with whole cloves, the bay leaf, thyme, a sprig of parsley, 1 teaspoon of the salt, and the peppercorns. Cover with water, bring to a boil, and boil 3 to 4 hours. Remove knuckle pieces and scrape any meat on the bones into a bowl. Finely mince veal meat and add to bowl. Season with 1 teaspoon salt and ½ teaspoon pepper. Discard onion, bay leaf, and peppercorns. Boil veal cooking liquid down to 1½ cups. Pour ¼ inch of liquid into bottom of a 1½-quart mold and let chill in refrigerator until just set. Arrange egg slices on the jelled stock with sprigs of parsley in between. Combine meat with minced parsley and spoon into mold. Pour cooled cooking liquid into mold and chill a few hours or overnight. Turn out onto a bed of parsley to serve. *Serves 4.*

GROUND VEAL LOAF

3 pounds ground veal
½ pound fat salt pork, ground
1 cup saltine cracker crumbs
4 tablespoons half-and-half
1 tablespoon lemon juice, strained
1 tablespoon salt
½ tablespoon pepper
1 tablespoon grated onion and juice

Combine ground veal and salt pork with cracker crumbs, half-and-half, and lemon juice in salt, pepper, and grated onion. Pack into a buttered bread pan and bake at 325° 3 hours. Cool, unmold, and slice before serving. *Serves 6 to 8.*

VEAL AND VEGETABLE CASSEROLE

2 pounds boneless rump of veal in 1-inch
  cubes
¼ cup flour
1 teaspoon salt
¼ teaspoon pepper
3 tablespoons margarine or butter
2 large onions, chopped
1 clove garlic, minced
2 tomatoes, chopped and seeded
2 green peppers, chopped and seeded
6 potatoes, peeled and quartered
1 cup chicken bouillon or water
1 cup dry white wine
Minced parsley

Preheat oven to 350°. Roll veal in flour mixed with salt and pepper. Melt 2 tablespoons margarine or butter in a big skillet over medium heat. Add onions, garlic, and cook until onions are transparent. Add tomatoes and peppers and cook until limp. Scrape into a casserole. Add the rest of the margarine or butter to the skillet and increase heat. Add meat and brown on all sides. Scrape into casserole and add potatoes, bouillon, and wine. Stir well, cover, and bake 1¾ hours. If sauce is thin, leave uncovered for last ½ hour of cooking. Garnish with minced parsley. *Serves 6.*

VEAL SHOULDER STUFFED WITH HAM

Serve with boiled sweet potatoes.

4 pounds veal shoulder
3 tablespoons white wine or white vinegar
3 tablespoons margarine or butter
¼ cup chopped onion
1 teaspoon salt
2 slices cooked ham, ground

Make a large pocket in the veal shoulder. Smear veal with wine or vinegar and let stand 2 hours. Heat oven to 450°. Heat margarine or butter in a pan and add onion and salt. Cook over low heat for about 10 minutes. Combine this mixture with the ham, then stuff in veal pocket. Roast for 15 minutes. Reduce heat to 350° and bake 1½ hours. Baste often. *Serves 8.*

VEAL AND SOUR CREAM

2 tablespoons margarine or butter
2 pounds veal shoulder in 1-inch cubes
½ cup chopped onions
¼ pound mushrooms, sliced
1 clove garlic, minced
1 tablespoon all-purpose flour
½ cup warm chicken bouillon
1 tablespoon paprika
1 teaspoon salt
⅛ teaspoon pepper
2 cups sour cream

Melt margarine or butter in skillet over medium heat. Add veal and brown on all sides. Remove veal and place in a medium baking dish. Add onions, mushrooms, and garlic to frying pan and cook until mushrooms are limp, about 5 minutes. Stir in flour and heat in the chicken bouillon until smooth. Add paprika, salt, and pepper and cook until thickened, about 4 minutes. Turn off the heat and mix in the sour cream. Pour over veal. Cover and bake at 300° for 1½ hours. *Serves 6.*

VEAL MEAT LOAF

2 pounds ground neck veal or ground veal
1 cup onion soup

½ cup milk
¼ cup celery, minced
1 teaspoon salt
⅛ teaspoon pepper
¼ teaspoon rosemary
½ green pepper, finely chopped

Place veal in a large mixing bowl, simmer onion soup, milk, celery, salt, pepper, and rosemary until reduced by about ⅓. Mix into veal and then chill for 30 minutes or more. Heat oven to 350°. Place veal in a bread loaf tin and garnish with pepper slices. Bake for 1 hour. *Serves 4 to 6.*

VEAL IN LEMON SAUCE

A nice and easy way to use up leftover cooked veal slices.

1½ cups Béchamel Sauce
1 egg yolk, slightly beaten
2 tablespoons strained lemon juice
2 cups cold roast veal, minced
1 cup canned mushrooms, drained (optional),
    or 2 tablespoons salad olives, chopped
    (optional)
2 tablespoons minced parsley

In a small saucepan, heat the Béchamel Sauce over low heat. Beat a few tablespoons of this sauce into egg yolk, then beat egg yolk back into sauce. Stir lemon juice into sauce, and heat to just below boiling. Add veal and stir 1 or 2 minutes. To stretch the meat or make it more festive, add 1 cup canned mushrooms and/or 2 tablespoons chopped salad olives. Stir 2 more minutes. Serve garnished with parsley. *Serves 4.*

VEAL CURRY

Follow the recipe for *Lamb Curry from Scratch* or *Curry of Cooked Lamb* but use veal instead of lamb. Can be served with rice or pasta.

VEAL AND CHICKEN CASSEROLE

This is a real economy dish but fit for your favorite guests. It is best made the day before, refrigerated in a baking dish, and baked in time for the meal.

6 slices leftover roast veal
2 or 3 cups diced chicken
2 tablespoons vinegar
½ teaspoon Italian herb mix
1 teaspoon salt
⅛ teaspoon black pepper
1 cup chicken bouillon
1 cup celery stalks in 1-inch cubes
1 cup thinly sliced carrots
1 cup blanched almonds (optional)
1 cup fresh mushrooms, cut in half
1 cup milk
⅛ teaspoon nutmeg
2 tablespoons all-purpose flour
1 cup grated cheese
1 egg, well beaten

Place veal, chicken, vinegar, Italian herb mix, salt, black pepper, and chicken bouillon in large kettle and bring to a boil, lower heat and simmer 10 minutes. Add celery stalks, carrots, almonds (optional), and boil 10 more minutes, or until vegetables are tender. Add mushrooms; remove from heat. Blend milk, nutmeg, and flour. Add to kettle, bring to a simmer until thickened. Remove from heat and let stand for a few minutes to cool. Add ½ cup grated cheese and beaten egg, stirring briskly. Adjust seasoning if necessary. Pour into baking dish. Sprinkle remaining ½ cup grated cheese, and bake in 375° oven 20 to 30 minutes, or until cheese is puffy and lightly browned. Serve in the baking dish. *Serves 6 to 8.*

Lamb and Mutton

Lamb, like beef, comes in cuts that range from ultra-luxurious to very economical. Thick lamb chops with the kidney in are a luxury; breast of lamb is generally a big bargain. Between these two extremes is a range of meats for roasting and stewing. The recipes here will give you some ideas on ways to use the various lamb cuts offered in the supermarket.

Mutton is a grown-up lamb—and rarely offered under that name in American markets, though it is common in Europe. The lamb here is generally slaughtered young. However, once the spring slaughtering season is over, look warily at "lamb" offerings—the lambs have sometimes grown beyond the lamb stage and come close to qualifying as mutton. The main difference between the two meats is that mutton is coarser and more strongly flavored. It is an excellent meat but requires strong seasoning.

If lamb seems tough, or to make lamb ready for use in quick-cooked shish kebab dishes, marinate it first in the sauce below.

YOGURT MARINADE FOR LAMB

2 cloves garlic, mashed
2 tablespoons lemon juice, strained
¼ teaspoon pepper
1 cup plain yogurt
¼ teaspoon ground anise seed (optional)

Combine the ingredients in a bowl.

The table below will give you some ideas on how to use the various cuts of lamb offered, and suggests possible substitutes for the cuts called for in the recipes.

LAMB CHOP CASSEROLE, NEW ZEALAND STYLE

4 shoulder lamb chops
Salt
2 apples, peeled, cored, and sliced
1½ cups chicken bouillon
½ teaspoon thyme
6 ounces mint jelly

Over high heat, sear chops until brown in a little salt. Put 2 chops into a baking dish. Cover with half the apple slices. Add remaining chops and cover with remaining apple slices. Pour in chicken bouillon, mixed with thyme. Put mint jelly, broken up, on top. Cover the dish. Bake in 350° oven 30 minutes, or until chops are tender. *Serves 4.*

LAMB CHOP GOURMET CASSEROLE

Dry rice makes a good accompaniment to this dish.

Basic Lamb Cuts

DESCRIPTION	COOKING METHOD
Lamb Shoulder Square Cut Whole (shoulder block, shoulder roast)	Roast, braise, stew
Cushion Roast	Roast, braise
Blade Roasts (or Chops) (shoulder blocks)	Roast, braise
Arm Roast (or Chops)	Roast, braise
Neck Slices of Stew	Braise, stew
Lamb Breast	Braise, stew, bone, and stuff
Lamb Breast Riblets and Spareribs	Braise, roast
Lamb Shank (foreshank, trotter)	Braise
Lamb Leg Whole (leg, sirloin on, leg-o'-lamb, full-trimmed leg roast)	Roast, poach
Lamb Shoulder, Blade Chops	Braise
Lamb Shoulder, Arm Chops	Braise
Lamb Rib Chops (rack lamb chops)	Broil, sauté
Lamb Leg, Center Slice (steak, leg chop)	Broil, sauté

4 shoulder lamb chops
Salt and pepper to taste
2 to 3 tablespoons vegetable oil
½ pound fresh mushrooms, sliced, or 1
    8-ounce can sliced mushrooms, drained
1½ cups chicken stock
2 tablespoons dry sherry (or to taste)
2 cups cooked or canned peas, drained

Sprinkle chops with salt and pepper. Heat oil to smoking and brown chops in it on both sides. Remove chops to a casserole. Pour off most of the oil. Sauté the mushrooms in remaining oil briefly. Spread over chops. Pour in chicken stock, sherry, and simmer, scraping up pan juices. Pour over all. Cook in 350° oven 25 to 30 minutes. Add peas during last 5 minutes of cooking. *Serves 4.*

LAMB CHOPS REFORMÉ

This is another of those dishes that are economical if you have a few leftovers, but turn out to be a luxurious dish for those extra special parties. Serve with noodles or boiled potatoes.

8 small lamb chops or 8 slices roast lamb
½ cup julienne-cut ham slices
½ cup julienne-cut canned carrots, drained
½ cup julienne-cut canned beets, drained
1 glass dry sherry
½ cup cooked julienne-cut tongue
1 tablespoon white vinegar
1 teaspoon sugar
1 onion, sliced in thin segments
2 tablespoons oil
½ cup sour cream
½ cup water with 2 bouillon cubes
Salt and pepper to taste

Broil lamb chops on high heat for a few minutes until seared on both sides. If using leftover roast lamb, place in a preheated baking dish in a moderate oven to keep warm. Mix ham, carrots, beets, sherry, tongue, vinegar, and sugar in a saucepan, and simmer gently. Sauté onion segments in oil until transparent and tender. Add to saucepan with sour cream and ½ cup water with 2 bouillon cubes. Bring

to a brisk boil to reduce until well thickened. Add salt and pepper if necessary. Pour saucepan contents over lamb. *Serves 4 to 6.*

LAMB PÔT À TOUT FAIRE

Cook lamb breast this way and use the cooked meat and cooking liquid as the basis for several other dishes—lamb curry, for instance. The broth can be thickened with additional vegetables or barley to make a hearty soup.

3 pounds lamb breast
1 clove garlic, mashed
2 tablespoons vegetable oil
Water to cover
1 whole onion
1 carrot, chopped
1 stalk celery with leaves, cut in 2-inch pieces
1 bay leaf
5 peppercorns
Sprig rosemary
1 teaspoon salt

Brown meat and garlic in oil. Add water to cover, and put in the other ingredients. Reduce heat and simmer 2 to 3 hours, or until meat is very tender. Strain the stock and chill so that fat is easy to remove. Carefully separate the meat from the fat and bone. Both meat and stock can be the basis of many dishes. *Serves 4.*

LAMB CURRY FROM SCRATCH

This is an excellent dish to cook ahead of time and refrigerate until you want to serve it. In that case, stir in a little more chicken before reheating. Serve with dry rice, chutney, and any other condiments that suit your fancy. A green vegetable, like peas or greens, will set off the curry to perfection—visually and with regard to taste. In India, this dish is often served with a few saucers of "cool" items on the side: grated coconut, finely diced banana, finely diced raw, seeded tomato or green pepper, and finely diced cucumber sprinkled with chopped dill—even nuts. A teaspoon of these is sprinkled over your plate, according to taste.

The colorful items make this a particularly suitable dish for a buffet supper.

2 pounds boneless lamb shoulder cut in small
    cubes
3 tablespoons margarine or butter
3 tablespoons vegetable oil
2 large onions, chopped
4 cloves garlic, crushed
1 to 2 tablespoons hot or mild curry powder
1 lemon, sliced and seeded
2 large tart apples, peeled, seeded, and
    chopped
1 cup chicken bouillon
1 teaspoon salt
⅛ teaspoon pepper

In a large skillet or Dutch oven, brown lamb in margarine or butter and oil. Remove the meat and set aside. Add onions and garlic to the fat remaining in the pan and sauté them, stirring constantly until onions are soft but not brown. Add 1 tablespoon of the curry powder and cook, still stirring, for 2 minutes more. Put the meat back into the pan. Stir in lemon slices, apples, chicken bouillon, salt, and pepper. Bring to a boil, reduce heat, cover, and simmer gently for 1 to 1½ hours, or until meat is tender and apples and onions have cooked down into the sauce. Stir from time to time. After about 45 minutes of cooking, check seasoning and add more curry powder if needed. If sauce seems thin, continue cooking uncovered until thick. *Serves 4 to 6.*

CURRY OF COOKED LAMB

A good way to use leftovers from a lamb roast, or meat left from lamb stock. Serve over rice with assorted condiments, such as chutney, peanuts, chopped celery, grated carrots, grated coconut, chopped bananas, bacon bits, sieved hard-boiled egg yolks, and chopped egg whites.

2 cups cooked lamb pieces
2 tablespoons margarine or butter
¼ cup raisins
1 large onion, thinly sliced
1 large cooking apple, peeled and sliced

1 tablespoon curry powder
2 cups lamb cooking liquid or chicken
    bouillon
Salt to taste
1½ tablespoons cornstarch dissolved in 2
    tablespoons cold water

Brown lamb pieces in margarine or butter. Then add raisins, onion, and apple, and continue cooking, stirring often, for 10 minutes. Add 1 tablespoon curry powder, or more if you like, and cook for 1 minute more. Stir in the stock, cover, and simmer about 30 minutes, stirring occasionally; add salt to taste. Turn up the heat, add cornstarch mixture, and boil for 1 minute. *Serves 6.*

LAMB CHOP RISOTTO SKILLET

Salt
6 shoulder lamb chops
2 tablespoons vegetable oil
1 onion, thinly sliced
1 green pepper, slivered
1 cup converted rice
2 cups chicken bouillon
Salt, pepper, and oregano to taste
1 tomato, cut into 6 wedges

Heat a large skillet which has a tight-fitting cover. Sprinkle a little salt over the surface of the skillet and brown chops on both sides. Cook until tender. Remove and keep warm. Heat oil in the same skillet. Brown onion and green pepper. Stir in rice. Add bouillon and seasonings. Bring to a boil. Add tomato, cover, reduce heat and simmer 14 minutes, or until rice is tender. Uncover, place chops on top of rice and heat through before serving. *Serves 6.*

LAMB SHANKS BRAISED

4 lamb shanks
½ cup all-purpose flour
1 teaspoon salt
⅛ teaspoon pepper
3 tablespoons vegetable oil
1 large onion, chopped
1 clove garlic, minced

1 cup chicken bouillon
1 carrot, chopped
3 stalks celery, chopped
1 large tomato, peeled and quartered
½ teaspoon rosemary
½ cup dry red wine
2 tablespoons chopped parsley
Grated rind of 1 lemon

Roll lamb shanks in combined flour, salt, and pepper. Heat oil in Dutch oven and brown meat on all sides. Add onion and garlic. When the onion is transparent, add bouillon and bring to boil. Reduce to simmer and add carrot, celery, tomato, and rosemary. Cover and simmer for about 1½ hours. Add wine 15 minutes before cooking ends, and simmer 10 minutes more. Place shanks in hot platter lined with vegetables and sauce. Pour over shanks. Garnish with parsley and lemon rind. *Serves 4 to 6.*

LAMB SHANKS IN TOMATO SAUCE

5 meaty lamb shanks
1 teaspoon salt
⅛ teaspoon pepper
2 cloves garlic, crushed
¼ teaspoon paprika
½ teaspoon basil
2 medium onions, sliced
1 28-ounce can whole tomatoes
1 green pepper, seeded and slivered

Into the shanks, rub mixed salt, pepper, garlic, paprika, and basil. Place sliced onions in bottom of roasting pan and put shanks on top of them. Set in 350° oven, uncovered, for 30 minutes. Add tomatoes and pepper. Bake 1½ hours. Turn shanks every 30 minutes and spoon tomato sauce over them. *Serves 6 to 8.*

LAMB STRIPS WITH LIMA BEANS, ORIENTAL STYLE

Lamb leg, especially the New Zealand variety, is often a good buy; next time you buy one, cut away a pound (a slice about 1 inch thick) and reserve it to make this easy, delicious dish.

2 tablespoons oil
3 cloves garlic, peeled
1 pound strips from leg of lamb
3 teaspoons soy sauce
½ package frozen lima beans

Measure 1 tablespoon oil. Crush garlic. Slice lamb into strips $2 \times 1 \times ¼$ inches. This is easiest when lamb is slightly frozen. Measure 2 teaspoons soy sauce and 1 more tablespoon oil. Thaw and dry limas. Measure another teaspoon soy sauce. Set ingredients in the order listed by the range, and warm a serving dish. Heat a large frying pan to almost smoking hot. Swirl in 1 tablespoon oil, count to 20, add crushed garlic and stir until brown. Turn heat to medium, add lamb and 2 teaspoons soy sauce, and stir-fry 3 minutes. Turn lamb into serving dish, and pour pan juices over it. Turn heat to medium high, add 1 tablespoon oil, count to 20. Add lima beans, stir-fry 2 minutes. Add 1 teaspoon soy sauce, stir-fry 1 minute more. Pour limas over lamb strips and serve at once. *Serves 4.*

LAMB AND CUCUMBER STEW, ARUBA STYLE

The cucumbers used in the Dutch islands are the small round ones called apple or lemon cucumbers. Use these, unpeeled, if your market has them; otherwise use regular cucumbers, peeled.

3 tablespoons vegetable oil
2 pounds lean, boneless shoulder of lamb
 cut into 1½-inch cubes, or cut the meat
 from lamb shanks
2 medium onions, finely chopped
1 clove garlic, chopped
½ cup celery, finely chopped
1 medium green bell pepper, seeded and
 chopped
2 medium tomatoes, peeled and chopped
Salt and freshly ground pepper to taste
½ teaspoon grated nutmeg
Water to cover
2 pounds cucumbers, cut into ¼-inch slices
2 pounds potatoes, peeled and cubed
Hot pepper sauce to taste

Heat oil in a heavy saucepan or casserole and lightly brown lamb cubes all over. Lift out and set aside. Add onions, garlic, celery, and green pepper and sauté until onion is tender but not browned. Return lamb to saucepan. Add tomatoes, salt and freshly ground pepper to taste, and nutmeg. Add water to cover and cook, covered, at a gentle simmer for 1½ hours. Add cucumbers and potatoes and cook for 20 minutes longer, or until the potatoes are done. Adjust seasonings and add hot pepper sauce to taste. *Serves 6.*

LAMB LOAF

A luxury edition of this is made with mushrooms instead of celery.

½ pound celery, minced
1 tablespoon chopped onion
1 tablespoon chopped green pepper
2 tablespoons chopped parsley
½ cup margarine or butter
2 pounds shoulder of lamb, ground
½ cup milk
1 egg
½ cup bread crumbs
Salt and freshly ground pepper to taste
¼ cup chicken bouillon or water

Sauté celery, onion, green pepper, and parsley in margarine or butter over low heat, stirring occasionally, for about 10 minutes so that they cook but do not brown. Mix all ingredients together with the lightest possible touch and form into a loaf. Place in buttered shallow baking dish. Add enough bouillon or water to cover the bottom of the dish. Bake in 350° oven 50 minutes, basting occasionally

and adding more bouillon or water if necessary. *Serves 4 to 6.*

LAMB WITH DILL

Boiled potatoes and spinach salad are excellent with this dish.

3 pounds neck of lamb
2 sprigs fresh dill
Boiling water to cover
1 teaspoon salt

Put lamb and dill into a pot with boiling water to cover and add the salt. Cover the pot and simmer until the meat is tender (about 2 hours). Remove the lamb and keep warm. Strain the stock and if necessary boil it down until it is reduced to about 2 cups for use in the *Dill Sauce* (below). *Serves 4.*

DILL SAUCE

2 tablespoons margarine or butter
2 tablespoons flour
2 cups lamb stock
4 teaspoons vinegar
2 teaspoons sugar
½ teaspoon salt
2 egg yolks
3 tablespoons chopped fresh dill

Melt margarine or butter and stir in flour smoothly. Add stock and cook, stirring constantly, until slightly thickened. Add vinegar, sugar, and salt and mix well. Beat egg yolks with a little of the hot sauce. Return to sauce and mix. Do not allow sauce to boil. Stir in chopped dill and serve over lamb.

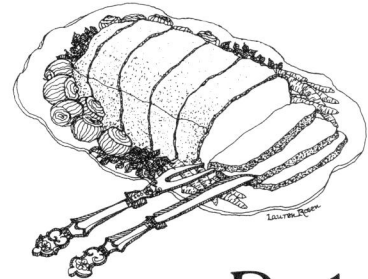

Pork

Pork roasts cost much more than they once did, and they can be a dubious bargain because of the amount of fat usually included. However, you can justify the purchase of a pork roast, however fat it may be, in several ways. For one, you can use the fat drippings to make *headcheese, Canadian style*, or a *pâté maison*. For another, pork leftovers are the basis of many really delicious Chinese dishes, which call for only a cupful or so of pork so that the leftovers from the roast will go much farther than the leftovers from a comparable beef or lamb roast. Look over the Oriental recipes in Section Seven which use odds and ends of leftover pork, and try a couple. Oriental dishes including pork needn't be used only with Oriental side dishes; they are also very good with plain boiled rice or with noodles and any green salad. Ham is another bargain when you consider the multiple uses there are for ham odds and ends.

Pig's feet and knuckles, and other bargain portions of the animal, make tasty dishes, too—but require some extra cooking time. The recipes here using these pork oddments are well worth trying, both for economy's sake and because many are considered delicacies by knowledgeable cooks.

Pork Chops

The prices of spareribs and pork chops, two economy standbys of the past, seem to be escalating along with everything else. The bargains now are in the end or shoulder cuts, either chops or country-style spareribs. When you find these meats at a good price, they're often packaged in large quantity. Don't pass them up, even if you live alone. Buy the whole package and freeze it. Use the chops one at a time if that's all you need.

If your freezer can't hold even another ice cube, use the budget pork in a stewlike recipe that can provide you with several meals. These dishes usually taste better reheated the second day. Be sure when reheating pork or any other meat to bring the cooking liquid to a boil before serving. This will prevent the growth of any decay-causing organisms.

The recipes here and the table of Basic Pork Cuts will give you some ideas on how to use various pork and ham products. Try substituting some of the other pork cuts that do appear on supermarket meat counters in your recipes.

DESCRIPTION	COOKING METHOD
Fresh Pork Shoulder Whole (New York style shoulder)	Roast or braise
Blade Boston Roast (pork butt, Boston butt, Boston shoulder)	Braise
Arm Picnic (picnic shoulder)	Bake, braise
Pork Hock (pork shank)	Braise, stew
Leg, Rump Portion (leg butt, leg sirloin portion)	Roast, braise
Leg, Shank Portion	Roast, braise
Pig's Feet (pig's trotters)	Braise, stew
Loin Back Ribs (country back bones, ribs for barbecue)	Roast, braise, stew
Pork Spareribs	Roast, braise, stew
Fresh Pork Side (belly, streak of lean, pork belly)	Boil, broil, sauté
Jowl (cheek, chap, chaw)	Boil, broil, sauté

ROAST PORK CHOPS

Dry vermouth is inexpensive and does wonders to all sorts of meat dishes. If no vermouth or wine is available, you can use tag ends of white wine, or a little wine vinegar or lemon juice.

10 end or shoulder cut pork chops
½ cup flour
2 teaspoons salt
¾ teaspoon pepper
10 large carrots
10 small potatoes
10 medium onions
4 cloves garlic
3 tablespoons margarine or butter
1 cup dry white vermouth or white wine
1 bay leaf
¼ teaspoon sage or thyme

Preheat oven to 325°. Dredge pork chops in flour mixed with 1 teaspoon salt and ¼ teaspoon pepper. Peel carrots, potatoes, onions, and garlic. Heat margarine or butter in a frying pan. Brown the chops in the hot fat. Remove from pan, and arrange them in a large roasting pan. Try not to stack them, though they may overlap a little. Put carrots, potatoes, and onions on top of meat and add garlic, vermouth, bay leaf, sage or thyme, 1 teaspoon salt, and ½ teaspoon pepper. Cover and cook in oven until juice of pork chops runs clear and yellow (not pink). It should take about 45 minutes. *Serves 10.*

HERB-STUFFED PORK CHOPS

If possible, use fresh herbs for this—fresh herbs make a real difference.

4 center cut pork chops, cut 2 inches thick
1¼ teaspoons salt
¼ teaspoon plus pinch pepper
¼ pound mushrooms, chopped
¼ stick melted margarine or butter
½ cup soft bread crumbs
¼ teaspoon thyme
½ teaspoon savory
½ teaspoon basil
¼ cup chopped parsley
Chicken bouillon (about 1 cup)

Have chops prepared with a pocket cut into the lean part. Wipe them and sprinkle with 1 teaspoon salt and ¼ teaspoon pepper. Sauté mushrooms in margarine or butter for 3 minutes. Mix in bread crumbs and herbs. Season lightly with ¼ teaspoon salt and pinch pepper. Stuff into the pockets. Fasten openings with skewers. Sear quickly in a hot skillet. Reduce heat. Pour in bouillon just up to the stuffing line and simmer gently for 1 hour, adding more if necessary. When done, remove chops to a hot platter, thicken gravy by simmering for 5 to 10 minutes, and pour it over the chops. *Serves 4.*

MARINATED PORK CHOPS

Cold leftover marinated pork chops make wonderful sandwiches.

3 teaspoons salt
⅓ teaspoon pepper
¾ teaspoon sage or thyme
2 bay leaves, crumbled
⅛ teaspoon allspice
3 or 4 cloves garlic, mashed
10 end or shoulder cut pork chops
4 tablespoons margarine

Mix all the seasonings together in a large bowl and rub some into each pork chop. Put meat into bowl and cover with a cloth or lid. You can refrigerate chops for up to 2 days, turning them occasionally. They will get better with time. Sauté chops in margarine over medium heat in a large skillet, turning once, for about 20 minutes, or until tender. Remove from heat and allow to rest a few minutes, covered, before serving. *Serves 10.*

BRAISED PORK CHOPS

This is another way to handle pork chops marinated as described above.

4 marinated pork chops
2 tablespoons margarine or butter
2 onions, minced
1 tablespoon all-purpose flour
1½ cups or 1 can peeled tomatoes
½ cup beef bouillon
½ teaspoon salt
⅛ teaspoon pepper

Preheat oven to 325°. Brown pork chops in margarine or butter and set aside. Cook onions in the same pan until they are transparent but not browned. Add flour and continue cooking and stirring for 2 minutes. Add tomatoes, bouillon, salt, and pepper. Cover and simmer for 5 more minutes. Arrange pork chops in a casserole or roasting pan and pour tomato sauce over them. Cover and heat on stove top until liquid bubbles. Place pan in oven and simmer slowly for about ½ hour, or until juice runs clear when you prick chops. *Serves 4.*

SLICED PORK, ORIENTAL STYLE

This is a great way to stretch—and enjoy—a tougher bit of pork meat. It's the Oriental trick of stir-frying small strips of meat with vegetables. It makes lesser cuts of meat delicious and stretches just a little meat to serve many. Nice with plain boiled rice or noodles.

¼ cup oil
½ pound pork, cut into fine strips
2 tablespoons soy sauce
¼ pound bean sprouts
1 4-ounce can water chestnuts
½ tablespoon finely chopped fresh ginger
1 large onion, cut into rings
½ cup 1-inch-thick celery slices
1 green pepper, cut into fine slices
1 tablespoon cornstarch
2 tablespoons water

Heat oil to very hot in a frying pan. Add pork and stir-fry for 2 minutes. Add soy sauce, bean sprouts, water chestnuts, ginger, and stir-fry 3 minutes more. Add onion, celery, and pepper, and stir-fry 3 more minutes. Combine cornstarch and water and pour into liquid in frying pan. Stir until all ingredients are glazed, then correct seasonings—adding soy sauce or salt as needed—and serve at once. *Serves 4.*

PIG'S KNUCKLES AND CABBAGE

An economy dish our grandmothers knew how to cook.

3 pig's knuckles
Boiling water to cover
½ tablespoon plus 1 teaspoon salt
1 cup celery tops
1 bay leaf
½ teaspoon thyme
¼ teaspoon pepper
1 clove garlic, peeled and minced
1 medium head green cabbage, cut in narrow
　　wedges

Cover knuckles with boiling water; add ½ tablespoon salt, celery, bay leaf, thyme, pepper, and garlic; cover and simmer 2 hours. Add cabbage and 1 teaspoon salt, cover, cook until cabbage is tender—about 10 to 15 minutes. Serve in a deep platter with cabbage around the sides. *Serves 4.*

SPARERIBS AND SAUERKRAUT

3 pounds spareribs
2 to 4 tablespoons vegetable oil
2 large onions, peeled and sliced
½ teaspoon salt
¼ teaspoon pepper
½ cup boiling water
1 quart sauerkraut, drained and washed in
　　cold water
½ teaspoon caraway seeds
1 apple, peeled, cored, and grated

In a large Dutch oven, sauté spareribs in oil until brown on all sides. Add onions; sauté 5 minutes. Season with salt and pepper, add water, cover and simmer 1 hour. Add sauerkraut, caraway seeds, and apple, and cook 30 minutes more. *Serves 6.*

BARBECUED SPARERIBS

1 6-ounce can tomato paste
½ cup water
2 cloves garlic, mashed
4 tablespoons Worcestershire sauce
½ teaspoon chili powder
½ teaspoon sugar
Salt and pepper to taste

Dash Tabasco sauce
3 or 4 pounds spareribs or country-style ribs

Preheat oven to 450°. Combine everything but the ribs in a small saucepan and simmer 5 to 10 minutes. Put the spareribs in a shallow baking dish and bake for about 20 minutes, until most of the visible fat has cooked off. Drain, lower heat to 350°, and bake for 1½ to 2 hours. Baste from time to time with the sauce until all the sauce is used. Serve with pan drippings scraped on the ribs. *Serves 4.*

SAUSAGE-STUFFED PEPPERS

A lot of eating for a small investment.

1 rounded cup yellow or green split peas
2⅓ cups water
½ teaspoon salt
1 small bay leaf
1 clove garlic, peeled and minced
2 tablespoons margarine or butter
1 small onion, peeled and minced
1 cup water
2 8-ounce cans tomato sauce
⅛ teaspoon poultry seasoning, oregano, or
　　thyme
1 pound pork sausage meat
8 medium green peppers
Boiling salted water
Dry bread crumbs

Cook peas in a saucepan with water, salt, bay leaf, and garlic. Bring to a boil, reduce heat, and cook 45 minutes, or until the peas are tender and all the water has evaporated. Remove bay leaf and set it aside. Heat margarine or butter in a skillet. Add onion and ½ cup water. Bring to a boil and cook until all the water has boiled away and the onion is soft and transparent. Stir the onion into the peas along with 1 can tomato sauce and the poultry seasoning. Break the sausage meat into chunks. Place in a heavy skillet, over medium heat, and brown. Combine with the split peas. Cut the tops off the peppers, then cut out the ribs and brush away the seeds. Drop into a kettle of boiling salted water for about 3 minutes. Lift from the kettle, drain, and cool.

Stuff each pepper with the split pea and sausage mixture, dividing it evenly. Sprinkle the tops with bread crumbs and place in a shallow pan. Mix the remaining can of tomato sauce with ½ cup water and pour around the stuffed peppers. Bake in a preheated 350° oven 45 minutes. Serve at once. *Serves 8.*

FRANKFURTER JUBILEE

A delicious way to use some of the best of our budget-saver ingredients.

1 pound frankfurters
1 small cabbage (about 1¼ pounds)
Water
¼ cup margarine
¼ cup all-purpose flour
1 teaspoon salt
Dash pepper
2 cups nonfat dry milk (reconstituted)
2 tablespoons prepared mustard

Cut frankfurters into 1-inch pieces. Coarsely shred cabbage. Add a small amount of water, cover tightly, and cook over low heat 5 minutes. Drain well. Melt margarine in a saucepan. Blend in flour, salt, and pepper. Gradually add milk and cook, stirring constantly, until thickened. Stir in mustard. Arrange half the cabbage in the bottom of a greased 1½-quart casserole. Arrange half the frankfurter pieces on top of the cabbage. Pour half the mustard sauce over this. Repeat layers. Cover and bake in 350° oven 35 to 40 minutes. *Serves 6 to 8.*

RED AND GREEN CASSEROLE FOR A CROWD

1 pound green noodles
Boiling salted water
2 pounds frankfurters
2 medium onions, chopped
2 tablespoons margarine
½ pound Cheddar cheese, shredded
4 tablespoons Worcestershire sauce
2 10-ounce cans condensed tomato soup

1 cup water
1 teaspoon salt

Boil noodles in salted water for 9 minutes. Drain. Cut franks into long, thin slices and brown, with the onions, in margarine. Add remaining ingredients and cook together, stirring frequently, until cheese melts. Combine with noodles. Place in a buttered casserole. Bake in a 400° oven 25 minutes. *Serves 12 to 16.*

HEADCHEESE FROM LEFTOVER PORK

This recipe appears in my *Take-It-Along Cookbook* as Galantine de Porc Marcel. It's a wonderful luncheon or picnic or buffet dish. Here, the recipe has been adapted to use bits of meat from cooked pork roast and its bones.

4 cups leftover cooked pork meat
1½ pounds pork hocks
1 onion, peeled, stuck with 8 whole cloves
3 cups water
2½ teaspoons salt
¼ teaspoon pepper
¼ teaspoon savory
¼ teaspoon ground thyme
⅛ teaspoon nutmeg
3 small cloves garlic, peeled
1 tablespoon minced parsley

In a large heavy kettle, combine meats, onion, water, salt, pepper, and spices. Bring to a boil and simmer, covered, until meat is thoroughly cooked, about 1½ to 2 hours. Remove meat and reserve cooking liquid. Remove rinds from pork hocks and blend rinds in electric blender with garlic, parsley, and 1 cup of the cooking liquid. Remove the pork hock meat from the bones and chop coarsely. Turn it into a large bowl and stir in the blendered rind mixture. Check the seasonings and add more salt and pepper if necessary. Pour into a 4-quart mold, rinsed with cold water, and refrigerate overnight before serving. *Serves 12 to 15* for appetizers, first course, or sandwiches.

CURRY OF COOKED PORK

Follow the recipe for *Curry of Cooked Lamb* but substitute 2 cups of cooked pork pieces for the lamb.

Hams

Ham can be an economy cut or a princely splurge. A specially cured Virginia ham may cost you more than prime ribs. The hams you see in the supermarket are certainly not as delicate as individually cured hams, but they can be turned into some good meals at budget prices.

The low-priced supermarket hams are most likely to be fully cooked hams. They can be eaten cold just as they are, or warmed and served as baked ham. Since water is added to these cuts (it says so on the label), they often taste much better with a little more cooking. It's important not to sweat away too much water, or else the ham will be too salty. Taste your fully cooked ham before you bake it. If it seems salty, serve it cold and use the leftovers in other dishes. If not, you can bake it until the internal temperature reaches 130° (about 15 minutes per pound).

One advantage of buying ham roasts when the price is right is that you can make an almost endless variety of dishes from leftover ham slices or ham bits. Throughout this book you'll find meat, vegetable, grain, and dried cereal dishes, as well as salads, in which leftovers from ham can be used.

If you want ham but don't want to invest in a whole roast, buy the little daisy ham rolls. Excellent in flavor, they serve 4 to 6 people generously and are reasonably priced. These are best boiled slowly, as in the recipe for *Delicious Daisy Ham*. Slices from an uncooked daisy ham roll can be used as cooked ham in the making of dishes calling for leftover ham. They also make great sautéed ham to go with eggs on those mornings when a big meal is called for. Or they are great sautéed with fried potatoes.

DELICIOUS DAISY HAM

This recipe is from my friend Sally Larkin Erath, author of *Cooking for Two*, and a wonderful food lady of the New England School. I've never tasted a daisy ham as good as when cooked this way. Use the broth that remains from the cooking to make split pea soup. It's terrific.

2 daisy ham rolls
3 quarts cold water
2 large onions, peeled
6 whole cloves
14 peppercorns
1 bay leaf
1 teaspoon dried thyme
¾ cup cider vinegar
1 cup dark brown sugar, firmly packed

Remove the outer casing of the ham and place in a kettle with all the ingredients listed. Cover and cook on low for 1½ to 2 hours. Allow hams to remain in broth until it has cooled if they are to be served the next day, then bake in a slow oven to reheat. *Serves 10 to 12.*

HAM AND POTATO CASSEROLE

A little ham can go a very long way when combined with vegetables, as in this recipe.

1 small onion
2 tablespoons margarine or butter
1 thick slice ham (about 3 ounces)
3 eggs
½ cup Swiss cheese
½ cup milk
1 scallion, chopped, or 1 slice onion, minced
Salt and pepper to taste
3 or 4 medium potatoes
Butter
½ teaspoon paprika or more to taste

Preheat oven to 375°. Peel and finely chop onion. Heat margarine or butter in a skillet until the foaming subsides. Add chopped onion and cook slowly until transparent but not browned. Dice ham and blend in a large bowl with eggs, cheese, milk, chopped scallion, salt, and pepper. Peel potatoes and grate them on the coarse side of a food grater. Add chopped onion and grated potatoes to ham mixture and blend. Pour mixture in a casserole, dot with butter, and sprinkle heavily with paprika. Bake for about 45 minutes. *Serves 4.*

HAM AND VEGETABLE CASSEROLE

1 medium eggplant, peeled
¼ cup all-purpose flour
½ teaspoon salt
⅛ teaspoon pepper
3 tablespoons vegetable oil
6 slices ham
2 large tomatoes, cut in 6 slices
6 teaspoons margarine or butter
Salt to taste
¼ teaspoon pepper
½ tablespoon brown sugar
Mozzarella cheese (6 thick slices)

Slice eggplant in 6 slices and place the slices between paper towels with a heavy weight on top for 1 hour. Heat broiler. Coat eggplant with flour seasoned with salt and pepper and brown lightly in hot oil. Place the slices in a shallow pan. Put 1 ham slice on top of each eggplant slice, then a slice of tomato. Add 1 teaspoon margarine or butter to each and sprinkle with salt, pepper, and brown sugar. Place under broiler for 5 minutes. Add a slice of mozzarella cheese to each tomato slice and broil 5 minutes more. *Serves 6.*

CREAMED LUNCHEON MEAT AND MUSHROOMS

¼ pound mushrooms
3 tablespoons vegetable oil
¼ cup all-purpose flour
1½ cups milk
¼ teaspoon salt
⅛ teaspoon pepper
1¼ cups canned luncheon meat, coarsely shredded
¼ teaspoon bottled thick meat sauce
4 pieces hot toast

Slice, then sauté mushrooms in oil in top of double boiler, over direct heat for about 5 minutes. Stir in flour, then milk, salt, and pepper, and heat over boiling water until smooth and thickened. Add luncheon meat and meat sauce. Heat through. Serve on squares of buttered toast. *Serves 4.*

CREAMED HAM AND PEAS

Make *Creamed Luncheon Meat and Mushrooms,* using 1 cup cooked or canned peas in place of mushrooms.

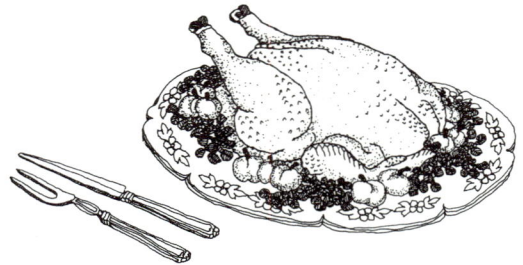

Poultry

Chicken remains one of the best buys. Roasted to a golden brown, it is delicious; stewed, it makes tasty casseroles that can be combined with the simplest or the most extravagant vegetables and condiments. Chicken can be used as a substitute in recipes calling for expensive veal or more exotic birds. And there need be no waste. Chicken bones, cooked or raw, can be used to make chicken soup and chicken stock for use in casseroles and stews; chicken livers make great dishes on their own; the giblets can be used as extenders for recipes calling for highly flavored meat parts such as kidney, or they can be used to make superb giblet stuffing or gravy for any poultry dish. Cooked leftover chicken can be the beginning of a whole new adventure in eating.

Buys in Chicken

As a rule, most markets charge more for cut-up chicken than for whole chicken, although whole chicken is the better buy when you know what can be made with the extras —back, neck, wing tips, liver, and giblets. So, cut your own. It really isn't hard. All you need is a large knife sharp enough to slice cleanly through the skin around the upper thigh. Once you have sliced through this skin, you will see where to place the knife to separate the thigh and leg from the breast. Once the thigh and leg have been cut away, the backbone is exposed. A sharp knife, given enough pressure, can easily cut the skinny backbone from the breast section, and when that's done your chicken is quartered.

Chicken wings are less of a buy than they once were. To some gourmets, the most delicate chicken meat is in the large portion of the wing section. Generally, chicken wings are sold with the wing tip attached. The wing tip isn't edible, so you must slice this away before you begin to cook. Don't discard the wing tip—add it to the backbone and other chicken scraps to make chicken soup and stock. When you buy a whole chicken for quartering, remove the wings from the breast portion; they won't be missed. Since most of us serve chicken at least once a week, it doesn't take long to accumulate enough chicken wings to make a meal.

When you run across sales of chicken, be wary of buying to freeze. Sales that don't specify fresh-killed chickens are almost sure to offer chicken that has already been frozen.

46

Make sure chicken you plan to freeze is fresh; otherwise the end product won't be the best chicken you've ever tasted. Do take advantage of the frozen bargains to cut the cost of an upcoming dinner—but don't plan to freeze for the future.

Buying Fowl

Fresh-killed fowl can be a very good buy, particularly in rural areas. Fowl generally are just older chickens. The meat is good but is tougher than that of roasting chicken. There is also more fat than on young fryers. Use fowl for casseroles and boiled chickens; use any extra cooking liquid to make soups and for bouillon or stocks for other casseroles. Try freezing chicken bouillon or stock in 1-cup portions. Before freezing let it chill overnight in the refrigerator, and next morning remove the chicken fat congealed on the surface. The bouillon then will be fat-free. You can use fresh chicken fat for cooking almost any time butter is called for. Saved-up chicken livers and chicken fat make an excellent Chopped Chicken Liver dish.

Other Buys in Birds

Occasionally supermarkets offer for sale frozen ducklings, small turkeys, turkey breast, and other birdy parts. These are possibilities for the home freezer when they are sold still frozen. Don't buy thawed birds and then refreeze; they won't be very good.

Duckling is an excellent meat, dark and more flavorful than chicken thighs. However, it is fatty meat—duck roasts have a lot of fatty drippings—and it is bony meat. The thigh and leg have less meat than chickens of comparable size.

Frozen small turkeys offer the most meat in the breast areas and usually are good buys because the leftovers are so useful.

Frozen cooked breast meat doesn't seem to have the flavor of breast meat on a roast turkey, but it can be a good buy and very useful if yours is a household where lots of sandwiches are in demand. Or you can add flavor to frozen cooked turkey breast by saucing it with saved-up turkey gravy from the freezer. Frozen turkey gravy, heated and offered with cooked turkey breast and chilled cranberry sauce, can be quite a treat when Thanksgiving and the other turkey days are far away on the calendar.

Goose and the game birds don't reach most American tables with great regularity. Goose is a delicious bird, but it is usually expensive and it holds a great deal of fat. Like chicken fat, goose fat is very finely flavored and may be saved up from drippings, stored in the refrigerator or freezer, and used for cooking other meats and for making pâtés and tureens.

The game birds are in a class by themselves, and usually only families with hunting members or friends get to serve them. As long as the game birds are marinated in a *basic marinade*, they can be cooked in a manner similar to that used to cook duck. Most game birds are lean and will require basting during the baking. Goose or chicken fat is excellent for this purpose. Most game birds are strongly flavored, and to enjoy them most serve a chutney, cranberries, or other relish with them.

Turkey Leftovers

What to do with leftover turkey is perhaps *the* problem of the holiday food department. That's partly because the wise budgeter will buy a larger turkey than needed, since the big ones cost relatively less per pound than the smaller sizes. There are, however, many possibilities. Turkey Hash St. Germain, as served for many years at the Ritz-Carlton Hotel in New York, is one. Just put your turkey meat through the grinder, then mix it with a good medium cream sauce and put it into flat individual baking dishes. Then pipe a border of pureed peas all around the border of each dish. Now run under the broiler to glaze the top of the hash.

Many people prefer cold turkey to hot. If you decide to serve it that way, be sure to use leftover cranberry sauce as an accompaniment. The combination is exceedingly good.

You can make wonderful casseroles from leftover turkey, mixing it with vegetables and whatever sauce you may invent at the moment. A sauce made from condensed canned cream of mushroom soup has a particular affinity for turkey. Or you might put it into your favorite tomato sauce. Shred the meat very finely, blender for a few minutes, and mix it with finely diced pickled cucumber, onion, radishes, sour cream, mayonnaise, pepper and salt to taste, and you have a fine dip. Vary the toppings for casseroles. Prepared packaged stuffing, dotted with butter before baking, is an especially good one for any poultry casserole. Use leftovers to make an aspic. Or cream it with small pieces of mushroom, cauliflower, and artichoke hearts, and fill pastry shells with the mixture, sprinkled with chopped parsley before serving—a real party dish.

BASIC ROAST CHICKEN

This way of cooking supermarket chicken improves the flavor and yields a nice pan gravy to serve with it. Save any leftover gravy to use in casseroles and for flavoring other dishes—frozen turkey breast, for instance.

1 2½- to 3-pound chicken, whole or cut up
1 teaspoon curry powder
1 teaspoon salt
¼ teaspoon pepper
½ cup chicken bouillon or water
½ small onion, peeled and halved

Preheat oven to 450°. Sprinkle chicken with curry, salt, and pepper. Bake at 450° for 20 minutes. Add bouillon and onion to pan, lower heat to 325°, and bake 45 to 60 minutes more. The chicken is done when the legs move very easily in their sockets. *Serves 4 to 6.*

FRENCH BAKED CHICKEN

This recipe may be doubled, but do not double the sherry. To make clarified butter, melt a stick of butter over low heat until the milky portion is separated from the oily portion. The oily portion is clarified butter.

1 3-pound roasting chicken, whole
Salt and freshly ground black pepper
4 to 6 tablespoons clarified butter (see above)
2 medium onions, chopped
½ cup dry sherry
Water
1 bay leaf
½ teaspoon thyme
⅛ teaspoon ground clove
1 teaspoon salt
2 tablespoons all-purpose flour

Sprinkle inside of chicken liberally with salt and pepper. Truss the bird with string. Heat clarified butter in a deep casserole or Dutch oven and sauté onions until soft and golden. Remove onions and set aside. In the remaining butter, brown the chicken slowly on all sides, adding more butter if necessary. When chicken is brown, return onions to pot and pour sherry over all. Cover tightly and bake 1 hour in a 325° oven. Meantime, simmer chicken giblets in water to cover with the bay leaf, thyme, ground clove, and 1 teaspoon salt for the entire time the chicken is cooking. Strain, reserving broth, and cut up the giblets fairly fine. When chicken is done, remove from pot and keep warm. Remove pot from heat. Add 2 tablespoons flour to the fat in bottom of pot and stir until smooth. Add a cup of giblet broth and the chopped giblets and cook, stirring constantly, until thickened. Serve in a gravy boat or bowl. *Serves 4.*

GIBLET GRAVY

You can use this recipe to make gravy from the giblets of any domestic fowl.

Giblets and neck
Boiling water to cover
1 bay leaf
¼ teaspoon thyme
1 small onion, peeled
4 whole cloves
1 teaspoon salt
⅛ teaspoon pepper

1 sprig parsley
4 tablespoons pan drippings
4 tablespoons flour
Water, if needed
Salt and pepper (optional)

Cook giblets and neck in boiling water with the next 7 ingredients, over low heat for 1 hour. Drain, reserving stock. Discard neck and chop the remaining giblets fine. Return to the stock. When the bird is done, pour off all but 4 tablespoons of the pan fat. Add flour and stir in smoothly, scraping up all the good brown pieces that stick to the pan. Add giblet stock and enough boiling water to make 2 cups. Stir until thickened. Add salt and pepper, if needed. *Makes 2 cups or more.*

CHICKEN CHARLOTTE

2 3-pound broiler-fryers, cut into frying pieces
¼ cup all-purpose flour
1 teaspoon salt
⅛ teaspoon pepper
4 tablespoons margarine or butter
½ pint milk or cream
2 1-ounce cans chopped clams and juice
Paprika to garnish

Toss chicken pieces with flour combined with salt and pepper. Melt margarine or butter in a Dutch oven or large skillet and sauté chicken pieces in it until golden. Add milk or cream and simmer gently 20 minutes. Add clams and simmer 5 minutes more. Serve with sauce poured over chicken, and sprinkled with paprika. *Serves 6.*

SOUTHERN CHICKEN PUDDING

If you have any left over, this dish is absolutely delicious cold. Its seasoning is delicate and very nice. Cranberry sauce (or currant jelly) is a fine accompaniment, together with a green salad.

1 3-pound broiler-fryer, cut into frying pieces
Cold water to cover chicken
2 teaspoons salt

1 tablespoon chopped fresh parsley
¼ teaspoon powdered thyme
1 small pod dried red pepper
1 medium onion, chopped
1 stalk celery, sliced (without tops)
4 eggs, well beaten
2 cups undiluted evaporated milk
½ cup melted margarine or butter
Freshly ground pepper to taste
2 cups flour (about)

In a 3-quart saucepan arrange the chicken pieces. Add enough cold water to cover 1 inch above the chicken. Season with 1 teaspoon salt. Bring to a boil, then turn heat to simmer. Skim froth. Add parsley, thyme, red pepper, chopped onion, and sliced celery. Cover and simmer 40 minutes, or until chicken is tender. Remove from heat; reserve broth. Butter a 1½-quart glass baking dish. Preheat oven to 450°. Remove chicken from broth and arrange in a baking pan. In a separate bowl mix beaten eggs, evaporated milk, melted margarine or butter, 1 teaspoon salt, and pepper. Add enough unsifted flour to make a batter the consistency of pancake batter. Beat until smooth. Pour batter over chicken; do not stir. Reduce heat to 350° and bake 30 minutes, or until golden brown. May be served as is or with chicken gravy made by simmering the cooking broth until it is reduced. *Serves 4.*

CHICKEN WITH OLIVE CONDITE

2 broiler-fryers cut into frying pieces
1 12-ounce jar Olive Condite, drained (reserve liquid)
1 clove garlic, crushed
1 tablespoon dried basil
1 tablespoon dried oregano
1 tablespoon minced fresh parsley
2 tablespoons white wine
3 ounces tomato paste
3 ounces water
Salt and freshly ground pepper to taste

Brown chicken on high heat in the liquid from the Olive Condite (about 1 cup). Add condite, garlic, basil, oregano, and parsley and simmer 15 minutes. Add wine, tomato paste,

water, salt, and pepper. Cover pan and simmer
½ hour. *Serves 8.*

CORN CRISPED CHICKEN

1 cup cornflakes, crumbled
1 teaspoon salt
⅛ teaspoon pepper
1 broiler-fryer, cut up
½ cup evaporated milk

Combine crumbled cornflakes with salt and
pepper. Line shallow baking pan with aluminum foil. Dip chicken pieces in evaporated
milk, then roll immediately in seasoned corn-
flake crumbs. Place chicken pieces, skin side
up, in foil-lined pan. Do not crowd. Bake in
a 350° oven about 1 hour, or until tender.
Serves 4.

CHICKEN FRICASSÉE

A real family favorite that used to take nearly
all afternoon to prepare. May be served with
steamed rice or dumplings.

2 tablespoons shortening
1 2- to 3-pound fryer, cut up
1 teaspoon salt
⅛ teaspoon pepper
½ cup water
2 slices bacon, diced
1 egg yolk
1 cup milk or cream
2 tablespoons minced parsley for garnish

Heat shortening in a Dutch oven. Brown
chicken and season with salt and pepper. Add
water and bacon. Close cover securely. Cook
over medium heat 35 to 45 minutes, turning
occasionally. Remove chicken pieces from
Dutch oven and keep warm. Beat egg yolk and
add milk or cream. Pour into Dutch oven and
heat, stirring until the mixture is slightly thickened. Do not boil. Return chicken to Dutch
oven and stir until well coated with sauce.
Simmer a few minutes more. Garnish with
parsley. *Serves 4 to 6.*

PILAU CHICKEN AND RICE,
ST. LUCIA STYLE

2 tablespoons margarine
1 3½- to 4-pound chicken, cut up
2 medium onions, finely chopped
1 clove garlic, chopped
1 sprig thyme or ½ teaspoon dried thyme
2 or 3 sprigs parsley
1 bay leaf
1 stalk celery, with leaves
1 small fresh hot red pepper, or 1 hot dried
   pepper
1 pound tomatoes, peeled and chopped, or use
   canned tomatoes
1 teaspoon salt
⅛ teaspoon pepper
Water
2 cups rice
1 10-ounce package frozen green peas, thawed

Heat margarine in a heavy covered skillet
and sauté chicken pieces until golden brown.
Remove from pan and set aside. Sauté onions
and garlic until tender but not browned. Return chicken pieces to skillet. Tie thyme,
parsley, bay leaf, celery, and hot pepper in a
small square of cheesecloth and add to skillet
with tomatoes, salt, and pepper. Add enough
water to barely cover. Simmer gently, covered,
for 20 minutes. Remove chicken from pan.
Strain stock and discard cheesecloth. Bring
quantity of stock up to 4 cups. Return chicken
pieces to pan, add stock, stir in rice, cover, and
cook for 15 minutes. Add peas, cover, and continue cooking for about 10 minutes longer, or
until rice is tender and all liquid is absorbed.
Serves 6 to 8.

CHICKEN TETRAZZINI,
ECONOMY STYLE

The economy version replaces cream in this
recipe with milk. Very nice with canned artichoke hearts, which have been marinated in
bottled Italian dressing, and crisp bread sticks.

1½ tablespoons plus 1 teaspoon salt
5 quarts boiling water
12 ounces spaghetti

1 medium onion, chopped
¼ cup plus 2 tablespoons margarine or butter
¼ cup all-purpose flour
1½ cups chicken bouillon
1 cup milk
⅛ teaspoon pepper
½ cup dry vermouth or white wine
¾ cup grated Parmesan cheese
½ pound mushrooms, sliced, or
    1 4-ounce can sliced mushrooms, drained
3 large chicken breasts, split and cooked

Add 1½ tablespoons salt to rapidly boiling water. Add spaghetti gradually so that water continues to boil. Cook, uncovered, and stirring occasionally, until tender (about 9 minutes). Drain. Meanwhile, in a saucepan over low heat, sauté onion in ¼ cup margarine or butter until almost tender. Stir in flour. Gradually beat in bouillon and milk. Cook and stir until sauce boils. Add 1 teaspoon salt, pepper, vermouth, and ¼ cup of the cheese. Set aside. In a large skillet sauté the mushrooms in 2 tablespoons margarine or butter until lightly browned. Combine spaghetti, mushrooms, and chicken in a 2½- to 3-quart casserole and pour sauce on top. Sprinkle with remaining cheese. Refrigerate until ready to bake. Bake in a 375° oven 30 to 35 minutes, or until bubbling. (If this dish has not been refrigerated, bake for only 20 minutes.) *Serves 6.*

HOMEMADE CHICKEN ROLL

This will keep in the refrigerator for a week. Save the broth for soup.

3 or 4 chicken livers
½ stick margarine, or 4 tablespoons chicken
    fat, rendered
2 large chicken breasts, boned
½ pound leftover cooked ham
4 eggs, beaten
Cracker crumbs
¾ teaspoon salt
¼ teaspoon nutmeg
¼ teaspoon white pepper

1 teaspoon cold water
4 to 6 ounces chicken bouillon

Sauté livers in margarine or chicken fat, drain, and put through a fine blade of the meat grinder with chicken breasts and ham. Combine meats with 3 beaten eggs, 3 tablespoons cracker crumbs, salt, nutmeg, and white pepper. Form the mixture into a roll about 2½ inches in diameter and 10 inches long. Coat generously with cracker crumbs, brush with 1 egg beaten with cold water, and coat again with crumbs. Roll up in a clean white cloth. Tie the ends of the roll. Bring the bouillon to a boil, put the roll in and simmer it for 1 hour, turning it midway during the cooking period. Remove from broth carefully and unwrap. Chill at least a day. *Serves 4.*

CHICKEN BAKED WITH SOUR CREAM

This may be prepared in advance and refrigerated until you are ready to cook it.

2 chicken breasts, halved
1 teaspoon salt
⅛ teaspoon pepper
½ pint sour cream
Prepared poultry stuffing
Margarine or butter

Season chicken breasts with salt and pepper. Place them on a baking sheet and spread them thickly with sour cream. Sprinkle well with poultry stuffing. Dot liberally with margarine or butter. Bake in 375° oven 40 minutes, or until crisp and brown. *Serves 4.*

CHICKEN WITH APRICOTS

Instead of apricot halves, vary this recipe by using mandarin orange segments, or fresh seedless green grapes. Serve with rice, green beans, and hot French bread, accompanied by a dry white wine.

2 chicken breasts, halved
¾ cup flour
1 teaspoon salt
⅛ teaspoon pepper

1 teaspoon ground ginger
1 stick margarine or butter
½ cup water
1 tablespoon dehydrated minced onion, rehy-
    drated
1 17-ounce can apricot halves
Chicken bouillon as needed
2 tablespoons cornstarch

Mix chicken, flour, salt, pepper, and ginger in a paper bag. Shake until breasts are well coated. Sauté in half the margarine or butter at a fairly brisk heat until golden brown. Remove breasts to an ovenproof casserole big enough so that each piece lies by itself with no over-lapping. Add water and the remaining butter. Bake ½ hour in a 375° oven, basting frequently. Sauté the onion in the butter in which the chicken was browned. Drain apricots, reserving juice. Measure the juice and add enough chicken bouillon to make 1 cup. Blend cornstarch with this mixed liquid. Add to the onion and bring to a boil, stirring constantly. Add the apricots. Serve over or surrounding the chicken. If using grapes, blend cornstarch with white wine. *Serves 4.*

LEMONY HERBED CHICKEN THIGHS

Nice with rice or just a tossed salad.

8 chicken thighs
Salt
1 stick margarine or butter
1 tablespoon lemon juice
2 tablespoons chopped parsley
1 teaspoon chopped chives
1 teaspoon chopped marjoram
Lemon slices

Bone the chicken thighs by cutting along the thinner side of each, scraping flesh away and removing bone. Sprinkle thighs with salt. Melt margarine or butter in a large skillet and add chicken, skin side down. Cook 10 minutes, turn, and sprinkle with lemon juice, parsley, chives, and marjoram. Cook 10 minutes longer. Garnish with lemon slices to serve. *Serves 4.*

CHICKEN WINGS MARCEL

This recipe is from my book *The Best of Electric Crock Cooking.* If you have a slow crock cooker, cook the wings on low for 4 to 5 hours. If cooking on the stove top, follow the recipe here. You must have fresh parsley to make it.

18 chicken wings
Water to cover
1 small onion, stuck with 4 whole cloves
1 bay leaf
½ teaspoon dried thyme
6 peppercorns
3 large sprigs fresh parsley
2 teaspoons salt
4 tablespoons margarine or butter
2 large cloves garlic, peeled and finely minced
1 cup finely minced fresh parsley

Remove end tips of chicken wings at joint, and place with large wing portions in a big kettle with water, onion stuck with cloves, bay leaf, thyme, peppercorns, parsley, and salt. Cover and cook 1 hour at simmer. Remove from heat and set aside. Just before serving, remove large wing portions from stock (freeze stock for future use in casseroles), discard tips of wings, onion, and peppercorns. Let wings drain well. Heat a large skillet over medium-high heat, and melt margarine or butter in it. Before margarine or butter begins to color, add chicken wings and sauté, turning often, until they are golden. This should take only 4 or 5 minutes. When they are done, add garlic and minced parsley, tossing wings rapidly over the heat, for about 2 minutes. The parsley should still be bright green when removed from stove. Serve at once. *Serves 6.*

CHICKEN WITH EGGPLANT

4 cups fine strips peeled eggplant
Boiling water
1 tablespoon cornstarch
2 tablespoons soy sauce
1 tablespoon sherry
½ pound raw chicken meat, cut into fine
    strips
4 tablespoons oil

4 hot peppers, cut into fine slices, or sweet
   green or red peppers
1 clove garlic
1 tablespoon chopped fresh ginger
½ cup chicken bouillon

Put eggplant into boiling water. Let stand 10 minutes, then drain well. Mix cornstarch, soy sauce, and sherry in a bowl. Dip chicken meat in this mixture. Heat oil in a large frying pan. Sauté peppers for 2 minutes, stirring. Remove from pan. Add chicken meat to the oil. Sauté until tender (3 to 4 minutes), stirring constantly. Add eggplant strips, peppers, garlic, ginger, and bouillon, and toss. Heat well and serve. *Serves 4.*

SPICY CHICKEN
BAKED WITH ONION

Serve with Oriental vegetables and rice.

2 pounds boned chicken breasts
1 tablespoon dry sherry
2 tablespoons soy sauce
½ teaspoon sugar
1 small Bermuda onion
1 teaspoon ground ginger

Cut chicken into pieces 1 inch long and ⅛ inch thick—across the grain. Mix sherry, soy sauce, and sugar in a bowl and slice peeled onion in ⅛-inch rounds into mixture. Toss with ginger. Spread mixture over chicken strips and marinate 15 minutes. Divide into 8 portions and wrap each portion in a 12-inch square of aluminum foil, folding the seam sides up. Bake 10 minutes in a 450° oven and serve. *Serves 4.*

FRIED SPRING CHICKEN

This is an Oriental way to cook cut-up bits of chicken, and is very good served with Chinese vegetables and rice.

Few drops ginger juice
2 scallions, or 1 slice onion, chopped
4 tablespoons soy sauce
1 tablespoon white wine

1 broiler-fryer, cut into 1½-inch pieces
½ cup cornstarch
1 cup oil
Salt and pepper to taste

In a bowl mix ginger juice, scallions or onion, soy sauce, and wine. Add chicken pieces and marinate 25 minutes. Drain chicken pieces and dredge them in cornstarch. Heat oil in a deep frying pan. Fry chicken 3 to 4 minutes, stirring constantly. Sprinkle with salt and pepper and serve at once. *Serves 8.*

EGG NOODLE CASSEROLE
WITH CHICKEN

Any white meat can be used in this recipe, but it is best with chicken. Or you can use some leftover ham, cut into ¼-inch cubes, to add variety to the dish. To make the dish look festive, sprinkle slivered almonds on top just before serving, with a tiny bouquet of parsley in the center, and a radish cut into a rosette.

½ broiler-fryer
3 cups water
½ carrot, peeled
½ onion
1 stalk celery
1 sprig parsley
½ pound egg noodles or thin spaghetti
Boiling salted water
3 tablespoons vegetable oil
1 onion, finely cut
3 cups 1½-inch-thick slices celery
1 green pepper, cut into thin slices (optional)
2 tablespoons soy sauce
2 tablespoons chicken stock or bouillon
1 tablespoon cornstarch
2 tablespoons water
Salt and pepper to taste

Put chicken in a saucepan with 3 cups water and add carrot, ½ onion, celery, and parsley. Cook until chicken is tender (15 to 20 minutes). Strain and save stock. Cut chicken meat into ¼-inch cubes. Set aside. Cook noodles in boiling salted water 3 to 5 minutes or according to directions on the label. Do not overcook. Drain. Heat 2 tablespoons oil in heavy frying pan. Add noodles and fry, shaking the pan and turning the noodles as they turn color with a slotted spoon, taking care not to break them (about 10 minutes). Transfer the fried noodles into an ovenproof serving dish and hold in a warm oven. Add 1 tablespoon oil to the same pan. Add onion and stir-fry 2 minutes. Add celery, fry, turning often, 2 minutes more; add green pepper, cubed chicken, soy sauce, and chicken stock. Mix cornstarch with water and add to pan. Add salt and pepper to taste. Cook 3 to 4 minutes, turning often. Place over warm noodles and serve. Garnish if you wish, as above. *Serves 4.*

CHICKEN CUSTARD

Although shrimp and mushrooms are expensive, you need so little of either that this elegant dish comes into the economy class. French fried potatoes and a salad are all that's needed to make this a party dish.

2 cups diced cooked chicken
4 large mushrooms, coarsely chopped
2 tablespoons margarine or butter
1 package frozen frenched green beans
Boiling salted water
8 shrimp, shelled and cleaned
3 cups chicken bouillon
1 tablespoon soy sauce
1 teaspoon salt
1 tablespoon sherry
4 eggs

Place diced chicken in the bottom of a casserole. Sauté mushrooms 5 minutes in margarine or butter. Sprinkle over chicken. Cook beans 3 minutes in boiling salted water and drain well. Spread over chicken and mushrooms. Place shrimp on top. Heat bouillon, soy sauce, salt, and sherry until just warm. Whip eggs, then beat them quickly into stock. Pour over ingredients in the casserole. Place in a pan of hot water and bake in a 350° oven until a knife inserted into the custard comes out clean (about 1 hour). *Serves 4.*

CHICKEN À LA KING

⅓ cup chicken fat
⅓ cup all-purpose flour
1 cup chicken stock, warm
1½ cups whole milk, warm
½ pound sliced sautéed mushrooms
½ teaspoon salt
1 pimiento, canned, in strips
2 tablespoons dry cooking sherry
4 cups cooked chicken in chunks, skinned and boned

In a double boiler top over simmering water, melt chicken fat and stir in flour. Slowly add chicken stock, stirring quickly to keep the sauce from becoming lumpy. Add milk, still stirring, and cook, stirring occasionally until sauce has thickened. While sauce is cooking, sauté mushrooms in a little chicken fat, then sprinkle with salt. Add mushrooms, pimiento, sherry, and chicken pieces to the sauce and heat through, but do not boil. *Serves 6.*

CHICKEN DIVAN

When you have half a recipe of Chicken à la King left over, try this with it. Instead of broccoli, you can use cauliflower or Brussels sprouts.

½ recipe Chicken à la King
¼ pint (about) half-and-half
½ teaspoon sweet paprika
⅛ cup dry sherry
1 package frozen broccoli
Grated Parmesan cheese
Margarine or butter

Warm Chicken à la King over hot water in the top of a double boiler. Add half-and-half (not enough to make the sauce runny), paprika, and sherry. Cook broccoli according to package directions. Drain. Arrange in the bottom of a large casserole. Pour chicken mixture over it. Top with Parmesan (freshly grated, preferably). Dot with margarine or butter and bake in a 400° oven until cheese is lightly browned (about 25 minutes). *Serves 3 or 4.*

CHICKEN CORDON BLEU

This recipe is also good with turkey, veal, or pork, but best done with chicken. Serve with hot buttered noodles and a salad.

*4 thin slices leftover chicken meat
    (white or brown)*
4 thin slices Swiss cheese
4 thin slices boiled ham
1 cup bread crumbs
1 egg, well beaten
1 teaspoon lemon juice, strained
Salt, pepper, and nutmeg to taste
4 teaspoons margarine or butter
Sprigs parsley for garnish (optional)

Make a sandwich of the slices of chicken meat, the cheese in the center, the ham on top. Place bread crumbs in a shallow bowl, egg in another bowl mixed with lemon juice, salt, pepper, and nutmeg to taste. Dredge sandwich in bread crumbs, then in egg mixture, and back in bread crumbs. Place in a shallow baking pan and top with 1 teaspoon margarine or butter to each sandwich. Bake in 375° oven 20 minutes; turn sandwiches with a spatula, and bake another 20 minutes at 450°, or until well browned. Garnish with sprigs of parsley if you wish. *Serves 2 to 4.*

Fowl and Stewing Chicken

BOILED FOWL

This is a good basic recipe. The bouillon or stock makes a good base for chicken soups of all kinds (add a couple of chicken bouillon cubes if you find the flavor of the stock insipid), and the cooked chicken itself is delicately flavored, especially in a cream sauce made from the bouillon, or cold, in salads, or reheated in recipes such as Chicken à la King.

1 4-pound fowl
8 to 10 cups boiling water
Tops of 5 or 6 celery stalks
1 large onion, peeled and sliced
1½ teaspoons salt
6 peppercorns

*1 large sprig fresh parsley, or ½ teaspoon dried
    parsley*
1 bay leaf
⅛ teaspoon ground thyme
1 whole clove

Leave the fowl whole, if you have a suitable cooking kettle, or cut it up to fit the kettle you have. Simmer, covered, with remaining ingredients, for 3 to 4 hours, adding water if necessary. When done, remove chicken from cooking liquid, allow to cool, then skim and cut up if you are planning to serve it in pieces. If the fowl is to be used in dishes to be made later, store it in its kettle, covered, in the refrigerator. Before using, skim away (and save for cooking) the fat congealed on the surface of the stock. *Serves 6 to 8.*

CURRIED CHICKEN MOUSSE

¼ cup margarine or butter
1 5-pound stewing chicken, disjointed
1 large Bermuda onion
2 tablespoons domestic brandy
1½ teaspoons salt
¼ teaspoon pepper
Water
1 tablespoon curry powder
1 cup milk or half-and-half
Watercress for garnish (optional)

Melt margarine or butter in a Dutch oven. Brown chicken pieces in it. Peel and slice onion and set aside. Warm the brandy and pour it over chicken pieces. Immediately set aflame with a match. When the flame dies, place onion slices over chicken. Sprinkle with salt and pepper, add water to half cover the chicken, cover pot and simmer until meat falls off bones. This will probably take from 1½ to 2 hours, depending upon the age of the bird. Test for tenderness with a fork. Sprinkle curry powder over chicken. Cool in the stock. Take chicken from pot. Boil stock briskly to reduce it to about 1½ cups. Remove the skin and bones from chicken and arrange good-sized portions of meat in the bottom of a mold or a square or oblong dish. Add milk or half-and-half to stock and bring just to a boil, but do not boil. Strain over chicken meat, cool, chill in refrigerator until jelled (at least several hours). Unmold and garnish with watercress or other greens of your choice. *Serves 6 to 8.*

CHICKEN GUMBO NEW ORLEANS

1 4-pound stewing chicken
Water to cover
2 celery stalks, chopped
1 teaspoon salt
⅛ teaspoon pepper
1 large onion, chopped
3 tablespoons margarine or butter
1 green pepper, chopped
1 bay leaf
1 cup stewed tomatoes
1 cup okra, canned or fresh
¼ cup converted rice
1 tablespoon chopped parsley

Put chicken in a large kettle with water to cover. Add celery, salt, pepper, onion; cover, cook 1 hour. Lift out chicken and cool; reserve broth. Bone and dice chicken meat. Melt margarine or butter in a big frying pan and sauté chopped pepper. Place diced chicken in 2 cups chicken broth along with bay leaf and cook over low heat until peppers have softened. Add peppers and margarine or butter to chicken with the tomatoes, okra, rice, and parsley. Simmer 30 minutes. Discard bay leaf before serving. *Serves 8 to 10.*

APPLE-STUFFED TURKEY

1 8-pound turkey
1 8-ounce package cream cheese, cold
2 large or 4 small tart apples, peeled and cored
1 teaspoon salt
¼ teaspoon pepper
Salt and pepper
Margarine or butter

Wash and wipe turkey and remove giblets. Cook as in *Giblet Gravy.* Rub cream cheese and apples through a grater. Combine,

and mix lightly with 1 teaspoon salt and ¼ teaspoon pepper. Stuff turkey cavity with mixture. Truss bird, salt and pepper it, rub turkey all over with margarine or butter, and place in a 450° oven 25 minutes. Reduce heat to 350° and bake 1½ hours more, or until the legs move easily. Offer Giblet Gravy on the side. *Serves 6 to 8.*

TURKEY STEW, DOMINICAN REPUBLIC STYLE

1 8- to 8½-pound turkey, cut into serving pieces
4 cloves garlic, crushed
1 teaspoon salt
¼ teaspoon pepper
2 tablespoons red wine vinegar
½ cup vegetable oil
1 cup tomato puree
1 green bell pepper, seeded and chopped
Water to cover
24 small pitted green olives
4 tablespoons capers
2 pounds potatoes, peeled and sliced
1 10-ounce package frozen peas, thawed

Season turkey pieces with garlic, salt, pepper, and vinegar. Leave for 1 hour at room temperature. Heat oil in a casserole or Dutch oven large enough to hold the turkey pieces comfortably, and sauté the pieces 2 or 3 at a time until lightly browned. Arrange turkey in the casserole and pour over it any marinade that remains. Add tomato puree, bell pepper, and enough water to cover. Cover and simmer 1 hour. Add olives, capers, and potatoes and cook 30 minutes longer, or until both potatoes and turkey are tender. Add peas and cook 5 minutes longer. *Serves 8 to 10.*

HUNTER'S TURKEY

Turkey legs, thighs, and wings can be a real boon for your food budget. And they're frequently put on sale to make it even nicer. Buttered noodles and a green salad make a good accompaniment.

2 to 3 pounds turkey pieces
½ cup all-purpose flour
1 teaspoon salt
¼ teaspoon pepper
3 tablespoons shortening
1 large onion, chopped
1 8-ounce can tomato sauce
1 bay leaf
¼ teaspoon thyme (about)
½ teaspoon marjoram (about)
1 teaspoon Worcestershire sauce

Heat a Dutch oven. Dredge turkey pieces in flour, salt, and pepper. Melt shortening in Dutch oven and brown turkey on all sides. Combine onion, tomato sauce, bay leaf, thyme, marjoram, and Worcestershire sauce and add to the turkey. Cover, and cook over medium heat 1½ hours. *Serves 6 to 8.*

PILAU OF TURKEY

2 cups cubed cooked turkey meat
1 cup Béchamel Sauce
¾ cup converted rice
1 teaspoon salt
½ teaspoon saffron (optional)
½ cup dried currants
Water to cover
¼ cup sugar
4 slices crisp bacon, crumbled

Warm turkey in Béchamel Sauce over gentle heat. Cook rice with salt and saffron as directed on package. Meanwhile, simmer currants in water to cover with sugar until there is a small amount of fairly thick syrup. Pack rice into a buttered ring mold and bake in 350° oven 10 to 15 minutes. Unmold onto a hot platter. Fill center with creamed turkey. Pour currants and sauce over and sprinkle with bacon. *Serves 4.*

ROAST GOOSE

Goose is far more widely available than it was just a few years ago and, when properly cooked, makes a delightful change from turkey, as the all-dark meat is more flavorful.

For a holiday dinner, when you are only a few, it can be a more economical undertaking than an oversized turkey. Any goose you buy is likely to be frozen. Probably the best method of thawing is in the refrigerator. A 10-pounder is likely to take more than 2 days to thaw completely, so buy it well ahead with that in mind. Place the frozen bird in a dish to catch the melted ice crystals.

1 10-pound goose
Water to cover giblets
1 bay leaf
1 small onion, sliced
¼ teaspoon thyme
3 whole cloves
1 teaspoon salt
¼ teaspoon pepper
Dressing (see below)
Salt and pepper

Remove neck and giblets from body cavity and simmer them in water with the next 6 ingredients, for about 1½ hours or until tender. Chop giblets, reserve them and broth to make gravy; strain broth. Meanwhile, remove excess fat from body cavity. Render fat for use in other cooking. Rinse bird and drain well. Stuff neck and body cavity loosely with Dressing; fasten opening with skewers; fasten neck skin to back with a skewer. Rub goose with salt and pepper. Place it, breast side up, on a rack in roasting pan. Insert a meat thermometer deep into inside thigh muscle. Roast uncovered in a preheated 400° oven 1 hour. Reduce heat to 325° and continue roasting about 2 to 2½ hours. Do not overcook or the bird will be tough. All during the roasting, draw off the fat with a bulb baster every ½ hour and baste often with drippings. When done, remove bird to a platter. Make Giblet Gravy with the cooked giblets. *Serves 8 to 10.*

DRESSING FOR GOOSE

After dinner, remove the stuffing from the cavity and refrigerate, covered. Remove the remaining meat from the carcass and refrigerate, covered. If desired, make stock from the carcass, adding an onion and carrot for flavor.

3 tablespoons rendered goose fat
3 large onions, chopped
1 clove garlic, mashed
Goose or turkey liver, chopped
2 stalks celery, chopped
1 large green pepper, chopped
12 black olives, pitted and chopped
½ pound mushrooms, chopped
2 cups diced cooked potatoes
Salt and freshly ground pepper to taste

Heat the fat. In it sauté onions, garlic, liver, celery, green pepper, olives, and mushrooms, about 10 minutes. Do not brown. Mix with potatoes. Add salt and pepper to taste. Stuff into bird.

SALMI OF GOOSE
MADE FROM LEFTOVERS

Try this elegant recipe to use up goose leftovers. The French salmi is made with wine and you may add wine to yours if you like, though the dish is very good just as is. There are mushrooms in a French salmi, but we omitted them as there are mushrooms in the dressing which you will serve with your salmi.

1 cup goose gravy
1 tablespoon tomato paste
1 cup light cream
Freshly ground pepper to taste
2 cups coarsely diced leftover goose
Dressing leftover from goose
Dry bread crumbs
Butter

Heat gravy until it softens. Add tomato paste and cream and continue heating, stirring to mix well. Add pepper. Add goose meat and heat to piping in the sauce, but do not let it boil. Put leftover dressing into a baking dish, top with dry bread crumbs, dot with butter, and bake in 350° oven until nicely browned on top (about 30 minutes). Serve with goose and gravy. *Serves 4.*

ROAST DUCKLING

When duck is on sale, try it this way. To serve 8 people you will need 2 ducklings, as most ducklings offered are only 3 to 4 pounds in weight and much of this is in fat and bones. Use this basic roasting recipe as the basis for duck flavored with tart fruit such as orange slices, mandarin orange segments, cranberries, sour (pie) cherries, seedless fresh green grapes.

1 3- to 4-pound duckling
½ teaspoon salt
⅛ teaspoon pepper
1 small sliced onion, crushed
1½ cups orange juice or other fruit juice
¾ cup orange slices, or other fruit

Preheat oven to 425°. Salt and pepper cavity of duckling, and rub it with crushed onion. Prick the skin of duckling around neck, back, and lower breast. Place duckling in roaster, uncovered, breast side up, and cook at 425° for 20 minutes. Remove fat from pan. Lower heat to 350° and roast for 60 to 80 minutes more, skimming away fat every 20 minutes or so. When duckling legs move easily and breast meat is fork tender, remove to warm serving platter and pour fruit juice and all but a little of the fruit into roasting pan. Place it over high heat on top of stove and stir and scrape roaster until stock is reduced by two-thirds and gravy has thickened. Serve this gravy on the side. Garnish bird with reserved fruit. *Makes 4 portions.*

GROUSE AND SPROUTS

This is a budget item if you have a hunter in the family. Pheasants may be substituted, using 2 birds of about 3 pounds each, cooking them in 2 large paper bags. Dot each bird with 1 tablespoon butter. Cook about 1 hour. Or 2 3-pound roasting chickens may be substituted. Cook these 1 hour and 15 minutes at 400°.

6 grouse, with giblets
2 cloves garlic, halved
10 tablespoons margarine or butter
½ cup chopped onion
½ pound mushrooms, sliced
¾ cup Madeira
½ cup chopped walnuts

¼ teaspoon rosemary leaves
1 teaspoon salt
Dash pepper
Shortening
⅔ cup chicken bouillon
2 1-ounce packages frozen Brussels sprouts, halved

Chop giblets. Brown garlic in 6 tablespoons margarine or butter, remove garlic and discard. Sauté onion and giblets about 5 minutes, add mushrooms, ½ cup Madeira, walnuts, and seasonings; cook until mushrooms are tender and liquid is reduced (about 10 minutes). Cool the stuffing slightly. Spoon cooled stuffing into birds and truss them. Dot each bird with butter, using about 1 teaspoonful for each. Place each bird in a small paper bag, fold over the ends, and brush with shortening on all sides. Place in a shallow roasting pan and roast in 350° oven 35 to 45 minutes. Meanwhile, bring bouillon and remaining Madeira to the boil, add Brussels sprouts and cook according to package directions until just tender. Drain and add 2 tablespoons margarine or butter. Serve with the birds. *Serves 6.*

GLAZED CHICKEN OR FOWL

This recipe is easy to make, and the only expensive ingredient is the bird you decide to use; it is just as good with chicken as with any of the darker-meat fowl. Serve it with boiled potatoes, boiled wild, brown, or converted rice, or even with buttered noodles. It is a fine dish to make for a large party, as it can be prepared the day before, and finished just before serving.

12 portions chicken or any other fowl
½ cup vegetable oil
2 bouillon cubes
3 large tomatoes, diced
3 large onions, diced
2 cups water
1 glass dry sherry
1 teaspoon salt (or more, to taste)
2 tablespoons soy sauce
½ teaspoon pepper
2 bay leaves
4 or 5 tablespoons marmalade or red currant jelly

Sauté meat portions in vegetable oil in a Dutch oven or big kettle. Add all the other ingredients except marmalade or jelly. Simmer for 1½ hours. Test meat for tenderness, and cook for ½ hour more, or until tender, with lid removed if the sauce is on the thin side. Remove bay leaves. Bring to a brisk boil and stir in marmalade or jelly. The sauce will instantly become very shiny. Place meat on a deep platter, pour sauce over it, and serve immediately. *Serves 6 to 8.*

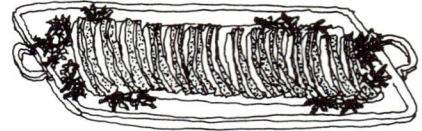

Variety Meats

There's a treasure in the economy section of your supermarket meat department that you may be overlooking.

Ris de Veau Braisés, Cervelles au Beurre Noir, and Rognons de Veau à la Bordelaise, to name just a few, appear on every European menu of any substance and are considered a delicacy by peasant and great chef alike.

These are what we call "variety meats" and, unfortunately, European enthusiasm for them is not shared in the United States where many of us are inclined to buy calf's liver (when we can afford it) and let it go at that. Sweetbreads, brains, and kidneys are left for the high-class restaurants.

Here is some basic information about some of the most easily obtainable variety meats, what they are, how to go about their preliminary preparation (if any), and then how to fix them in just a few of many classic, interesting, and delectable ways.

Liver

Most people like calf's liver. It's tender, juicy, wonderfully tasty, and usually requires only a minimum of preparation. If it's really fresh,
you can do just about anything with beef liver (pork and lamb, too) that you can do with calf's liver and have the same delicious results for about one-quarter the price—and sometimes less. Chicken liver may appeal to your family more than beef, and it often is offered at very reasonable prices.

When cooking any liver, the most important thing to keep in mind is not to overcook it. Liver from any animal, regardless of age, is not naturally tough and unappetizing, but overcooking will certainly make it just like shoe leather with about as much taste. When liver is served, it should be crisply brown on the outside and slightly pink inside. Juices should run a pale rose color when it is cut.

If you feel that beef liver is slightly stronger than calf's liver, then soak it in milk for 1 or 2 hours before cooking. Drain it well and pat dry on paper towels. Peel off any thin filament that may surround the liver and cause it to curl as it cooks.

Many good cooks don't realize how interchangeable different animal livers are in recipes. This fact can be important to the budget cook, since prices vary widely, making chicken livers more expensive one week, beef the next. The following recipes will give you an idea of the versatility and utility of liver.

RICE AND
CHICKEN LIVER CASSEROLE

An interesting way to use up leftover tongue, but you can serve the casserole without the tongue, or substitute ham.

¼ cup minced onion
2 slices bacon, diced
4 chicken livers
1¼ cups converted rice
Salt, pepper, and nutmeg to taste
2 cups chicken bouillon
2 tablespoons chopped parsley
¼ cup milk or half-and-half
2 slices julienne-cut tongue (optional)

Sauté onion and bacon in 2-quart shallow casserole until onion is transparent. Add chicken livers. Sauté until brown. Dice livers with a sharp knife. Add rice and stir with a wooden spoon until well glazed, and golden, 3 to 4 minutes. Add seasonings. Gradually add bouillon and parsley, stirring with a fork. Cover, bake in 375° oven 25 minutes. Stir in milk or half-and-half. Sprinkle with tongue strips. *Serves 4.*

LIVER WITH ONION BUTTER

1 pound beef liver or 20 chicken livers
¼ cup all-purpose flour
1 teaspoon salt
⅛ teaspoon pepper
4 tablespoons margarine or butter
½ cup sliced onions

Slice beef liver in even ⅓-inch slices or cut chicken livers in half. Season flour with salt and pepper, and dredge each piece of liver. Set aside. Heat 2 tablespoons margarine or butter until the foaming subsides. Gently sauté onion slices until transparent and tender. Set aside. Now melt 2 tablespoons margarine or butter over high heat. Fry the liver quickly, about 1 minute to each side. If you prefer liver medium-done, allow 2 minutes to a side. Put liver on a plate, pour onion butter over the top, and serve at once. *Serves 4.*

LIVER REFORMÉ

See the recipe for *Lamb Chops Reformé*, but substitute liver, and omit the vinegar and sugar and add a pinch of thyme. Serve this with buttered noodles and chopped dill or parsley, and you will have a fine dish for a party.

BAKED BEEF LIVER,
FRENCH STYLE

1 2-pound piece beef liver
1 teaspoon salt
⅛ teaspoon pepper
⅛ teaspoon each ground sage, thyme, and
    allspice
3 tablespoons margarine or butter
2 cups hot beef bouillon
3 sprigs parsley
1 bay leaf
2 whole cloves
1 small clove garlic, minced
12 tiny white onions
8 mushrooms, caps left whole and stems
    chopped
1 cup diagonally sliced celery
2 tablespoons dry sherry
2 tablespoons all-purpose flour

Sprinkle liver lightly with salt, pepper, sage, thyme, and allspice. Melt margarine or butter in a large skillet, add liver and brown on both sides. Transfer liver to a shallow baking dish. Add remaining ingredients except flour, cover tightly, and bake in a 350° oven 1½ hours. Transfer liver to a serving platter. Surround with any large pieces vegetables, or Brussels sprouts. Strain juice, thicken with a little flour and pour over liver. Carve liver in thin slices to serve. *Serves 6 to 8.*

BEEF LIVER, ITALIAN STYLE

Good served over rice or mashed potatoes.

1 pound beef liver, sliced and cut into short
    strips
Flour for dredging
1 teaspoon salt

⅛ teaspoon pepper
2 tablespoons margarine or butter
1 medium onion, chopped
1 clove garlic, minced
2 tablespoons all-purpose flour
½ cup dry red wine
1 cup beef bouillon
Salt and pepper to taste
½ cup sliced, cooked, or canned mushrooms
Chopped parsley (garnish)

Dredge liver with flour, salt, pepper, and set aside. In a large skillet, melt margarine or butter, add onion and garlic, and sauté, stirring now and then until chopped onion is soft and golden. Remove onion from skillet and set aside. In the fat remaining in the skillet (you may have to add a little butter), sauté the liver pieces until they are brown and crisp on all sides. Remove liver from skillet and set aside. To the pan juice, add 2 tablespoons flour, stirring constantly. Gradually add wine and bouillon. Cook, stirring, until the sauce is thickened and smooth. Season with salt and pepper to taste. Return onions and liver to pan, add mushrooms, and heat thoroughly. Sprinkle with parsley to serve. *Serves 4 to 6.*

BEEF LIVER HASH

1 pound beef liver
2 cups salted water
2 tablespoons margarine or butter
2 tablespoons all-purpose flour
1 cup beef bouillon
1 teaspoon salt
⅛ teaspoon pepper
½ teaspoon dried thyme
2 tablespoons dry sherry
Toast triangles

Wipe liver with a damp cloth and remove outside skin and veins. Cook in simmering salted water for ½ hour; drain. Put liver through the finest cutter of the meat chopper. Melt margarine or butter and blend flour in smoothly, add bouillon and stir constantly until thickened. Add seasonings, sherry, ground liver, and let stand over very low heat for about 5 minutes so that it may reheat and

absorb the flavors. Serve over toast triangles. *Serves 4.*

LIVER PÂTÉ ARDENNAIS

This is a very economical dish, as you can use the cheapest liver on the market. It can be eaten hot, with any vegetable and potatoes, rice, or pasta. It is also delicious as a snack, or wrap a slice in a sandwich bag and it makes a fine light luncheon. For variety, add chopped mushrooms and olives.

½ pound liver, cut into slices
1 teaspoon salt
5 slices stale bread
½ cup condensed milk
Pepper and nutmeg to taste
1 cup diced onion
1 cup diced bacon
2 tablespoons vegetable oil
⅛ teaspoon thyme
1 bouillon cube dissolved in hot water
2 eggs, well beaten

Grind liver in a meat grinder, being sure to remove all veins and skins. Add salt. Soak bread in milk, add pepper and nutmeg to taste, and add to liver. Sauté onion and bacon in vegetable oil and add to liver. Add thyme, bouillon cube, and 2 eggs. Blend well. Pour mixture into bread loaf pan and bake in 200° oven 1½ to 2 hours, or until knife inserted in center removes clean. Serve hot (see above), or keep up to 2 weeks in refrigerator if well wrapped. *Serves 5 to 10.*

Kidneys

Beef and pork kidneys are extremely tasty, but because they're too strongly flavored for every palate, I'm not including any recipes for them.

Lamb and veal kidneys are easy to cook, and either may substitute for the other. Neither requires any more advance preparation than liver. Just remove the filament that surrounds them and cut away the little knob of fat at the bottom.

Good kidneys from any young animal should smell fresh and sweet with only the faintest, if any, suggestion of ammonia. Soak them in ice water or milk overnight before cooking. Cut away fatty parts.

There's a tendency to overcook kidneys. Don't—they lose their character even more quickly than liver when overcooked. Veal and lamb kidneys should be faintly pink on the inside after cooking.

LIVER AND KIDNEYS IN RED WINE

Serve riced potatoes with this.

3 tablespoons margarine or butter
2 tablespoons finely chopped onion
⅓ cup dry red wine
1 teaspoon wine vinegar
1 veal kidney (about 1 pound) trimmed and
    cut into ½-inch cubes
½ pound beef liver, trimmed and cut into
    ½-inch squares
½ teaspoon salt
4 tablespoons finely chopped fresh parsley

In a small skillet, melt 1 tablespoon margarine or butter over moderate heat. Add onion and cook, stirring frequently, for about 5 minutes, or until soft but not brown. Pour in wine and wine vinegar and, stirring constantly, bring to a boil over high heat. Cook uncovered until thick and syrupy. Remove pan from heat. Melt remaining margarine or butter in a large skillet. When foam subsides, add kidney and liver. Turn the pieces of meat constantly and sauté for about 5 minutes, until they are lightly cooked and evenly browned. Stir in reserved sauce and, still stirring, cook for 1 minute longer. Add salt and taste for seasoning. Transfer to a serving platter and sprinkle with chopped parsley to serve. Serves 4.

SAUTÉED KIDNEYS
WITH MUSTARD SAUCE

10 tablespoons margarine or butter
3 or 4 veal kidneys or 12 lamb kidneys, peeled,
    fat removed

2 tablespoons finely chopped scallions
¾ cup dry white wine
2 tablespoons Dijon-style mustard
½ teaspoon salt
¼ teaspoon pepper
2 tablespoons lemon juice
3 tablespoons chopped parsley

In a large skillet, melt 6 tablespoons margarine or butter over moderate heat. When foam subsides, sauté the kidneys, uncovered, turning them frequently, until they are lightly browned. (Veal kidneys will take about 10 minutes; lamb kidneys, 4 or 5 minutes.) Transfer to a hot platter and keep warm. Stir the scallions into the margarine or butter remaining in skillet and cook, stirring, for 1 minute. Add the wine and bring to a boil, stirring constantly to incorporate any brown bits that cling to the skillet. Boil briskly for about 5 minutes, or until the wine is reduced to ¼ cup. Remove skillet from heat. Cream 4 tablespoons margarine or butter by beating it hard against the sides of a small bowl. When it's fluffy, beat in the mustard, salt, and pepper. Off the heat, swirl spoonfuls of the creamed margarine or butter into the skillet. Work quickly and cut the kidneys into crosswise slices about ⅛ inch thick. Return them to the skillet, sprinkle with lemon juice and parsley and toss over low heat for 1 or 2 minutes to just heat everything through. Serve immediately. Serves 4.

DEVILED LAMB KIDNEYS

12 lamb kidneys
¾ cup margarine or butter
¾ cup chopped parsley
1 teaspoon dried tarragon
1 medium onion, minced
¼ cup dry sherry
1½ tablespoons Worcestershire sauce
1 teaspoon salt
⅛ teaspoon pepper
¼ teaspoon cayenne pepper
4 slices buttered toast, cut in half

Split kidneys without cutting through. Make a paste of the margarine or butter, parsley, tarragon, onion, sherry, Worcestershire sauce, salt, pepper, and cayenne. Put 1 tablespoon of this paste into each kidney. Place kidneys on a cool broiler-pan and broil 5 inches from the heat for about 6 minutes. Serve 2 to a person on buttered toast triangles. *Serves 6.*

BEEF AND KIDNEY STEW

2 pounds boneless shin of beef, in 1-inch cubes
¼ cup flour
¼ cup margarine or butter
1 cup chopped onion
¼ pound fresh mushrooms, washed and
*   halved, or 1 4-ounce can sliced*
*   mushrooms, drained*
4 lamb kidneys, thinly sliced
2 10¾-ounce cans beef gravy
2 tablespoons chopped parsley
1 teaspoon dried thyme
1 teaspoon salt
½ bay leaf
Freshly ground black pepper
Chopped parsley (optional)

On a sheet of waxed paper, roll beef in flour until well coated. In hot margarine or butter in a Dutch oven, brown the beef well on all sides, removing it as it browns; add onion and mushrooms to pan and sauté until golden. Return beef to pan. Add kidneys, beef gravy, parsley, thyme, about 1 teaspoon salt, bay leaf, pepper to taste, and bring to boiling. Reduce heat and simmer, covered, for 2 to 2½ hours, or until the beef is tender. Turn into a heated serving dish. Sprinkle with chopped parsley, if desired. *Serves 6.*

Brains and Sweetbreads

A popular misconception says that sweetbreads and brains are one and the same. Not so. Brains are what they are. Sweetbreads are the thymus gland of the calf (or young steer). As the calf grows, the thymus gland gets smaller and finally disappears.

However, the two do have much the same "nutty" taste and smooth texture, but brains are more delicate and tender. Both are highly perishable and require almost identical two-step preliminary preparation. They are first soaked in cold water to soften the filament which covers them, to dissolve any dark patches of blood, and to whiten them. Then they are blanched in acidulated water.

There are a number of slightly varying schools of thought on this preliminary preparation process.

Brains

Figure on about 1 brain per person; plan on serving them as close to purchasing time as possible, not more than 48 hours after blanching.

Rinse the brains, place in a bowl, and soak for 2 or 3 hours in several changes of cold water. Drain and carefully pull off as much of the thin filament which encloses them as you can without tearing the flesh. This is a slow process. Soak them again, for about 1½ to 2 hours, this time with 1 tablespoon of white vinegar per quart of water. After the white opaque bits at the base are removed, the brains are ready to be blanched.

Place the brains in a saucepan and cover with about 2 inches of boiling water. For each quart of water covering them, add 1 teaspoon salt and 1 tablespoon lemon juice or dry white wine. When the water returns to boiling, lower the heat and simmer very gently for 20 minutes. Allow the brains to cool for about 20 minutes in their cooking liquid. If they are not to be used immediately, refrigerate in the cooking liquid and cover the pan. When ready to prepare them, drain thoroughly and pat dry on paper towels.

Sweetbreads

Plan on 1 pair of sweetbreads or about 1 pound for 2 persons.

Soon after purchasing them, place the

sweetbreads in a bowl and cover with cold water. Soak for about 1 hour in several changes of cold water. Drain and cut away the tube which separates them. You'll notice that one half is smoother and rounder than the other, which is rather long and split. The rounder of the two is the heart or *noix*, and the choicest part. When you serve it, remember to divide the two pieces in half so that each person receives part of each. Now pull off as much of the fat and filament as you can without damaging the sweetbreads. Don't worry if it doesn't all come off. Return the sweetbreads to the bowl and soak for another hour in cold water to which you've added 1 tablespoon of vinegar for each quart of water. The sweetbreads are now ready to be blanched.

Depending on the recipe you will be using in preparing the sweetbreads, blanching time will vary. If the final recipe calls for the sweetbreads to be cooked, you will only need to blanch them for 5 minutes or so to firm them up a little and make them easier to handle. If the sweetbreads are to be cut up and added to a hot sauce, they should be blanched for 15 minutes.

Place the sweetbreads in a saucepan and cover with about 2 inches of cold water. Add 1 teaspoon of salt and 1 tablespoon of white vinegar for each quart of water. Bring to a simmer and cook uncovered at the barest simmer for either 5 or 15 minutes. Drain and plunge the sweetbreads immediately into ice water for 5 minutes. They are ready for further preparation after draining and patting dry on paper towels. If you refrigerate them, be sure to cover them tightly.

Some cooks like to weight their sweetbreads. That means to place them on a dish, cover them with another flat dish, and set a heavy weight on top for 1 or 2 hours in the refrigerator. This breaks down the fibers and keeps the sweetbreads from shrinking as they cook. Do this if cooking them whole or if the recipe calls for them to be sliced.

So the next time you see brains and sweetbreads at your supermarket, don't run away from them. They are truly a gourmet's delight at a budget price per serving.

BRAINS VINAIGRETTE

For adventuresome diners, an unusual and delicious way to serve brains. Serve this as a luncheon dish with coleslaw, mixed vegetables, and mayonnaise; or serve it as an appetizer with French bread.

4 calves' brains
Cold water to cover
2 tablespoons white vinegar or juice of 1 lemon
1 teaspoon salt
6 peppercorns
½ onion, sliced
1 small carrot, sliced
2 sprigs parsley
½ teaspoon thyme
1 bay leaf
¼ cup wine vinegar
½ cup olive oil
1 tablespoon finely chopped parsley
2 scallions, finely chopped
2 tablespoons capers
Salt and freshly ground pepper to taste
1 hard-boiled egg yolk, minced

Soak brains as described on page 64, place in a shallow pan and add cold water to barely cover. Add white vinegar, salt, peppercorns, onion, carrot, parsley sprigs, thyme, and bay leaf. Bring just to a boil and simmer 25 minutes. Remove pan from heat and let the brains cool in the cooking liquid. Just before serving, remove the brains, drain and pat dry with paper towels. Combine wine vinegar and oil and beat until homogenized. Add remaining ingredients and beat again. Spoon the sauce over the brains. *Serves 4.*

CALVES' BRAINS AU BEURRE NOIR

6 pairs calves' brains
Flour
½ cup butter
2 tablespoons tarragon vinegar
2 tablespoons capers, drained
Dash of Tabasco sauce

Prepare brains as described on page 64. Dust lightly with flour and sauté in 3 tablespoons butter until lightly browned on both sides. Remove to a hot platter and keep warm. Add remaining butter to pan and brown it, being careful not to burn. Add tarragon vinegar, capers, and Tabasco. Heat for a couple of minutes and pour over brains. *Serves 6.*

BRAISED SWEETBREADS

This classic method of preparation could shine at your next small dinner party. If you are planning to do just one pair of sweetbreads, use the same amount of sauce ingredients as for 2 pairs. If you will be cooking either 3 or 4 pairs, double the sauce ingredients. Peas and potato puffs go nicely with this.

2 pairs sweetbreads
2 tablespoons margarine or butter
1 medium-size carrot, sliced
2 tablespoons chopped onion
1 strip bacon, in small pieces
2 sprigs parsley
1 teaspoon salt
¼ teaspoon freshly ground black pepper
1 small bay leaf
½ cup chicken bouillon
½ cup water

Soak and prepare sweetbreads as described on page 65. Simmer for only 5 minutes (they will finish cooking as they are braising). After draining, place sweetbreads in a shallow dish and cover with a heavy plate pressing directly on them in order to break down the fibers and prevent them from contracting during cooking. In an ovenproof dish, melt margarine or butter, add carrot, onion, bacon, parsley, salt, pepper, and bay leaf. Bake at 450° for 10 minutes. Add sweetbreads, bouillon, water, and continue baking, basting occasionally, for 45 minutes more, or until the meat is well browned on top. Remove sweetbreads to a heated serving dish and pour sauce over them. *Serves 4.*

SWEETBREADS IN SHERRY SAUCE

3 pairs sweetbreads
Milk

Water
3 scallions, chopped
2 tablespoons margarine or butter
1 tablespoon chopped chives
1 tablespoon chopped parsley
2 cups Medium White Sauce (see below)
½ cup dry sherry
Salt and freshly ground black pepper to taste
3 cups cooked rice
1 cup cooked green peas
1 pimiento, chopped
2 tablespoons slivered almonds (optional)

Soak sweetbreads overnight in milk to cover. Drain them and rinse in cold water. Cook sweetbreads in simmering water for 15 minutes, or until they are just tender. Drain, remove all membranes and tubes, and cut into large cubes. Cook scallions in margarine or butter until they are just tender. Stir in chopped chives and parsley. Add this mixture to Medium White Sauce, stir in sherry, and season with salt and pepper to taste. To serve, arrange a mound of hot cooked rice in the center of a serving platter. Spoon half the sauce over the rice, put sweetbreads on top and cover with remaining sauce. Garnish the platter with hot peas, and sprinkle with chopped pimiento and slivered almonds, if you wish. *Serves 6.*

MEDIUM WHITE SAUCE

4 tablespoons butter
4 tablespoons flour
2 cups milk

Melt butter, add flour, and stir until well blended. Meanwhile, bring milk to a simmer and add to the butter-flour mixture all at once. Stir until mixture comes to a boil and simmer for 5 minutes. *Makes 2 cups sauce.*

SWEETBREADS VIRGINIA

3 pairs sweetbreads
5 tablespoons margarine or butter
¾ pound fresh mushrooms, sliced
6 slices cooked ham, about ⅛ inch thick

2 tablespoons all-purpose flour
1½ cups chicken bouillon
1 egg yolk
¾ cup half-and-half
Salt and paprika to taste

Soak and simmer sweetbreads for 15 minutes as described on page 65. After they have been drained and cooled, cut into bite-size pieces. Melt 3 tablespoons margarine or butter in a skillet, add sweetbreads and mushrooms, and cook, stirring, for about 6 minutes, or until they are browned. Meanwhile, place ham slices in a 350° oven and heat thoroughly. Melt remaining margarine or butter in a heavy saucepan, stir in flour and blend until smooth. Gradually add chicken bouillon and stir until smooth. Beat egg yoke and half-and-half together and slowly add to sauce. Cook, stirring, until thick and smooth. Do not boil. Season to taste with salt and paprika. Arrange ham slices on a hot platter, cover with mushrooms and sweetbreads, and top with sauce. *Serves 6.*

SWEETBREADS
À LA MAID OF HONOR

This is a very economical dish or a super-deluxe dish, according to the ingredients you use. Vary the vegetable ingredients according to your taste, but "white" vegetables—cauliflower buds, diced sautéed onion, artichoke hearts, mushrooms (canned, drained, or small fresh ones lightly sautéed)—are most suitable. You can also add a cup of finely diced chicken leftovers.

1 cup finely diced cooked sweetbreads
1 cup chopped blanched almonds
1 cup finely diced celery, cooked until just
    tender
Salt and pepper to taste
⅛ teaspoon nutmeg
½ cup mushrooms (as above)
½ cup diced onion, sautéed in 1 tablespoon
    vegetable oil
4 artichoke hearts, quartered
1 tablespoon dry sherry

12 pastry shells (individual ones)
2 cups Medium White Sauce
2 tablespoons heavy cream (optional)

In a deep ovenproof bowl, blend all ingredients except last three. Set bowl in pan of hot water and place in 350° oven for 30 minutes, or until thoroughly heated. Place pastry shells on a flat baking tray, and spoon the mixture into each pastry shell. Blend Medium White Sauce with heavy cream, if you wish, and spoon over each filled pastry shell. Place in the oven for 10 to 20 minutes to heat thoroughly. *Serves 6 to 8.*

Heart

Beef or veal heart is an "inner" meat that isn't cheap anymore, especially if you have to ask the butcher to get one for you. But if a heart does appear at a good price in your supermarket meat case, you'll discover it to be one of the most versatile variety meats.

The usefulness of heart meat comes from its firm, dry texture, much more like muscle than like other organs. Because of this texture, you can use heart in recipes calling for ground beef, especially those that require slow cooking. Since heart tends to be tough, it probably isn't at its best in hamburgers. But try it in stuffed peppers or meat loaf.

The classic way to cook heart is to stuff and bake it. Baking is ideal to soften its stubborn fibers. Use any favorite stuffing recipe. Cook the heart covered with a small amount of liquid, such as tomato sauce or beef bouillon. A good trick is to lay 3 or 4 slices of bacon over the heart while cooking, since it has no natural self-basting layer of fat.

Heart slices can be cooked many ways. Two of the best are *Steamed Heart* and *Chicken-Fried Heart.* Here are the basic recipes.

STUFFED BEEF HEART

You may thicken the delicious pan juices with flour and water for good gravy. Mashed potatoes with this would be just right.

1 small beef heart or 3 veal hearts
Cold salted water
4 tablespoons margarine or butter
1 large onion, chopped
1 stalk celery, minced
2 tablespoons minced parsley
3 cups packaged dressing mix
1 cup beef bouillon
Salt and freshly ground black pepper

Cut a pocket in the heart(s). Remove skin and soak in cold salted water for about 15 minutes. Wipe dry. In the margarine or butter, sauté onion for 3 minutes. Add celery and parsley with dressing mix; toss lightly. Stuff the heart(s). Fasten with skewers and string as you would poultry. Brown the heart(s) lightly in margarine or butter in the stuffing skillet. Add bouillon, season with salt and pepper, cover, and simmer in a 400-degree oven about 2 hours, or until tender. *Serves 4 to 6.*

STEAMED HEART

1 2-pound beef heart cut in ¼-inch slices
2 carrots, diced
2 stalks celery, diced
1 large onion, diced
½ teaspoon salt
1 cup boiling water

Cut the heart into even slices, across the grain. Put vegetables and salt with about 1 cup boiling water in the bottom of a roasting pan. Place the heart slices on a rack above the water and cover tightly. Steam for 1½ to 2 hours, or until meat is tender. *Serves 4.*

CHICKEN-FRIED HEART

¼ cup all-purpose flour
1 teaspoon salt
¼ teaspoon pepper

1 2-pound beef heart, sliced as for Steamed
    Heart
¼ cup vegetable oil
⅛ cup beef bouillon

Season flour with salt and pepper. Coat the heart slices with flour. Heat the oil until a drop of water spatters in the pan. Brown the slices, turning once. Add bouillon and cover. Reduce heat and cook slowly for about 2 hours. Add liquid as necessary. *Serves 4.*

HEART CHASSEUR

This is best served with mashed potatoes or buttered noodles.

1 1-pound heart cut into ½-inch cubes
1 cup diced green pepper
1 cup diced onion
1 cup diced bacon
2 or 3 tablespoons oil
1 cup diced tomatoes
1 tablespoon tomato paste
2 tablespoons Worcestershire sauce
Hot water
2 tablespoons cornstarch mixed with
    2 tablespoons dry sherry
1 small can peas and carrots, or mushrooms
    (optional)
Salt and pepper to taste

Stir-fry in a large skillet the heart, pepper, onion, and bacon in 2 tablespoons oil. When the onion and pepper are tender, add tomatoes. If necessary, add another tablespoon oil. Turn into kettle, add tomato paste and Worcestershire sauce, and simmer, adding hot water as necessary to prevent drying out, for 20 to 30 minutes, or until tender. Add 2 tablespoons cornstarch mixed with sherry to thicken gravy; add vegetables if desired. Salt and pepper to taste. *Serves 4.*

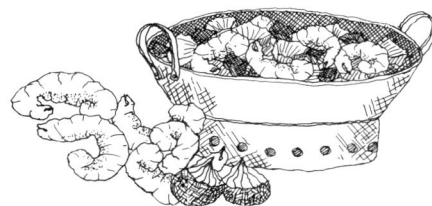

Fish

Although the price of fish continues to rise, there are still a good many fish, especially frozen ones, which are far less expensive than most meats. And fish—fresh or frozen—is still an inexpensive source of highest-quality protein. In frozen filets, there are no bones, no fat, no shrinkage. With fish, what you see is what you get to eat. As people become more aware of the high cost of food and more interested in cooking, fish is finally coming into its own.

Because weather, pollution, and storms affect the supply of fresh fish in the markets, it is impossible to say which kinds of fresh fish you will find most plentiful in any season in any part of the country. Except for the catch your fisherman may bring home to you, most fresh fish is concentrated in the markets of the coastal areas.

If your favorite fresh fish is not available, be prepared to substitute frozen fish. Whiting, pollock, ocean perch, Greenland turbot —whose flavor is a sort of cross between flounder and halibut—and many other species are usually available in frozen filets, sticks, or other portions all across the country.

When you buy frozen fish, defrost it in the refrigerator and cook it as soon as possible after it has defrosted. (Fish deteriorates more quickly than meat.) Allow about 24 hours to defrost a 1-pound package. Never defrost fish at room temperature or in warm water. In an emergency, you can put a 1-pound wrapped package into a deep pot, and leave it under cold running water for 1 to 2 hours to thaw it. Do not defrost fish sticks or portions before cooking.

Fish may be baked, broiled, sautéed, deep fried, steamed, or poached. In every case, your main objective should be to cook it quickly to maintain texture and flavor. Fish is delicate and needs only brief cooking to be moist and delicious. If cooked too long, it becomes dry and tasteless. To test for doneness, use the flaking method. Insert the tines of a fork gently into the flesh and move them, again gently. If the fish is done it will flake easily. When using this test on a whole fish or fish steaks containing bones (such as salmon), be sure to insert the fork near the bone, since that is where the flesh takes longest to cook.

How Much Fish to Buy

Whole: 1 pound serves 2 people
Dressed: 1 pound serves 2 people

Steaks and filets: 1 pound serves 2 people
Canned: 1 pound serves 6 people
Sticks: 1 pound serves 4 people

How to Use Fish

As the French have always known and we are finding out, the secret of good fish cooking is a supply of basic fish recipes that can be used for all kinds of fish. No flounder to be had? Try cod, or turbot, or even whiting. Salmon has no equal of course, but good salmon, like good beefsteak, hardly needs any cooking.

Although certain national cuisines have classic dishes that call for specific fishes, you are not required to stick strictly to the letter of the law unless the Ambassador is coming for dinner. Use whatever is plentiful and/or cheap in your area or whatever your son brought back from his fishing trip. The Budget Recipes fish system uses 5 basic cooking methods. Once you learn the basic recipe, you are equipped to do all the variations—and probably can think of more. We suggest, therefore, that you try each basic recipe first. Because of the delicate flavor of fish, the basic recipes are often the best. Basic Recipe C, for example, the simplest of all, can turn out as truly gourmet fare. What a pleasure to delight your guests, who are accustomed to dry restaurant fish dishes, with something so simple to cook.

What to Serve with Fish

As the flavor of fish is rather delicate, it is best not to serve it with anything that has an overpowering flavor. Mashed potatoes, boiled rice, or buttered pasta are fine. Lightly sautéed mushrooms are tasty with most fish recipes. Of course, any creamed vegetable is also quite popular with fish, especially if served with mashed or boiled potatoes. In summer, sometimes just the fish, plainly prepared, and served with a salad and French bread or toast is enough for a light lunch.

Put Fish Leftovers to Work

Cold poached fish can be used in salads, aspics, or mixed with mayonnaise. Or use mixed leftover fish saved up from various recipes. When you have enough fish for 4 persons, blend with 1 cup milk, 1 cup mixed vegetables, 1 egg, salt and pepper to taste, 1 cup grated cheese, and bake. Use fish trimmings for stock to make fish soups and fish aspics. Serve boiled whole fish with some of the famous fish sauces below. Cold leftover boiled or poached fish is also good with their sauce, and with Tartar sauce.

AIOLI

Aioli is a famous sauce from the sunny area of France called the Provence. It's really nothing more than garlic mayonnaise. But garlic mayonnaise can be splendid. If you make your own mayonnaise, you can have the purist's version of aioli. But you can certainly use a good commercial variety if you take the trouble to crush the garlic with a mortar and pestle. This is what gives aioli its characteristic strong-but-not-harsh garlic flavor.

4 to 8 cloves garlic, peeled
1 slice stale white bread
2 cups mayonnaise
Few drops lemon juice
Salt
Pepper

Slice garlic and place in a small bowl or mortar with stale white bread. Pound with a pestle for 5 minutes or more until you have a very smooth paste. Check carefully for large pieces of garlic. Don't try to pound with the back of a spoon or any other utensil. A pestle is a worthwhile investment, decorative, and essential for aioli. Add garlic paste to mayonnaise and mix thoroughly. Season to taste with lemon juice, salt, and pepper. *Makes 2 cups.*

HERB YOGURT SAUCE

Yogurt can be used in your favorite sauce or dressing recipes as a substitute for sour cream and buttermilk, and even as a partial substitute for mayonnaise. For buttermilk, thin yogurt with a little water so that the consistency is more like that of milk. When replacing mayonnaise in a recipe, use half yogurt and half mayonnaise. Use for fish or seafood, especially shrimp or salmon.

½ cup chopped fresh parsley
½ cup chopped scallions
2 tablespoons white tarragon vinegar
1 cup plain yogurt
½ teaspoon dillweed
Pinch garlic salt
Pinch pepper

Put parsley, scallions, vinegar, and half the yogurt in a blender. Blend at high speed for 30 seconds. Or mix in a bowl at high speed with an electric mixer. Gently fold in remaining yogurt, dillweed, and seasonings. *Makes 1 cup.*

RED LOBSTER SAUCE

This sauce is served on linguine, among other pastas. Spoon liberal amounts of sauce over each portion and center a piece of lobster meat atop the pasta in each dish.

1 live lobster (1 pound)
3 tablespoons olive oil
1 8-ounce bottle clam juice
1 whole white onion, peeled
1 celery rib
4 cups Marinara Sauce

Rinse lobster well in cold water; ½ inch down on the underside of the head, pierce it with a rigid, sharp pointed knife. When lobster is motionless, split it from that point down to the tail. Remove solid dark-green string in tail. Separate claws and tail from body. Heat oil in a frying pan and place pieces of lobster, still in shell and undersides down, in oil. Cook over medium heat until shell gets red, or for about 10 minutes, turning often. Pour in clam juice, add onion and celery, cover pan, and simmer 10 minutes.

Prepare Marinara Sauce in a large saucepan. Remove onion and celery from lobster pan and discard them. Add lobster and its liquid to

Marinara Sauce. Stir well, simmer uncovered 20 minutes, lifting lobster pieces from the pan frequently to drain liquid in shells into sauce. When sauce has thickened, stir, then remove from heat. Remove lobster meat from shells, discard shells, and put lobster back into sauce. *Makes about 4½ cups.*

Other Sea Foods

Food from the sea isn't limited to scale fish. Some of the most elegant dishes in fine restaurants include shellfish—oysters, clams, shrimp, lobsters, crab. On a budget, none of these in their fresh state is a sound investment. However, for special occasions shellfish frozen, canned, shucked, or what you have can be a good buy used as a tidbit of luxury in a salad or a sauce. If you make an investment in the fresh product once in a while, encourage leftovers and put them to work in salads, sauces, or aspics the next day.

The Right Way to Cook Fish

There are 5 basic approaches to cooking fish, the Basic Recipes below. Nearly all other fish recipes are variations on these major themes. Here is the code for our fish cooking system, followed by the variations.

Pan Fried—Whole filets or pieces are sautéed, served with pan juices
Deep Fried—Deep fried pieces, plain or specially prepared, served with sauces
Broiled—Filets, plain or with seasonings, are put under broiler
Poached—Filets, covered, are poached in liquid which is used to make sauce
Baked—Whole fish, filets, or specially prepared fish, are baked with or without liquid

Basic Recipe A

PAN FRIED OR SAUTÉED FISH

This is a very simple, and for most people the tastiest, way to prepare fish. For small fish—sole, turbot, small flounder—filets can be prepared whole. The secret is to cook the fish with just the right degree of doneness. It should be barely firm and not have an excessively wet look. This is when it tastes best. Taste it often. If the fish is large—sea bass or snapper, for instance—the filets should be cut into pieces of about 1 inch if the fish is very firm, or 3 to 4 inches if less firm, and proceed as described below. If the fish is thick, like sea bass, cooking will take somewhat longer.

4 fish filets (about ⅛ pound each)
2 to 3 tablespoons all-purpose flour
1 teaspoon salt
⅛ teaspoon pepper
2 to 3 tablespoons butter or oil

Dust fish with flour, salt, and pepper. Heat butter or oil quite hot and fry fish 5 minutes on each side, or until done. Remove to a platter, scrape up pan juices, and pour over fish. *Serves 2.*

FISH FILET MEUNIÈRE

This is a classic French method for preparing fish filets and is the simplest variation of Recipe A.

1½ pounds fish filets
All-purpose flour
4 tablespoons butter or oil
1 teaspoon lemon juice
1 tablespoon chopped parsley

Coat fish with flour and fry according to Recipe A in 2 tablespoons butter or oil. Remove fish when done. Add remaining butter to pan and scrape up browned bits. Pour butter over fish and sprinkle with lemon juice and parsley. *Serves 4.*

FRIED FISH
WITH GARLIC AND HERBS

This recipe is best with a hearty fish like sea bass, but others will do. Although it calls for a lot of garlic, it is not overpowering. For those who like hearty and spicy food, it might provide a good transition from meat-and-potato meals. Serve with spaghetti or noodles.

1½ pounds fish filets
All-purpose flour
6 to 10 cloves garlic
3 tablespoons olive oil
4 tablespoons parsley
2 tablespoons basil
1 tablespoon oregano
1 teaspoon salt
⅛ teaspoon pepper

Cut fish into 2-inch pieces and coat with flour. Fry garlic in oil at low heat for 5 minutes. Raise heat, add fish and herbs. Cook according to Recipe A but stir more frequently. Salt and pepper after cooking. *Serves 4.*

SAUTÉED FISH, CHINESE STYLE

1½ pounds fish filets
All-purpose flour
3 tablespoons oil (peanut or soy)
3 to 4 scallions
3 to 4 diced Chinese mushrooms (optional)
3 tablespoons soy sauce
1 tablespoon ginger (optional)

Cut fish into 3-inch pieces and coat with flour. Fry over high heat as in Recipe A, but add scallions also cut into 3-inch pieces to the pan as the fish cooks. Stir more frequently than in Recipe A. When fish is cooked, remove from pan. Add other ingredients, scraping up browned bits—you may have to add a little water—and pour over fish. *Serves 4.*

BRAISED FISH IN SOY SAUCE

3 tablespoons white wine
¼ cup soy sauce
4 slices white meat fish filets
3 tablespoons oil
1 scallion, chopped
2 slices ginger

Mix 1 tablespoon wine and the soy sauce in a shallow bowl. Add fish slices and marinate

15 minutes. Heat oil in a frying pan. Add scallion and ginger. Add fish slices and fry until golden on both sides, as in Recipe A. Add remaining wine and marinade. Simmer 5 to 10 minutes and serve. *Serves 4.*

SAUTÉED SALMON STEAKS

Frozen salmon steaks as well as other packaged frozen fish come in what can be an annoying variety of sizes in the same package. Keep this in mind when cooking them, as the smaller ones may be done before the larger, and in that case should be removed at once from the pan.

1 1¾-pound package frozen salmon steaks, defrosted
All-purpose flour
1 teaspoon salt
⅛ teaspoon pepper
1 tablespoon vegetable oil
3 tablespoons margarine or butter
1 tablespoon minced parsley
2 tablespoons lemon juice, strained

Flour steaks lightly. Season with salt and pepper. Heat oil and margarine or butter. Sauté steaks to brown on both sides. Remove steaks from pan after 8 to 10 minutes, or when flesh flakes easily with a fork. Place fish on a platter and pour pan juices over. Sprinkle with parsley and lemon juice. *Serves 4 or 5.*

Basic Recipe B

DEEP FRIED

There are two simple ways to deep fry fish: (1) Coat the fish filets cut into large pieces with flour, salt, and pepper, and fry in oil; (2) Dip the cut-up filets in batter and deep fry. Either way the oil should be 340° to 360°. It's better to err on the side of too hot than not hot enough. Insufficiently hot oil makes greasy, unappetizing fried food. Remember, too, that as you add cold foods to hot oil, the oil will get cooler. If you are frying a large amount of food, allow the oil to reheat between batches. A good standard batter is the following.

1 cup all-purpose flour
1 medium egg
⅔ cup milk
1 teaspoon salt
⅛ teaspoon pepper

Mix ingredients and let stand 20 minutes before using.

1½ pounds fish filets
3 cups vegetable oil
Lemon wedges
Parsley sprigs

Cut fish filets into 3- to 4-inch pieces. Coat well in batter. Fry in hot oil (see above) 5 to 6 minutes, or until golden brown and easy to flake. Drain on paper towels set on a plate in a warm oven. Serve at once, with lemon wedges, garnished with parsley. *Serves 4.*

FISH-AND-CHIPS

The British "Fish-and-Chips" means deep fried fish served with French fried potatoes, which in England are called chips. What we call potato chips are called crisps in England. The fish is prepared according to the basic Recipe B using flour-and-egg batter.

FISH ORLY

Orly is a classic French way of preparing fish or seafood by deep frying and serving it with tomato sauce.

2 tablespoons margarine or butter
1 small onion, finely chopped
1 clove garlic, finely chopped
1 16-ounce can tomatoes
3 ounces tomato paste
1 teaspoon salt
⅛ teaspoon pepper
1 teaspoon sugar

1 cup all-purpose flour
1 medium egg
⅔ cup milk
1 teaspoon salt
⅛ teaspoon pepper

2 pounds fish filets
3 cups vegetable oil

In a saucepan, fry chopped onion and garlic over low heat until just cooked. Add tomatoes from can, reserving liquid. Add tomato paste, salt, pepper, and sugar. Allow sauce to simmer 20 minutes or longer, adding liquid from tomato can if it becomes too thick. Mix ingredients for batter, coat fish and deep fry according to Recipe B. Drain and serve with tomato sauce. *Serves 4 to 6.*

FISH WITH SOUR CREAM, RUSSIAN STYLE

1½ pounds fish filets
All-purpose flour
1 teaspoon salt
⅛ teaspoon pepper
⅓ pound mushrooms
2 tablespoons margarine or butter
2 hard-boiled eggs, sliced
⅔ pint sour cream
¾ tablespoon grated Swiss cheese

Coat fish with flour mixed with salt and pepper and fry according to Recipe B. Slice mushrooms and fry very quickly in margarine or butter over high heat for about 5 minutes. Place cooked fish in a baking dish, layer with mushrooms, sliced eggs, and cover with sour cream. Before serving, sprinkle with cheese and warm under the broiler for a few minutes until brown. *Serves 4.*

PORGY À LA TAJ

4 porgies
Salt to taste
¼ cup lime juice
All-purpose flour
1 egg beaten with 1 tablespoon water
Fine bread crumbs
3 cups vegetable oil
Fried parsley
Tartar sauce (optional)

Clean porgies but leave them whole. Sprinkle with salt and douse with lime juice.

Dip into flour, then beaten egg, then crumbs. Fry in oil at 450° for 4 to 5 minutes. Serve with fried parsley (see below) and with tartar sauce, if desired. *Serves 4.*

FRIED PARSLEY

½ bunch parsley
½ cup vegetable oil

Pull clusters of parsley leaves with a little stem attached for "handles" from the top of a bunch. Throw a few at a time into hot oil for less than a minute. Drain on absorbent paper.

Basic Recipe C

BROILED FISH

This is the simplest of the basic recipes. If you have to eat as soon as you come home from work or are otherwise in a hurry, this is the fastest method for getting a good fish meal.

1½ pounds fish filets
All-purpose flour
2 tablespoons margarine or butter, or oil
1 teaspoon salt
⅛ teaspoon pepper

Dust the filets with flour, salt and pepper, and dot with butter. Place under the broiler 10 to 15 minutes until the top is brown and done well but the inside is just cooked, not dry or flaky. *Serves 4.*

BROILED FISH WITH TOMATOES AND SAUSAGE

6 sausage links (or 1 medium or 2 small Italian sausages)
2 pounds fish filets
All-purpose flour
1 teaspoon salt
⅛ teaspoon pepper
1 medium can tomatoes
3 tablespoons scallions
2 tablespoons dillweed

Cook sausages in a dry skillet until done, about 10 minutes. Cover filets with flour mixed with salt and pepper and place in a greased baking dish. Add the sausage broken up into small pieces, tomatoes, scallions, and dillweed. Broil according to Recipe C 10 to 15 minutes. *Serves 4 to 5.*

BROILED SALMON STEAKS WITH GREEN YOGURT SAUCE

4 salmon steaks, ½ inch thick
¼ cup melted butter
1½ teaspoons seasoned salt
Green Yogurt Sauce

Rinse salmon and dry. Add seasoned salt to butter. Place salmon on broiler pan rack; brush with half the butter mixture. Broil according to Recipe C 4 inches from heated broiler for 10 minutes. Turn salmon, brush with remaining butter, and broil 8 minutes more. Serve with Green Yogurt Sauce. *Serves 4.*

GREEN YOGURT SAUCE

½ cup chopped fresh parsley
½ cup chopped scallions
Juice of ½ lemon
1 cup plain yogurt
½ cup fresh dill
Dash cayenne pepper

Place parsley, scallions, lemon juice, and half of yogurt in blender. Reserve the dill. Blend at high speed for 30 seconds. Fold in remaining yogurt but do not blend. Fold in dill and cayenne. *Serves 4.*

BROILED FISH, HOME STYLE

This is a simple but very popular way to prepare fish and allows many additions and variations. Sautéed chopped green peppers or fried mushroom pieces can be added just before broiling.

¾ cup pieces of bacon
4 tablespoons butter
⅔ cup small onions, cut into rings

1½ pounds fish
3 tablespoons bread crumbs
½ cup parsley for garnish

Chop bacon into small pieces and cook until just crisp. Reserve bacon and pour off all but 1 tablespoon fat. Add 1 tablespoon butter and fry onions cut into slices until golden but not brown. Grease an ovenproof dish or low casserole. Place fish in casserole. Add onion rings, then bacon, finally bread crumbs. Dot with remaining butter and place under broiler as described in Recipe C. Garnish with parsley. *Serves 4.*

Basic Recipe D

POACHED FISH

Here is a classic French method for preparing fish. The fish is poached in liquid. The liquid is used to make a sauce which is then poured over the fish. It is slightly more complicated than the other basic methods outlined here and, unlike the others, the basic recipe can't be done in 10 minutes. But it is still not a difficult method and makes delicious fish dishes.

2 pounds fish filets
2 tablespoons chopped scallions or onion
1½ cups dry white wine or water
3 tablespoons margarine or butter
2 tablespoons all-purpose flour
½ cup milk or half-and-half
¼ cup grated Swiss cheese

Preheat oven to 350°. Place filets in a buttered dish, add scallions and wine. Heat almost to the simmer on top of stove and then place in oven. Cook for about 10 minutes. Test it to make sure the flesh is just cooked, not dry. Remove to a warm platter to keep hot. Heat remaining liquid over very high heat until boiled down to 1 cup. Meanwhile, on top of stove in a saucepan melt margarine or butter and stir in flour. Stir reduced cooking liquid into the flour and butter mixture. Cook a few minutes until thickened. Add milk or half-and-half and cook until as thick as heavy cream. Pour over fish. Sprinkle the top with cheese

and put under broiler for a few minutes.
Serves 4.

NORWEGIAN FISH BALLS IN SAUCE

2 pounds pollock filets, fresh or frozen,
    defrosted
1 teaspoon salt
2 tablespoons potato flour or cornstarch
⅛ teaspoon grated nutmeg
2 cups milk
Salted water for poaching
Béchamel Sauce made with milk
Minced fresh dill

Sprinkle fish with salt. Put through the
finest knife of the grinder. Add potato flour or
cornstarch and put through the grinder 3 more
times. Season to taste with nutmeg. Put in milk
until mixture is the right consistency to form
into balls. It may not take the full 2 cups. Form
into balls and poach them in simmering salted
(1 tablespoon) water 15 to 20 minutes. Serve
covered in Béchamel Sauce, sprinkled with
dill. *Serves 4 to 6.*

FISH WITH PAPRIKA SAUCE

2 pounds filets
2 tablespoons chopped scallions
Water to barely cover fish
2 tablespoons margarine or butter
1 medium onion, finely chopped
2 tablespoons all-purpose flour
⅓ tablespoon paprika (depending on
    strength)
½ cup milk

Preheat oven to 350°. Cook filets with scallions and water according to Recipe D. When
filets are done, remove and boil down liquid to
1 or 1½ cups. Melt margarine or butter and
cook onion until just golden but not brown.
Add flour and cook over low heat for a few
minutes. Stir reduced cooking liquid into flour
mixture with paprika. Cook, stirring, until
thickened, thinning it with milk. Adjust seasoning. It should be slightly spicy but not hot.
Pour sauce over fish. *Serves 4.*

FISH DUGLÉRÉ

2 pounds filets
1 small can tomatoes
1 clove garlic, finely chopped
3 tablespoons parsley, chopped
1 teaspoon thyme
½ bay leaf
3 tablespoons margarine or butter
2 tablespoons all-purpose flour

Preheat oven to 350°. Place filets, tomatoes,
and garlic in a pan and cover with herbs, reserving 1 teaspoon parsley. Remove bay leaf.
Proceed with Recipe D, using margarine or
butter with the cooking sauce to make a thick
sauce. Pour finished sauce over fish and garnish with remaining parsley. *Serves 4 to 6.*

FISH BONNE FEMME

2 pounds filets
½ pound sliced fresh mushrooms
2 tablespoons chopped scallions
Liquid to barely cover fish (white vermouth is
    best)
5 tablespoons margarine or butter
2 tablespoons all-purpose flour
½ cup milk or half-and-half
2 egg yolks
6 whole mushroom caps

Preheat oven to 350°. Place filets in a baking
dish with mushrooms and scallions, barely
cover with liquid and cook according to Recipe D. Prepare sauce with 3 tablespoons margarine or butter, flour, and cooking liquid from
the fish, as in Recipe D, and just before
serving slowly beat egg yolks into sauce. Pour
over fish and decorate with mushroom caps
which have been lightly sautéed in 2 tablespoons margarine or butter. *Serves 4 to 6.*

FISH WITH BROWN SAUCE

2 pounds fish filets
2 tablespoons scallions or onion
1½ cups water
2 tablespoons margarine or butter
1 tablespoon chopped onion

2 tablespoons all-purpose flour
1½ cups stock from cooking fish
Salt and freshly ground pepper to taste
¼ teaspoon dried thyme

Poach fish with scallions, in water, as described in Recipe D. Drain and keep warm; reserve cooking liquid, reduced to 1½ cups if you have more. Melt margarine or butter. Sauté onion until lightly brown. Blend in flour and brown it with butter and onion, stirring constantly. Add stock and seasonings and continue stirring until thickened. *Serves 4 to 6.*

Basic Recipe E

BAKED FISH

This is another very simple method. The fish is placed whole or as filets in a pan in the oven and baked at 400° for 10 to 15 minutes for filets, or at 350° for up to 40 minutes for a whole fish. Whole fish usually has to be basted to prevent drying out. Water or stock added to the pan while cooking is good basting liquid, or oil can be used.

2 pounds fish filets
¼ cup water or dry white wine
1 teaspoon salt
⅛ teaspoon pepper
2 tablespoons margarine or butter or
    vegetable oil

Preheat oven to 400°. Place fish in a baking dish, add water or wine, season fish with salt and pepper, dot with margarine or butter, or brush with oil. Bake in a preheated oven at 400° 10 to 15 minutes. *Serves 4 to 6.*

MEXICAN PARSLEYED FISH

1 10-ounce can Mexican green tomatoes
1 medium onion, finely chopped
2 cloves garlic, peeled and finely chopped
1 cup fresh chopped parsley
1 teaspoon salt
⅛ teaspoon pepper
1½ pounds fish filets

Preheat oven to 400°. Mix tomatoes, onion, garlic, parsley, salt, and pepper. Put a layer of this mixture in a greased casserole. Add fish filets and cover with rest of mixture. Bake according to Recipe E for 15 to 20 minutes. *Serves 4.*

BAKED FILETS OF HADDOCK OR COD

Serve this hot or cold with boiled potatoes and beet salad.

4 fish filets, 1 inch thick
1 teaspoon salt
2 tablespoons vegetable oil
⅛ teaspoon pepper
5 scallions, including green tops, coarsely
    chopped
2 fresh tomatoes, sliced, or
    2 tablespoons tomato paste diluted in ½
    cup water
½ lemon, thinly sliced
½ cup white wine (optional)
½ cup chopped parsley for garnish

Wash and salt filets. Leave to drain, dry with paper towels. Oil a baking dish that can be brought to the table. Place fish filets in baking dish in an orderly way next to one another. Sprinkle with pepper, spread on scallions. Place tomato slices on top of filets or pour on tomato paste. Decorate with lemon slices. Bake in 350° oven 30 minutes, or until fish is tender. Add wine and bake 3 minutes more. Garnish with parsley. *Serves 4.*

BAKED FILETS OF SEA BASS

1½ pounds filets of sea bass, fresh or frozen,
    defrosted
Salt and pepper
8 stuffed green olives
¾ cup chicken stock
Brown Sauce

Season filets with salt and pepper. Place in a shallow baking pan with olives and pour stock over. Bake in 425° oven 10 minutes. Arrange

filets and olives carefully on a hot platter. Reserve stock for sauce. Pour Brown Sauce over.
Serves 3 to 4.

BAKED STUFFED WHITING

1 frozen 26-ounce whiting, defrosted
1 teaspoon salt
⅛ teaspoon pepper
3½ tablespoons margarine or butter
¼ cup boiling water
½ cup prepared stuffing mix
¼ pound mushrooms, finely chopped
1 stalk celery, chopped fine
1 tablespoon chopped shallot
1 tablespoon chopped parsley
2 tablespoons melted margarine or butter
¼ cup dry vermouth

Remove backbone and wipe fish with a
damp cloth. Season inside and out with salt
and pepper. Melt 2 tablespoons margarine or
butter in boiling water. Add stuffing and mix
well. Sauté mushrooms, celery, shallot, and
parsley in 1½ tablespoons margarine or butter
for about 5 minutes. Mix with stuffing. Fill
lightly into fish and fasten with toothpicks or
skewers. Lace with kitchen string. Place in a
well-greased baking pan and brush with
melted margarine or butter. Pour in vermouth.
Bake in 425° oven 12 to 15 minutes, or until
fish flakes easily with a fork. Baste occasionally. *Serves 2 to 3.*

BAKED FISH, VIKING STYLE

This is a brilliantly simple way of perking up
frozen fish filets. Invented by Erik Murer, a
Norwegian scientist living in Philadelphia, it
can be cooked with frozen filets without
thawing. For variation, top the fish before
cooking with thin slices of lemon, crumbled
bacon, sautéed mushrooms, nuts, or whatever
other flavorful garnish you like.

2 tablespoons olive oil
2 pounds frozen fish filets
2 tablespoons sage
2 tablespoons savory

Pepper
Salt

Preheat oven to 350°. Oil a baking pan. Place
frozen fish in pan. Sprinkle filets with seasonings. Bake according to Recipe E for 20 to
30 minutes until cooked but not dry. *Serves 2.*

SOLE OF DECEPTION

This recipe comes from an amusing cookbook
called *The Madison Avenue Cookbook,* which
is supposed to help you impress your friends
without knowing how to cook. The author,
Alan Koehler, likes it "because the stature of a
cook is instantly jacked up a notch when a
guest comes upon a whole cooked grape in
anything." We like it because it points out how
easy it is to use Recipe E. As Koehler men-
tions, any white fish filet can be used, but
"you bill it as Dover sole flown from England
the night before."

½ cup sour cream
½ cup mayonnaise
Juice of ¼ lemon
3 or 4 mushroom caps
2 dozen seedless grapes
2 tablespoons butter
1 pound fish filets

Mix sour cream and mayonnaise. Add lemon
juice. Sauté mushroom caps and grapes lightly
in butter. Spread sour cream and mayonnaise
mixture over fish in a greased shallow dish.
Add sautéed mushrooms and grapes. Bake according to Recipe E for 15 to 20 minutes.
Serves 2 to 4.

BAKED FISH,
FLORENTINE STYLE

Any fish, including salmon, can be cooked this
way. The recipe given is for a 4-pound fish.
Adjust the amount of stuffing to fit smaller or
larger fishes.

1 small onion
4 tablespoons butter

½ pound fresh spinach or 1 package frozen
  spinach, drained
2 cups bread crumbs
Dash lemon juice
2 teaspoons salt
¼ teaspoon pepper
2 tablespoons cream or half-and-half
½ to 1 cup white vermouth (or water and vermouth)

Preheat oven to 400°. Fry onion, finely
chopped, over low heat in 2 tablespoons
butter. Add spinach, finely chopped, and cook
until wilted. Add bread crumbs, lemon juice,
salt, and pepper. Sauté 1 minute, and add
cream or half-and-half. Stuff fish with this mixture and place in an ovenproof dish. Add ½
cup vermouth and rub fish with remaining
butter. Bake according to Recipe E, adding
more vermouth if it evaporates. *Serves 8.*

CREOLE FISH

This is best with a whole fish but filets, or
even steaks, of firm-fleshed fish such as cod
can be used. The creole sauce could also be
used for other dishes such as meat.

3 tablespoons oil
1 green pepper, seeded and chopped coarsely
2 medium onions, chopped
1 medium can tomatoes
½ cup fresh or frozen okra (optional)
1 hot red pepper crushed (or less, to taste)
2 cloves garlic, chopped
3 tablespoons parsley
1 bay leaf
1 clove
1 teaspoon salt
⅛ teaspoon pepper
1 3-pound fish or 2 pounds filets

Preheat oven to 400°. Heat oil in skillet and
add green pepper. Cook over moderate heat
until slightly softened. Add onions, cook until
golden but not brown. Add all other ingredients except fish and simmer 5 to 10 minutes.
Place fish in a greased ovenproof dish. Pour
creole sauce over. Bake according to Recipe E
for 30 to 40 minutes for whole fish, 10 to 15

minutes for filets. The fish should just flake
when tested with a fork but should not be dry.
Serves 4 to 6.

SHELLFISH JAMBALAYA

A real stretcher—and elegant enough for a
party with a crisp green salad and crusty
French bread. Made in a pressure cooker, it's
grand eating in a hurry!

3 tablespoons shortening
1 to 2 cloves garlic, cut in half
½ cup chopped onion
½ pound smoked cooked ham, diced
1 cup long-grain rice
2 teaspoons salt
⅛ teaspoon freshly ground black pepper
⅛ teaspoon allspice
Pinch each cayenne, chili powder, and basil
½ cup water
1 16-ounce can tomatoes
1 6-ounce can mushroom pieces, drained
1 pound peeled, cleaned cooked shrimp (fresh
  or frozen) or lobster
½ green pepper, slivered

Heat pressure cooker and add shortening.
Sauté garlic and onion until golden. Stir in
ham and rice. Cook until rice is golden. Remove garlic if you wish. Add seasonings,
water, tomatoes, mushrooms, and mix well;
add shrimp or lobster and sprinkle with green
pepper slivers. Close cover securely. Place
pressure regulator on vent pipe and cook 5
minutes. Cool cooker at once by running cold
water over the top of it. *Serves 8.*

SHRIMP AND CRABMEAT DELUXE

With this you might like to serve cooked or
canned green beans dressed with sour cream
and a bit of dill accompanied by hot cornbread.

1½ pounds crabmeat, picked over
1 pound cooked shrimp (fresh or frozen)
½ green pepper, chopped
⅓ cup chopped parsley
2 cups cooked rice

1½ cups mayonnaise
2 packages frozen peas, cooked according to
*   package directions*
Salt and freshly ground black pepper to taste

Place all ingredients in a large bowl and mix together gently. Turn into a lightly buttered, large casserole. Refrigerate until ready to bake. Bake, covered, at 350° for 1 hour. *Serves 6.*

STUFFED TOMATOES NEPTUNE

This is a real budget item, which can be varied in quite a few ways: Stuff the tomatoes with just fish or shellfish and mayonnaise, or mix half-and-half with peas and carrots; use pure mayonnaise, or mix half-and-half with sour cream; or you can even use *Green Goddess Dressing.* Top the tomatoes with a sprig of parsley, a rosette of radish, an olive, one shrimp, or a pecan. The variations are endless. Serve on a bed of watercress.

4 tomatoes, stems removed, all seeds and
*   centers removed*
1 cup leftover fish, flaked, mixed with
*   shellfish*
*   or shrimp cut into bits*
4 green olives, chopped
1 teaspoon finely chopped scallion
1 teaspoon finely chopped parsley
1 cup (approximately) mayonnaise or other
*   dressing (see above)*
1 cup canned peas and carrots, rinsed and
*   well drained*
Salt and pepper to taste

Prepare tomatoes, and place them upside down in a colander to drain any remaining liquid. Mix all other ingredients except salt and pepper in a bowl. Taste, and add salt and pepper if necessary. Spoon into each tomato until very full. Top with garnish (as above), and serve tomatoes on a bed of watercress, surrounded by spoonfuls of any remaining stuffing. *Serves 4.*

SECTION TWO · VEGETABLES, SALADS, AND DRESSINGS

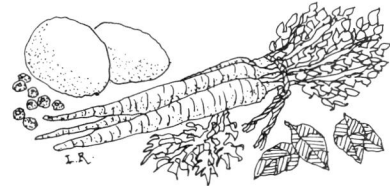

Vegetables

Vegetables, fresh in season, or canned or dried vegetables all year, begin to look like the best buy around. Add vegetable courses to your main meals, and cut down on meat portions. Use them liberally—especially celery, cabbage, carrots, and potatoes—as casserole and stew stretchers and reduce meat contents proportionately.

Fresh vegetables are a real bargain in both vitamin content and cost when the local crops are being harvested. But don't dismiss the canned goods, or the dried vegetables, as so many of us have in the past. Dried legumes, such as beans and peas, and lentils, cost very little and are the basis for some very good vegetable dishes and soups. And there is a lot you can do with the canned product; you can use canned vegetables wherever a recipe calls for fresh precooked vegetables, for instance.

Commercially canned vegetables retain a high percentage of their vitamin content; if the flavor isn't all you could ask, there are ways to improve it. You can remove some of the canned flavor by rinsing the vegetables well in cold water, and adding salt and pepper before using. Or salt, pepper, and warm canned vegetables in margarine or milk.

Home-canned vegetables often have a very fine flavor. If you have a vegetable garden, you should consider canning or freezing some produce. Freezing of fresh vegetables, if you work in small lots, is relatively simple. You can cook twice as much as you will serve for dinner, and freeze the rest, following instructions on page 7.

Here are three simple ways to improve some of the best buys in canned vegetables. Try these tricks on other canned vegetables.

CANNED BEET RELISH

1 16-ounce can whole beets, drained
2 large cloves garlic, peeled and minced
2 tablespoons oil
1 tablespoon olive oil
2 tablespoons vinegar
Salt to taste
½ cup minced fresh parsley

Dice beets into a medium bowl, and combine with remaining ingredients. Toss several times, and chill slightly before serving. *Serves 4 to 6.*

DILLED CANNED GREEN BEAN SALAD

1 16-ounce can whole green beans
2 tablespoons minced fresh dill or 1 table-
spoon dillweed, dried
1 tablespoon minced onion
½ teaspoon prepared mustard
3 tablespoons oil
1 tablespoon vinegar
Salt and pepper to taste

Drain and rinse beans, and warm them over medium heat in a saucepan. Turn into a salad bowl, and at once toss with all remaining ingredients. Let beans cool at room temperature in their sauce, then chill slightly before serving. *Serves 4 to 6.*

CANNED CREAMED ONIONS

2 16-ounce cans onions
3 tablespoons butter
3 tablespoons all-purpose flour
1½ cups whole milk, heated
Salt and pepper to taste
¼ teaspoon nutmeg

Drain and rinse onions thoroughly in cold water. In a small saucepan over low heat, melt butter, and stir in flour. Stir in warm milk quickly to keep sauce from lumping. Add onions, salt, pepper, and nutmeg, and heat the onions through. *Serves 4 to 6.*

Variations on Fresh Vegetable Themes

Nearly all vegetables have a season in which they are a good buy. If you tire of the same old flavor, vary it with herbs, lemon juice, soy sauce—or by cooking the vegetables in a little bouillon made with beef or chicken bouillon cubes or packaged granules.

There are innumerable ways to use up left-over cooked vegetables. Sweet potato puffs, parsnip cakes, and parsnip sticks—to use only three examples—are recipes you can adapt to other leftover vegetables as well.

The Best Meat Stretchers

How do you make a stew expand to serve a last-minute guest? How do you stretch a salad, a vegetable dish, a whole meal? More often than not, one of three inexpensive and serviceable vegetables can help you out. A meat loaf is just a meat loaf, but add hot, fluffy baked potatoes and a salad, and it's dinner. Then there's the chicken salad that grows and grows as you add crisp, green celery or shredded cabbage. Potatoes, celery, and cabbage are so homely, so useful, that we tend to take them for granted and to forget them when it comes to creative cooking. So here let us review the virtues of these "ordinary" vegetables.

There used to be a joke going around that cabbage and celery were the only vegetables with minus calories. You actually use more energy chewing than the vegetables supply. Although that's something of an exaggeration, one rib of celery, enough for two or three celery sticks, has about five calories. Potatoes, on the other hand, have an undeserved reputation as diet spoilers. One medium potato has about 100 calories, fewer than a cup of cooked peas. Probably some of the unfounded rumors about potatoes come from our tendency in this country to lavish a single potato with five tablespoons of butter or half a cup of sour cream. But good potatoes have a marvelous nutty flavor all their own, and they add an indispensable heartiness to dishes like beef stew or corned beef hash. And did you know that potatoes are a good source of Vitamin C?

Besides being low in price and high in versatility, potatoes, celery, and cabbage have very long storage lives once you get them home. A few tips:

- Don't store potatoes in the refrigerator. When they're too cold (below 40°F) some of the starch in potatoes changes to sugar, giving them a sweetish taste.
- Do keep celery and cabbage refrigerated, preferably in a hydrator and a plastic bag to maximize moisture. If you make celery sticks, keep them in a glass of cold water.
- Don't use "new" potatoes for baking or mashing. They are really slightly imma-

ture and take best to boiling and sautéing.

- If you find that your red-skinned potatoes have red flesh, too, it's because they've been artificially dyed. If your potatoes have been ruined by this practice, your grocer should refund your money.
- You can use every part of a stalk of celery making it a waste-free food. The leaves? Use them to flavor soups and stews, add them as an unusual green to tossed salads, use them in place of parsley for garnish.
- Try soy sauce, Worcestershire-sauce, dill-weed, turmeric, or just plain salt and pepper to flavor a baked potato when you're counting calories. If it seems too dry, add a little milk.
- Soup or stew too salty? Cut in an extra potato during the cooking to absorb some of the unwanted salinity.

SPICED RED CABBAGE

Delicious with beef or pork.

6 cups chopped red cabbage
3 tablespoons margarine or butter
2 apples, cut into wedges
12 whole cloves
1 teaspoon salt
¼ cup sugar
¼ cup water
¼ cup wine vinegar or cider vinegar

Place chopped cabbage in pan with tight-fitting lid. Cut margarine or butter in pieces over it. Add apple wedges and cloves. Add salt and sugar. Pour water over all. Cook 5 to 8 minutes, covered, until crisp-tender. Add vinegar, replace lid, and turn off heat. Let stand 5 minutes before serving. *Serves 6 to 8.*

CARROTS COOKED IN BOUILLON

Carrots are a great year-round buy, and there are loads of imaginative ways to vary their flavor. Try adding one of the following to this recipe as it cooks:

¼ teaspoon tarragon; ¼ teaspoon sweet

basil; ½ teaspoon dillweed; 1 teaspoon soy sauce (omit the salt when using soy sauce); dash Worcestershire sauce; or 1 teaspoon dried parsley flakes
4 large carrots
1 cup chicken or beef bouillon
¼ teaspoon sugar
Pinch salt
1 teaspoon margarine or butter

Bring the bouillon to a boil. Scrape and slice the carrots and add to the liquid. Add sugar and salt and simmer, covered, until barely tender. Remove carrots to a warm dish, add margarine or butter, and cover. Turn up the heat and boil down the liquid until it begins to thicken. Serve carrots topped with the hot sauce from the cooking liquid.

CARROTS IN GARLIC SAUCE

1 pound carrots
½ pound onions
4 tablespoons oil
2 or 3 cloves garlic, mashed
2 teaspoons all-purpose flour
¼ cup beef bouillon
¼ cup milk
1 teaspoon sugar
Salt and pepper to taste
Pinch nutmeg

Scrape and cut carrots into thin rounds. Heat oil in the bottom of a saucepan and cook carrots and onions in it gently until they are only translucent. Add garlic and cook 5 minutes more. Remove from heat, stir in flour, and mix well. Cook 3 minutes more. Heat broth and milk in separate pans just to the boiling point. Away from heat, stir first hot broth, then hot milk into vegetables. Add seasonings and simmer uncovered about 25 minutes or until carrots are completely tender. *Serves 4 to 6.*

LEMON CARROTS

3 tablespoons lemon juice
⅓ cup water
4 large carrots

Salt to taste
1 teaspoon margarine or butter

Combine lemon juice and water and bring to a boil. Scrape and thinly slice carrots and add to boiling liquid. Simmer until carrots are barely tender when pricked with a fork. Salt very lightly and add margarine or butter. *Serves 4.*

ORANGE CARROTS

3 ounces orange juice
*   concentrate (undiluted)*
¼ cup water
4 large carrots
1 tablespoon brown sugar

Combine orange juice concentrate and water and bring to a boil. Scrape and thinly slice carrots. Add carrot slices and sugar to hot liquid and cook, covered, until barely tender. Add more water by the tablespoon if pan threatens to go dry. Serve piping hot, adding boiled-down pan juices for glaze. *Serves 4.*

CARROT–POTATO FRITTERS

You can make this from scratch following the recipe here. But the economical way to make the fritters is to use carrot and potato leftovers.

1 pound carrots
1 pound potatoes
Boiling water to cover
1 medium onion
3 tablespoons cooking oil
1 clove garlic, mashed or minced
3 tablespoons tomato catsup
1 teaspoon dillweed
Flour
1 tablespoon parsley (optional)

Scrape and quarter carrots. Peel potatoes and cut into large chunks. Place vegetables in boiling water to cover, and boil until barely tender (about 20 minutes). While carrots and potatoes are cooking, chop onion and sauté until translucent in 1 tablespoon oil. Add garlic and cook slowly for 5 minutes more.

Puree or mash cooked carrots and potatoes. Add onion mixture, catsup, and dillweed. Shape mixture into patties with your hands and dredge each one in flour. Fry in remaining oil until golden-brown, about 5 minutes on each side. Sprinkle lightly with parsley if you wish. *Serves 4 to 6.*

CANDIED CARROTS

6 medium carrots
Boiling salted water
¼ cup (½ stick) margarine or butter
¼ cup sugar

Scrape and dice carrots, and cook in boiling salted water until tender (8 to 10 minutes). Drain thoroughly. Melt margarine or butter, add carrots and sprinkle with sugar. Heat, stirring frequently, until sugar is entirely melted and carrots are well coated with mixture. *Serves 4.*

CARROTS IN CREAM

An elegant side dish for company dinners.

1 pound carrots
Cold water to cover
¼ teaspoon sugar
Pinch salt
3 tablespoons butter
1 pint heavy cream or half-and-half

Scrape carrots and cut them in half. Place carrots in a saucepan with cold water to cover and add sugar, salt, and 2 tablespoons butter. Bring to a boil, reduce heat and simmer until the liquid is reduced and thickened and carrots are barely tender. Heat cream or half-and-half to boiling in a saucepan. Pour hot cream over cooked carrots, heat to boiling, then reduce heat again and simmer 5 minutes. Just before serving, stir in the last tablespoon of butter. *Serves 4 to 6.*

SUPER SIMPLE SIMMERED CELERY

Celery is one of the good year-round vegetables that costs little and can be served many ways. This recipe is strongly flavored—and makes a perfect diet vegetable dish. Save celery leaves to flavor soups, salads, and stews.

2 bunches celery
½ cup chicken bouillon
¼ cup soy sauce
¼ teaspoon Tabasco sauce

Trim away celery leaves. Cut each rib into ½-inch slices. In a saucepan, heat chicken bouillon, soy sauce, and Tabasco until mixture starts to bubble. Add celery slices, reduce heat, cover, and cook very slowly until just tender (about 12 to 15 minutes). *Serves 6.*

BRAISED CELERY AND CARROTS

A hearty celery side dish flavored with carrots and onions—pretty enough for company.

16 celery stalks
2 tablespoons bacon drippings or margarine
¼ cup sliced onion
¼ cup carrot rounds
3 cups beef stock or bouillon
1 bay leaf
2 whole cloves
8 peppercorns
Salt to taste

Wash celery, trim off tops, cut into 3-inch pieces. Heat drippings or margarine in a 2-quart baking dish. Add onion, carrot rounds, and celery. Toss to coat, and simmer 5 minutes. Add stock or bouillon, bay leaf, cloves, peppercorns, and salt to taste. Bring to a boil, then put into oven and bake at 375°, covered, until tender (about 40 minutes). Remove vegetables from baking dish, boil to reduce liquid until there is just enough to coat celery. *Serves 6 to 8.*

CORN FRITTERS

Don't throw away uneaten ears of corn—make fritters instead.

4 or 5 ears cooked corn on the cob
2 eggs
1 teaspoon minced green pepper

¼ teaspoon salt
¼ teaspoon pepper
4 to 6 tablespoons margarine or butter
Salt to taste

Score the rows of kernels with a paring knife, then squeeze out pulp by pressing the blunt side of knife down on the rows. Beat eggs until thick and lemon-colored, and don't skimp on the beating. Add green pepper, salt, and pepper. Whip beaten egg mixture into corn. Spoon into margarine or butter in a hot frying pan and cook until brown on one side. Turn, brown on the other side, and salt to taste before serving. *Serves 4 to 6.*

STUFFED CUCUMBERS

If you get bored with cucumbers when they are in season, try them stuffed. It's a great way to use up ham leftovers. You can stuff summer squash and zucchini the same way.

2 tablespoons margarine or butter
2 tablespoons flour
1 cup milk
6 medium cucumbers, unpeeled
¼ pound cooked ham
Salt and pepper to taste
2 drops gravy seasoning
¼ pound Cheddar cheese, grated

Melt margarine or butter and stir in flour until smooth. Add milk and cook, stirring constantly, until thickened. Set aside. Cut cucumbers in half lengthwise. Scoop out seeds and pulp. Discard seeds—reserve shells and cucumber meat. Put cucumber pulp through a food chopper. Chop ham and add cucumber. Add, with seasonings, to the prepared sauce. Mix well. Fill cucumber shells, top with cheese and bake in 375° oven 30 minutes, or until top is lightly browned. *Serves 6.*

CREAMED FRESH ONIONS

Onions are another year-round bargain vegetable—and very good done this way.

12 medium onions
Boiling salted water

4 tablespoons margarine or butter
4 tablespoons flour
2 cups milk
Salt and pepper to taste
½ cup (approximately) dry bread crumbs
Margarine or butter

Peel onions and cook in boiling salted water until tender (about 30 minutes). Drain well and put into a casserole. Meantime, melt 4 tablespoons margarine or butter and stir in flour until smooth. Add milk, salt, and pepper and cook, stirring constantly, until thickened and smooth. Pour over onions and sprinkle bread crumbs to your taste over the top. Dot liberally with margarine or butter and put under the broiler to brown until golden. *Serves 6 to 8.*

PARSNIP CAKES

Parsnips are primarily a late winter vegetable, though they are available in limited quantity all year. But in winter, after they have been exposed to cold temperatures, they are of sweeter flavor—excellent in stews instead of carrots, great braised in a little beef bouillon, or boiled and flavored with margarine or butter and a few drops of lemon juice. Leftover parsnips make very good fried patties.

1 pound parsnips, peeled
Boiling salted water to cover
1 tablespoon flour
5 tablespoons margarine or butter
1 teaspoon salt
2 egg yolks

Cook parsnips in boiling salted water to cover until done. Mash parsnips. Add flour, 1 tablespoon margarine or butter, salt, and egg yolks and form into flat cakes. Fry in 4 tablespoons margarine or butter until nicely browned on both sides. *Serves 4.*

FRIED PARSNIP STICKS

You can make this from scratch, as in this recipe, or use boiled parsnip leftovers.

8 medium parsnips
Boiling water to cover
1 egg, lightly beaten
½ cup flour
¼ cup vegetable oil
Salt to taste
¼ cup minced parsley

Wash and scrape parsnips. Cook in boiling water 30 minutes to 1 hour, or until done. Drain well and cut lengthwise into ½-inch-thick slices. Dip into beaten egg, then flour. Heat oil in a large skillet and in it fry parsnips until golden brown on both sides. Sprinkle lightly with salt, then with parsley, and serve at once. *Serves 4.*

SWEET POTATO PUFFS

A wonderful way to use up leftover mashed sweet potatoes. Care should be used in selecting sweet potatoes because they are more perishable than white ones. They should be well shaped and firm with smooth, bright, uniformly colored skins, free from signs of decay.

2 cups mashed sweet potatoes
Milk
1 egg, beaten
Salt and pepper to taste
Dash nutmeg
2 cups crushed cornflakes

Mash potatoes with just enough milk to make them smooth. Do not make the consistency too soft. Add egg and seasonings and mix well. With floured hands, form into balls about 3 inches in diameter. Roll in cornflakes. Fry in 375° deep fat to a golden brown. Drain on absorbent paper. *Serves 4.*

SPICED BAKED STUFFED POTATOES

Try other spices and spice combinations, and your baked potatoes could taste different every time you serve them. Try spiced mashed potatoes, too.

6 large potatoes, baked
1 tablespoon margarine, butter, or sour cream

Salt, pepper, and instant onion flakes to taste
¾ teaspoon dillweed, or ½ teaspoon turmeric,
*   or 2 teaspoons crushed tarragon, or*
*   1½ teaspoons crumbled marjoram leaves*
⅓ cup Parmesan cheese

Scoop out the insides of the halved baked potatoes, and mix potato meat with all the ingredients except the cheese. Restuff the skins with potato mixture, sprinkle with cheese, and put in a hot (425°) oven or under broiler for a few minutes, until cheese melts and just begins to brown. *Serves 6.*

HASHED BROWN POTATOES

3 tablespoons cooking oil
3 cups potatoes, diced
1 small onion, finely chopped
½ teaspoon salt
¼ teaspoon pepper

Warm the oil in a skillet. Combine potatoes, onion, salt, and pepper and put on top of the oil, spreading the potatoes out to cover the whole pan. Fry slowly for 5 minutes, then cover, lower heat, and fry a few minutes more, until the bottoms of the potatoes are browned. Press potatoes down from time to time with the back of a spatula but be sure they don't burn. You should have a fairly cohesive pancake by the time you're ready to turn the potatoes over. When the bottom is browned, cut the pancake in half and turn each half. Brown the second side with the pan uncovered, watching to prevent burning. *Serves 4 to 6.*

HOMEMADE FRENCH FRIES

Budget French fries are those you make yourself. The cooking oil, strained and refrigerated, can be reused many, many times—in fact, until it has become quite dark. To fry well, potatoes must be mature. Choose large baking potatoes, and slice them as evenly and as long as you possibly can. The effect should be one of long, skinny, perfectly rectangular potato sticks.

Large baking potatoes
1 quart vegetable oil
Salt to taste

No quantity of potatoes is suggested. You'll probably find that you or your guests can eat almost any amount up to the cook's exhaustion point. Peel the potatoes and trim them into large rectangles. Then slice each rectangle evenly into thin rectangular slices, and cut long "matchsticks" out of each slice. Soak the potato sticks in cold water for 15 to 30 minutes. Drain on paper towels, and dry completely.

Heat cooking oil to 300°. When the oil is ready, lower potatoes into hot fat, either with a slotted spoon or a frying basket, and dip them up and down a few times before leaving in the fat. Add only a handful of potato sticks at a time by this method, since they sizzle violently when they hit the fat. Fry all the potatoes until they are limp and the oil has stopped sputtering. They'll begin to float. Remove and drain on paper towels.

Heat the fat to 375° and put all the potato sticks back in the frying basket. Fry them again for 3 to 5 minutes, just until golden brown. Remove and drain until crisp. Salt to taste, and serve at once.

STUFFED ACORN SQUASH

A light entrée that uses a minimum of the meat budget.

2 acorn squash
¾ pound sausage meat
Water to cover

Cut squash in half. Remove seeds and a little pulp if the hole in each will not be deep enough to hold a fourth of the stuffing. Fill each cavity with sausage meat. Place in a baking pan and add enough water to cover the bottom, about ½ inch deep. Bake in 375° oven 1 hour, or until squash is done and sausage browned. *Serves 4.*

Whether or not you peel tomatoes is a matter of choice. If you are broiling or baking tomatoes, leave the skin on; it helps them keep their shape. To peel tomatoes, dip them into boiling water for about a minute, then into cold water and slip off the skin.

BROILED TOMATOES

4 medium tomatoes
1 teaspoon sugar
½ teaspoon basil
1 cup (2 slices) soft bread crumbs
2 tablespoons melted margarine or butter
½ cup crumbled cream cheese

Halve tomatoes crosswise; sprinkle tops with sugar and basil. Broil 4 to 6 inches from heat for 3 minutes or just until bubbly. Toss bread crumbs with melted margarine or butter in a small bowl; stir in cheese. Spoon over hot tomatoes. Broil 2 minutes more, or until topping is toast brown. *Serves 4.*

SAUTÉED TOMATOES

4 medium ripe tomatoes
1 teaspoon sugar
½ cup all-purpose flour
1½ teaspoons salt
1½ teaspoons oregano (optional)
6 tablespoons margarine or butter
1¼ cups milk
Parsley for garnish (optional)

Cut the tomatoes in ½-inch-thick slices; sprinkle with sugar. Mix flour, salt, and oregano, then measure 2 tablespoons and set aside. Dip tomato slices in remaining flour mixture to coat both sides. Sauté, half at a time, in margarine or butter until golden in a large frying pan; lift out onto a heated serving platter; keep warm. Blend the 2 tablespoons flour mixture into the pan fat. Stir in milk. Cook, stirring constantly, until gravy thickens and boils 1 minute. Pour over tomatoes. Garnish with parsley if you wish. *Serves 4.*

MASHED TURNIPS

Yellow turnips are a great bargain in winter, and so are the small white turnips available during the growing season. They are a delicious vegetable overlooked by many. Combined half-and-half with diced carrots and boiled, they are very good. For company, try them this way.

3 medium turnips
Boiling salted water to cover
½ cup dry sherry
2 tablespoons milk
1 tablespoon melted margarine or butter
Dash white pepper
Minced parsley

Peel turnips and cut into uniform cubes. Cover with boiling water, add salt, and cook until tender. Drain, toss in the cooking pot over high heat to dry the water. Add sherry, milk, margarine or butter, and pepper and mash until fluffy. Sprinkle with minced parsley. *Serves 4.*

YAM-STUFFED ORANGES

Yam-stuffed oranges make an elegant meat garnish for gala dinners. Save the orange pulp to make *Ambrosia.*

4 large yams
⅓ cup milk
3 tablespoons margarine or butter
Salt and pepper to taste
3 tablespoons sherry
4 large oranges

Boil yams in their jackets, covered, 20 to 30 minutes, or until tender. Peel and mash perfectly smooth. Heat milk and margarine or butter together. Beat into mashed yams until light and fluffy. Season with salt and pepper. Add sherry and mix well. More milk may be added if mixture seems too stiff. Cut off tops of oranges. Scoop out pulp. Fill orange skins with yam mixture. Bake in 375° oven 30 minutes. *Serves 4.*

Vegetable Sauces

CELERY CREAM SAUCE FOR COOKED VEGETABLES

A low-calorie sauce excellent with all sorts of warmed meat leftovers, or with plain boiled vegetables, or over soufflés.

½ pound celery
1 tablespoon margarine or butter
1 tablespoon all-purpose flour
2 cups milk, whole or skim
Salt and pepper to taste
½ teaspoon paprika, or nutmeg
2 cups cooked sliced vegetables

Wash celery and chop it finely. Heat margarine or butter until foaming in a large frying pan. Add chopped celery and sauté on low heat, stirring often, until limp and tender (about 10 minutes). Add flour and heat 3 to 5 minutes more, stirring constantly. Add milk and seasonings, and cook, stirring, until mixture reaches the desired thickness. *Makes about 1½ cups.*

BÉCHAMEL SAUCE (CREAM SAUCE) FOR VEGETABLES OR MEAT

This sauce can be made with the cooking water of vegetables or the stock or bouillon of boiled meats or fish. It is also made with milk. Serve it over boiled vegetables, meats, or fish, or use it as the base for other sauces.

2 tablespoons margarine or butter
2 tablespoons all-purpose flour
1 cup cooking liquid (see above) or warm milk
1 teaspoon salt (unless cooking liquid is seasoned)

Melt margarine or butter in a small saucepan over low heat. Stir in flour until smooth. Add cooking liquid or milk and heat until smooth. Simmer until desired thickness, and season with salt if needed. *Makes 1 cup.*

Vegetable Recipes
That Make One-Dish Dinners

Aspics, Soufflés, and Gratinées

Vegetable aspics—cooked vegetables molded in colorful gelatins—make festive party dishes and are a success out of all proportion to cost. Soufflés, made with cooked vegetables, are easier than they look, and make nice luncheon entrées. Gratinées of cooked vegetables, flavored with cheese and browned under the broiler, are delicious. All these begin with leftovers. The most economical way to make them is to cook extras so you'll have leftovers available.

Casseroles

Vegetables combined with other vegetables, with meat leftovers, or with rice and other grains make delicious casseroles. Try some of the dishes here as replacements for the meat course when vegetables are in season and a bargain.

Don't stick devotedly to the vegetables given in each recipe. Many are interchangeable, so use whatever is available or best tailored to your budget. Carrots and parsnips are similar, and turnips can be used instead of either; sweet potatoes and yams are hard to tell apart (well, almost); squash and zucchini are very similar, and both resemble cucumber; shredded iceberg lettuce and cabbage have a lot in common.

STOCK FOR ASPICS

Canned jellied consommé provides the jellied stock for aspics. If it doesn't seem firm enough, add an envelope of unflavored gelatin. Or make your own stock by simmering chicken or beef or veal bones in several cups of water for 3 to 4 hours.

Vegetable Aspics

ALL-PURPOSE STOCK

This recipe is from my book, *The How to Grow and Cook It Book of Vegetables, Herbs, Fruits, and Nuts.*

The experienced cook always likes to have

on hand a constant supply of good stock. Dissolved bouillon cubes are a substitute, of course, but why settle for something inferior when you daily throw out many of the ingredients that can go into the making of excellent stock? With the exception of charcoal-broiled bones and mutton bones, any leftover meats and bones combined with herbs and flavorings make fine stock. The gelatin that the cooking extracts from the ingredients is highly nutritious. You can intensify flavor by pouring ½ cup hot water into the bottom of a pan in which meat has roasted or been sautéed, scraping and adding this thinned-out pan gravy to the stock pot. You can add more beef or chicken bouillon cubes to strengthen the flavor. Reduce the stock to make a wonderful aspic with vegetables.

1 pound beef and bones
1 pound chicken bones and meat
Chicken giblets
1 pound veal bones and meat
1 carrot
1 bay leaf
½ teaspoon thyme
1 onion stuck with 4 cloves
½ teaspoon marjoram
1 stalk celery and leaves
2 sprigs parsley
½ teaspoon dried chervil
1 tablespoon salt
6 peppercorns
3 beef bouillon cubes
Cold water to cover

Place all ingredients in cold water to cover. Bring to a boil and simmer 4 hours. Strain, reserve meat, discard bones and herbs. Serve meat and soup stock for a meal with a crisp garden salad and French bread and butter. Store remaining strained stock in refrigerator. It will jell and a coat of congealed fat will form on top. Skim off the fat before using the stock.

VEGETABLES
IN MEAT-FLAVORED ASPIC

2 cups jellied beef or chicken stock or consommé

2 cups cooked vegetables
Cooked carrot, shrimp, and parsley for garnish
Watercress or lettuce
Vinaigrette Sauce

Skim and discard any fat from the top of the stock or consommé. Melt the consommé. You need a firm jelly, so reduce the stock a little if it seems too liquid. Measure 2 cups. Pour ¼ inch of stock or consommé in the bottom of a 1½- or 2-quart mold. Chill until firm. Put slices of cooked carrot, or tiny shrimp, or sprigs of parsley in the bottom of a small mold. Add cooked vegetables (with boneless morsels of meat or fish if you wish). Gently pour in the remaining liquid stock and refrigerate until it jells. Set the mold briefly in a pan of hot water to loosen the gelatin. Then turn it out onto a bed of watercress or lettuce. Serve with Vinaigrette Sauce. *Serves 4 to 6.*

TOMATO IN GELATIN ASPIC

You can also make aspics from fruit-flavored jellos. These are usually served with commercial mayonnaise instead of a Vinaigrette Sauce.

2 packages lemon-flavored gelatin
2 cups warm water
2 cups stewed or canned tomatoes, drained thoroughly
2 teaspoons salt
2 tablespoons vinegar
2 teaspoons Worcestershire sauce
1 teaspoon dried basil

Dissolve gelatin in warm water. Add remaining ingredients and mix well. Pour into a ring mold, washed out in cold water, and chill thoroughly. *Serves 8.*

JELLIED RAW VEGETABLE RING

Raw vegetables in aspic make nice substitutes for summer salads. These are usually made from fruit-flavored gelatins, and may be served with commercial mayonnaise.

1 package lemon-flavored gelatin
1 cup boiling water
1 cup cold water
1 teaspoon salt
1 tablespoon vinegar
1 cup diced cucumber
1 cup thinly sliced radishes
½ cup thinly sliced onion
Watercress
Coleslaw

Dissolve gelatin in boiling water. Add cold water, salt, and vinegar. Cool. When slightly thickened, stir in vegetables. Put into a ring mold, rinsed in cold water, and chill until firm. Unmold on a bed of watercress and place coleslaw in the center. *Serves 4 to 6.*

Soufflés and Gratinées

VEGETABLE SOUFFLÉ

This is a basic recipe for making a vegetable soufflé. If you are making it with a cooked vegetable and have not saved the vegetable cooking liquid, use water instead.

1 cup cooked vegetable
¼ cup margarine or butter
¼ cup all-purpose flour
⅓ cup vegetable cooking water
⅓ cup cream or half-and-half
3 eggs, separated, plus 1 egg white
Salt and pepper to taste

Preheat oven to 375°. Cook and drain vegetable and reserve liquid. Shake vegetable dry over heat. Mash through a ricer or rub through a sieve, so the vegetable comes out as light as possible. Melt margarine or butter in an enameled saucepan. Stir in flour, then add vegetable water. Stir in cream or half-and-half and simmer, stirring, for 5 to 10 minutes. Beat 3 egg yolks until thick. Beat 4 egg whites until stiff but not dry. Lower the heat under cream mixture. Remove from heat. Pour a little of the hot cream mixture into egg yolks, then stir yolks back into sauce until smooth. Remove from heat. Fold in egg whites, vegetable, and

seasonings. Turn into a buttered 6-cup soufflé mold and bake 30 to 45 minutes. Do not open oven door until done. *Serves 4.*

BEET SOUFFLÉ

You can make soufflés from canned vegetables, too. This one is especially pretty.

4 tablespoons margarine or butter
4 tablespoons all-purpose flour
1 cup milk
1 teaspoon salt
⅛ teaspoon pepper
4 eggs, separated, plus 1 egg white
2 cups canned beets, ground

Preheat oven to 375°. Melt margarine or butter and blend in flour smoothly. Add milk, salt, and pepper, and stir constantly until thickened. Beat 4 egg yolks and combine with above mixture, as described in Vegetable Soufflé, above. Add beets. Cool slightly. Beat 5 egg whites stiff and fold into beet mixture. Place in a well-buttered soufflé dish. Set in a pan of hot water and bake 35 minutes. Do not open oven door until done. *Serves 4.*

CORN PUDDING

A nice soufflé-light supper dish to serve with a little leftover ham.

4 egg yolks
2 cups canned, drained corn kernels
Salt and freshly ground pepper to taste
1 teaspoon sugar
1 small green pepper, minced
⅛ teaspoon Paprika
⅛ teaspoon nutmeg
2 tablespoons all-purpose flour
1 teaspoon baking powder
2 tablespoons melted margarine or butter
2 cups milk, scalded
4 egg whites

Preheat oven to 375°. Beat egg yolks until thick and lemon-colored, add to corn, beating it in with salt, pepper, sugar, minced green pepper, paprika, and nutmeg. Mix with flour, baking powder, and melted margarine or butter; then whip in the milk. Beat egg whites until stiff but not dry, and fold into corn mixture. Turn into a 2-quart buttered baking dish, set in hot water on the bottom third of the oven, and bake until a knife inserted in the middle comes out clean (about 45 minutes). *Serves 6 to 8.*

SCALLOPED VEGETABLES AU GRATIN

2 cups cooked vegetables
Salt and pepper to taste
4 tablespoons margarine or butter plus extra
    butter
½ to 1 tablespoon minced onion
4 tablespoons all-purpose flour
2 cups light cream or milk
½ cup bread crumbs
½ cup grated Parmesan or Swiss cheese

Slice vegetables thinly, and season to taste with salt and pepper. Melt 4 tablespoons margarine or butter in an enameled saucepan; in it sauté onion until translucent. Stir in flour, then cream or milk. Simmer, stirring, for 5 to 10 minutes. Season to taste. Butter a baking dish. Cover the bottom with a little of the sauce, then arrange alternate layers of vegetables and cream sauce, ending with a layer of cream sauce. Sprinkle with bread crumbs, dot with butter, and sprinkle cheese over all. Bake in a 375° oven 25 to 35 minutes. Place briefly under the broiler to brown. *Serves 6 to 8.*

PUMPKIN AU GRATIN

Don't throw away scoopings from jack-o'-lanterns. Pumpkin is a bargain vegetable, has a delicate flavor, and adapts to many uses. Cook it like squash—make it into *Pumpkin Bread,* or serve it au gratin as here.

1 can pumpkin or 1 cup cooked pumpkin,
    drained
½ teaspoon salt
¼ teaspoon black pepper
Dash nutmeg

¼ teaspoon ground cloves
2 tablespoons melted margarine or butter
1 egg
½ cup heavy cream or half-and-half
2 tablespoons grated Parmesan cheese

Thoroughly combine pumpkin, seasonings, and margarine or butter. Place in a small buttered casserole. Beat the egg lightly and mix in the cream or half-and-half and Parmesan cheese. Pour over pumpkin. Bake in a 400° oven 30 minutes, or until the top is puffed and lightly browned. *Served 4 to 6.*

POTATOES AU GRATIN

1 small onion, chopped
2 tablespoons margarine or butter
Salt and freshly ground pepper to taste
2 cups boiled cubed potatoes
1 cup Béchamel Sauce
1 cup grated Cheddar or Parmesan cheese
Paprika

Sauté onion in 1 tablespoon margarine or butter until pale golden. Season to taste. Mix with potatoes and Béchamel Sauce. Put into a shallow baking dish and cover the top with grated cheese. Dot with remaining margarine or butter and sprinkle lightly with paprika. Bake in 375° oven 20 to 25 minutes, until nicely browned on top. *Serves 4.*

Casseroles

STUFFED CABBAGE

If you make this with white cabbage instead of green, parboil the whole head for 5 minutes. Then drain and cool, before proceeding with the recipe. Otherwise you will find the 8 large leaves impossible to remove intact. Winter, or white, cabbage is tightly curled.

1 medium head green cabbage
1 pound lean ground beef
1 small onion, minced
1 clove garlic, mashed
1 tablespoon dried parsley

¾ teaspoon salt
¼ teaspoon pepper
2 cups canned tomatoes (reserve juice)

Cut core out of cabbage and remove 8 large leaves. Shred the rest of the head as for coleslaw. Soak leaves a few minutes in boiling water to make them less brittle and easy to roll. Combine meat, onion, garlic, parsley, and seasonings. When leaves are soft, put a portion of meat (⅛ pound) on each leaf and roll. Tuck the ends in or secure with toothpicks. Put shredded cabbage in a large saucepan or kettle with tomatoes and ½ cup tomato juice. Place stuffed leaves on top, close together. Cover and simmer over low heat 1½ to 2 hours, or until cabbage is tender. Add more juice from tomatoes if the pot seems to be going dry. *Serves 4.*

CABBAGE A LA MILAN

1½ pounds lean ground beef
1 cup chopped onion
1 cup chopped celery
1½ teaspoons salt
1 teaspoon paprika
¼ teaspoon pepper
1 medium head cabbage, cut into 6 wedges
1 16-ounce can tomato sauce
½ teaspoon dried basil
½ teaspoon dried oregano
½ teaspoon garlic powder
1 cup grated mozzarella cheese
3 cups hot cooked rice

In an oven-proof skillet, sauté beef, onion, celery, salt, paprika, and pepper until meat is no longer pink and vegetables are tender-crisp, stirring frequently to crumble meat. Arrange cabbage wedges on top of meat mixture. Blend tomato sauce, basil, oregano, and garlic powder. Pour over cabbage wedges. Cover tightly and bake in 350° oven 45 minutes, or until cabbage is tender. Remove cover. Sprinkle with cheese. Return to oven for 5 minutes. Serve on a bed of fluffy rice. *Serves 6.*

BROWNED CABBAGE AND NOODLES

A Hungarian dish. Nice with beef dishes that include a sauce—casseroles and stews, for instance.

1 large head cabbage
2 stalks celery
¼ pound (or more) margarine or butter
Salt and pepper to taste
3 cups broken up broad noodles
Boiling salted water

Shred cabbage. Dice celery. Brown thoroughly in margarine or butter, stirring often, and adding more margarine or butter if needed (this will take about 1 hour). Add salt and pepper and simmer for another hour. Cook noodles in boiling salted water for 9 minutes. Drain well and toss with cabbage before serving. Or arrange in a ring around the cabbage. *Serves 6 to 8.*

CARROT PLAKI

Vegetables combine well with rice. Use this as a basic vegetable and rice dish, and substitute any vegetable in season for the carrots. Serve cold as an appetizer or salad. Squeeze lemon juice on top. Can be served hot as a light luncheon dish.

6 medium carrots
2 medium onions, finely sliced
½ cup salad oil
½ cup raw rice
½ tablespoon sugar
Salt to taste
2½ cups water
2 tablespoons chopped parsley
1 lemon, cut into wedges

Scrape and wash carrots. Cut slantwise into ¼-inch-thick oval slices. Place onions in saucepan. Add oil and sauté over medium heat for 6 minutes. Add carrots and sauté for 3 minutes more. Add rice, sugar, salt, and water. Mix well, then cover and cook over medium heat for about 45 minutes, or until carrots are tender. (If necessary, more water may be added.) Remove from heat. Allow to cool in saucepan. Transfer to a serving platter. Decorate with parsley and lemon wedges. *Serves 4 to 6.*

STUFFED EGGPLANT ENTRÉE

The eggs and cheese in this entrée provide protein, which makes it a perfect main course dish. A mashed clove of garlic may be added to the puree mixture, if desired.

2 large eggplants
1 onion, chopped
4 tomatoes, peeled and chopped
3 green peppers, chopped
1 stalk celery, chopped
¼ cup olive oil
2 eggs, beaten
Salt and pepper to taste
Dash cayenne pepper
¾ cup grated cheese

Cut eggplants in half and scrape out seeds. Parboil 15 minutes. Drain well and place in a shallow casserole 12 × 24 inches. Meantime cook onion, tomatoes, peppers, and celery in olive oil over gentle heat, stirring frequently, until they form a puree. Remove from heat and add eggs, salt and pepper to taste, and the cayenne. Fill eggplant halves with the mixture and sprinkle with cheese. If there is any stuffing left over, place it around eggplant halves. Bake in 350° oven 25 to 30 minutes, or until eggplant is tender and cheese is brown. *Serves 4.*

WOODS HOLE CASSEROLE

½ pound carrots
1 tablespoon margarine or butter
½ pound spinach, fresh or frozen, drained
2 scallions
1 medium eggplant, peeled
Salt and pepper to taste
Flour
2 tablespoons oil
3 slices or 3 ounces Swiss cheese

Scrape carrots and slice them on the diagonal into long, thin ovals. Sauté the slices in margarine or butter in a covered saucepan for about 20 minutes, stirring occasionally. Chop spinach and scallions and add to the pan. Stir until spinach wilts and then simmer 5 minutes more. If you use precooked frozen spinach, just add it and stir until combined. While carrots are cooking, slice eggplant thinly, and sprinkle with salt and pepper to taste. After about 10 minutes eggplant should be mostly dehydrated. Dry the slices with a paper towel, dredge lightly in flour and fry gently in the oil for about 5 minutes on each side, or until tender. Combine cooked vegetables in a casserole, a layer of eggplant slices, a layer of carrot and spinach mixture on top, another layer of eggplant, and so on until all the vegetables are used. The top layer should be eggplant. Cover the top with slices of cheese and brush with oil. Before serving, heat in a 350° oven 15 to 20 minutes, until cheese is melted and casserole bubbles. *Serves 4 to 6.*

EGGPLANT PARMESAN

The eggplant, under much fancier names, is a standard substitute for meat in many Mediterranean countries. As in this recipe, this vegetable is usually combined with cheese or other protein foods. Although not a high-protein food itself, the eggplant tastes good and cooks well. Eggplant Parmesan is an economical and delicious substitute for Veal Parmesan.

1 16-ounce can plum tomatoes (reserve juice)
4 ounces tomato paste
2 cloves garlic, mashed
1 teaspoon basil
1 teaspoon oregano
1 teaspoon sugar
½ teaspoon salt
¼ teaspoon pepper

1 medium eggplant, peeled
1 egg, lightly beaten
½ cup bread crumbs
¼ teaspoon salt
⅛ teaspoon pepper

¼ cup cooking oil
4 ounces thinly sliced mozzarella cheese
¼ cup grated Parmesan cheese

Preheat oven to 375°. Combine the first 8 ingredients in a large skillet or saucepan and simmer for about 30 minutes, or until flavors are blended. Dilute, if necessary, with a little of the tomato juice. Set aside. This is the sauce. Cut eggplant into thin, even slices. Dip slices in beaten egg, then in bread crumbs, combined with salt and pepper and fry in hot oil until browned, adding more oil if necessary. Drain well. Lightly grease a shallow baking dish and layer in half the eggplant slices with half the slices of mozzarella, half the tomato sauce, and half the Parmesan cheese. Repeat for second layer. Bake in preheated oven until cheese melts and tomato sauce bubbles. *Serves 4.*

ONION TART OR QUICHE

Endive, or other strongly flavored vegetables, can be made into a quiche, following this basic recipe. Quiche is a real treat, either as a first course for a party dinner or as a luncheon entrée. It is an economical dish when it is used as a substitute for a meat course.

Pastry for a 9-inch pie shell
Rice or beans for cooking pie crust
2 pounds yellow onions
½ cup margarine or butter
4 eggs
1 cup heavy cream
1 teaspoon salt
⅛ teaspoon pepper
⅛ teaspoon nutmeg
½ cup diced ham (optional)

Line a pie pan with the rolled-out crust and flute the edge. Line the crust with aluminum foil and fill with rice or beans to keep crust flat. Bake in 400° oven until pastry is set (about 8 minutes). Remove foil and rice or beans, prick crust, and return to oven for 2 to 3 minutes. Peel onions and cut up coarsely. Cook over low heat in margarine or butter until soft, but not brown. Beat eggs until thick

and lemon-colored. Add cream, salt, pepper, and nutmeg. Mix well with cooked onions and diced ham. Pour onion mixture into the crust and bake in preheated 375° oven until puffed and brown (35 to 40 minutes). Serve warm or at room temperature. *Serves 6.*

VEGETABLE AND EGG DINNER

This recipe is subject to almost infinite variation. Keeping the potato as a base, try different vegetables according to your taste and the season. Keep in mind that in this dish, freshness is everything. Old or overcooked vegetables won't do.

4 tablespoons oil or butter
4 medium potatoes, peeled and sliced
4 small onions, sliced
2 red or green bell peppers, seeded and sliced
4 small yellow goosenecked squash, sliced
4 eggs, fried or poached or soft-boiled

Heat the oil or butter and add potato slices. Cook on low heat. When potatoes are half done, add other sliced vegetables. Fry until all the vegetables are tender. Serve with 1 cooked egg over each portion. *Serves 4.*

MIXED VEGETABLE LOAF

1½ cups peeled and grated carrots
1½ cups stemmed and grated string beans
½ cup roasted peanuts
1 cup chopped celery
½ cup chopped onion
½ cup finely chopped green pepper
4 tablespoons margarine or butter
2 tablespoons cornstarch
2 tablespoons soy sauce
2 tablespoons cooking oil

Preheat oven to 350°. Combine carrots and beans. Crush peanuts in a grinder or blender. Sauté celery, onion, green pepper, and carrot and bean mixture in margarine or butter until tender, then set them aside. Dissolve cornstarch in soy sauce and add to the pan, stirring vigorously to keep it from sticking. When the cornstarch is blended, add carrot and bean mixture, peanuts, and oil, and sauté 3 minutes more. Remove from heat. Oil a loaf pan and spoon in vegetable mixture. Bake 30 minutes. *Serves 4.*

RATATOUILLE

This is a great recipe to use when the late summer vegetables are abundant. Use whatever is available—don't limit yourself to those described here. The tomatoes are essential, but summer squash, leeks, cucumbers, and beans are all good in a ratatouille. In southern France, the farmers toss into the pot any vegetable handy.

⅓ cup olive or vegetable oil
3 large cloves garlic, minced
4 large ripe tomatoes
1 medium eggplant, peeled
2 red or green peppers, seeded
2 medium zucchini, stemmed
3 medium onions, peeled
2 teaspoons salt
Dash pepper
½ teaspoon oregano
½ teaspoon thyme

Heat the oil in a large heavy kettle, add garlic, and cook about 3 minutes. Cut tomatoes into 2-inch chunks, toss into the hot oil. Cut eggplant, peppers, zucchini, and onions into 2-inch pieces. Add to the kettle when the tomatoes are soft. Add salt, pepper, oregano, and thyme. Mix gently and simmer, uncovered, until all the vegetables are soft. Stir often—the tomatoes tend to burn. Turn up the heat and cook, stirring, to dry up any excess liquid. It is ready when the mélange is thick. *Serves 6 to 8.*

CANADIAN SUPPER PIE

A neat vegetable meal based on leftover ham. You can use inexpensive canned luncheon meat or sliced, canned hash instead of cooked ham.

3 green onions with stems, chopped
1 medium green or red pepper, diced
4 tablespoons margarine or butter
3 tablespoons all-purpose flour
1½ cups milk
2 tablespoons mayonnaise
2 teaspoons prepared mustard
⅛ teaspoon pepper
2 cups chopped cooked ham
1 teaspoon salt
Pastry for a 1-crust pie

Sauté onions and diced pepper in margarine or butter for 3 or 4 minutes, until onions are tender. Stir in flour; gradually add milk, stirring until smooth and slightly thickened. Blend in mayonnaise, mustard, pepper, and ham. Add salt. Spoon the mixture into a greased 2-quart shallow baking dish. Roll out pastry to fit the baking dish. Cover and press along the edges to seal. Prick the center. Bake at 425° about 20 minutes, until pastry is golden brown. *Serves 4.*

Dressings, Salads

One trick to use when you want to serve exciting meals on a low budget is to make magic with leftovers. Salads are just meant for using up odds and ends from other meals. Of course you can go out and buy all the ingredients called for, but the smart cook does it the other way around, and serves these salads when the leftovers make them an economy instead of a luxury.

Salads need not be used only as accessories to meat and potato dishes. They can be entrées as well. Have a close look at the recipes here and remember for future reference the types of ingredients used. As you read, translate the ingredients. Where the recipe calls for a bland meat such as chicken, make a note that the white meat of any fowl can be used instead—and so can pork or veal. Chicken and tuna are often interchangeable. Though their flavors differ, they are in the same range between bland and sharp. Grapefruit that is left over can be used instead of orange in a salad. White beans can be used in the place of potatoes, as can rice. In other words, think of these recipes as guides to the construction of salads, and let your store of leftovers govern what goes into them.

If you make a lot of substitutes in the preparation of a salad, be sure you taste the end product carefully so the seasonings in the recipe work well with the recipe's ingredients as listed. The ingredients you substitute may require a little more oil, vinegar, or salt.

The Great Dressings

The dressing makes, or breaks, the salad and it is no place to skimp. Making your own salad dressing is a real economy. Bottled dressings and packaged dried dressing flavorings are a needless expense. From-scratch dressings, carefully sealed in bottles, keep in the refrigerator for weeks on end. Double, triple, or quadruple recipes when you are making dressing so you'll have a supply handy in the refrigerator.

Olive oil of good quality adds great flavor to salads, and is almost essential to getting the flavor of an Italian or Mediterranean salad just right. However, it costs a fortune. If you splurge for some special dressing, buy a small bottle and be sure to store it in the refrigerator. Because olive oil is not only distinctly flavored, but also often strongly flavored, you can bring the cost of the olive oil dressing down by mixing olive oil half-and-half with a bland vegetable oil. Or be more economical yet and use only a spoonful or so of olive oil with your salads—it should be enough to add just a hint of its special flavor to the rest of the ingredients.

The *French Dressing* recipe is a basic oil-and-vinegar dressing that can be used as a base for almost any flavor direction that appeals to you. You can add ½ teaspoon or more of vinegar or pinch in some dry mustard for a sharper flavor. Strained lemon or lime juice can be used instead of vinegar (especially fine with fish salads). You can make the flavor meatier by adding a few drops of Worcestershire or soy sauce. But the most interesting variations come from the addition of herbs, fresh or dried. Herbs are a good investment, one that yields a great deal of flavor for little cost.

FRENCH (OIL AND VINEGAR) DRESSING

This is a basic dressing you can vary by adding herbs and other flavorings. I use ½ teaspoon of dried herbs, and up to 2 teaspoons of fresh, minced herbs in the dressing. You may prefer stronger flavors; if so, just keep adding the herb (or herbs) until you find the taste just right. Omit the garlic if you dislike it.

1 medium clove fresh garlic, peeled
1 teaspoon salt
1 cup oil
¼ cup vinegar
¼ teaspoon sugar
⅛ teaspoon pepper
Chopped parsley (optional)

Slice garlic clove into salad bowl, and sprinkle salt over it. With the back of a flattish spoon, crush garlic with salt until it is completely mashed. Stir in oil, vinegar, sugar, and pepper and mix well. Chill until ready to serve. Mix in 1 teaspoon chopped parsley if you wish, or sprinkle on top. *Makes about 1¼ cups.*

ITALIAN DRESSING

Another basic dressing.

1 cup olive or salad oil
¼ cup wine vinegar
1 teaspoon salt
1 teaspoon sugar
¼ teaspoon dried basil
2 cloves garlic, split
1 teaspoon paprika
½ teaspoon dry mustard
1 tablespoon grated onion
1 tablespoon Worcestershire sauce

Place ingredients in a jar and shake well. Let set, shaking occasionally, for several hours. Before serving, remove garlic. *Makes about 1½ cups.*

FRESH MAYONNAISE

This is a luxury, both in the time it takes to make and in cost. But it is the world's greatest cold dressing for leftover meat, fish, and cooked vegetables, or raw vegetables such as tomatoes or hard-boiled eggs. This version is from my book, *The How to Grow and Cook It Book of Vegetables, Herbs, Fruits, and Nuts.* Use this mayonnaise as a base for *Green Goddess Dressing,* and other recipes in this section, instead of commercial mayonnaise. It makes leftovers into a gourmet event.

2 egg yolks
½ teaspoon salt
½ teaspoon dry mustard
1 tablespoon vinegar
1 cup or more vegetable oil
2 to 3 tablespoons lemon juice

Drop egg yolks into a medium-size bowl that narrows at the bottom. This keeps the yolks together and seems to work better. Beat yolks with a whisk or fork until they are thick; beat in salt, mustard, and vinegar. The vinegar thins out the yolks. Now dribble in a *little* of the oil, beating hard as the oil goes in. Be sure the yolks have absorbed each dribble of oil before you add more. As mayonnaise thickens it is hard to keep the bowl from skidding, so I place it inside a larger bowl, lined with wet crumpled towels, and set it in a corner of the sink. (It took me years to figure that out.) Keep dribbling in oil until about half of it is gone and the mixture is quite stiff. Now thin it by beating in the lemon juice. Then add oil in larger dribbles until the mayonnaise is as thick as you want it. It can be made stiff enough to stand up like soft butter. (If made as stiff as you can get it, you can use cake decorator forms to make patterns on an aspic or platter of food to give a festive air.) Any spices, herbs, or special flavorings you want should go in after the lemon juice. Taste often. It usually needs more salt, depending on what it is to be served with. NOTE: Mayonnaise made with vinegar instead of lemon juice, tightly capped and stored in the refrigerator, will keep at least 2 weeks. *Makes about 1 cup.*

AIOLI

Mash up to 4 cloves of peeled garlic in the bottom of the bowl in which you will make the mayonnaise and proceed with the *Fresh Mayonnaise* recipe. This is served in southern France with boiled white fish and potatoes.

MAYONNAISE CHANTILLY

Fold ½ cup of whipped cream into the finished mayonnaise. For fruit salads.

HERB MAYONNAISE

Add 2 tablespoons fresh, finely chopped dill, parsley, and chervil. Great served as a dollop on filet mignon, or as a party dressing.

FRENCH DRESSING WITH CREAM CHEESE

1 package cream cheese
1 teaspoon finely minced onion
½ teaspoon dry mustard
1 teaspoon salt

Freshly ground black pepper
2 tablespoons chopped parsley
¼ cup salad oil
1½ tablespoons vinegar

Place cream cheese in a small bowl and mash until soft or beat with an electric beater. Whip in onion, mustard, salt, pepper, and parsley. A little at a time, beat in the oil, then the vinegar. *Makes about ⅞ cup.*

RUSSIAN DRESSING

1 cup mayonnaise
1 tablespoon grated horseradish
1 teaspoon Worcestershire sauce
¼ cup chili sauce or tomato catsup
1 teaspoon grated onion

Combine ingredients. *Makes about 1¾ cups.*

BLUE CHEESE DRESSING

½ cup French dressing
2 tablespoons or more crumbled blue cheese

Combine ingredients. *Makes about ⅔ cup.*

GREEN GODDESS DRESSING

You can make this with commercial mayonnaise, but for special events make it with *Fresh Mayonnaise.*

1 cup Fresh Mayonnaise
1 clove garlic, minced
3 anchovy filets, minced
¼ cup finely minced chives or green onions
¼ cup minced parsley
1 tablespoon lemon juice
1 tablespoon tarragon vinegar
½ teaspoon salt
Freshly ground black pepper
½ cup cultured sour cream

Combine ingredients. *Makes about 2 cups.*

THOUSAND ISLAND DRESSING

1 cup mayonnaise
¼ cup chili sauce or tomato catsup
2 tablespoons minced stuffed olives
1 tablespoon chopped green pepper
1 tablespoon minced onion or chives
1 hard-boiled egg, chopped
2 teaspoons chopped parsley

Combine ingredients. *Makes 1½ cups.*

LOW-CALORIE
THOUSAND ISLAND DRESSING

¾ cup tarragon vinegar
1 10½-ounce can condensed tomato soup
1 clove garlic, minced
⅛ teaspoon cayenne pepper
2 tablespoons chopped dill pickle
2 tablespoons finely chopped celery
2 tablespoons finely chopped parsley
1 tablespoon Worcestershire or soy sauce
1 teaspoon paprika
1 teaspoon prepared mustard

Combine ingredients. *Makes about 2 cups.*

HONEY DRESSING
FOR FRUIT SALADS

½ cup vegetable oil
1 teaspoon grated lemon peel
¼ cup lemon juice
2 tablespoons water
2 tablespoons honey
1 teaspoon garlic salt
½ teaspoon dried savory leaves

Combine ingredients in a jar. Cover tightly. Shake well to blend before serving. *Makes 1 cup.*

MAYONNAISE DRESSING

¾ cup commercial mayonnaise
¼ cup tomato catsup
2 tablespoons chopped pimiento-stuffed olives
2 tablespoons chopped salted peanuts

Put mayonnaise and catsup in blender container. Blend 10 seconds. Stir in olives and peanuts. Chill. *Makes about 1¼ cups.*

ORANGE MAYONNAISE
FOR FRUIT SALADS

⅔ cup commercial mayonnaise
¼ teaspoon grated orange peel
⅓ cup orange juice

In a small bowl, combine ingredients and blend well with a wire whisk. *Makes about 1 cup.*

SOUR CREAM DRESSING

1 8-ounce container sour cream
½ cup mayonnaise
1 tablespoon poppy seeds
⅛ teaspoon onion salt

In a small bowl, combine ingredients and blend well with a wire whisk. *Makes about 1½ cups.*

YOGURT–GARLIC SALAD DRESSING

Make your own *yogurt* and this becomes a budget-minded dressing.

2 cloves garlic, mashed
2 teaspoons salt
2 egg yolks
1 teaspoon Worcestershire sauce
4 tablespoons lemon juice
2 cups salad or olive oil
1 teaspoon prepared mustard, Dijon if
    possible
⅓ cup plain yogurt
¼ cup tomato paste
3 tablespoons water

Mix together all ingredients except yogurt, tomato paste, and water. Stir thoroughly with a spoon or blend at low speed with an electric mixer. Stir in yogurt and tomato paste. Thin with water as desired, up to 3 tablespoons. Refrigerate before serving. *Makes 3 cups.*

The Great Cold Sauces

There are a handful of inexpensive sauces that turn cold cuts, plain fish, and vegetables into a taste treat. *Tartare Sauce* and *Horseradish Dressing* are familiar to most American cooks and can be purchased. But they are less expensive and better if you make them following the recipes here. *Ravigote Sauce* and *Fresh Mayonnaise* are sauces European cooks use, and which you should add to your bag of cooking tricks.

TARTARE SAUCE

1 cup firm mayonnaise
1 teaspoon mustard
1 tablespoon finely chopped parsley
1 teaspoon minced shallots or onion
1 tablespoon chopped, drained sweet pickle
1 tablespoon chopped, drained green olives (optional)
1 hard-boiled egg, finely chopped
1 tablespoon chopped, drained capers
Salt and pepper to taste

Combine ingredients. *Makes about 1⅓ cups.*

HORSERADISH DRESSING

½ cup French dressing
1 tablespoon or more fresh or prepared horseradish

Combine ingredients. *Makes about ½ cup.*

RAVIGOTE SAUCE

1 cup French dressing
½ cup finely chopped onion
1 tablespoon finely chopped capers
1 teaspoon chopped parsley
½ teaspoon chopped fresh tarragon
½ teaspoon chopped fresh chervil

Combine ingredients. *Makes about 1⅓ cups.*

COCKTAIL SAUCE

¾ cup tomato catsup
⅛ to ¼ cup prepared horseradish
Juice of 1 lemon
Dash hot pepper sauce

Combine ingredients. *Makes about 1 cup.*

HAWAIIAN DELIGHT

This recipe can be served in a pineapple shell half (place the pineapple lengthwise on a wooden board and slice in half horizontally), or can be used as a topping for a vegetable or fruit aspic, or with cold meats.

1 cup finely crushed pineapple, well drained
½ cup stiff Fresh Mayonnaise
½ cup finely crushed mixed nuts
1 tablespoon finely chopped green olives
½ cup sour cream
1 tablespoon chopped fresh parsley
1 teaspoon chopped fresh dill
1 tablespoon finely minced raw carrot, or onion, or both
Salt and pepper to taste

Combine well, and serve as above. *Makes about 2½ cups.*

Fruit Salads As a Main Course

Fruit, a meal in itself if prepared properly, gives a needed variety in any diet. Its freshness and crispness add to the enjoyment of eating something light but satisfying, especially when you entertain. Fruit dishes are perfect for parties! And with rising meat prices, fruit is becoming even more popular and less expensive. Also, in most fruit dishes, few ingredients are necessary and they take little time to prepare.

There are more ways to fix fruit dishes than one might suspect from a look at the average dinner table, whether it is set for family or for guests. Assorted fresh fruits combined and decoratively arranged with different types of nutritious nuts, cheese, poultry, eggs, or fish—all of which are full of protein—can make a delightful and easily prepared main dish instead of the traditional main dish of meat.

Here are some fruit favorites that are fresh, light, and complete meals.

ORANGE–CHICKEN FRUIT SALAD

This is an elegant salad to serve at a luncheon party. Serve it in late summer when cantaloupe is inexpensive and avocados are in season.

1 quart iceberg lettuce, leaves torn and loosely packed
1 quart romaine lettuce, leaves torn and loosely packed
Orange-Chicken Salad
1 small cantaloupe, peeled and cut into lengthwise slices
2 avocados, peeled, sliced, and brushed with lemon juice
Frosted Grapes
Orange Mayonnaise

In a large salad bowl or individual bowls, mix together iceberg and romaine lettuce leaves. On the greens, arrange in a decorative design the Orange–Chicken Salad, cantaloupe slices, avocado slices, and Frosted Grapes. Serve with Orange Mayonnaise. *Serves 6 to 8.*

FROSTED GRAPES

1 pound dark grapes
1 egg white, slightly beaten
⅓ to ½ cup granulated sugar

Wash and dry grapes thoroughly. Separate bunches into smaller ones. Dip grapes into egg white and then into sugar to coat. A spoon may be used to sprinkle sugar into areas too difficult to reach by just dipping into sugar. Chill several hours, or until sugar coating appears crystalized on the grapes. *Serves 6 to 8.*

ORANGE–CHICKEN SALAD

1 quart (about 1½ pounds) ½-inch cubes cooked chicken
¼ cup bottled clear French or Russian salad dressing
½ cup diced celery
2 cups well-drained diced oranges (or tangerines)
⅓ cup mayonnaise
⅛ teaspoon salt
1 tablespoon grated onion

In a large bowl, mix together chicken and dressing and marinate in refrigerator about 1 hour, stirring occasionally. At serving time, add celery and oranges to chicken. In a small bowl blend together mayonnaise, salt, and grated onion. Stir into chicken mixture. *Serves 6.*

SAVORY EGG SALAD

This also makes a great filling for sandwiches.

4 hard-boiled eggs, finely chopped
⅓ cup finely chopped celery
¼ cup mayonnaise
1 teaspoon dried instant minced onion
¼ teaspoon dry mustard
⅛ teaspoon salt
Dash pepper
8 whole crisp lettuce leaves

In a medium-size bowl, mix together eggs and celery. In a small bowl, blend together mayonnaise, onion, mustard, salt, and pepper. Stir into egg mixture and mix well. Arrange 2 lettuce leaves to each plate, and divide egg mixture among them. *Serves 4.*

FRESH FRUIT SALAD LUNCHEON

An elegant "ladies' luncheon" dish—attractive and economical.

4 large plums, halved and pitted
1 8-ounce package cream cheese, softened
¼ cup finely chopped pecans
2 tablespoons finely chopped ripe olives
⅛ teaspoon celery salt

1 3-ounce package black raspberry-flavored
    gelatin
4 cups crisp iceberg lettuce, leaves torn and
    loosely packed
4 cups crisp romaine lettuce, leaves torn and
    loosely packed
1 cup orange sections
1½ cups (about ½ pound) seedless green
    grapes
Whipped cream for topping (optional)

Begin by making the stuffed plums. In a medium-size bowl, mix together cream cheese, pecans, olives, and celery salt. Put about 2 tablespoons of the mixture in each plum. Then prepare gelatin according to directions on the package, but reduce cold water to ¾ cup. Pour mixture into an 8-inch square baking pan. Chill until set. At serving time, cut gelatin into 8 squares. In individual salad bowls or in one large bowl, mix together iceberg and romaine lettuce leaves. On greens, arrange in a decorative design gelatin squares, stuffed plums, orange sections, and grapes. Serve with whipped cream. *Serves 4.*

WINTER FRUIT SALAD

Make this with those tangerines that don't get eaten Christmas Day.

4 tangerines
1 large red onion
½ head iceberg lettuce, shredded
French dressing to taste

Peel and section tangerines. Peel onion and slice it thin. Place tangerine sections and onion rings on beds of lettuce on individual salad plates and pour a little dressing over each. *Serves 4.*

CRANBERRY TUNA SALAD

A great way to use up leftover cranberry sauce, if you have any left over to use up—my family rarely does!

1 3-ounce package lemon-flavored gelatin
½ cup orange juice

1 cup water
1 16-ounce can jellied cranberry sauce
Red food coloring
1 7-ounce can tuna, drained and flaked
1 hard-boiled egg, chopped
¼ cup celery, minced
¼ cup sliced stuffed green olives
1 tablespoon chopped onion
1 cup mayonnaise
½ teaspoon salt
Dash pepper
1 envelope (1 tablespoon) unflavored gelatin

Combine lemon-flavored gelatin, orange juice, and ½ cup water; cook and stir until boiling and gelatin dissolves. Beat cranberry sauce and 2 to 3 drops red food coloring until smooth; stir into orange juice mixture. Chill in a 2-quart mold. Combine tuna, egg, celery, green olives, and onion. Fold in mayonnaise, salt, and pepper. Soften envelope of unflavored gelatin in ½ cup cold water; heat until dissolved. Stir into half-firm tuna mixture. Spoon over cranberry layer. Chill overnight. *Serves 5 or 6.*

COTTAGE CHEESE AND FRUIT SALAD

An elegant luncheon salad to make when fresh fruit prices are low.

1 quart crisp Bibb lettuce, leaves torn and
    loosely packed
1 quart (about 1 bunch) crisp watercress
    sprigs, loosely packed
Cottage Cheese and Apple Salad (below)
4 medium-size peaches, peeled and sliced
2 large-size grapefruits, in sections
1 pint strawberries, washed and drained
1 small-size cantaloupe, sliced
Sour Cream Dressing

In a large salad bowl or individual bowls, mix together lettuce and watercress. On the greens, arrange in a decorative design the cottage cheese dish, peach slices, grapefruit sections, strawberries, and cantaloupe slices. Serve with Sour Cream Dressing spooned over it. *Serves 4.*

COTTAGE CHEESE AND APPLE SALAD

1 16-ounce container creamed cottage cheese
½ cup shredded peeled apple
¼ cup dark seedless raisins
¼ teaspoon salt

In a medium-size bowl, combine ingredients and blend well. *Makes about 2½ cups.*

HAM AND APPLE SALAD

This dish is especially good in the fall because of the availability of really crisp new apples. Avoid soft apples like McIntosh or Delicious.

½ pound cooked ham
4 hard eating apples
1 pound cooked potatoes
2 stalks celery
4 ounces Cheddar cheese
1 head leaf or romaine lettuce
1 cup mayonnaise

Cut ham, apples, potatoes, celery, and cheese into small cubes. Tear lettuce into bite-size pieces. Combine ingredients and toss with mayonnaise until evenly coated. Chill before serving. *Serves 4.*

HUNGARIAN SALAD

Let your guests guess what's in it. . . . This is an ideal appetizer for a festive occasion, served in individual dishes. It is just as good made the day before, and served when needed.

1 cup finely diced leftover pork and/or veal
  roast
1 cup finely diced pickled herring
½ cup finely diced onion
1 cup sour cream
1 cup Fresh Mayonnaise
1 cup finely diced celery
1 cup finely diced tart apples
½ cup finely diced sour pickle
Salt and pepper to taste
1½ cups finely diced cooked beets
Parsley or watercress (optional)

Combine all ingredients except beets and chill. Spoon into individual dishes and sprinkle beets around the rim before serving. This is sometimes served with the beets mixed into the recipe, and a sprig of parsley or watercress on top. *Serves 8 to 10.*

APPLE–SALMON SALAD
IN LIME DRESSING

4 tablespoons fresh lime juice, strained
⅛ cup brown sugar, firmly packed
⅛ teaspoon salt
⅓ cup vegetable oil
1 16-ounce can red salmon, drained and boned
2 cups cooked macaroni
1 cup cubed apple
½ cup shredded Cheddar cheese
½ cup chopped celery
¼ cup chopped green pepper
¼ cup chopped onion
½ cup mayonnaise
¼ teaspoon prepared horseradish
⅛ teaspoon salt
Dash pepper
6 large lettuce leaves

Make a lime dressing by combining lime juice, brown sugar, salt, and oil in container of an electric blender. Blend for 15 seconds. Stir before serving. In a large bowl mix together salmon, macaroni, and lime dressing. Marinate for ½ hour, stirring occasionally. Add apple, cheese, celery, green pepper, and onion. In a small bowl beat together mayonnaise, horseradish, salt, and pepper. Stir into salmon mixture. Serve in lettuce leaf cups. *Serves 6.*

WALDORF SALAD

1 cup cubed apple
½ cup chopped celery
¼ cup chopped English walnuts
½ cup mayonnaise
½ head iceberg lettuce, shredded

Toss apple, celery, and walnuts together in a medium-size bowl. Add mayonnaise. Serve on shredded lettuce. *Serves 4.*

The Hearty Meat and Fish Salads

Here are recipes for some of the best-known and most popular salads for main courses. Remember that you need not slavishly follow the list of ingredients. The white meat of almost any fowl can be used instead of chicken; and other types of cooked fish, if originally poached rather than broiled or fried, can be used in the place of tuna fish.

CHEF'S SALAD I

2 large heads Boston lettuce, washed and
    crisped
1 cup julienne-cut chicken
1 cup julienne-cut tongue
1 cup julienne-cut Swiss cheese
1 tablespoon capers
½ cup French dressing

Shred lettuce. Add chicken, tongue, cheese, and capers. Just before serving add dressing and toss lightly but thoroughly. *Serves 6 to 8.*

CHEF'S SALAD II

If you cook your own kidney beans from scratch, this becomes even more economical.

1 20-ounce can red kidney beans
½ cup French dressing
1 quart crisp iceberg lettuce, leaves torn and
    loosely packed
1 quart crisp raw mustard greens or spinach,
    loosely packed
1½ cups cooked chicken, cut in long strips
1½-ounce can luncheon meat, cut into strips
¼ pound Muenster cheese or other flavorful
    white cheese, cut into strips
2 tomatoes, cut into wedges
4 whole green onions
Blue Cheese Dressing (optional)

In a medium bowl, combine kidney beans and dressing. Place lettuce and mustard greens or spinach in a large salad bowl. Arrange marinated beans on top, and over them chicken, luncheon meat, cheese, tomatoes, and green onions. Just before serving, toss well. Offer Blue Cheese Dressing on the side. *Serves 4.*

CHICKEN SALAD

3 cups diced cooked chicken
½ pound mushrooms, coarsely chopped, or
    2 cups minced celery
2 scallions, chopped
Salt and freshly ground pepper to taste
1 cup mayonnaise
Boston lettuce, washed and crisped
Paprika

Mix all ingredients except lettuce and paprika. Line a bowl with lettuce leaves and place chicken-mushroom or chicken-celery mixture in the center. Sprinkle lightly with paprika. *Serves 4 to 6.*

EVERYTHING SALAD

1 head Boston lettuce
1 small head escarole
4 strips crisp bacon (optional)
½ cup diced celery
½ cup julienne-cut tongue
2 hard-boiled eggs, sliced
1 medium Spanish onion, sliced
6 tablespoons olive oil
2 tablespoons red wine vinegar
Salt and pepper to taste

Tear washed and crisped greens into a salad bowl. Crumble bacon over. Add celery, tongue, eggs, and onion and toss gently to mix. Coat all with oil and vinegar. Salt and pepper to taste. *Serves 4 to 6.*

RICE SALAD

A great way to use leftover cooked rice.

1 cup cooked rice
½ cup olive oil
3 tablespoons vinegar
1 teaspoon salt

Freshly ground pepper to taste
1 7-ounce can tuna fish, drained and flaked
2 medium ripe tomatoes, coarsely chopped
1 medium cucumber, peeled and cubed
2 tablespoons chopped scallion
2 hard-boiled eggs, sliced (optional)
8 large stuffed green olives (optional)

To the rice, add oil, vinegar, salt, and pepper and mix well. Add tuna fish, tomatoes, cucumber, and scallion and mix gently but well. Mount on a serving dish and decorate with egg slices and olives. *Serves 4 to 6.*

POTATO SALAD

This salad is especially good to serve with hamburgers and/or frankfurters at an outdoor party. It also goes well with cold cuts. Make extra potatoes the night before, so you won't have to cook them from scratch.

10 medium potatoes
1 bunch scallions
2 stalks celery with leaves
¾ cup French dressing
6 hard-boiled eggs
8 slices crisp bacon, crumbled (optional)
1 teaspoon celery seed
Mayonnaise to taste

Boil potatoes in their jackets until done but still firm. While still warm, peel and slice into a large bowl. Chop both green and white parts of scallions with celery and add to bowl. Pour dressing over, toss well, and refrigerate, turning occasionally. Shell and slice eggs; add eggs, bacon, and celery seed when ready to serve. Garnish with dollops of mayonnaise, and mix just before serving. *Serves 6 to 8.*

SALADE NIÇOISE

This is a recipe from the Mediterranean coast of France, and is often seen on the menus of good French restaurants here. It makes a great luncheon salad.

1 head Boston lettuce, torn into bite-size bits
1 head romaine lettuce, torn into bite-size bits

3 ripe tomatoes, quartered
1 green pepper, seeded and chopped
1 7-ounce can tuna fish, drained and flaked
10 black olives, pitted and sliced
1 large red onion, thinly sliced
10 radishes, stemmed and thinly sliced
2 cups finely chopped red cabbage
1 1¾-ounce can flat anchovy filets, chopped and drained
½ to ¾ cup French dressing

Put all ingredients into a large salad bowl. Pour dressing over and toss well. *Serves 6 to 8.*

POACHED EGGS
AND TONGUE SALAD

A nice way to turn leftover tongue into a luncheon salad.

4 eggs, poached
1 head Boston lettuce, washed and crisped
1 cup slivered red cabbage
1 cup chopped apple
½ cup julienne-cut tongue
¼ cup French dressing
½ cup mayonnaise

Poach eggs 4 minutes. Remove from the water with a slotted spoon or spatula and place in cold water to cool and stop the cooking. Drain and chill. In a bowl, make a bed of lettuce leaves. Mix cabbage, apple, and tongue with the dressing and place on the lettuce. Top with the cold poached eggs and cover with mayonnaise. *Serves 4.*

RUSSIAN SALAD

When you have a refrigerator full of leftovers, try this.

3 cups diced ham
2 cups diced cooked potatoes
1 cup cooked peas
1 cup diced onion
1 cup diced cooked carrots
1 pickled herring, diced
1 tablespoon capers
1 cup French dressing
1 to 2 cups mayonnaise

Put ham, vegetables, herring, and capers into a bowl, and pour dressing over them. Let stand in the refrigerator at least 4 hours. Pour off extra dressing and mix ham, vegetables, herring, and capers with mayonnaise to taste. Serve thoroughly chilled. *Serves 8 to 10.*

The Wonderful Vegetable and Green Salads

Vegetable salad was designed to clear the refrigerator of tidbits of leftover vegetables, cheese, and pasta, and they are a great way to prepare bargains using canned vegetables. Before using canned vegetables for a salad, rinse them well under cold running water.

Use imagination in the selection of greens for your salads. Iceberg lettuce is wonderfully crisp, and quite bland as a flavor. A few clean, crisp leaves of spinach that is really fresh can be added to almost any vegetable or green salad with wonderful effect. (Ever try leftover spinach, chopped, mixed with sour cream and chopped walnuts?) Celery tops, finely minced, snippets of carrot ends, shreds of raw cabbage—trimmings from the vegetable ingredients for soups—can be added to almost any of the recipes here to change the flavor and texture, and bring variety to your meals.

CAESAR SALAD

4 tablespoons olive oil
1 clove garlic, peeled and mashed
2 cups croutons
1 head iceberg lettuce
1 head romaine lettuce
¼ cup lemon juice
½ cup olive oil
Salt and pepper
1 tablespoon Worcestershire sauce
¼ cup grated Parmesan cheese
¼ cup crumbled blue cheese
1 raw egg

In a large skillet over medium heat, warm oil and sauté garlic 2 minutes, then remove garlic. Sauté croutons until golden, then re-
move and drain on absorbent paper. Tear up the greens. In a cup combine lemon juice, olive oil, salt, pepper, and Worcestershire sauce. Add cheeses to the greens. In a large salad bowl, beat egg until frothy; a little at a time, beat the dressing into the egg. Add greens and cheese mixture and toss 20 times. Garnish with croutons and toss again before serving. *Serves 6.*

THREE BEAN SALAD

When canned vegetables are on sale, keep this salad in mind. This recipe makes about 2 quarts. Whatever you don't use may be stored almost indefinitely in covered jars in the refrigerator.

1 16- or 17-ounce can cut green beans
1 16- or 17-ounce can cut wax beans
1 16- or 17-ounce can kidney beans
1 small onion, grated
2 carrots, thinly sliced
1 cup diced celery
½ cup sugar
⅓ cup salad oil
⅔ cup cider vinegar
1 teaspoon salt
1 teaspoon pepper

Drain canned vegetables and rinse in cold, running water. Drain well. Place them in a large bowl and add the other vegetables and toss. Mix sugar, oil, vinegar, salt, and pepper and stir until sugar is dissolved. Pour over mixed vegetables and let stand at room temperature for several hours before serving, stirring occasionally. *Serves 8 to 10.*

COTTAGE CHEESE AND VEGETABLE SALAD FOR DIETERS

8 radishes
4 scallions
1 medium cucumber
2 ripe tomatoes
3 cups creamed cottage cheese
Diet sour cream

Wash radishes and scallions and slice them thin. Peel cucumber. Cut into cubes. Cut tomatos into cubes. Mix vegetables with cottage cheese and serve in a mound. Have a bowl of sour cream and a pepper grinder nearby to use as desired. *Serves 4.*

FROZEN CHEESE SALAD
FOR DIETERS

½ pound cottage cheese
¼ pound blue cheese
Half-and-half or milk as needed
1 tablespoon chopped chives
½ teaspoon Worcestershire sauce
Salt and pepper to taste
Lettuce

Mix and mash the two cheeses together, removing all lumps. Add half-and-half or milk to make the mixture smooth, but not too soft. Add chives, Worcestershire sauce, salt, and pepper and mix in thoroughly. Place in ice tray and freeze 2 to 3 hours. When ready to serve, cut into thin slices and serve several to each person on a bed of lettuce. *Serves 4.*

COLESLAW WITH CARROTS

Make coleslaw well ahead of time and let it rest in the refrigerator.

1 small head cabbage
1 carrot
1 tablespoon sugar
½ cup vinegar
3 tablespoons mayonnaise
Salt and pepper to taste

Shred cabbage with a sharp knife. Grate carrot into strips on the coarse side of a grater. Dissolve sugar in vinegar, then stir in mayon-naise. Add salt and pepper to taste. Pour dressing over vegetables, and toss thoroughly. Check seasoning. *Serves 6 to 8.*

DIET COLESLAW

Shred cabbage and carrot as above. In addition, grate 1 small onion. Dress with ¼ cup vinegar, ¼ cup water, and 1 tablespoon sugar. No mayonnaise. *Serves 6 to 8.*

CHIFFONADE SALAD

1 head iceberg lettuce
1 bunch watercress
1 cup canned julienne-cut beets
½ cup French dressing

Wash and crisp lettuce and watercress, then chill. Chill beets. Tear greens into a salad bowl. Add beets and mix. Pour dressing over and toss well before serving. *Serves 6.*

RED AND GREEN SALAD

3 cucumbers, sliced
4 large tomatoes, peeled and sliced
3 red onions, peeled, sliced, and separated
    into rings
⅔ cup dry bread crumbs
¾ cup Italian dressing
Parsley or watercress to garnish

In a salad bowl, alternate layers of cucumber, tomato, and onion slices, sprinkling bread crumbs between the layers. Refrigerate. When ready to serve, pour dressing over vegetables and toss. Garnish with parsley or watercress. *Serves 6.*

BEANS, RICE, AND PASTAS

Dried Beans and Vegetables

Occasionally you will find in foreign food markets packages of dried, mixed vegetables which are great in stews and casseroles. The most available dried vegetables are beans, which are consistently listed by USDA bulletins as the best protein buy available. There are at least 12 popular varieties sold. They are delicious in casseroles and salads and make good substitutes for meat.

Dried peas and lentils are also available and are most popular in soups. By halving the liquids in soups that are made with dried peas and lentils, you can make an excellent pea or lentil puree to serve as a vegetable dish. They are particularly good with broiled meats.

Cooking Dried Beans from Scratch

It is possible to cook dried beans without soaking, but they cook much faster and hold their shape better when they are presoaked. The old-time way was to soak beans overnight in plenty of plain cold water. That is still a good way. But newer methods developed in the U.S. Department of Agriculture laboratories in Washington, D.C., and in California, are worth a try:

One-hour hot soak: To 1 pound dried beans, any variety, add 6 to 8 cups hot water. Heat to boiling, boil 2 minutes, then set aside for an hour or so.

Overnight salt soak: To 1 pound dried beans add 6 cups cold water and 2 teaspoons salt. Let stand overnight, or for several hours.

Cooking Soaked Beans

For plain boiled beans to serve as a hot vegetable or to use in casseroles and other dishes, drain the soaked beans. (They will have swollen to twice or three times their original measure.) Put them into a large pot or Dutch oven and cover with 6 cups hot water or to about an inch above the beans. Add 1 to 2 tablespoons oil, bacon drippings, or butter, and 2 teaspoons salt and other seasonings if wished. Cook gently with lid tilted (or without a lid if foaming is a problem) until tender when taste-tested. Add hot water as needed to keep beans just covered with liquid. If ham or other salty meat is cooked with the beans, use only 1 teaspoon salt; add more to taste when almost done.

How Long to Cook

The recipes here tell approximately how long it takes for cooking the beans if you are starting from scratch with dried beans. However, it is impossible to give accurate timing because much depends on altitude, hardness of water, and length of time beans have been on the grocer's shelves or in your own kitchen cupboard. The best rule is to test frequently during cooking, then come to your own decision as to when beans are tender and taste "done."

If you have a pressure saucepan, follow directions in the instruction book. To avoid possible clogging of the vent pipe by foam, it's important not to fill the cooker more than one-third full of soaked beans and liquid. If you are cooking dried beans in a slow-cooking electric crockery pot, they need not be soaked.

If water in your locality is very hard, adding not more than ⅛ to ¼ teaspoon baking soda for each cup of beans will soften the water and make the beans cook more quickly. Too much soda, however, will soften them too much and also affect their flavor. Incidentally, it's best to wait until beans are tender before adding vinegar, tomatoes, or other acid foods. Too much acid slows down cooking.

Beans and Rice

CHILI BEANS

Serve with corn chips and long cold drinks.

4 cups (about 1¾ pounds) pinto or red beans
12 cups water
4 teaspoons salt
1 large whole onion, peeled
1 large bay leaf
1 fat clove garlic, peeled and sliced thin
4 tablespoons margarine or butter
1½ pounds lean ground beef
1 cup beef stock or tomato juice
3 to 4 tablespoons good chili powder
1½ teaspoons cumin

Place beans in a large kettle. Add 12 cups (3 quarts) water and soak overnight. The follow-

ing day add salt, onion, and bay leaf. Place over a high heat and bring to a boil rapidly. Reduce heat to simmer, cover tightly, and cook about 2 hours, or until beans are almost but not quite tender. Lift out and discard onion and bay leaf. Melt margarine or butter in a heavy skillet. Add meat, breaking it up with a fork, and brown quickly. Add beef stock or tomato juice and bring to a boil. Stir into beans. Mix chili powder and cumin together with a little of the liquid from bean pot. Then stir it into bean pot. Bring to a boil over high heat, reduce heat to simmer, cover tightly and cook for 1 to 1½ hours, or until beans are tender. *Serves 8.*

CHILI CON CARNE

An old-time chili recipe popular in the California–Arizona–Mexico border area.

2 cups (1 pound) pink beans or light red kidney beans, soaked
6 cups boiling water
1 medium onion, chopped (about ¾ cup)
1 to 3 large cloves garlic, minced
⅓ cup bacon drippings or oil
1½ teaspoons salt
1 8-ounce can tomato sauce
1½ teaspoons chili powder
¼ teaspoon cumin seed or powder

Combine ingredients in a large kettle and cook slowly, covered, about 3 hours, until beans are tender and a rich sauce is formed. Add more hot water if necessary; they should be neither too dry nor too juicy. While beans are cooking, prepare sauce.

CHILI CON CARNE SAUCE

2 tablespoons oil or bacon drippings
2 pounds ground beef
3 or 4 cloves garlic, minced
1 large onion, chopped (about 1 cup)
1 8-ounce can tomato sauce
1½ teaspoons salt
2 to 3 tablespoons chili powder
½ teaspoon cumin seed

4 cups hot water, plus more as needed
¼ cup flour
⅓ cup warm water

Heat oil. Add ground beef and cook, stirring and turning, until it loses its red color. Stir in garlic, onion, tomato sauce, salt, chili powder, cumin, and 3 cups of hot water. Cover, and cook slowly 3 hours or longer, to a thick, rich consistency. Before adding sauce to beans, add to it 1 cup hot water, then thicken slightly, using ¼ cup flour mixed smooth with ⅓ cup warm water. Stir gently into beans. Taste; add salt if needed, and cook a few minutes longer. *Serves 10 to 12.*

BAKED BEANS

Serve with Boston Brown Bread (from cans) or hot rolls. Baked beans are best made in a large earthenware casserole that has a lid or in an old-fashioned bean crock. Or you can make them in a slow-cooking crockery pot or a large Dutch oven.

4 cups (about 1¾ pounds) dried white pea
    beans or Great Northern beans, soaked
Cold water
¾ cup (about 6 ounces) salt pork
1 large onion, peeled
2 tablespoons tomato paste
2 tablespoons cider vinegar
Good pinch powdered cloves
½ cup dark molasses
1 generous teaspoon freshly ground black
    pepper
1 cup dark brown sugar

Place soaked beans in a large kettle, cover with fresh cold water by at least 2 inches. Bring to a boil slowly, then simmer until beans are almost tender. In the event the water boils away, add more boiling water to keep them well covered. Drain, setting cooking water aside to use later. While this is going on, scald pork in boiling water. Cut in half. Then cut one of the halves into 1-inch squares. Leave the other half whole. Place onion in whatever container you are using. Add half the drained beans, the cubes of pork, then the remainder

of the beans. Place the chunk of pork on top. Mix together remaining ingredients and pour over beans. Heat 2 cups of cooking water and pour over all. Cover and place in a preheated 250° oven for 6 to 8 hours, or until tender. Look at the beans every once in a while to see if they are still covered with liquid. If not, add more of the cooking water or plain water heated to the boiling point. Beans must be covered at all times. During the last hour of cooking, uncover the pot. At this point do not add more liquid. *Serves 6 to 8.*

MIXED BEAN CASSEROLE

½ to 1 pound ham
1 clove garlic, minced or juiced
1 large onion, chopped
2 cups drained cooked or canned light red
    kidney beans
2 cups drained cooked or canned garbanzos
1 16-ounce can baked beans (without tomato
    sauce)
2 to 4 tablespoons brown sugar
1 to 2 teaspoons prepared mustard
½ cup catsup
½ cup red wine (or ½ cup water plus
    3 tablespoons vinegar)
Salt and pepper to taste
Onion slices

Trim fat from ham and render fat in a large skillet. Cut ham in small strips and brown lightly in hot fat. (If ham is extra lean, add 2 tablespoons bacon drippings.) Add garlic and chopped onion; cook until limp. Add beans and other ingredients except onion slices. Taste; add more seasonings and more liquid if needed. Turn into 2½-quart casserole, top with onion slices, and bake at 350° about 45 minutes. *Serves 6 to 8.*

BLACK-EYED CHICKEN

1 meaty fryer, cut up
4 tablespoons all-purpose flour
1 teaspoon salt

¼ teaspoon pepper
⅛ teaspoon paprika
2 to 3 tablespoons oil
2 to 3 teaspoons margarine or butter
¼ to ½ pound fresh mushrooms or celery
3 or 4 tablespoons finely chopped onion
1 teaspoon garlic salt
¼ teaspoon mixed fine herbs
½ cup dry white wine or chicken bouillon
2 to 3 cups cooked or canned black-eyed
    beans, drained
1 tomato, coarsely diced, or ½ cup diced
    canned tomatoes
Tomato juice (about ¼ cup)
Chicken bouillon (about ½ cup)

Dry chicken pieces with paper towels. Shake chicken with flour, salt, pepper, and paprika in a plastic bag. Heat oil and margarine or butter in a large skillet and brown chicken slowly on both sides. When golden brown, take up and keep warm. In same skillet, adding a little more oil and margarine if needed, cook whole or halved mushrooms or celery with chopped onion for about 10 minutes. Sprinkle lightly with garlic salt and fine herbs while cooking. Add wine or broth and drained black-eyed beans. Heat just to boiling. Arrange browned chicken over top, partially sinking pieces into beans. Scatter diced tomato over beans; add tomato juice plus just enough chicken broth or water to show through beans. Cover and simmer 10 to 20 minutes on top of range until chicken is fork-tender. *Serves 4 to 6.*

CALIFORNIA BEEF-AND-BEAN POT

1 cup (½ pound) small white beans
1 quart cold water
1¾ teaspoons salt plus extra salt
3 cups hot water
2 pounds fat short ribs of beef cut in 2-inch
    pieces
3 large onions, chopped
2 cups sliced celery
1 large clove garlic, minced
2 to 3 tablespoons tomato paste

Soak beans overnight in 1 quart cold water with 1 teaspoon salt. About 3 hours before serving, drain beans, add 3 cups hot water and ¾ teaspoon salt, and let cook slowly, covered, while you start the meat cooking. Brown short ribs on all sides in a Dutch oven or heavy pot, starting them fat side down. Salt lightly while turning and cooking slowly. Add onions, celery, garlic, and tomato paste; cook about 5 minutes. Then add beans and their liquid, cover, and cook slowly 2½ to 3 hours, or until both meat and beans are tender. Don't let beans cook dry; add a little hot water if needed while cooking. *Serves 6 to 8.*

BEANS AND FRANKS

2 or 3 frankfurters, sliced crosswise
1 tablespoon butter or bacon drippings
2 cups drained cooked garbanzos
2 tablespoons minced onion
1 tablespoon brown sugar
1 tablespoon prepared mustard
¼ cup catsup

Brown frank slices in butter in skillet. Add rest of ingredients. Mix and heat 10 minutes or more. *Serves 4.*

QUICK TOMATO BEAN RAREBIT

1 10½-ounce can condensed cream of tomato
    soup
2 cups cooked pink beans, drained and
    slightly mashed
1 tablespoon minced onion
2 tablespoons catsup
1 cup chopped Cheddar cheese
Dash cayenne pepper or Tabasco sauce
Hot toast for 4

Prepare soup as directed on can. Add beans, onion, and catsup, and heat in a double boiler or fondue pot. Stir often. When steaming, add cheese and blend well. Stir constantly but slowly for 5 minutes. Season with cayenne or Tabasco and serve on hot toast. *Serves 4.*

LENTIL LOAF WITH CHEESE SAUCE

The walnuts in this recipe make it expensive—to cut cost, omit them. It's good even without them.

¾ cup lentils
2 cups hot water
1 teaspoon salt
¼ teaspoon thyme
Margarine or butter
2 cups shelled walnuts (optional)
4 slices dry white bread
1 16-ounce can whole tomatoes, drained
2 eggs, lightly beaten
2 tablespoons onion juice
⅛ teaspoon black pepper
Cheese Sauce

Place lentils in a saucepan with 2 cups hot water, salt, and thyme. Bring to a boil, then simmer uncovered for 5 minutes. Take off heat and allow to stand for 1 hour. Return to heat, bring to a boil again, then simmer for 15 minutes, or until tender. Drain. Butter well an 8½ × 4½ × 2½-inch loaf pan. Set aside. Drop walnuts, if using them, into a saucepan of rapidly boiling water and boil for 3 minutes. Drain thoroughly. Spread in a shallow pan. Grate bread and place in another shallow pan. Toast both walnuts and bread in a preheated 400° oven for 15 to 20 minutes, or until lightly browned. Place half the lentils and the drained tomatoes in the container of an electric blender and blend to a fine puree. Blend the other half. Chop walnuts fairly fine. Now mix everything together except the Cheese Sauce. Taste for seasoning—you may need both salt and pepper. Spoon into the prepared pan and bake in a preheated 350° oven 30 minutes, or until firm. Allow to stand about 5 minutes before turning out onto a heated platter. Offer Cheese Sauce on the side. *Serves 6.*

CHEESE SAUCE

2 tablespoons margarine or butter
2 tablespoons all-purpose flour
1¾ cups hot milk
1 cup (about 2 ounces) grated Cheddar cheese
Salt to taste
½ teaspoon prepared mustard
¼ teaspoon Worcestershire sauce
Few drops Tabasco sauce

Melt margarine or butter and stir in flour until smooth. Cook, stirring constantly, over moderate heat for about 3 minutes. Do not brown. Add milk gradually, whipping constantly with a wire whisk. Continue cooking, whipping with the whisk until sauce comes to a boil and thickens. Take off heat and stir in remaining ingredients. Taste for salt; if not served immediately, seal surface with Saran wrap to keep a skin from forming. Keep warm over simmering water. *Makes about 2 cups.*

Rice and Cornmeal

Rice has been the staple of the Orient for centuries. It combines well with almost any meat or vegetable, and stretches either. Oriental cooking depends on a little of a highly flavored sauce or stew to flavor a lot of plain boiled rice. In the Near and Far East, rice is cooked with other ingredients into pilafs. Borrow from these cuisines and stretch luxury foods with rice. In Italy, risotto is the economy rice dish.

The late Adele Davis recommended unprocessed brown rice and converted white rice as the most nutritious of the rices.

Cornmeal is a staple of Southern "soul food" and is also used in Italian and East European cooking. The flavor is great and the cost minimal. I've included a few cornmeal recipes here to suggest some of the creative ways in which it can be used.

RICE PILAF

You can make this basic rice pilaf with either white or brown rice. Brown rice takes a little longer to cook.

2 tablespoons vegetable oil
1 cup converted or brown rice
1 medium onion, chopped
2 cloves garlic, mashed
½ cup chopped green pepper
½ cup chopped mild red pepper
1 teaspoon salt
2 vegetable bouillon cubes
2 cups water
¼ teaspoon Tabasco sauce
¼ cup pine nuts (optional)

Heat oil in a saucepan. Add rice, onion, and garlic, and sauté, stirring constantly, until onion is transparent. Add the remaining ingredients except the pine nuts, and bring to a boil. Reduce heat, cover, and cook over very low heat for about 45 minutes, or until rice is tender and all the water is absorbed. Sprinkle with pine nuts just before serving. *Serves 6.*

COLD CURRIED RICE WITH PEAS

½ cup margarine or butter
2 cups converted rice
3 cups chicken bouillon
1 tablespoon curry powder
1 cup cold cooked peas
Preserved ginger (optional)

Melt margarine or butter and stir rice in it

until every grain is coated and a golden color. Add chicken bouillon and curry powder and boil 15 minutes. Drain, cool, and chill. Mix with peas and serve with bits of preserved ginger scattered on top, if desired. *Serves 8 to 10.*

RICE CASSEROLE

A dish rather like paella but without the costly shellfish used in paella.

1 fryer chicken, cut into 8 pieces
½ cup ham
2 small chorizos, or substitute pepperoni
1 cup dried chick-peas, soaked overnight
8 cups water
½ teaspoon salt
⅛ teaspoon black pepper
2 tablespoons vegetable oil
½ onion, finely chopped
1 sweet sausage
2 cups converted rice

In a heavy pan, combine chicken, ham, chorizos, chick-peas, water, salt, and pepper. Bring to a boil, reduce heat and simmer, uncovered, for about 2½ hours, or until chick-peas are tender. Drain and reserve cooking liquid. Heat oil in a large, shallow pan. Sauté onion and sausage for about 8 minutes. Remove sausage and slice into bite-size pieces. Slice chicken, ham, and chorizos. Add rice to paella pan and stir for 3 minutes. Reheat reserved cooking liquid. Add sliced meats, chick-peas, and 4 cups of cooking liquid. Stir, then boil 3 minutes over high heat. Reduce heat and simmer, uncovered, 15 to 20 minutes more, or until rice has absorbed all the liquid. *Serves 8.*

RICE WITH TOMATOES

4 tablespoons margarine or butter
2 onions, finely chopped
2 cups converted rice
4 cups beef bouillon
1 8-ounce can tomato sauce
1 teaspoon salt
¼ teaspoon black pepper

Heat margarine or butter in a saucepan. Add onions and sauté over medium-high heat for 3 minutes. Add rice and stir until it begins to brown. Add beef broth, tomato sauce, salt, and pepper. Simmer, uncovered, over low heat for 20 minutes without stirring, until the rice is tender and all the liquid has been absorbed. *Serves 6 to 8.*

RICE WITH TUNA CASSEROLE

2 cups water
½ teaspoon salt
1 cup converted rice
1 10-ounce can tuna
3 tablespoons margarine or butter
3 tablespoons all-purpose flour
1½ cups milk
3 egg yolks
1 teaspoon curry powder
½ teaspoon salt
Freshly ground black pepper

Bring water to a boil. Add salt and rice. Cover and cook over low heat 25 minutes, or until all the liquid is absorbed. With a fork, break tuna into broad flakes. Melt margarine or butter in a saucepan and stir in the flour. Cook over low heat for 1 minute. Add milk gradually, stirring constantly. Beat egg yolks and add 1 tablespoon of the hot sauce. Stir egg yolks and curry powder into sauce. Season with salt and pepper. Arrange rice on a platter, place pieces of tuna on top, and pour sauce over the fish. *Serves 4 to 6.*

RISOTTO WITH VEGETABLES

2 cups converted rice
3 tomatoes, peeled, seeded, and chopped
1 green pepper, seeded and chopped
1 medium onion, chopped
⅛ teaspoon black pepper
¼ cup margarine or butter
4 beef bouillon cubes
1 quart hot water
Grated Parmesan cheese

Combine rice, vegetables, and pepper in a casserole; mix well. Place pats of margarine or butter on rice mixture. Dissolve bouillon cubes in hot water; stir into rice mixture. Cover. Bake in a moderate oven (375°) about 30 minutes. Remove cover, stir, bake another 30 minutes. Sprinkle with grated Parmesan cheese; bake 5 to 10 minutes longer, or until cheese is golden brown. *Serves 6.*

HEARTY RICE SALAD

A great way to use leftover cooked rice.

2 cups cold cooked rice
½ cup cooked peas
4 ounces Swiss cheese, diced
1 1¾-ounce can anchovy filets, chopped
1 4-ounce can Vienna sausages, diced
4 lettuce leaves
1 pimiento, cut into strips
½ yellow or green pepper, cut into strips
3 gherkin pickles, sliced
Italian dressing to taste

Combine rice, peas, cheese, anchovies, and sausages; toss lightly. Arrange on a bed of lettuce. Garnish with pimiento, pepper strips, and pickle slices. Chill. Pour dressing over salad just before serving and toss well. *Serves 6.*

RICE CROQUETTES

A marvelous accompaniment to any meat.

2 cups cooked rice
½ cup Béchamel Sauce
1 egg, separated
¼ cup grated Parmesan cheese
1 teaspoon salt
Dry bread crumbs

Mix rice with Béchamel Sauce and well-beaten egg yolk. Add cheese and salt. Spread mixture out on a platter and cool well. Shape into croquettes. Dip in beaten egg white, then in bread crumbs. Fry in 375° deep fat 3 to 4 minutes, or until golden. *Serves 4 to 6.*

QUICK GREEN RICE

This dish is good with almost any kind of roast meat or poultry dish—and very pretty.

3 cups cooked rice
¼ cup grated Parmesan cheese
⅓ cup minced parsley
½ cup minced spinach, drained
2 eggs, well beaten
1 cup milk
¼ cup melted margarine or butter
1½ teaspoons salt
1 tablespoon Worcestershire sauce
2 tablespoons grated onion

Mix all ingredients well and place in a 2-quart casserole. Bake in 325° oven 45 minutes. *Serves 6.*

CORNMEAL WITH OKRA, BARBADOS STYLE

This dish supplies both green vegetable and starch and is all that is needed to complete any meal based on a plainly cooked meat, poultry, or fish dish, such as fried chicken or pan-broiled flank steak.

12 pods small young okra
6 cups water
Salt to taste
2 cups yellow cornmeal
3 tablespoons unsalted margarine

Wash okra, cut off stems, and slice crosswise about ¼ inch thick. Pour water into a saucepan and bring to a boil. Add okra and salt to taste and cook, covered, for about 10 minutes. Pour cornmeal into saucepan in a steady stream, stirring with a wooden spoon. Cook, stirring, until the mixture is thick (about 5 minutes). Taste for seasoning, adding more salt if necessary. Turn into a warmed serving dish, molding to an attractive shape. Spread margarine on top. *Serves 6.*

POLENTA

This is the basic approach to the Italian use of cornmeal. Once cooled, polenta can be sliced and fried, baked, or served with Italian meat or tomato sauce.

1½ cups cornmeal
3 cups water
1 teaspoon salt

Combine cornmeal and 2 cups water in a heavy saucepan; mix well. Stir in remaining water and salt. Bring to a boil, stirring constantly. Be sure cornmeal does not lump. Continue to cook, stirring constantly, until the mixture is so thick that the spoon will stand up, unsupported, in the middle of the pan. Pour into a buttered 1½-quart bowl or mold. Cool. *Serves 8.*

Pasta

There are a number of popular misconceptions about pasta, one of the world's most perfect foods. It was *not* discovered in China by Marco Polo. Something resembling ravioli was being eaten in Rome in 1284, almost 20 years before Polo's famous travels. Pasta was not brought to this country all tangled up in meatballs by Italian immigrants. Thomas Jefferson introduced it here in 1786, bringing back one spaghetti die from Italy, which he used to make small amounts of pasta, serving it only to family and friends. The classic pasta dish is *not* spaghetti and meatballs, any more than chop suey is typically Chinese. In fact, pasta and meatballs can rarely be found in Italy.

Let's straighten out another bent fact —pasta is *not* a weight builder. Naturally, if you overeat any food you'll pile on the pounds. Pasta itself is a very low-fat food, its fat content averaging ¼ percent. Two ounces of uncooked macaroni contain only 200 calories. In addition, pasta is superior to the potato as an energy-giving carbohydrate because it contains more protein. In this pasta-protein, six of the eight essential amino acids are found. The other two required acids are usually in the pasta sauce; so a dish of pasta with meat, cheese, seafood, tomato, or eggs means that you are serving up a perfectly balanced diet.

In addition to all this, not only does pasta magically mate with about any food, but it is a budget item without peer. Try to name another food that will supply a quick supper or an elegant dinner for four, or even six, that you can put on the table for about $2, often half that.

In most cities of any size, you'll find either a drogheria or a salumeria (an Italian grocery or delicatessen—often combined) where you can buy fresh pasta, usually noodles, spaghetti, or ravioli. If you can find such a place, buy the fresh pasta. Nothing out of a box can compare with it. If you can't buy it, try your hand at making it, for homemade is the best of all pastas.

No matter what pasta you use, it won't be at its peak if you cook it improperly. Most of us overcook it. Seven quarts of water in a deep pot so the pound of pasta can properly swim is the first requirement. Secondly, put 2 tablespoons salt in after the water is boiling, just before you push the pasta in. If water and salt boil together for any length of time before the pasta is in the pot, there is a disagreeable odor, rather like that of carbolic acid. If you use a large pasta like lasagne, add 1 tablespoon olive

124

oil to keep the pasta from sticking. Now the cooking.

As an example, let's use the most popular pasta—spaghetti—which is a "string" pasta as opposed to a shell, an elbow macaroni, or any of the other myriad shapes. Push the spaghetti gently into the boiling water until all of it is submerged. Never break it. Then, using a wooden fork, gently stir until the strands are separated. The master pasta cooks, the Italians (in Italy, not here), like their national dish al dente (to the tooth), slightly chewy, firm, not soft and overdone the American way. Like wine, of course, you will have pasta to suit your own taste. But you'll find it nuttier and tastier if you do not overcook it.

Two tricks learned in Italian kitchens: While the pasta is cooking, have a large bowl warming with sweet butter (½ stick for each pound of pasta). The butter will melt in the bowl. While the pasta cooks, also have serving bowls, soup bowls, or ramekins warming. Pasta cools quickly, and although a great food it isn't all that great cold.

When done, fork the pasta out using special pasta tongs you can buy in many places, or an ordinary tined fork. Shake the water off the pasta over the pot and place it into the bowl with the butter. (Pasta should never be drained in a colander, and never, never rinsed. This brings pasta together and usually makes it gummy.) Once all the pasta is in the warm bowl with the butter, toss it well. Now all you have to do is quickly sauce it and serve it immediately in warm bowls.

Tips on Cooking Spaghetti

All experts agree that spaghetti should be cooked al dente, which means with a little bit of chewiness left in. You have to watch the pot and taste the spaghetti frequently to catch the moment of perfect doneness.

Make the tomato sauce for pasta dishes from scratch for best flavor. Use canned, peeled plum tomatoes, combined with canned tomato paste and herbs such as oregano, rosemary, and basil to taste. Canned tomato sauce is fla-vored with a lot of things that can alter the taste of your sauce. It's also expensive. Tomato paste diluted with water is more pure and costs less.

Probably the single pasta question that causes the most arguments is whether to add sugar to tomato sauce for pastas. Some purists are horrified at the idea of "artificially" sweet-ened sauce. Others insist that red spaghetti sauce just doesn't taste good without a little sugar. The right answer seems to be that it de-pends on the tomatoes. If you're using freshly picked tomatoes, all the sugar a good spaghetti sauce needs is right in the fruit. But older or canned tomatoes usually need a little help. Spaghetti sauce should never have a sugary taste—½ to 1 teaspoon should be enough.

Meat sauce is often greasy. This problem, one that bothers a lot of people, has a simple solution. Cook your ground beef separately from the sauce, pour off the grease, and add the meat to the sauce to simmer. If you think you lose meat flavor this way, put a soup bone into the sauce along with the meat. Or add an instant beef bouillon cube. Cooking meat sauces a day ahead of serving time also gives a better blend of flavors.

All the kinds of pasta are, or can be, made from the same dough. But the number of shapes this dough is molded into is huge. The Italian names of the different kinds of pasta refer to the shapes. Vermicelli, for example, which is very thin spaghetti, means little worms in Italian. Flat spaghetti is linguine, or tongue spaghetti, and ditali, short pieces of macaroni, are fingers. Except for specialized pasta like lasagne and manicotti, most are in-terchangeable within a given size group. Even lasagne can be very good made with large shell macaroni. You might feel that the more delicate shapes are more suited to light sauces, while robust dishes call for big pieces of pasta. Experiment with any kind that takes your fancy. Pasta shapes have proliferated just be-cause they're so good at adding variety to meals.

Spaghetti sauce keeps beautifully. In fact, it's better the second day. Add it to soups or cooked vegetables if you don't want to make spaghetti again. Or freeze it. To reheat cooked spaghetti or other forms of pasta, toss into a pot of boiling, salted water, stir, then lift out the pasta at once. It won't be as perfect as the first time it was cooked, but it will be okay.

CLASSIC SPAGHETTI
IN MEAT SAUCE

2 tablespoons shortening
1 pound ground beef
1 large onion, chopped
1 to 2 cloves garlic, minced
½ cup chopped celery
1 green pepper, diced
2 teaspoons salt
1 6-ounce can tomato paste
1 cup water
1 teaspoon chili powder, or more to taste
⅛ teaspoon cayenne pepper
⅛ teaspoon curry powder
Cooked spaghetti for 6
Grated Parmesan cheese

Heat a large saucepan and add shortening. Crumble beef into cooker and brown lightly. Add onion, garlic, celery, green pepper, and salt. Combine tomato paste, water, chili powder, cayenne pepper, and curry powder, and add to saucepan. Cover, and cook 1 hour or more. Place spaghetti in a big serving bowl and ladle sauce over the top. Offer Parmesan on the side. *Serves 6.*

SPAGHETTI WITH MARINARA SAUCE

2 tablespoons olive or vegetable oil
2 small white onions, chopped
2 small carrots, chopped
1 clove garlic, minced
½ teaspoon black pepper
2 35-ounce cans whole tomatoes
1 teaspoon salt
3 tablespoons margarine or butter
¼ teaspoon dried hot red pepper (optional)
Cooked spaghetti for 8 to 10

Sauté onions, carrots, and garlic in oil until onions are soft. Mill in black pepper, and add

tomatoes. Stir sauce well, add salt, and cook, uncovered, for 20 minutes. Now push sauce through a food mill. It will emerge velvety. Melt margarine or butter in a pan and add strained sauce. Stirring often, cook for 15 minutes. At this stage you can stir in the hot red pepper. *Serves 8 to 10.*

SPAGHETTI ALLA CARBONARA

¼ pound bacon
½ pound raw spaghetti
Salted water
½ cup Parmesan cheese
2 tablespoons parsley, dried or fresh chopped
2 eggs
2 cloves garlic, minced
2 tablespoons olive or vegetable oil

Cut bacon into small squares and cook slowly, just until crisp. Remove from heat and pour off all but 1 or 2 tablespoons of the grease. Cook spaghetti in a big pot of salted water. Add cooled bacon, cheese, and parsley to the eggs and beat until blended. Just before spaghetti is done, sauté garlic briefly in the oil and bacon grease. Have a heated serving bowl ready. When the spaghetti is drained, put it in the bowl and pour in the hot fat and egg mixture. Toss immediately and thoroughly, so that the eggs cook in the heat of the other ingredients. Eat at once. *Serves 4.*

RIGATONI "TUTTO GIARDINO"

Rigatoni with the Whole Garden is the translation of this name. Rigatoni is a spaghetti variant—you can use spaghetti instead or one of the other pastas.

½ cup parsley leaves
2 cloves garlic
2 white onions
8 thin slices prosciutto, or boiled ham
2 red radishes
3 small carrots
2 small leeks
6 fresh basil leaves
3 tablespoons butter

3 tablespoons olive oil
1 cup finely chopped cabbage
1 medium zucchini, diced
4 ripe tomatoes, peeled and diced
1 cup chicken broth
Salt and pepper to taste
1 pound rigatoni
⅓ cup grated Romano cheese
⅓ cup grated Parmesan cheese
6 tablespoons soft margarine or butter

Finely mince parsley, garlic, onions, prosciutto or ham, radishes, carrots, leeks, and basil, mixing together into what Italians call a soffrito. Heat butter and oil in a large pot, stir vegetable mixture into it, simmering until onions and carrots are soft. Blend in cabbage, zucchini, tomatoes, and chicken broth, seasoning with salt and pepper. Simmer on top of stove, covered, for about 20 minutes, stirring often until vegetables are tender. Cook rigatoni al dente, drain and place in a large hot bowl. Sprinkle cheese over pasta in the bowl, stir in soft margarine or butter, toss well. Add vegetable sauce and toss again. Serve right away in hot soup bowls. *Serves 6 to 8.*

LINGUINE WITH WHITE CLAM SAUCE

Devotees of this classic but simple sauce mistakenly believe that it can be made only with fresh clams. Not so. Canned clams can be even better—much less expensive and (unless you are expert with clams) more tender than the fresh—and they present no problem with prying clam shells open. Linguine is another pasta variant sold in most markets.

4 tablespoons olive oil
8 large cloves garlic (4 whole, 4 minced)
2 8-ounce bottles clam juice
2 8-ounce cans minced clams
½ cup dry white wine
3 tablespoons minced parsley
1 pound linguine
½ stick soft margarine or butter

Heat olive oil in frying pan. Add 4 whole cloves garlic, sautéing until garlic is brown. Take pan from heat, discard garlic. Pour contents of 2 bottles clam juice plus juice from 2 cans minced clams (clams are added later) and ½ cup wine into frying pan. Place pan on medium heat and reduce clam juice and wine by half. Reducing the liquid is important. Stir in minced garlic, cooking until it is soft. Now add minced clams; bring sauce to a soft boil, immediately remove pan from heat so clams won't toughen. Cook linguine al dente. Remove from water and toss with margarine or butter in the bowl; add clam sauce, toss well again. Add minced parsley and toss once more. Serve immediately in warm soup bowls or ramekins. *Serves 4 to 6.*

MACARONI AND CHEESE À LA BAUSERMAN

1 pound elbow macaroni
6 tablespoons margarine or butter
2 cups crushed saltine crackers
Salt and white pepper
14 ¼ × 1 × 2-inch-long slices very sharp
    Cheddar such as aged Canadian
Milk
1 35-ounce can tomatoes, well chilled

Cook macaroni al dente and drain. Spread 3 tablespoons margarine or butter in a casserole, arrange a layer of crushed crackers and one of macaroni, season with salt and pepper, then add a layer of cheese. Repeat procedure, ending with a layer of cheese. Pour in milk to two-thirds depth of dish, dot the top with remaining margarine or butter, and bake uncovered in a preheated 350° oven until golden brown on top; set under the broiler to get a crusty brown top. *Serves 6.*

TETRAZZINI CASSEROLE

Pasta pairs perfectly with leftovers. Here is a famous version obtained from a noted restauranteur in Florence, Italy.

20 small mushrooms, quartered (optional)
4 tablespoons margarine or butter
2 cups diced leftover cooked chicken
    (or other white meat)

Salt to taste
2 teaspoons flour
½ cup heavy cream
1½ cups milk
2 egg yolks
½ pound fettuccine
½ cup grated Parmesan cheese

Sauté mushrooms in 2 tablespoons margarine or butter for 5 minutes; stir in diced chicken, sprinkle in salt and flour, blend well. Pour in cream and ½ cup milk, simmer, stirring and blending well. Beat egg yolks with remaining milk and pour in. Stir quickly over low heat until sauce is slightly thickened. Don't boil. Cook pasta al dente. Toss with 1 tablespoon margarine or butter and half of the cheese. Butter 4 ramekins; arrange pasta in each; cover with chicken sauce. Sprinkle remaining cheese on top, dot with the rest of the margarine or butter. Place under broiler until heated through and brown. *Serves 4.*

NEAPOLITAN TOMATO SAUCE

Most Americans believe that all sauces from the south of Italy are ragu—very heavy. This is untrue; many southern sauces are not only light but delicate. Marinara is an inspired example—so is this one which many Italian restaurant owners cook for themselves and their staff, usually on Sundays. If you have found the place to buy homemade pasta, or better still have made it yourself, this is the sauce to mate it with.

4 heaping tablespoons minced prosciutto
    (Italian ham) fat, or baked ham fat; or
    bacon fat after you have blanched the
    bacon so its flavor won't dominate
3 tablespoons olive oil
2 tablespoons margarine or butter
4 large white onions, chopped
8 large fresh sweet basil leaves, minced,
    or 2 tablespoons dried basil
12 large ripe plum tomatoes, peeled, seeded,
    and diced, or 2 35-ounce cans Italian
    plum tomatoes put through a food mill
¼ teaspoon pepper
Salt to taste

1 teaspoon sugar
1 pound pasta of your choice
¼ stick margarine or butter
Asiago or Parmesan cheese, grated

Sauté minced fat in oil and margarine or butter until slightly crisp but not brown. Stir in onions and basil and simmer for 6 minutes. Add tomatoes, and blend well with a wooden spoon. Simmer over medium heat, uncovered, for 20 minutes, stirring often. Add pepper, salt, sugar, and stir well. Increase heat, stir often, cooking off excess liquid. Cook pasta and toss with butter in bowl. Add some sauce and toss. Serve with a lavish spoon of sauce atop each portion. Offer grated cheese on the side. *Serves 6.*

ZUCCHINI IN NOODLE RING

2 pounds zucchini
1½ cups finely chopped onion
1 clove garlic, mashed
¼ cup vegetable oil
1½ teaspoons salt
¼ teaspoon pepper
2 cups stewed tomatoes

Cut zucchini lengthwise and then into pieces about 3 inches long. Brown the pieces, cut side down, with onion and garlic in oil. Turn them over, add salt and pepper, then tomatoes, and simmer 40 minutes, or until done. Serve in *Noodle Ring. Serves 4 to 6.*

NOODLE RING

8 ounces flat noodles
Boiling salted water
2 egg yolks
1 cup milk
¼ cup dry bread crumbs
½ teaspoon salt
2 egg whites, stiffly beaten

Cook noodles in boiling salted water about 9 minutes. Drain well. Beat egg yolks until thick and light. Add milk, noodles, bread crumbs, and salt. Fold in stiffly beaten egg whites. Turn into buttered ring mold and bake in 350°

oven about 45 minutes, or until mixture is solid. Unmold on hot platter and fill with zucchini mixture.

LASAGNE AND CHICKEN CASSEROLE

4 tablespoons margarine or butter
4 tablespoons oil
1 large onion, chopped
2 cloves garlic, minced
¼ pound mushrooms, chopped
1 large chicken, cooked, boned, and cubed
¼ pound chicken livers, chopped
1 teaspoon salt
¼ teaspoon pepper
½ cup dry red wine
3 cups tomato puree
1 teaspoon dried basil
½ teaspoon dried rosemary
1 teaspoon parsley flakes
10 ounces lasagne noodles, cooked
½ cup grated Parmesan cheese

Melt margarine or butter in large skillet over medium heat; add oil. Sauté onion, garlic, and mushrooms in hot oil mixture until onion is transparent. Add chicken and chicken livers. Cook 2 to 3 minutes. Add salt, pepper, and wine. Continue to cook until wine is reduced by half. Skim off excess fat. Add tomato puree and herbs; cook 25 to 30 minutes. Butter a 13½ × 8¾ × 2-inch baking dish. Arrange alternate layers of noodles and meat mixture. Top with meat mixture and sprinkle with Parmesan. Bake in 350° oven 25 to 30 minutes. *Serves 8 to 10.*

LASAGNE AND CHEESE CASSEROLE

1 pound ground beef
1 clove garlic, minced
1 tablespoon dried basil
1 teaspoon salt
1 16-ounce can tomatoes
2 6-ounce cans tomato paste
3 cups cottage cheese
½ cup grated Parmesan cheese
2 tablespoons parsley

1 teaspoon salt
⅛ teaspoon black pepper
10 ounces lasagne noodles, cooked
1 pound mozzarella cheese, thinly sliced

Brown ground beef in a heavy skillet. Add garlic, basil, salt, tomatoes, tomato paste, and simmer, uncovered, for about 30 minutes, stirring frequently. Combine cheeses, parsley, salt, and pepper. Blend well. Layer half the lasagne in a long buttered baking dish; spread with half the cheese mixture. Add half the mozzarella cheese; then half the meat sauce. Repeat. Bake at 375° for 30 minutes. *Serves 8 to 10.*

LASAGNE MILANESE

This is a dish often served in northern Italy, and is a welcome change from the usual ground meat and tomato sauce.

2 cups cottage cheese
10 ounces lasagne noodles, cooked
1 pound prosciutto or boiled ham, thinly sliced
1 pound mozzarella cheese, thinly sliced
Salt to taste
Garlic salt to taste
2 tablespoons finely chopped parsley

In a large, deep baking dish, spread a layer of cottage cheese, then a layer of noodles, a layer of ham, a layer of mozzarella cheese, and sprinkle with salt and parsley; keep alternating until you have used all the ingredients. Bake in a 375° oven 30 minutes. *Serves 8 to 10.*

SPAGHETTI WITH GARLIC

1 pound spaghetti, cooked
½ cup margarine or butter
½ cup olive oil
4 cloves garlic, minced
¼ cup finely chopped parsley
½ teaspoon dried basil
½ teaspoon dried oregano
½ teaspoon salt
⅛ teaspoon pepper
Grated Parmesan cheese

Keep cooked spaghetti hot. Melt margarine or butter in heavy saucepan, add oil, and heat. Sauté garlic until lightly browned. Stir in parsley, basil, oregano, salt, and pepper. Toss spaghetti and sauce and serve with grated Parmesan cheese. *Serves 4.*

SOUPS, EGGS, CHEESE, SANDWICHES, AND SNACKS

Soups and Soup Dinners

Soup and sandwich for lunch is an old story, but have you ever tried this combination for supper? In Britain, there's a meal known as "high tea" that is a boon to the budget—it is a light supper of snack foods, including sandwiches, washed down with tea. In France "le souper" is similar, except that it is started with soup. The *soupe* in *souper* is, literally, soup. Originally the word *souper* was used strictly for the meal taken after opera, theater, or balls, and consisted often of the famous French onion soup. Now it has come to mean not a midnight snack but an early evening meal —or, as we know it, supper. Combine these concepts—soup and supper—when your budget needs a break. Your family will welcome the change of pace in a meal composed of soup, sandwiches, or a meaty snack, and topped with fresh fruit or with a nice baked dish for dessert.

Soup from Scratch Is Easy on the Pocketbook

You don't need a recipe to make soup—all you need is a big kettle and an onion. Or so the saying goes. The truth this is meant to convey is that you can make good soup of almost anything: steak or roast bones, carrot peelings, celery tops, the tough inner core of cabbage, leftover mashed potatoes, a tag end of canned tomatoes or tomato paste. Once-a-week soup can be a catch-all for clearing the refrigerator before next week's groceries arrive.

BASIC VEGETABLE SOUP BASE

This is a good soup base into which you can incorporate almost any leftover vegetables you have.

2 tablespoons margarine or butter
1 large onion, peeled and chopped
4 cups water, or stock, or vegetable cooking
    water
2 teaspoons salt (or more)
⅛ teaspoon pepper
Large sprig parsley
1 large old potato, peeled and diced

In a large kettle over medium heat melt margarine or butter and simmer onion until translucent. Add other ingredients, cover, and cook over medium-high heat until potatoes look round and soup is slightly thickened. *This will serve 4.*

But you haven't finished. To this chowder-like base all sorts of leftovers can be added: fish or shellfish along with a pinch of thyme; a can of creamed corn and a strip of diced fresh green pepper (cook 10 minutes more); leftover carrots, diced, and a little nutmeg; leftover green beans and a little dill; yesterday's green salad remains (cook 15 minutes rapidly); cooked rice, or bits of diced leftover chicken and any leftover chicken drippings or gravy; bits of cooked ham and nutmeg (simmer 15 minutes more). If the flavor is still a little thin after your addition, and the second period of cooking, flavor with Worcestershire or soy sauce, or a pinch of a favorite herb, mustard, or a glass of sherry. Experiment, and continue seasoning until it's just right. Sometimes a dab of sour cream does wonders.

Soup in an Electric Crockery Cooker

The popular electric crockery cookers now on the market make heavenly soup with little investment of time on your part. Combine all the ingredients described above with six cups water in the morning, turn the cooker to low, and allow to cook all day. Just before serving, taste, correct seasonings to suit yourself—add a chicken bouillon cube or beef bouillon cubes if you think the flavor still is thin—and serve.

The recipes that follow suggest ways of combining ingredients to make soups. Use them to develop a whole line of personal soups based on the most common leftovers in your household or the best buys at the market. The principles of soup-making are super simple, the results delicious, and nutritious—and the cost is relatively minimal.

CHICKEN BOUILLON MADE FROM LEFTOVERS

You can make this stock, an excellent base for chicken soup recipes of all sorts, from chicken backs and parts, fresh or frozen—or you can mix odds and ends of chicken parts together with bones, necks, and oddments from roasted chicken. It is a catch-all recipe meant to use up every available scrap of chicken, cooked or raw. The recipe is adapted from my book, *The Best of Electric Crock Cooking*; if you make it in a crockery cooker, cook on low for 8 to 12 hours.

Carcass, cooked or raw, of 2 or 3 small
  chickens, including drippings from baked
  chicken, if any
1 medium carrot, scraped
1 medium parsnip, scraped
2 medium cloves garlic, peeled
6 black peppercorns
2 teaspoons fresh parsley or 1 teaspoon dried
1 bay leaf
½ teaspoon thyme
2 teaspoons salt
8 cups water
3 chicken bouillon cubes

Place ingredients in a large kettle over medium-high heat, cover, and cook 4 to 5 hours. Add salt and another bouillon cube if flavor seems thin. Strain before serving or using.

BEEF BOUILLON

One pound of stew beef, seared until dark brown, and bones from roasted beef or sautéed steaks are used instead of chicken with recipe above, along with drippings from roast beef or pan juices from sautéed steak. Add beef bouillon cubes instead of chicken bouillon cubes. Serve the boiled beef, cut up, in the broth to make a complete meal. You can also add some leftover julienne or diced vegetables. For a festive occasion, add a glass of red wine or dry sherry.

BEEF AND BARLEY SOUP

3 tablespoons barley
Water
4 cups beef bouillon
1 teaspoon salt
⅛ teaspoon pepper

1 carrot, sliced
1 medium onion, chopped
½ cup sour cream
2 cups plain yogurt
1 egg
1 tablespoon wine vinegar

Soak barley in water for 12 hours. Drain and add to bouillon, salt, pepper, carrot, and onion in a large pot. Simmer 1½ to 2 hours until barley is tender. Beat together sour cream, yogurt, and egg. Slowly stir in ½ cup hot stock, being careful not to add it so fast that you scramble the egg. Now pour egg mixture into soup pot, beating constantly. Heat soup until it steams but doesn't boil. Correct seasoning and stir in wine vinegar. Serve at once. *Serves 4 to 6.*

LENTIL SOUP, ITALIAN STYLE

Lentils are available dried in most markets and make a very good dark brown meat-flavored soup. With big pieces of crisp French bread and a salad, this makes a meal.

2 cups dried lentils
2½ quarts water
1 ⅛-pound piece salt pork, diced
1 tablespoon tomato paste
1 teaspoon salt
⅛ teaspoon pepper
½ teaspoon marjoram

Combine lentils with remaining ingredients in a big kettle, cover, bring to a boil, then reduce heat and simmer 4 to 5 hours. *Serves 6 to 8.*

USE-IT-ALL-UP LENTIL SOUP

2 cups dried lentils
2½ quarts cooking water from a daisy ham
1 carrot, scraped and cut up
2 stalks celery leaves

Combine lentils with remaining ingredients in a big kettle, cover, bring to a boil, then reduce heat and simmer 4 to 5 hours. Taste, and add salt and pepper if needed. *Serves 6 to 8.*

KIDNEY BEAN SOUP

This is adapted from my book on electric crockery cooking, *The Best of Electric Crock Cooking.* In the slow cooker, start with dried beans and cook the soup on low 10 to 12 hours.

1 cup light red kidney beans, dried or canned
1 medium onion, peeled and minced
1 carrot, peeled and grated
6 cups beef bouillon
¾ cup whole milk
1 egg yolk, slightly beaten
1 teaspoon salt
¼ teaspoon pepper

Soak beans as directed on page 115, if using dried beans. Combine beans, onion, carrot, and broth in a big kettle, cover, bring to a boil, then reduce heat and simmer 4 to 5 hours. Drain beans and vegetables, reserving broth, and process in blender with a little of the bouillon at low speed for 1 or 2 minutes. Turn into a medium kettle with remaining bouillon and bring to a slow boil. Combine milk and egg yolk with salt and pepper in a small bowl and beat ½ cup bouillon into mixture. Pour back into bouillon, stirring quickly and constantly; remove from heat as soon as all the egg mixture is in. *Serves 6 to 8.*

SPLIT PEA SOUP

This is a truly delicious way to use up a ham bone. A bit of leftover daisy ham roll can be used instead of a ham bone. Or use a single slice of packaged ham. To freeze, pour into suitable freezer containers and seal securely. Add the milk after thawing.

4 cups (2 pounds) split peas
Ham bone
2 onions, peeled, each stuck with 2 cloves
2 cloves garlic, peeled and crushed
2 bay leaves
Freshly ground pepper
3 celery ribs, with tops coarsely chopped
3 large carrots, washed and coarsely chopped
Cold water
2 tablespoons tomato paste
Milk

Minced parsley
Thyme (optional)

Place first 8 ingredients in a large heavy kettle. Add 2 to 3 quarts cold water. Bring to a boil over moderate heat. Reduce heat, then simmer, covered, until peas are very soft. This will take from 2 to 3 hours. Lift ham bone from kettle. Cut off any meat, sliver it and reserve. Discard bone. Push soup and all vegetables through a fine sieve or whirl in blender to make a thick puree. Then stir in tomato paste. You will have in the neighborhood of 3 to 4 quarts. Before serving, bring thick puree to a boil over moderate heat, then add enough milk to dilute it to the right consistency—about 1 cup to a quart. Taste for seasoning. Bring up to a boil again but do not cook further. Serve soup in heated soup plates or bowls with a garnish of slivered ham, minced parsley, and some good, sturdy bread. If you wish, you may add a pinch of thyme just before serving. *Serves 12 to 14.*

CLEAR-THE-FRIDGE SOUP

This is another soup from *The Best of Electric Crock Cooking*. The base for this soup is leftover meat or tomato sauce from spaghetti.

½ to 1 cup meat sauce for spaghetti
2 to 4 chicken necks, wing tips, or backs
1 large onion, peeled and chopped
1 to 2 coarse outer stalks of celery and leaves
½ cup light red kidney beans or other beans
2½ quarts beef bouillon
½ cup leftover rice, spaghetti, or macaroni
3 sprigs parsley, minced, or several parsley
    stems
1 large clove garlic, peeled and minced
Salt and pepper (optional)
⅓ cup grated Parmesan or Swiss cheese,
    or cottage cheese

Combine all ingredients except cheese in a kettle, cover, bring to a boil, reduce heat and cook 4 to 5 hours. Remove chicken bones. Taste, and add salt and pepper if needed. Serve with 1 or 2 tablespoons cheese. *Serves 6 to 8.*

HAM HOCK SOUP, CREOLE STYLE

This makes a meal all by itself. Great on cold winter nights.

2 cups light red kidney beans
1½ pounds smoked ham hocks
2 large onions, peeled and chopped
1 cup chopped celery and leaves
1 large bay leaf
1 teaspoon salt
¼ teaspoon pepper
3 quarts water
¼ cup dry red wine
2 egg yolks, slightly beaten
2 scallions, chopped in rounds
2 lemons, sliced into thin rounds (optional)

In a large kettle, combine beans, ham hocks, onions, celery, bay leaf, salt, and pepper with water; cover, bring to a boil, reduce heat, and simmer for 4 to 5 hours. Remove ham hocks, discard half the skin of the hocks. Place the other half, cut into small pieces, in blender with a little of the cooking liquid and blend 2 or 3 minutes. Strain, and puree beans and vegetables in blender with a little cooking liquid for 1 to 2 minutes. Place pureed hock skin, vegetables, cut-up hock meat, and cooking liquid in a medium casserole, and heat to simmering. Add wine and bring to a boil. Beat a little of the broth into egg yolks, then return to broth, stirring quickly and constantly. Remove from heat without letting broth boil again. Serve, garnished with chopped scallions and thin lemon rounds. *Serves 8 to 10.*

VICHYSSOISE

Served chilled with chives, this is the most elegant of all summer soups. In the basic recipe, 1 cup of heavy cream is added. Make an economy version by floating a single tablespoon of cream on top just before serving.

¼ cup margarine or butter
1 large bunch leeks or 2 bunches scallions,
    trimmed and sliced
2 medium onions, chopped
1 pound potatoes, peeled and cut into ½-inch
    cubes

3 cups chicken bouillon
Salt and white pepper to taste
2½ cups whole milk
¼ cup heavy cream
Chopped chives or scallions for garnish

Heat margarine or butter in a large kettle until foaming subsides. Add leeks or scallions and chopped onions, and sauté until transparent but not browned. Add potato cubes, chicken bouillon, salt, and pepper, and bring mixture to a boil. Reduce heat, cover, and simmer slowly for about 1 hour, or until potatoes are very soft. Remove potatoes from heat and puree in a blender until smooth and creamy. Scald milk. Stir milk into potato puree and mix well. At this point you have an excellent hot potato soup for 4 to 6 people. Garnish with chopped chives and serve at once. Or, if you want real (meaning cold) vichyssoise, chill ungarnished soup overnight. Just before serving, float 1 tablespoon heavy cream, whipped until slightly thickened, on top of soup and garnish with chopped chives. *Serves 4 to 6.*

CREAM OF CELERY SOUP

A light soup to serve for lunch or as a first course.

2 tablespoons margarine or butter
1½ cups chopped celery and celery leaves
1 small onion, thinly sliced
2 cups chicken bouillon
1 tablespoon cornstarch
2 cups milk
Paprika (optional)

Melt margarine or butter in bottom of large saucepan and add celery and onion, frying slowly until onion slices are limp and slightly transparent. Add chicken bouillon and simmer slowly for 15 minutes. Remove from heat and pour through a strainer. Dissolve cornstarch in a few tablespoons of milk. Heat remaining milk in a small pan, just to the boiling point. Stir milk and then the cornstarch mixture into hot soup and return to the heat. Bring to a boil, and cook, stirring constantly, until soup is the

desired thickness (1 to 2 minutes). Serve topped with paprika, if desired. *Serves 4.*

CARROT–POTATO SOUP

2 tablespoons margarine or butter
2 medium onions, thinly sliced
3 medium potatoes, peeled and sliced
6 carrots, scraped and sliced
Water (approximately 2 cups)
Milk (approximately 2 cups)
Salt and pepper to taste

Melt margarine or butter in a large kettle and add onion slices. Sauté onions gently until transparent. Add potatoes, carrots, and enough water to almost cover vegetables. Cover and simmer until carrots and potatoes are tender. Drain vegetables and puree in a blender or food mill. Or push mixture through a large sieve. Put strained vegetables back in the pot and add milk until soup is the thickness you like. Heat to boiling point and add salt and pepper to taste. *Serves 4.*

POTATO SOUP

3 tablespoons vegetable oil
3 leeks, chopped
1 medium onion, chopped
4 large potatoes, peeled and diced
4 cups chicken bouillon
1 teaspoon salt
Pinch pepper
1 cup milk
1 cup plain yogurt
¼ cup chives or scallions, minced

Heat oil in a large saucepan. Gently cook chopped leeks and onion until transparent but not browned. Add potatoes, bouillon, salt, and pepper. Cover and simmer about ½ hour, or until potatoes are tender. Put soup into an electric blender and puree or use a mixer. Return soup to saucepan and add milk. Heat until soup steams but does not boil. Just before serving, stir in yogurt and garnish each serving with chives or scallions. *Serves 6.*

CABBAGE SOUP

This soup can be topped with sour cream or yogurt.

1 large onion, chopped
1 clove garlic, mashed
1½ tablespoons margarine or butter
6 cups beef bouillon
1 small head green cabbage, finely shredded
½ teaspoon salt
½ teaspoon pepper

Sauté onion and garlic in margarine or butter until onion is transparent but not browned. Bring beef bouillon to a boil. Add bouillon and cabbage to onion mixture and season with salt and pepper. Simmer for about 10 minutes, or until cabbage is tender. *Serves 6 to 8.*

CABBAGE BORSCHT

1 pound winter cabbage (small head, cored)
2 large onions, chopped
2 to 3 medium carrots
2 pounds soup beef and bones, 2½ pounds
   if very bony
1 teaspoon salt
⅛ teaspoon pepper
Water to cover
4 to 5 cooked or canned medium beets, grated
¼ medium cucumber, seeded and grated
1 cup sour cream or low-calorie yogurt

Shred cabbage finely as for coleslaw. Chop onions, and grate carrots on coarse side of grater. Put first 6 ingredients in a pot with water to cover and simmer gently for about 2 hours. When meat is tender, add grated beets and cook until soup is thickened. Serve each bowl with a spoonful of grated cucumber and a dollop of sour cream or yogurt. *Serves 6 to 8.*

SCOTCH BROTH

Scotch Broth is the creation of a thrifty race, combining simple and inexpensive local ingredients. It is both comforting and sustaining in the cold Scottish climate. Served for lun-cheon, it is a meal in itself. The addition of salad and fruit will complete a supper menu nicely. Double the recipe, freeze it for another day, and you will have on hand a satisfying and thrifty meal suitable for any occasion calling for a dish of hearty proportions.

½ pound neck of lamb, soaked in cold salted
   water
Water to cover
⅓ cup barley, soaked overnight
1 teaspoon salt
⅛ teaspoon pepper
2 medium onions, chopped
2 carrots, diced
Herb bouquet consisting of parsley stalks,
   a bay leaf, and a sprig of thyme

Soak the neck in cold salted water for 12 hours, changing water once or twice. Place in a large kettle, cover with water. Bring slowly to the boil, skimming often. Add barley, salt, and pepper; cover and simmer 40 minutes. Add onions, carrots, and herb bouquet. Continue to simmer until barley and vegetables are well cooked, approximately 45 minutes more. Remove herbs, lift out pieces of neck, remove bone, and replace meat cut into small pieces. Adjust seasoning and serve very hot. *Serves 4 to 6.*

MINESTRONE MILANESE

3 tablespoons vegetable oil
⅓ cup diced salt pork
1 medium onion, peeled and chopped
2½ quarts beef bouillon
1 large carrot, peeled and diced
⅓ cup diced celery
2 small zucchini, diced
1 cup light red kidney beans
1 cup converted rice
3 sprigs parsley, minced
1 medium clove garlic, minced
¼ teaspoon dried basil
¼ teaspoon dried thyme
⅓ cup grated Parmesan cheese

In a large kettle over medium heat, heat oil and sauté salt pork and onion until onion is transparent. Add beef bouillon with all ingredients except cheese. Cover, bring to a boil, reduce heat and simmer 2 hours. Taste, and add salt if needed. Before serving, add cheese. *Serves 8.*

QUICK CROAKER CHOWDER

2 10½-ounce cans cream of potato soup
3 cups milk
2 tablespoons plus 6 pats margarine or butter
2 teaspoons dehydrated minced onion
1 teaspoon dried thyme
1 small bay leaf
Pepper to taste
1 12-ounce can corn and peppers
3 cups flaked cooked croaker
Paprika to taste

Combine soup, milk, 2 tablespoons margarine or butter, minced onion, thyme, bay leaf, and pepper. Heat well, stirring occasionally. Add corn and fish, and heat well. Remove bay leaf. Serve in large soup dishes with a pat of margarine or butter in each and a sprinkling of paprika. *Serves 6.*

QUICK CURRIED SOUP

1 10-ounce can condensed tomato soup
1 10-ounce can condensed pea soup
2 cans milk
1 teaspoon curry powder
⅓ cup dry sherry

Put soups into a large double boiler. Using a can as measure, add milk. Add curry powder and beat with a rotary beater until smooth. Heat over hot water and just before serving, add sherry. *Serves 6 to 8.*

CHEESE SOUP

This soup is even more delicate and delicious served cold.

¼ cup chopped onions
1 stalk celery, chopped
1 small carrot, peeled and chopped
2 cups chicken bouillon
2 tablespoons margarine or butter
2 tablespoons all-purpose flour
2 cups milk
1½ cups grated Swiss or Cheddar cheese
Salt and pepper to taste

Cook vegetables in chicken bouillon until tender (about 15 minutes). Melt margarine or butter. Blend in flour until smooth. Add milk. Strain chicken bouillon and add it. Bring to the boil slowly, stirring constantly. Add grated cheese. Cook and stir until cheese has melted. Season to taste with salt and pepper. *Serves 4.*

Omelets, Soufflés, and Egg Dishes

Eggs

The generally high price of eggs should do much to alter the American conviction that eggs are extras to be served at the breakfast table. In other countries they are treated with the respect given to meat or fish, and are served frequently for lunch and supper. No single item of food offers wider scope for the creative artistry of a cook than eggs. There are literally hundreds of delectable and elegant egg dishes that can be successfully included in your menu to help control the devastation brought to your food budget by escalating meat prices.

While eggs of all sizes are a good value, you can save even more with a little calculation. Extra-large eggs are a better value than large when they sell at a price up to one-eighth more. Medium eggs are your buy when they are tagged one-eighth less than large. When small are one-fourth cheaper than large, they are the bargain.

The ounce count clarifies the figures another way. Three ounces is the difference between each size. If the cost per ounce information is available on the price label, it is simple arithmetic to determine the cost advantage.

ONE DOZEN EGGS

Size	Ounces
Jumbo	30
Extra-large	27
Large	24
Medium	21
Small	18

The egg recipes which follow are not mere breakfast dishes, though they make quite a hit when served for that first meal of the day. They also are sturdy and filling main courses for lunch or dinner.

EGG AND PARSLEY RING WITH SPANISH SAUCE

A memorable company lunch or supper —served with rice and a tossed green salad.

5 eggs
¼ cup grated Parmesan cheese
3 tablespoons finely chopped parsley
½ teaspoon salt
⅛ teaspoon pepper
3 cups milk
3 tablespoons margarine or butter
1½ tablespoons all-purpose flour
2 tablespoons tomato paste
⅓ cup milk
2 tablespoons sour cream
¼ cup sherry (optional)
Salt, pepper, and nutmeg to taste
Hot cooked rice (optional)

Beat eggs until foamy. Stir in cheese, parsley, salt, and pepper. Add milk and beat until thoroughly blended. Pour into a well-greased 1½-quart ring mold. Bake in a pan of hot water in 325° oven until set (about 50 to 60 minutes). To make sauce, heat margarine or butter and stir in flour until smooth. Add tomato paste, milk, and sour cream. Cook and stir until thick and smooth; *do not boil*. Blend in sherry and seasonings. Unmold egg ring on a heated serving dish. Serve sauce separately. *Serves 4.*

EGGS GRIMES COVE

Nice with toast or plain buttered rice.

10 hard-boiled eggs
½ cup mayonnaise
1 tablespoon dry mustard
1 teaspoon Worcestershire sauce
¼ teaspoon salt
Dash freshly ground pepper
2 tablespoons sweet pickle relish
2 10-ounce cans condensed tomato soup,
    undiluted
½ pound (about 2 cups) sharp
    Cheddar cheese, grated

Cut eggs in half and remove yolks. Mix yolks with mayonnaise, mustard, Worcestershire sauce, salt, pepper, and relish. Fill egg whites with yolk mixture and place in a baking dish. Meanwhile, put soup and cheese in the top of a double boiler and heat until cheese is melted

and mixture is hot. Pour over eggs and bake in 300° oven about 20 minutes. *Serves 5.*

EGG, HAM, AND POTATO CASSEROLE

A four-protein dish—eggs, ham, cheese, and milk—choose a green vegetable to complete the main course.

2 tablespoons finely chopped onion
2 tablespoons margarine or butter
2 tablespoons all-purpose flour
1 cup milk
½ teaspoon salt
⅛ teaspoon pepper
2 tablespoons parsley, minced
2 tablespoons diced pimiento
2 cups sliced cooked potatoes
1 cup finely chopped cooked ham
1½ cups shredded Cheddar cheese
4 hard-boiled eggs, sliced
½ cup soft bread crumbs

Sauté onion in margarine or butter for 3 minutes until transparent. Blend in flour; gradually add milk, stirring until medium thick. Season with salt and pepper. Stir in parsley and pimiento. Place a layer each of potatoes, ham, 1 cup cheese, and eggs. Pour cream sauce over. Sprinkle with bread crumbs and remaining ½ cup cheese. Bake in 375° oven for about 15 minutes, or until golden brown and bubbling. *Serves 4.*

HAM QUICHE

An elegant luncheon dish, or a great first course for a party meal.

4 ounces cooked ham
1 tablespoon margarine or butter plus extra
    cold butter
1 8-inch partially cooked pastry shell
4 eggs
2 cups light cream
½ teaspoon salt
Pinch pepper
Pinch nutmeg

Preheat oven to 375°. Cut ham into small cubes and sauté for about 1 minute in margarine or butter. Press the pieces into the soft bottom of pastry shell. Beat together eggs, cream, and seasonings. Pour into shell and dot the top with cold butter. Set in the upper third of oven and bake 30 minutes, or until the top is puffy and brown. It will deflate somewhat after it comes from the oven, so serve as quickly as possible. *Serves 6.*

DEVILED EGGS RISOTTO

This recipe is one of 20 imaginative and delectable rice recipes called "Serve Rice 'n Save" which can be obtained free of charge from the Rice Council, P.O. Box 22802, Houston, Texas 77027. It sounds as though it might have been written for *Budget Recipes*, which it wasn't, but it was certainly written for anyone who wants to reduce his or her food budget and still serve tasty food.

6 hard-boiled eggs
2 tablespoons mayonnaise
1 teaspoon Worcestershire sauce
1 teaspoon onion salt
⅛ teaspoon pepper
3 cups hot cooked rice
Butter
1 teaspoon prepared mustard
2½ cups hot Béchamel Sauce
1 cup grated Swiss cheese
Paprika

Cut eggs in half lengthwise. Remove yolks and blend with mayonnaise, Worcestershire sauce, onion salt, and pepper. Stuff egg whites with this mixture. Turn rice into buttered shallow casserole or 6 individual casseroles. Arrange eggs on rice (2 halves in each individual dish). Stir mustard into Béchamel Sauce and spoon over eggs. Sprinkle with cheese and dust with paprika. Bake in 350° oven 10 to 15 minutes. *Serves 6.*

DEVILED EGGS IN TOMATO ASPIC

A pretty party dish that takes a little time but makes a nice showing.

4 cups stewed tomatoes
1 medium onion, chopped
¼ cup chopped celery leaves
1 small piece bay leaf
2 cloves
3 teaspoons salt
2 tablespoons brown sugar
3 tablespoons lemon juice
2 envelopes unflavored gelatin
¼ cup cold water
8 hard-boiled eggs
¼ teaspoon dry mustard
¼ teaspoon pepper
2 tablespoons margarine or butter,
*   softened*
¼ cup chopped green olives
2 pimientos, chopped
2 tablespoons minced onion
1 cooked carrot, thinly sliced
2 tablespoons parsley, minced
Lettuce or watercress for garnish
*   (optional)*
Mayonnaise

Simmer tomatoes with onion, celery leaves, bay leaf, cloves, 2 teaspoons salt, and brown sugar for 40 minutes. Put through a fine sieve. Add lemon juice. Soften gelatin in cold water about 5 minutes. Add to tomato mixture and stir until dissolved. Chill until thick but not set. Cut eggs in half lengthwise. Remove yolks carefully. Mash yolks and season with 1 teaspoon salt, mustard, and pepper. Add margarine or butter, olives, pimientos, and minced onion. Mix well. Fill egg whites and fit halves together. Rinse a mold in cold water. Arrange carrot slices in a pretty pattern on the bottom and sprinkle with parsley. Carefully spoon in 1 cup of thickened tomato mixture. Place eggs in this and cover with remaining tomato mixture. Chill until firm. Unmold and garnish platter with lettuce or watercress. Offer mayonnaise on the side. *Serves 8.*

EGGS HONGROIS

The treasure of a Hungarian cook's imagination —spicy, pink, and interesting; serve with spinach salad for delightful texture balance.

¼ cup chopped onion
3 tablespoons margarine or butter
2 tablespoons paprika
4 tablespoons all-purpose flour
1½ cups milk
½ cup chicken bouillon
Salt and pepper to taste
½ cup sour or heavy cream
6 hard-boiled eggs, quartered
Rice or buttered toast for 4
4 sautéed mushroom caps (optional)

Sauté onion in margarine or butter until lightly browned. Stir in paprika and flour until blended. Gradually add milk and chicken bouillon, stirring until smooth and thickened. Season to taste with salt and pepper. Blend in sour cream and cook over low heat until heated through; do not boil. Arrange egg quarters over rice or buttered toast. Pour hot sauce over; garnish with mushroom caps. Serve at once. *Serves 4.*

Soufflés

A soufflé, served with salad and a dessert, makes a delicious and surprisingly filling dinner. Don't be afraid to try one. True, they fall with great frequency, but if you follow the directions below carefully, yours shouldn't fall until everyone at the table has had a chance to admire this beautiful and tasty confection of airy bubbles and eggs.

First, an overview of the procedure. You begin by making a soufflé base sauce. This can be prepared ahead and incorporated into the egg white mixture that makes it rise at the last moment. Just before cooking, heat the oven and grease a soufflé mold. Then beat the egg whites until they are stiff but still shiny and velvety looking. Mix this concoction with the soufflé base sauce. Flattening the whites as little as possible, pour the mix into the soufflé mold, and bake.

General Notes for Soufflés

To make a collar for a soufflé, fold foil into 4 thicknesses 3 inches wide and long enough to go around the soufflé dish with generous overlap. Attach to the dish with sealing tape, leaving 1 inch of the foil around the dish to make a collar 2 inches high.

With average soufflé dishes, a soufflé volume of 3 or 4 cups in excess of the volume of the dish will make the soufflé above the rim of the dish. If desired, use larger soufflé dishes than specified in recipes and omit the collar.

Soufflé mixtures may be turned into molds, serving bowls, or individual serving dishes, as long as they are oven-proof. Reduce cooking times for individually baked soufflés by about 5 to 8 minutes. Half of a soufflé recipe may be used as filling for a 9-inch pastry or crumb shell. Butter soufflé dishes and collars before using.

BASIC CHEESE SOUFFLÉ

Here's a basic soufflé recipe you can adapt by replacing the cheese with cooked vegetables or fruits.

BASE SAUCE

3½ tablespoons butter
4½ tablespoons all-purpose flour
1½ cups hot milk
6 large egg yolks
½ teaspoon salt
⅛ teaspoon pepper
⅛ teaspoon nutmeg

In a medium saucepan over moderate to low heat, melt butter and blend flour into it with a fork or a whisk. The blending process should take about 2 minutes. Take saucepan from heat and allow it to cool a moment. Then blend in hot milk, salt, pepper, and nutmeg all at once, beating quickly to keep sauce smooth. Stirring constantly, return to heat and simmer about 1 minute. The sauce should be very thick. Remove from heat and beat in egg yolks one at a time. If you make this portion of the soufflé ahead, spear a little butter on a fork and spread over the top of the sauce before it cools to keep a skin from forming. Reheat the sauce gently before continuing with the rest of the recipe.

EGG WHITES AND FLAVORING

8 egg whites
½ teaspoon cream of tartar
⅛ teaspoon salt
1 cup firmly packed, coarse-grated dry cheese
   of the type called Gruyère, or other
   flavoring ingredient

Preheat oven to 400°. Egg whites beat up best at room temperature. If yours are chilled, warm to room temperature by setting in warm water. Beat eggs until foaming, then continue to beat as you add cream of tartar and salt. Beat until eggs form shiny peaks. Don't beat so much they become dry-looking. Very gently stir ¼ of the Base Sauce into egg whites with a rubber spatula. Add remaining sauce a little at a time, adding a portion of grated cheese each time. Keep egg whites as airy as possible. Don't beat, mash, or overmix. The folding operation should be accomplished as quickly as possible. Turn mixture into a greased soufflé dish. Set mold over a burner on stovetop at high heat for a few seconds (less than ½ minute) before placing it on lowest rack in oven. Turn heat down to 375° as soon as souffle is in, and do not open oven door for 35 minutes. It will be done in 35 to 45 minutes. Test for doneness by inserting a straw—if it comes out clean, or almost clean, the soufflé is ready. Remove the collar, if you have used one, and serve within the next 3 to 5 minutes. *Serves 4 to 6.*

BROCCOLI SOUFFLÉ

Substitute broccoli, cooked and minced fine, for cheese in the basic recipe.

CHICKEN SOUFFLÉ

Substitute cooked chicken, beaten to a pulp in the blender and pressed through a coarse sieve, for cheese in the basic recipe.

SPINACH SOUFFLÉ

Substitute spinach, cooked and minced fine, for cheese in the basic recipe.

SHRIMP SOUFFLÉ

Substitute cooked shrimp, beaten to a pulp in the blender and pressed through a coarse sieve, for cheese in the basic recipe.

YAM SOUFFLÉ

Substitute a cooked buttered yam, pressed through a sieve, for the cheese in the basic recipe.

The Pluperfect Omelet

Omelets are festive, fast, and inexpensive. Once you learn how, classic French omelets are easy, too. With this dish, you can serve your dinner guests an elegant example of Continental cuisine, made to their order. For your family, omelets make a simple budget meal.

A perfect French omelet for one can be made in 1 minute or less. Excess heat ruins eggs, and extended cooking makes them dry and tasteless. First, an overview of the omelet. Since it all happens so fast, it's a good idea to get a mental picture of the entire process before getting down to specifics.

The first step is to heat margarine or butter to a very high temperature, almost to the point of smoking. You might have to burn a few tablespoons of butter before you learn to recognize this stage. Eggs are added to the hot margarine or butter. They cook for a few seconds until partially set into a pancake. Filling is added, the pancake is rolled up and served. Total time: 30 seconds to 1 minute.

What do you need to cook omelets? Almost any flat-bottomed pan with sloping sides can be used. Best is a No. 24 cast-iron omelet pan, but this isn't mandatory. Teflon-coated aluminum pans with sloping sides do very well. The diameter of the pan should be 6 to 8 inches for one- or two-egg omelets. (It's easier to make two omelets of two eggs each than to make a four-egg omelet.) If you use a cast-iron pan for omelets, you should never use it for anything else. When you first buy a cast-iron omelet pan, it should be seasoned by heating with oil.

Allow it to cool and clean it by wiping with a paper towel. Omelet pans should never be washed, but merely wiped clean. Spots that stick can be scoured with salt.

There are several different types of omelets. Three basic entrée omelets are described here.

FOLDED OMELET (using a fork)

Break 1 or 2 eggs into a mixing bowl, add ½ teaspoon salt and pepper if desired. Beat eggs with a fork for about 15 seconds, or until blended but not full of air. Heat about 1 teaspoon margarine or butter (other oils can be used, but butter tastes best—not too much is required) and heat on a high flame until butter stops bubbling and is just about to burn. Quickly add eggs and tip pan to spread eggs over entire bottom of pan. As omelet cooks, pull cooked part back from edges with your fork, letting uncooked egg run into pan. The egg should be formed into a wrinkled pancake with just a thin film of uncooked egg on top. So far the cooking has taken about 20 seconds. At this point, filling would be added if desired. After filling, omelet is folded by tipping pan forward, lifting one edge of omelet with a fork, and folding it over onto rest of omelet. You now have a semi-circle.

ROLLED OMELET

This kind of omelet, the one that everyone likes to watch the French chefs do, sounds like it's much harder to make than the folded omelet. But with a little practice it's really easier. This method depends on the fact that, once the eggs have cooked to the "pancake" stage, they should be moved around in the pan without a fork, and finally, with vigorous arm movements, rolled up. The rolling is accomplished by pulling the pan out from under the omelet—something like pulling off the tablecloth without breaking the dishes.

Here's how it's done. Heat butter as in folded-omelet method and add eggs. When eggs start to set, jerk pan toward you so that set portion of eggs moves over and lets uncooked part run into pan. This requires a strong, abrupt arm motion. Think of the tablecloth.

When eggs are almost completely set, as described above, add filling, and roll. You use the same kind of strong, jerking motions here, to push omelet toward lip of pan. Keep jerking and front edge of omelet should fold back over the rest. In other words, omelet will roll itself up. It sounds difficult, but it really isn't once you try it a few times. You can always bring a fork into play if you see that the rolling method isn't working. Of course, you should practice alone before you invite guests. You can always eat the omelet yourself and enjoy it, even if it isn't perfectly rolled.

FILLED OMELETS

Fillings can be added to omelets either by mixing them into the eggs when they're being beaten, or by adding fillings just before you roll or fold the omelet. Here's a partial list to give you ideas. All recipes are for two-egg omelets. If a large amount of filling is added, it should be preheated, if it is not mixed into the beaten eggs.

BACON OMELET

Add 2 tablespoons of crisp-cooked bacon bits to egg mixture.

CHEESE OMELET

Cheese can only be added just before rolling—never in egg mixture. Almost any cheese can be used, but best for a classic French omelet is 2 tablespoons freshly grated Parmesan cheese and 1 tablespoon grated Swiss cheese.

SPINACH OR COLLARD GREEN OMELET

Add 3 tablespoons cooked, chopped spinach or collard greens to eggs before beating. Collard greens, although not well known as an omelet filling, are especially tasty.

HAM OMELET

Sliced ham cut into small pieces can be added either to egg mixture or, better, just before rolling omelet.

OMELET LECSO

Pronounced let-cho, this is a Hungarian tomato, pepper, and onion mixture. (The characteristic flavor of Lecso comes from Hungarian smoked bacon. Although this is unavailable in the United States, bacon grease or bacon grease mixed with oil will substitute.)

1 onion, coarsely chopped
1 green pepper, coarsely chopped
2 tablespoons bacon grease
½ 16-ounce can cooked tomatoes, drained
3 tablespoons paprika

Cook chopped onion and green pepper in grease. Cook over low heat, covered, until pepper is soft (about 30 minutes). Add tomatoes and paprika and cook another 5 minutes. Add 2 tablespoons of the cooked mixture to each omelet just before rolling. When omelet is done, put it on a plate and pour some more Lecso over it.

OMELET NULLJAILS

Nobody knows where this name comes from, but it's a very tasty omelet. Before rolling the omelet, add a mixture of:

1 tablespoon chopped cooked bacon
2 tablespoons marinated artichoke hearts, well drained and chopped into small pieces
1 tablespoon chopped fresh parsley
1 teaspoon chopped chives or scallions

CHICKEN LIVER OMELET

Cooked chicken livers chopped in small pieces can be added before rolling and also on top of the cooked omelet. Livers should be sautéed in margarine or butter over high heat. Don't overcook the livers. They should be pink inside when you chop them.

MUSHROOM OMELET

Three tablespoons of cooked mushrooms are added to omelet just before rolling. More cooked mushrooms can be poured over top of omelet when you serve it. The best way to cook mushrooms for omelets is in a little butter over very high heat. Slice small mushrooms and chop large ones. Sauté, stirring constantly, until tender. One way to recognize that the mushrooms are done is that they begin to "sweat" oil. It takes 5 to 8 minutes. Salt very lightly as they finish cooking.

ONION OMELET

Take 1 small onion, cut it into rings, and cook slowly with 1 tablespoon margarine or butter until soft and transparent, but not browned. Reserve half the rings and chop the other half. Add chopped onion to an omelet before rolling and put remaining rings on top of finished omelet.

SPINACH FRITTATA

This glorified Italian near-omelet may include almost any cooked vegetables or meat leftovers. Good with hot garlic bread.

1 10-ounce package frozen chopped spinach, or other vegetable or meat
2 tablespoons vegetable oil
1 tablespoon margarine or butter
1 medium onion, finely chopped
1 2-ounce can mushroom pieces, drained (optional)
6 eggs
¼ cup grated cheese
½ teaspoon dried basil
Salt, pepper, and nutmeg to taste

Thaw spinach, then drain thoroughly. In a large skillet, heat oil and margarine or butter;

sauté onion and mushrooms until onion is tender. Stir in spinach. Beat eggs until foamy; blend in cheese and seasonings. Pour egg mixture over mushroom and spinach mixture in skillet; stir to blend. Cook over low heat until underside is light brown. Turn out on a plate. Add more margarine or butter if necessary. Slide omelet, browned side up, back into pan; brown the second side. Serve at once. *Serves 6.*

EGGS MARVIN GARDENS

¼ *medium onion, chopped*
1 *tablespoon vegetable oil*
1 *medium-size boiled potato, cut in ¼-inch*
  slices
¼ *firm ripe avocado, cut in ¼-inch slices*
¼ *cup leftover roast chicken*
Salt and pepper to taste
¼ *teaspoon cumin*
Dash Tabasco sauce
2 *tablespoons grated cheese, preferably*
  Cheddar
2 *eggs, lightly beaten*
1 *tablespoon bacon fat*

Sauté onion in oil until transparent, but not browned. Add potato and avocado slices and cook over medium heat until they start to brown. Add chicken and fry until hot. Beat salt, pepper, cumin, Tabasco, and grated cheese into eggs, and add to mixture in pan along with 1 tablespoon bacon fat. Reduce heat and scramble eggs slowly until creamy. *Serves 1 or 2.*

PIPÉRADE

Scrambled eggs French style, a quick, complete supper with hot toasted rolls.

2 *green or red peppers, thinly sliced*
1 *medium onion, thinly sliced*
3 *tablespoons vegetable oil*
2 *medium tomatoes, peeled and chopped*
1 *small clove garlic, crushed*
1 *teaspoon salt*
¼ *teaspoon each pepper and dried thyme*
8 *eggs, beaten*

8 *thin slices ham or bologna*
2 *tablespoons margarine or butter*

Sauté peppers and onion in oil for about 5 minutes, until onion is soft but not brown. Add tomatoes, garlic, salt, pepper, and thyme; simmer, stirring frequently, for about 15 minutes until mixture reaches puree stage. Add beaten eggs; stir until eggs are just set but still moist. Sauté ham slices briefly in margarine or butter. Arrange 2 ham slices on each of 4 plates. Spoon the pipérade over. Serve very hot. *Serves 4.*

EGGS EN COCOTTE WITH TUNA

A 15-minute winner—adaptable for breakfast, lunch, or supper.

2 *tablespoons chopped onion*
1 *tablespoon margarine or butter*
½ *cup light cream or evaporated milk*
1 *teaspoon chopped parsley*
½ *teaspoon grated lemon rind*
Salt and pepper to taste
1 *7-ounce can tuna, drained and flaked*
4 *eggs*
Grated Swiss or Parmesan cheese

Sauté onion in margarine or butter for 5 minutes. Add cream, parsley, lemon rind, salt, and pepper. Heat through but do not boil. Thoroughly blend in tuna. Line bottom and sides of 4 greased ramekins with mixture, leaving a hollow in center of each. Slip an egg in each hollow. Sprinkle with grated cheese. Bake in 450° oven 10 minutes, until eggs are just set, being careful not to overcook. Put under broiler, if necessary, to melt cheese. *Serves 4.*

EGGS PARMENTIER

These egg-crowned potatoes are man-pleasers. A good accompaniment is canned whole tomatoes heated with basil.

2 *large potatoes, baked*
3 *tablespoons plus 1 teaspoon melted*
  margarine or butter

2 tablespoons milk
½ teaspoon salt
⅛ teaspoon pepper
2 strips bacon, fried crisp and crumbled
4 eggs
Grated cheese
Paprika
Sour cream (optional)

When potatoes are cool enough to handle, cut evenly in half, lengthwise. Scoop out insides, being careful not to break skins. Mash potato pulp with 2 tablespoons melted margarine or butter, milk, salt, and pepper until fluffy and smooth. Pile back into potato shells, building sides high with a well in center of each. Pour 1 teaspoon melted margarine or butter and sprinkle ¼ of the bacon into each center; then slip an egg into each. Sprinkle eggs with grated cheese and paprika. Bake in 425° oven 15 minutes, until potatoes are lightly browned and eggs are set. Serve with sour cream, if desired. *Serves 4.*

Cheese Dishes, Sandwiches, and Snacks

The popularity of cheese has zoomed in the past decade, and the general public has expanded its cheese-eating habits to a remarkable degree. One reason for this is that cheese has the same high-quality protein as that in meat, fish, and eggs. In addition, the price of cheese has not risen as drastically as that of meat and fish.

Another reason for the growing interest in cheese is that the variety available has expanded greatly. Cheese shops and departments have proliferated, and customers are offered tastes of cheese for their approval and, hopefully, purchase.

The Two Types of Cheese

There are two main categories of cheese—natural and processed. Natural cheese is made by coagulating milk and then separating the curd (the solid part) from the whey (watery part). Some natural cheeses are ripened (aged) to develop their natural flavor and texture. Others are used unripened. Processed cheeses are a blend of fresh and aged natural cheeses which have been melted, pasteurized, and mixed with an emulsifier. Natural cheeses are preferable, though the making of processed cheese has improved in recent years. Each natural cheese has its own distinctive flavor, while all processed cheeses taste much alike, except for the fruits, vegetables, nuts, meats, or spices which are sometimes added to them.

The kinds of cheese people like and are inclined to serve are basically a matter of personal taste. But there are good reasons why some cheeses are especially appropriate with wine or cocktails before dinner and why others seem made for winding up a meal—often in place of dessert. Try as many cheeses which are new to you as you possibly can—and make your own decision as to when to serve them.

The Soft Cheeses—Dessert Cheeses

The soft cheeses, such as Brie, Camembert, Crema Daníca from Denmark, and Belle Étoile, a favorite triple cream French cheese, are usually regarded as dessert cheeses. But lots of people serve them with crackers at cocktail time—and why not? One soft cheese appropriate only with drinks before dinner is Liederkranz because its flavor is too strong for dessert. Bel paese is marvelous with pears—or almost any fruit. Petit suisse is good with strawberries. Any of the semi-soft cheeses do well with fruit for dessert—or, with the addition of some hard sausage and wine, for an alfresco luncheon.

Cheeses for Grating

Grating cheeses like Parmesan, Asiago, Cheddar, and Swiss (Emmenthaler) are handy to have in the refrigerator. Grate your own. It's so easy with a little Mouli grater, and the resulting product is head and shoulder in flavor over the grated variety which comes in cardboard tubes.

Storing Cheese

Cheese should be stored in the refrigerator. Those like cottage and cream cheese are exceedingly perishable and should be eaten up quickly. Cheddar, Swiss, Parmesan, and the like keep much longer if they are protected from drying out. Leave cheese in its original wrapper, if possible. Cover cut surfaces tightly with foil or plastic wrap or store in a tightly covered container. If surface mold develops on hard natural cheese, it can be scraped off completely before the cheese is used and it will be quite all right. By and large, freezing of cheese is not recommended.

When you are going to serve cheese, remove it from the refrigerator and let it come to room temperature for at least 1 hour. Cheeses like Camembert and Brie should stand out for 2 to 3 hours so that they can be served soft and runny.

The Cheese Board

A cheese board is important to serve with wine or other drinks and for middle-of-the-night food, too. A big cutting board does very well for this. Depending upon the number of people you wish to serve, offer a choice of from two to four different kinds of cheese and be sure that their flavor and texture is varied. For example: a fine Vermont (or other) Cheddar and a Belle Étoile; Rumanian Kashkaval, Liederkranz, Swiss, and Edam; Camembert, Monterey Jack, and domestic blue; Muenster, Canadian smoked cheese, and Brie. Serve sweet butter and crackers or crusty French bread with these if you want to be very in the know.

WELSH RAREBIT

1 pound sharp Cheddar
1 tablespoon margarine or butter
1 cup light beer
1 egg, slightly beaten
1 teaspoon Worcestershire sauce
1 teaspoon salt
¼ teaspoon prepared mustard
6 to 8 pieces hot toast

Grate cheese. In the top of a double boiler over simmering water, melt margarine or butter and stir in beer. When beer has warmed, begin to add cheese, stirring constantly as cheese melts. Add egg and seasonings, still stirring. Don't let rarebit boil after adding egg. Remove from heat and serve at once over hot toast points. *Serves 6 to 8.*

CHEESE FONDUE

This is a variation on the popular Swiss cheese fondue served bubbling over a wick lamp or a Sterno container and eaten with stale or semi-stale stick or chunks of French bread. For dieters you can offer celery sticks or zucchini instead of bread sticks.

1 pound Emmenthaler or ½ pound
   Emmenthaler and ½ pound Gruyère
   cheese
1 clove garlic
2 cups dry white wine
3 tablespoons Kirsch
1 teaspoon cornstarch
20 to 24 chunks stale bread

Grate cheese or cheeses, and cut garlic clove

in half. Rub a heavy small saucepan with the cut halves of garlic. Pour into the saucepan the dry white wine and heat over a medium flame. Mix Kirsch with cornstarch. Stirring the wine constantly, and keeping it at close to simmer but not boiling, begin adding grated cheese a little at a time. During the entire process, wine must not actually boil. When cheese is beginning to thicken in the bottom of saucepan, pour in Kirsch and cornstarch mixture. Continue to cook until fondue begins to thicken, then pour it into serving dish and set dish over a low flame to keep it warm. Serve with stale bread sticks for dipping. *Serves 4.*

AMERICAN CHEESE PUDDING

1½ cups milk
2 cups soft bread crumbs
1½ cups grated Cheddar cheese
1 teaspoon salt
Dash cayenne pepper
2 tablespoons melted margarine or butter
3 egg yolks, well beaten
3 egg whites, beaten stiff

Pour milk over bread crumbs and let stand at least 30 minutes. Add cheese, seasoning, margarine or butter, and egg yolks and mix well. Fold in egg whites. Turn into buttered baking dish and bake in 350° oven until puffed and brown (about 45 minutes). *Serves 4 to 6.*

CHICKEN CHEESE MELTS

1 4¾-ounce can chicken spread
2 tablespoons mayonnaise
⅔ cup grated Cheddar cheese
1 tablespoon pickle relish
1 teaspoon minced onion
4 teaspoons chopped green pepper
2 tablespoons chopped stuffed olives
4 hamburger rolls, split

Combine all ingredients except rolls. Spread on bottom halves of rolls. Cover with top halves. Wrap in foil and bake in 375° oven 10 minutes. *Serves 4.*

MACARONI AND CHEESE FROM SCRATCH

This is an excellent way to use up hardened cheese leftovers. It is best made with Cheddar, mild or sharp.

2 cups cooked macaroni
½ cup milk or cream
¾ cup grated cheese

Place cooked, hot macaroni in a large saucepan, over medium heat, and stir in milk or cream. Sprinkle grated cheese over macaroni a little at a time, stirring constantly. When all the cheese has melted, serve at once. *Serves 6.*

Sandwiches

Sandwich time is all-year-round, but probably in summer most of us consume more sandwiches than at any other time because it's picnic season. Whether you take sandwiches on picnics, as a lunch to eat in the office or at school, or offer them to guests and/or family at home, stress variety in your planning. Sandwiches can be nutritious and delicious. Use as many different kinds of bread as you can find (and there are many), and use rolls or buns occasionally for a change of pace. You can make sandwiches of almost any leftover meat, including meat loaf.

If your family uses a great many sandwiches, you should plan sandwich-making sessions once a week and freeze the result of your labor. Most sandwiches freeze well. Use only a small amount of mayonnaise and avoid raw vegetables like tomatoes or lettuce; these wilt when frozen. To make sandwiches, day-old bread is actually better than very fresh. Good freezing sandwiches include meat salad, egg salad (yolks only), tuna, salmon, ham or ham salad, cheese, roast beef, chicken or turkey, deviled ham, olive, pickle, peanut butter, and hamburger.

If you like butter on your sandwiches, spread each slice of bread with a thin layer to keep the bread from getting soggy. Or try a bit of cream cheese. Wrap the sandwiches tightly and freeze. To thaw, leave them in the wrapping at room temperature for 3 to 4 hours.

The wrapping of sandwiches, especially if you're going to freeze them, is most important. They must be tightly sealed either in the convenient Pliofilm sandwich bags, which are so readily available, or in properly folded plastic wrap, foil, or waxed paper. The "drugstore" wrap is the best for the last three, but the sandwich bags are unquestionably the simplest and the least trouble to use.

CROQUE MADAME

To make a Croque Monsieur, substitute slices of ham for the slices of chicken used below.

12 slices white bread
12 slices Swiss cheese
6 slices cooked breast of chicken
1 stick soft margarine or butter

On each of 6 slices of bread place a slice of cheese, a slice of chicken, and another slice of cheese. Spread top of sandwiches generously with margarine or butter. Melt about 8 tablespoons butter in a large skillet or skillets. Put in sandwiches, unspread side down. Sauté over low heat until golden. Turn and sauté second side until golden. *Serves 6.*

THE SEBASTIAN

12 slices enriched rye bread
1 stick margarine or butter
⅔ cup mayonnaise
⅓ cup chopped chutney
1 tablespoon curry powder
1 teaspoon salt
3 cups shredded cabbage
1 pound baked ham, very thinly sliced
6 slices Cheddar cheese

Butter both sides of bread. Combine mayonnaise, chutney, curry, salt, and cabbage. On each of 6 slices of bread place equal amounts of sliced ham, about ½ cup cabbage mixture, and 1 slice cheese. Top with remaining bread slices. Grill both sides of bread in remaining

margarine or butter until golden brown. Use 1 or more hot skillets. *Serves 6.*

FRENCH TOASTED DEVILED HAM AND CHEESE

8 thin slices white bread
2 tablespoons prepared mustard
1 4½-ounce can deviled ham
4 slices Cheddar cheese
2 eggs, slightly beaten
½ cup milk
Salt and pepper to taste
Margarine or butter

Spread each of 4 slices of bread with mustard, then with deviled ham. Top with slices of cheese, then with remaining bread slices. Press firmly together. Combine eggs, milk, and seasonings in a shallow dish. Dip each sandwich in mixture to coat both sides. Sauté in margarine or butter until well browned on both sides. *Serves 4.*

DEVILED HAM AND CHUTNEY SANDWICHES

This mixture is also very good on rye or whole wheat bread.

2 4½-ounce cans deviled ham
2 tablespoons Major Grey's chutney, minced
12 slices white bread
Mayonnaise

Mix deviled ham with chutney. Spread on 6 slices of bread. Spread remaining slices with mayonnaise. Press together, cut in half and serve. *Serves 6.*

HAM AND CHEESE ON RYE

This is one of the most popular sandwiches in America. The secret to success is the mustard.

8 slices rye bread
Soft margarine or butter
4 slices boiled ham
4 slices Swiss cheese
Prepared mustard (optional)

Spread 4 slices of bread with margarine or butter. Place a slice of ham and a slice of cheese on each. If desired, add mustard to taste. Top with remaining bread slices. *Serves 4.*

CORNED BEEF ROLLS

6 bulky rolls or other hard rolls
2 4½-ounce cans corned beef spread
6 green pepper rings
⅔ cup chopped Spanish onion
4 teaspoons vegetable oil
1 teaspoon vinegar
¼ teaspoon pepper

Split rolls horizontally and hollow out tops. Spread corned beef on bottom halves of rolls. Top with pepper rings. Combine remaining ingredients. Place seasoned chopped onion on top of pepper rings. Close rolls. *Serves 6.*

TONGUE SANDWICHES

1½ cups ground cold cooked tongue
4½ teaspoons chopped pickles
4½ teaspoons chopped chives
1 hard-boiled egg, peeled and chopped
1½ teaspoons prepared mustard
Soft margarine or butter
12 slices rye bread

Mix all ingredients except bread. Spread on 6 slices of bread. Cover with remaining slices. Cut in half. *Serves 6.*

APPLE AND HAM SANDWICHES

12 slices white bread
Soft margarine or butter
12 thin slices boiled ham
24 thin slices red apple (unpeeled)
3 tablespoons lemon juice, strained

Spread bread with margarine or butter. On each of 6 slices place 2 slices ham, then 4 slices apple. Toss apple with lemon juice to preserve color. Top with remaining bread. Cut in half. *Serves 6.*

CURRIED CHICKEN SANDWICHES

1 4¾-ounce can chicken spread
1 teaspoon curry powder
2 tablespoons mayonnaise
Dash red pepper flakes (optional)
1 tablespoon juice from chutney jar
8 slices white bread

Mix all ingredients except bread. Spread on 4 slices of bread. Top with remaining slices. Cut in half. *Serves 4.*

OPEN-FACE DIETERS' SANDWICHES

4 slices white toast
Soft margarine or butter
1 cup watercress or lettuce leaves
4 slices cooked chicken
½ cup plain yogurt
2 tablespoons finely chopped green pepper
½ teaspoon curry powder
¼ teaspoon instant minced onion, dehydrated

Spread toast lightly with margarine or butter. Arrange watercress or lettuce on toast. Top with chicken slices. Combine yogurt, green pepper, curry powder, and onion. Top each sandwich with a dollop of yogurt mixture. Cut in half. *Serves 4.*

HERO SANDWICHES

You can get quite a round of applause for this if you have a little meat sauce to spread on the bread instead of butter.

4 loaves brown-and-serve French bread
Soft margarine or butter
8 slices Swiss cheese
8 slices Italian-style salami

Bake bread according to package directions. When done, cool slightly and split in half lengthwise. Spread generously with margarine or butter. Place 2 slices cheese and 2 slices salami on the bottom of each bread loaf. Place top over all. Cut each loaf in half, diagonally. *Serves 4 to 8.*

BAKED BEAN SANDWICHES

1½ cups canned baked beans, drained
3 tablespoons chopped dill pickle
4½ teaspoons mayonnaise
12 slices Boston brown bread
Soft margarine or butter
12 slices crisp bacon, or 6 slices bologna

Combine baked beans with pickle and mayonnaise and mix well. Spread bread slices with margarine or butter. Spread half of the slices with bean mixture. Top each with 2 slices bacon or 1 slice bologna. Cover with remaining bread slices. Cut in half. *Serves 6.*

EGG AND BACON SANDWICHES

4 hard-boiled eggs, chopped
6 slices crisp bacon, crumbled
½ stick margarine or butter
1 to 2 tablespoons mayonnaise
1 tablespoon minced chives
8 slices white bread

Shell eggs and chop coarsely. Mix with bacon, margarine or butter, mayonnaise, and chives. Spread on 4 bread slices. Cover with remaining bread slices. Cut in half. *Serves 4.*

DEVILED EGG SANDWICHES

6 hard-boiled eggs, peeled
1 teaspoon prepared mustard
Salt and freshly ground pepper to taste
2 tablespoons mayonnaise (or to taste)
1 tablespoon pickle relish
12 slices cracked wheat bread

Chop eggs coarsely. Add mustard, salt, pepper, mayonnaise, and pickle relish, and mix well to blend. Spread on 6 slices bread. Top with remaining slices. Cut in half. *Serves 6.*

CUCUMBER SANDWICHES

These are "ladies' special" sandwiches. In England they are made from paper-thin bread, crusts removed, and buttered, rather than spread with mayonnaise.

2 large cucumbers, peeled
12 thin slices white bread
Mayonnaise to taste
Salt to taste
⅛ teaspoon pepper

Slice cucumbers paper thin. Spread 6 slices bread with mayonnaise to taste. Place cucumber slices on these slices of bread. Sprinkle with salt and pepper. Place remaining slices of bread on top. Cut in quarters. *Serves 6.*

TUNA AND WATER CHESTNUT SANDWICHES

1 5-ounce can water chestnuts, drained
1 7-ounce can tuna fish, drained
¼ cup mayonnaise
¼ teaspoon salt
2 tablespoons lemon juice, strained
8 slices whole wheat bread
Soft margarine or butter
4 lettuce leaves

Chop water chestnuts coarsely. Mix with tuna fish, mayonnaise, salt, and lemon juice. Spread bread generously with margarine or butter. Spread tuna mixture on 4 slices. Top with lettuce and cover with remaining bread slices. Cut in half. *Serves 4.*

CLAM AND CREAM CHEESE SANDWICHES

The cream cheese mixture here also makes a great dip for potato chips, if thinned with a little clam juice and lemon juice.

1 7-ounce can chopped clams
1 8-ounce package soft cream cheese
Dash Worcestershire sauce
1 clove garlic, mashed
12 thin slices white bread
Soft margarine or butter

Drain clams, reserving juice. Mash cheese and add clams. Add enough clam juice to make the mixture of spreading consistency. Add

Worcestershire sauce and garlic. Spread 6 slices bread with mixture. Spread remaining slices with margarine or butter and place on top. Cut in half. *Serves 6.*

Snack Foods

In today's fast-paced world, snack foods take on more importance every year. "There's nothing to snack on" is a frequent complaint even when the refrigerator is full of potential snacks. The complaint occurs because the hungry ones aren't looking with enough imagination.

One way out, and a good way to fill stomachs as you empty the refrigerator of leftovers, is to package leftovers as snacks. Cut cheese, chicken, or roast tag ends into attractive morsels, and pack in clear plastic with a stick or two of celery, raw carrot, green pepper, or pickle. Store bits of leftover stew or casseroles in ovenproof containers covered with plastic, so the hungry folk can "see" this will only take a moment to heat. Store leftover vegetables in salad dressing and cover with foil—these "dressed vegetables" are excellent with bread and butter and cheese, and they are ready to eat just as they are.

Keep handy relishes, chutneys, pickles, and other family favorites that go well with snack foods. These aren't expensive items, but they can turn a chip of cold dried lamb or a hamburger into exactly what some hungry member of the family was hoping for when he or she opened the door of the refrigerator.

If your family is heavy on snacks, it will be worthwhile when planning meals to program snacks into the cooking. Roast an extra half chicken at dinner, boil six eggs while you cook breakfast, make two pies instead of one for dessert.

Or adapt the basic principles in the snack recipes below and make your own variations.

VIENNA SUPPER LOAF

1 12-ounce can pork-ham luncheon loaf
¼ cup chopped ripe olives

1 10-ounce can cream of mushroom soup
1 long loaf unsliced Vienna bread
Soft margarine or butter
2 tablespoons catsup
2 teaspoons prepared mustard

Coarsely grind luncheon meat. Combine with ripe olives and undiluted soup. Slice bread the long way into 3 layers. Spread margarine or butter on cut sides. Spread bottom layer with catsup and ½ the meat mixture. Top with second layer and spread with mustard and remaining filling. Top with upper crust layer. Wrap loaf loosely in foil, sealing ends. Heat on a baking sheet in a 400° oven 20 to 25 minutes. Remove to serving tray and cut loaf into 12 or 14 generous slices. *Serves 6 or 7.*

SWISS SUPPER LOAF

A great snack for a hungry crowd.

1 loaf unsliced cornmeal or rye bread
½ cup margarine or butter
½ cup minced onion
½ cup chili sauce
1 tablespoon poppy seed
6 slices crisply fried bacon, crumbled
10 slices Swiss or mozzarella cheese
1 cup fresh spinach, chopped

Cut bread into 10 slices. Melt margarine or butter, add onion and sauté until lightly browned. Add chili sauce, poppy seed, and ½ the crumbled bacon. Heat 5 minutes longer. Spread hot mixture on bread slices. Place a slice of cheese and sprinkling of bacon and spinach on each slice of bread. On a sheet of foil, reassemble slices into a loaf, crinkle foil around loaf, and place on a baking sheet. Pour remaining chili sauce mixture over top. Heat in a 350° oven 20 to 30 minutes. Sprinkle with additional bacon to serve. *Serves 10.*

APPLESAUCE HAM LOAF

1 pound ground ham
1 pound ground pork
1 cup bread crumbs

1 egg
½ cup plus 2 tablespoons applesauce
2 tablespoons sour cream
1 tablespoon minced onion
1 tablespoon minced celery leaves
½ teaspoon salt
¼ teaspoon pepper
2 tablespoons catsup
1 teaspoon Dijon mustard

Put first 3 ingredients in mixing bowl. Mix rest of ingredients except catsup and mustard and add to mixing bowl, blending well. Pack into 9×5×3-inch buttered loaf pan. Spread 2 tablespoons catsup mixed with 1 teaspoon Dijon mustard over top for glaze. Bake 1½ hours at 350°. Let set 10 to 15 minutes before transferring to serving platter. *Serves 6 to 8.*

SURPRISE LOAF

This will keep several days in the refrigerator, tightly wrapped in sandwich wrap, or in the freezer for at least a week.

6 slices any bread except rye or cracked wheat
2 eggs
1 6-ounce can condensed milk
Pepper and salt to taste
*Any leftover meat, vegetable, or recipes
    containing either*
½ cup drained salad olives
Herbs and spices (optional)

Mix ingredients thoroughly, then blend to get a fairly fine puree. Add herbs and spices if you wish, to strengthen the flavor of ingredients. Bake 20 to 30 minutes in 375° oven in an aluminum-foil form in the shape of a loaf. This can be sliced and eaten as a snack or party food. Great to take along to picnics. *Serves 4 to 8.*

BACON AND CHEESE TOASTS

1 pound bacon
1 10-ounce can sharp Cheddar cheese
1 green pepper
Italian or French bread, thinly sliced

Put bacon, cheese, and pepper through a meat grinder. Spread on slices of bread. Broil until browned. *Serves 20 to 30 slices.*

POPOVER SURPRISE

This is great for glamorizing a picnic, an in-between-meal party, a midnight snack, besides using up leftovers of stew, creamed meat, or vegetables; or mixed chopped vegetables and cold meats blended with grated cheese. Make in advance and reheat.

1 package frozen dough
1 egg, well beaten
Filling (as above)

Roll out dough and cut out rounds 5 inches across and ⅛ inch thick. Place 2 tablespoons filling in the center, and fold over. With a pastry brush, wet inside edge of the round with beaten egg so each half will adhere to the other. Fold closed and pinch the edge tightly together. Bake 20 to 30 minutes in 375° oven, until well browned if they are to be eaten right away, or until pale brown if they are to be refrigerated (you can then finish browning them when ready to eat). They can be reheated by placing on the side of a barbecue grill at picnics. *Serves 4.*

SECTION FIVE · **BAKED GOODS**

Bread and Quick Breads

You can save a fortune at the bakery by making your own breads, coffee cakes, and buns. All you need are a few facts, a couple of trial runs, a warm place where the breads can rise. There's no mystery—and relatively little cost—involved. The basic ingredients are flour, liquids, and flavorings. The other essential ingredient is leavening—the agent that puts in the air bubbles that make a raised baked product.

Breads, coffee cakes, and buns are "raised" by the action of yeast in dough. Once you've made a single yeast bread, you will know how to make luscious coffee cakes, wonderful hot buns and dinner rolls, every baked goods you've dreamed of—for all are simply variations on a single basic recipe.

The variations, by the way, are endless. There are many kinds of flour, sweeteners, nutritional additions, flavoring seeds and sweets, shortenings, and every variation on leavening styles. To invent your own variations on the basic principle, you need some understanding of how the many variants on the basic ingredients work. The list of basic ingredients below will answer some of your questions on the subject of variations, substitutions, and additions to the basic bread principle.

In the following pages, you will find a step-by-step group of recipes for the making of plain and sweet breads, coffee cakes, and buns. Try the Master Recipe for Basic White Bread first. Once you've made this successfully, you are ready to try some of the variations.

Quick Breads

The baked products called "quick breads" in most cookbooks are really types of cakes, and are raised by the action of baking soda or powder, rather than by the action of yeast. Since yeast breads require several hours of coddling in a warm spot for the yeast to act on the dough, the baking powder-raised breads are faster and easier to make. They usually are served as "tea breads," or coffee cakes, so a few classic recipes for these are included in this section, along with yeast-raised breads.

The Basic Ingredients: Flours

All-Purpose. This blend of hard and soft wheat flour has been bleached, chemically preserved, and literally processed to death. Use only if you can't find anything else.

Unbleached White. The germ and bran have been removed to "refine" the flour. No chemical treatments or preservatives have ruined it completely as a food. Use this as your basic white bread and general cooking flour. Add to whole grain flours to lighten the loaf if desired. Also called "bread flour."

Whole Wheat. Contains all parts of the kernel and has the highest proportion of wheat gluten. Try replacing 1 or 2 cups of white flour with this for better nutrition and heartier flavor in any bread recipe. Look for "stone-ground" and "finely milled" for a superior product. Also known as graham flour. Less kneading is required than with white flour. Refrigerate if possible.

Non-Wheat Flours. Only wheat flour has the particular gluten that will give the results you generally expect from a flour. Therefore, use a combination of about 2 cups wheat to 1 cup other flour for a less dense loaf. Never sift whole grain flours. Refrigerate them if possible.

Granulated, Pre-Sifted, and Self-Rising. In general, not good for breadmaking or eating in any form.

Soy Flour. Very high in protein. Use in small quantities for added nutrition. Will tend to make your loaf heavy and brown.

Barley Flour. Substitute up to ½ of other flour in any recipe. Lightly roast in a 400° oven before using for finer flavor.

Rye Flour. Fine texture and taste, but very heavy. Must be used with plenty of wheat flour to get a rise out of it. Used by itself, it makes your loaf a fat, heavy cracker.

Brown Rice Flour. Similar to soy in results, but sweeter. Very nutritious.

Carob Flour. Sweet flavor similar to chocolate, but much better for you. A valuable source of many vitamins and protein. Use in very small quantities like soy.

Potato Flour. Will help your loaf to keep longer. Substitute 1 cup of it for 1 cup regular flour.

Buckwheat Flour. Strong of flavor, very popular in hotcakes. Substitute in moderate amounts for other flours.

White Rice Flour. Also called "mochi." Not suitable for western-style breadmaking.

Grains, Meals, and Seeds

Cornmeal, White and Yellow. May be used interchangeably according to your preference. Substitute for up to ½ of total flour called for. Smaller amounts in any recipe add a sweet graininess. As with any other meal, you may heat your liquid, add the meal and soak until lukewarm. Then dissolve your yeast in a little warm water, add to meal, mix and proceed as usual.

Cornmeal, Whole. This is "live" meal with the germ retained. Not suitable for supermarket shelves since it spoils. Find it in health food stores, refrigerate and use as you would regular flour. Often referred to as "stone-ground" and is more nutritious. Try a cup in rye bread.

Rolled Oats. One of the most nutritious grains. Substitute 1 heaping cup for 1 flat cup of flour in any bread recipe for a chewy, sweet taste.

Oatmeal. This meal (and oat flour) is more highly processed. You can use instant oatmeal, too.

Millet, Meal or Cracked. Will add a special richness to your bread. Add in moderate quantities like cornmeal—raw or cooked for less chewy texture.

Wheat Germ. The heart of the wheat kernel and of great nutritive value. Add in small amounts with the flour, or knead in larger amounts toward end of recipe. Will make loaf dense and brown. Supermarket varieties are generally processed, preserved, and toasted. The toasting is all right but try for a fresher kind with more of the Vitamin E intact, if possible. Refrigerate, especially the fresh wheat germ.

Wheat Berries. Popular on the West Coast. Add as wheat germ, mentioned above.

Bran, Flakes and Meal. Add the flakes in same proportions as rolled oats. The meal benefits from soaking or cooking.

Cracked Wheat. Also called "burghal." Comes in various degrees of coarseness. Add in small amounts as wheat germ. When using larger amounts, cook first.

Buckwheat Groats. Cook first, then add as any meal. Strong taste. Also called "kasha."

Hominy Grits. Cook or just soak the quick variety. Very mild flavor. Add as above.

Rye Meal or Grits. Add in small amounts. Will make loaf heavy as will rye flour. May be cooked or soaked first.

Other Starches, Flours, and Meals. Various nut flours and meals are healthful and may be added in small amounts. Starches, such as cornstarch, arrowroot, etc., are not suitable for breadmaking.

Sunflower Seeds, Hulled. (Also squash and melon seeds.) These are a delicious addition, high in vitamins. They may be toasted first. Add in small amounts, as all other seeds, toward the end of the first kneading.

Sesame Seeds. Sprinkle on top of any loaf before baking and after glazing, or toast and add as you would sunflower seeds. Also called "benne seed" in the South.

Poppy Seeds. Generally used as a topping, like sesame seeds. They may also be ground and combined with sugar, cream, and butter and used as a filling for sweet rolls. Also called "mohn" filling.

Caraway Seeds. Best known as an addition to rye bread. Use 2 tablespoons per loaf.

Dill Seeds. An excellent addition to rye loaves. Used with caraway or by itself. Two tablespoons per loaf.

Cumin Seeds. Try 1 tablespoon or so in rye bread, cornbread, Italian and Mexican flat breads. When ground, cumin is the basis for curry and chili powders.

Fennel Seeds. Used in some Italian breads. Lends them an exotic taste.

Liquids

Water. With flour or meal and salt, it is the basis of all bread. The great classic breads contain no other liquid. A crisper crust results than when using milk.

Potato Water. Boil 1 pared, sliced potato in 2 cups water until tender. Drain. The resulting water makes the liveliest sourdough starter. A loaf will be higher and slightly coarser using potato water.

Milk. Skim milk powder, flakes, crystals, or evaporated milk, all mixed with the proper amount of water, are excellent for breadmaking. Whole milk or any reconstituted milk may be used interchangeably with water. A softer, longer-lasting, more nutritious loaf results, but expect a less earthy flavor. Heat milk to soften hard shortening or use warm water with powdered milk. Forget about scalding milk; it is not necessary with today's products.

Sour Cream. Substitute 1 cup sour cream for 1 cup milk in most bread recipes, for a tender crumb and fine flavor. Delicate to the taste.

Sweet Cream. Good if your arteries and budget can handle it.

Buttermilk. Use as you would yogurt.

Soy Milk. You may use it instead of other milk, allowing for deeper browning of loaf.

Artificial Cream, Whips, or Toppings. In general, forget them!

Sweeteners

Honey. A neutral, light-colored honey is the preferred sweetening for all breads, except where the stronger flavor of molasses or brown sugar is desired. Your loaf will keep longer, have a fine fragrance, and be more nutritious. (See "Baking Soda.") Some honey will be more acid than other; check by the way the loaf browns.

Raw Sugar. This unrefined, cleaned sugar is another good choice in any recipe.

White Sugar. All the nutrition has been processed out, leaving "empty" calories. Use only if nothing else is available. Cut down on sugar from ⅜ to ¼ total called for in most recipes, as a general practice of good health. Be kind to your children: they don't need all that sugar and neither do you. You may substitute any other sweetening except syrups in equal portions to the white sugar.

Molasses. Strongly flavored and a good source of some vitamins and minerals. Use as desired, particularly in rye and dark wheat breads.

Syrups. Not suitable for breads. Small amounts of maple may be added as a flavoring.

Powdered or Confectioners' Sugar. Use for glazing, not for breadmaking. Cornstarch has been added.

Sugar Substitutes. Sugar helps feed the yeast and assists fermentation. Substitutes cannot do this and cannot be used in breads for this reason. Add them only for a desired sweeter flavor.

Shortening

Vegetable Oils, Neutral. Any of these are desirable shortening for bread. Corn, cottonseed, peanut, safflower, or blends are interchangeable with one another and solid shortenings. Use slightly less oil than solid shortening for delicate recipes.

Vegetable Oils, Cold Pressed. These have little special value except their high price. Substitute in the same amount as regular oil. Store carefully (cool) as they may become rancid rapidly. Corn germ oil may be a little

more valuable as a food because the whole germ is used.

Olive Oil. Strongly flavored and subject to rancidity. Desirable in many Italian breads and in any loaf for those who like the taste. Store carefully in a dark place. Virgin oil is preferable.

Sesame Oil. Very strong in flavor. Use in small amounts as a flavoring agent, especially in earthy, grainy breads.

Vegetable Oils, Solid. These are hydrogenated and therefore more saturated than liquid oils. Margarine is a little better as it is generally enriched and has a little milk. Solid oils give a softer, lighter loaf than liquid oils.

Butter. A highly saturated fat like the hydrogenated oils, it is nevertheless desirable for its fine flavor and delicate results. As with sweet cream, if your arteries and budget can handle it, use it.

Lard and Other Animal Fats. While not generally used for breadmaking, there are some exceptions as in drippings for Yorkshire pudding or bacon fat for cornbread. In these instances the fat is used as a flavoring agent and as shortening.

Leavening

Yeast, Granulated. Can be found in individual packets containing the equivalent of 1 cake compressed yeast. The dry form keeps longer and more easily. If bought in bulk, use 1 tablespoon for each cake or package called for. Dissolve in a small amount of warm liquid or sprinkle directly over warm liquid in bread bowl, stirring well.

Yeast, Compressed. This is found in small cakes of ⅝ ounces in most markets. It is now becoming less common since the dry form is easier to store. There is no real difference between the two, in spite of the personal preferences of some "authorities." You may use any yeast in proportions of up to 1 package per cup of liquid for faster rising. If for some reason you wish to use less, 1 package will rise about 7 to 8 cups of flour. Dissolve first.

Air. It plays a large part in the rising of breads. In fact, if you trap enough air in your product, that's all you need! Just think of popovers or soufflés. Air is incorporated in every stage of breadmaking, particularly during stirring, folding, and kneading.

Eggs. They help to stabilize and enlarge the carbon dioxide-filled bubbles formed by the activity of the yeast. This makes the loaf higher and lighter. Eggs also add color and change the texture. For best results, bring eggs to room temperature and whip a few seconds before adding. Addition of eggs will require some adjustment in the quantity of flour. All recipes here refer to Grade A Medium eggs.

Egg Substitutes. The new frozen egg substitutes used according to directions work well in breads calling for more than 1 egg. Use 1 real egg for every 2 needed, except for rich holiday breads. For these, use 2 real eggs and you can substitute the rest. Dried eggs may be added to the flour to increase the protein, but don't expect any leavening action.

Baking Powder. A combination of ingredients that react to form carbon dioxide in a different way from yeast. Caught short, you can mix 2 tablespoons cream of tartar, 1 tablespoon baking soda, and 1½ teaspoons salt for the average loaf of quick bread. Use it soon and bake right away. The most common double-acting powders work on contact with moisture (as all baking powders do) and again when heated (as other powders don't). Use the double-acting.

Baking Soda. May be used instead of the powder in the presence of an acid such as yogurt, molasses, or spices. The same acid-alkaline reaction results. As a precaution, in large recipes where you want to be sure of a good rise, use both. A pinch of soda will counteract the acid in a strong honey and is a nice touch.

Salt. While not a leavening, salt helps control bacteria action and fermentation. In sourdoughs, unleavened, and salt-rising bread, it helps kill the harmful bacteria while the necessary (and more salt-tolerant) ones continue to work. Too much salt will over-control the yeast, so be light-handed. Add it toward the end of dense, tricky loaves to be sure. Recipes refer to standard table salt.

Sea Salt. Also called coarse or kosher. Has a fine flavor and valuable minerals. Grind before adding in place of table salt. Sprinkle on top of breadsticks, pretzels, etc.

Sourdough. An ancient process wherein a simple batter of flour and liquid is set out to entrap the wild yeast spores in the air. After some trial and error you may get a batch that consistently gives good results. Perpetuate and carefully nurture it. You have now stabilized and domesticated a wild yeast strain (See "Basic Sourdough Bread.")

Brewer's Yeast. For nutrition only; it has no leavening power. Use in small amounts.

Flavorings and Additions

Fruits, Dried. Currants, raisins, dates, figs, prunes—diced. May be added in amounts of 1 cup per any loaf without changing other proportions. You may wish to reduce your sweetening as a result.

Vegetables, Cooked. Add 2 cups sautéed, chopped onions to any nonsweet bread, or 1 cup mashed potato to any bread.

Fruits, Fresh. Any peeled, sliced fresh fruit may be laid in as a filling for coffee cakes. Don't measure; just cover thickly.

Candied Fruits, Peels, and Citron. Generally 1 cup per loaf of sweet bread. Usually a mixture is used.

Nuts, Chopped. One-half to 2 cups may be added to any bread. Almonds are lowest of all nuts in fat.

Peels, Grated. One lemon, orange, lime, or tangerine per loaf.

Extracts. One teaspoon vanilla, almond, etc., per loaf of sweet bread. Seldom used.

Liquors. Brandy, rum, bourbon, Kirsch, etc., are a fine addition to any sweet bread. Use up to ¼ cup.

Ground Spices. One tablespoon mixed, sweet spices or 1 tablespoon of any mild single sweet spice may be added to any sweet bread to make a spice bread. (See "Baking Soda.") Smaller amounts used as desired. Pepper can be added to a spice blend for sweet breads or used in cheese bread by itself—up to 2 teaspoons per loaf. One teaspoon cardamom will give a Scandinavian touch to your holiday bread, while 2 teaspoons saffron soaked in hot water will add a favorite English accent.

Herbs. One-half teaspoon mild (basil, marjoram, etc.), ¼ teaspoon strong (oregano, thyme), 1 teaspoon fresh (parsley, chives, etc.), to add up to about 2 tablespoons per loaf is a nice formula. If all the herbs are fresh, increase the total amount to 2 or 3 tablespoons. Zather, a Middle Eastern blend of sumac and thyme is used lavishly—up to 4 tablespoons in or on many Arabic breads. Chili powder, or a freshly mashed blend of equal parts cumin, oregano, and hot peppers (with some salt and garlic), is also used in quantity; try 2 tablespoons in a cornbread.

Cheeses. One to 2 cups hard grated cheese such as Parmesan, Romano, Gruyère, etc., are added to warm liquid for savory bread. Softer grated or diced cheese may be added in layers to melt during baking. Cottage cheese may replace the liquid in a recipe—perhaps adding another egg to thin, if necessary.

Other Goodies. Chili peppers, sauerkraut, cooked rice, meats or fish, bean sprouts, celery, porridges, granola, bread crumbs, and marmalade—just about anything you can conceive of can be incorporated as a filling for breads. Go ahead, invent something!

Basic White Bread

MASTER RECIPE

3 cups warm water or milk
3 packages yeast

¼ cup honey or raw sugar
8 to 11 cups unbleached white flour
1 tablespoon salt
¼ cup cooking or olive oil

Sprinkle yeast over water, add honey and stir until dissolved. Add 4 cups flour and the salt. Stir until moist, then beat until batter is smooth. Fold in 1 to 2 cups more flour until dough begins to leave sides of bowl. Turn out on floured surface and knead about 10 minutes, adding flour as necessary until dough is elastic and no longer sticky. Flatten dough gently and make indentations with your fingertips all over. Pour on oil and knead it in until absorbed. Form into ball. Pour 1 tablespoon oil into large clean bowl. Place ball in bowl upside down, swirl and turn over so sides of bowl and top of dough are oiled. Cover with clean towel and set to rise. When doubled, punch down, turn out onto lightly oiled surface and knead briefly. Cut as desired and let rest under the towel 10 minutes. Shape as directed and place in baking utensil. Cover and let rise to double. Glaze and bake at 350° until done, about 1 hour. I have never seen a failure with this recipe.

Each recipe will make 2 loaves bread or 24 to 28 large onion buns. One quarter of a recipe will make 1 pizza; 1 coffee cake; 8 cloverleaf rolls or sticky buns; or 12 breadsticks. Do not reduce the recipe. Instead, cut dough in half, and portion out for variations. Thus, you may decide to make 1 loaf bread, 12 breadsticks, and a coffee cake, or 4 pizzas for a party; 32 rolls for a buffet supper or 2 loaves for your family.

Variations

PROFESSIONAL ONION BUNS

These are most impressive; they are simple to do and make the novice baker look like she was born with flour up to her elbows.

Chop 4 to 5 large onions in ¼ cup margarine and cook until limp and golden. Salt to taste and cool. After first rising, cut dough in half, and then in fourths. Roll each quarter piece into a log and cut into 7 pieces. Roll a little piece into a ball and press a deep indentation into the center. Fill the hole with about 1 tablespoon onion, then carefully pinch hole closed. Lay seam side down on a greased baking tray leaving plenty of room for expansion. Repeat with each piece. Let rise until doubled, glaze with beaten egg and water and sprinkle with poppy seeds. Bake at 350° about 40 minutes, or until done and beautifully golden brown. You may cut this recipe in half or fourth to make 14 or 7 buns, respectively.

SIMPLE COFFEE CAKE

All measurements are approximate; use more if you wish, less if you have less.

Oil a quarter piece of dough and table top. Knead and stretch dough into a large, thin rectangle. Spread with ¼ cup softened margarine or butter. Sprinkle evenly with 1 cup raw or light brown sugar, leaving a 1-inch edge all around. Sprinkle on ½ to 1 cup chopped nuts and raisins, currants, or dates. Sprinkle evenly and generously with cinnamon and a little allspice. Dot with ¼ cup additional margarine. Carefully roll dough away from you on long side of table as you would a jelly roll. Pinch the seam closed. Press the two ends into points and pinch closed. Lay on a greased cookie sheet and nudge into a crescent shape. If you have never handled dough before, make your rectangle on a piece of waxed paper and use it as a support when rolling up and transferring to pan. Pinch all holes closed. Brush with egg glaze evenly and dust with cinnamon. Let rise and bake at 350° for 40 minutes, or until done. This is best served warm with more butter. You may also knead all the above ingredients directly into the dough and pat into a circle. Bake in a cake pan. Add icing if desired.

STICKY BUNS

Prepare as above to jelly-roll stage using nuts without raisins. When dough is log shaped, slice into 12 equal pieces. Place 1 tablespoon oil or melted margarine and 1 tablespoon raw sugar or honey in bottom of each of 12 Teflon coated or well-greased cupcake cups. Lay a slice of rolled dough in each. Let rise and bake at 350° for 30 minutes. Watch carefully to avoid scorching. Turn out upside down.

CLOVERLEAF ROLLS

Cut dough as for Onion Buns except make 8 pieces from each log. Take each little ball and divide into 3 tiny balls. Dip each tiny ball into melted margarine or oil and place 3 in a greased cupcake cup. Let rise and brush with more butter. Bake at 350° for 30 minutes. Reduce recipe as desired.

SOFT PRETZELS

Cut dough as for Onion Buns, making 8 pieces from each log. Roll each piece into long thin pencils. Twist into pretzel shape and let rise. Brush with egg glaze and sprinkle heavily with sea or coarse salt. Place on greased baking sheet and bake in 425° oven for 10 minutes, or until done.

HOMEMADE PIZZA

Incomparable! It is as easy to make 4 pies as 1. Simply assemble your ingredients in a row, stretch out the dough and bake 2 at a time. You may make the dough the night before if you wish. Refrigerate with a heavy plate over the bowl, and bring to room temperature as you need it. Here are the proportions for 1 pie.

DOUGH

Oil a large pizza pan generously. Take a quarter piece of dough and knead it into a flat circle. Oil dough and hands well. By pulling and stretching around the perimeter while dangling it from your hands and turning, the circle will enlarge enough to fit about half of the pan's area. This is not as hard as it sounds.

Lay dough in pan and let rest a few minutes. Now, using fingertips, stretch dough carefully out to the edge. Pinch together holes. Form a rim of dough around the edge. Drizzle 3 tablespoons olive oil over surface and fill.

FILLING

Drain and chop a large can of plum tomatoes (or spoon out ¼ of a very large can of puree) and space evenly over dough. Sprinkle lightly with salt and fresh black pepper. Crumble 2 teaspoons basil and 1 teaspoon oregano all over. Add 1 teaspoon garlic powder or 2 cloves fresh minced garlic. Dot with thinly sliced pepperoni (½ pound crumbled cooked Italian sausage) and ½ cup sliced canned mushrooms. Drain 1 cup unpitted black olives and add. Thinly slice and separate into rings 1 small onion and 1 green pepper. Grate ½ cup each fresh Parmesan and Romano cheeses and sprinkle evenly over all. Add 1 cup coarsely grated mozzarella. Bake at 350° for 20 minutes, or until bottom is slightly browned and edges are firm and crusty. Serve with tossed salad and Chianti.

STUFFED ROLLS

Any good filling will do for these little turnovers, but this one is a treasured recipe.

Drain, squeeze, and chop contents of 1 large (27-ounce) can sauerkraut. Soak, drain, and chop 4 dried mushrooms. European or Chinese, it doesn't matter, but these are essential. Dice 1 large onion. Mix all together and sauté in 2 tablespoons butter and 1 tablespoon bacon fat. Fry for about 15 minutes over low heat. Do not brown. Salt and pepper heavily. Use half of recipe's dough and cut as for Onion Buns. Roll each piece into a thin circle. Divide filling among dough. (About 2 tablespoons filling per roll.) Fold circle over to make a half moon shape. Press edges together well and cut off any excess edge. Press again. Place on greased baking sheet and let rise 10 minutes. Brush with melted butter. Bake at 375° for 20 minutes, or until done.

Basic Rich White Bread

Use same proportions as Master Recipe adding 3 eggs, and using milk instead of water. Adjust flour, using 1 or 2 cups more to get proper consistency. Dough will be softer. Use rich bread for any of the white bread variations, or try these:

SPAGHETTI-DINNER BREAD

Try this bread to perk up a budget supper. Makes 4 cake pans of bread; will *serve 8 to 10.*

Heat 3 cups milk. Do not boil. Stir in 1 cup freshly grated Parmesan cheese. It will dissolve partially. Stir in honey. When lukewarm, add yeast and proceed as directed. After first rising, turn out, knead, and cut into 4 pieces. Cut each portion of dough into about 12 pieces. Roll each piece into a ball and dip into ½ cup melted butter or margarine containing 2 to 4 minced cloves garlic. Fill a greased standard cake pan with dough balls. Sprinkle with sesame seeds and a little coarse salt. You may also add freshly ground pepper and a large pinch oregano if you wish. Let rise to double and bake at 350° for 35 minutes, or until done.

COTTAGE HERB BREAD

Replace liquid with 3 cups cottage cheese. Dissolve yeast separately in ¼ cup water. Add a large pinch baking soda to flour, and decrease salt to 1 teaspoon. Proceed as directed. After second rising, either knead Herb Mix (see below) into dough, or flatten dough into a rectangle as in coffee cake. Blend Herb Mix with ½ cup softened butter or margarine and spread over dough. Roll up jelly-roll fashion, shape it in a greased bread pan, let rise, and bake as usual.

HERB MIX

1 teaspoon each marjoram and thyme, or 1 tablespoon fresh basil; 1 tablespoon each minced fresh parsley, green onions, or chives.

Basic Sweet Bread

MASTER RECIPE

3 cups warm milk
1 to 2 cups shortening, soft
3 packages yeast
¾ to 1½ cups raw or white sugar
3 to 12 eggs
2 teaspoons salt
9 or more cups unbleached flour
2 grated lemon rinds or 2 teaspoons vanilla

You may notice a distinct similarity between this recipe and that of the Basic Rich White Bread; that is because they *are* the same. The addition of more shortening and sugar makes a richer dough, while the greater amount of eggs gives a wetter texture—almost a batter-like consistency. This recipe is easily divisible, so we will work with it in thirds.

LOAF 1

1 cup milk
1 cup softened margarine or butter
½ cup raw or white sugar
1 package yeast
4 eggs, beaten
½ teaspoon salt
3 cups unbleached flour

Heat milk and partially dissolve margarine or butter in it. Add sugar. When lukewarm, sprinkle on yeast. Beat in eggs; add salt; beat in flour, 1 cup at a time. Beat vigorously 3 to 5 minutes with back of wooden spoon. Slap and stretch dough 5 to 10 minutes more. Let rise to double in the bowl. Stir down gently and treat any of the following ways.

1. Swirl 1 teaspoon cinnamon through dough. Pour dough into 2 well-greased 2-quart molds. Let rise until almost double and bake at 350° about 45 minutes. Makes 2 small loaves.

2. Spoon dough into well-greased cupcake cups (24) until ⅔ full. Let rise a little and bake at 375° for 15 minutes, or until done. Remove from pan and poke holes in top of each. Place in deep platter or baking dish and pour syrup over, under, and around. Remove to a plate before they lose their shape. Glaze and serve with a separate bowl of whipped cream or strawberries and cream.

Syrup: Boil together 2 cups sugar and 4 cups water for a few seconds. Stir to dissolve sugar. Add ½ cup Triple Sec and 2 teaspoons rum extract, or flavor with 1 cup rum. Use any extra to soak fruit in.

Glaze: Melt over low heat a small jar of currant jelly or strained apricot preserves. Paint over babas with pastry brush while warm.

Cream: Whip 1 pint chilled heavy cream until soft-stiff, flavoring with a little sugar.

Fruit: Soak 2 pints fresh strawberries in leftover syrup or a little sugar and liqueur for 15 minutes. Drain and place berries over and around cakes. Pass whipped cream. This is what strawberry shortcake was derived from.

3. Bake half the dough in a well-greased 2-quart ring mold. Make babas from the rest. Flavor syrup with Kirsch and glaze. Serve with fresh fruits and cream as above. You may decorate with Maraschino cherries and sliced almonds dipped in glaze. These classic French recipes contradict any advice against sugar I've given, so don't serve them every night.

LOAF 2

1 cup milk
¾ cup softened margarine or butter
½ cup raw sugar
1 package yeast
2 eggs, beaten
½ teaspoon salt
3 cups unbleached flour
Grated rind of 1 lemon

Follow directions for Loaf 1.

Fold in 1 cup chopped candied fruit, fruit peel, or citron and ½ cup chopped nuts. Pour into greased Bundt pan and bake at 350° for 1 hour. Glaze with Lemon-Sugar Glaze.

Lemon-Sugar Glaze: Blend 1 cup confectioners' sugar, 2 tablespoons milk, and 2 tablespoons lemon juice. Spoon over warm (not hot) bread or rolls.

FOR DOUGHNUTS

Increase flour by 1½ to 2 cups until you have a soft dough you can just barely knead. You may replace lemon rind with 1 teaspoon vanilla extract or a large pinch each nutmeg and cinnamon. Chill dough 1 hour or longer. Turn out on lightly floured surface and pat into ½ inch thickness. Heat a kettle of oil for deep frying to 375°. Cut doughnuts with cutter or use a glass and thimble and let rest 5 minutes. Fry no more than 3 at a time, turning once until golden brown. To transfer from table to kettle, dip metal spatula in hot fat first. Roll the drained doughnuts in powdered sugar, cinnamon sugar, or glaze.

Classic Doughnut Glaze: Boil together 2 cups white sugar and 2 cups water for a few minutes. Cool and stir in 1 teaspoon vanilla extract. Dip and drain doughnuts.

LOAF 3

1 cup milk
½ cup soft margarine or butter
¼ cup raw sugar
½ teaspoon salt
1 package yeast
1 egg, beaten
4 cups unbleached flour
Grated rind of 1 lemon

Follow directions for Loaf 1.

Pour half the dough into a well-greased 9 × 13 × 2-inch baking pan. Mix together 2 cups (1 pound) cottage cheese, 1 cup drained crushed pineapple, and ½ cup raw sugar or light brown sugar. Beat in 3 eggs and sprinkle ¼ cup flour. Beat together and spread over dough. Sprinkle heavily with cinnamon and bake immediately at 350° for about 45 minutes, or until custard is set and the bread done.

Pour half the dough as above. Wash, core, and slice 4 to 5 nice tart apples. Lay over dough.

Stir together ½ cup each of raw or brown sugar, flour, and softened margarine or butter. Strew over apples. Sprinkle well with cinnamon and a little clove or allspice. Bake as above.

Pour dough as above. Drain 1 large can sliced peaches or 2 packages frozen peaches. Lay over dough and sprinkle lightly with raw or brown sugar and ½ teaspoon each of nutmeg and mace. Beat 3 eggs well and blend in 1 cup sour cream. Pour over all. Bake as above.

Pour dough as above. Top with any fresh fruits in season, or any mixed or drained canned fruits you have. Dot with butter and sprinkle with sugar and spices to your taste. Add some chopped nuts if they are handy. Bake as above.

Work 2 cups or more flour into dough before rising to make a soft-stiff dough. Turn out and knead well. Place in large greased bowl, cover, and let rise. Punch down, turn out, and knead in 1 cup currants or raisins, ½ cup candied mixed peel, and 1 cup chopped nuts. Cut as for Onion Buns (into about 28 pieces) and let rise on well-greased baking sheet. Brush with egg white or milk and sprinkle with sugar. Bake at 375° for 20 to 30 minutes. Glaze with Lemon-Sugar Glaze.

Basic Wheat Bread

MASTER RECIPE

3 cups warm milk
3 packages yeast
¼ cup honey or raw sugar
3 eggs, beaten
3 to 4 cups whole wheat flour
2 to 3 cups flour: white, wheat, or blend
¼ cup oil
2 teaspoons salt

Dissolve yeast in milk. Add honey and eggs. Beat in flour, 1 cup at a time; dough should be fairly thick. Beat well until batter is smooth, about 5 minutes. At this point, cover the dough and let rise about 1 hour, or until doubled. This is called the "sponge method." When the sponge has risen, begin folding in the rest of the flour, small amounts at a time, until it begins to leave the sides of bowl. Turn out on floured surface and begin kneading. You may add more flour if you have to. But remember, the more you use, the heavier the bread. If you need less than the recipe calls for, feel free to stint. Now, pour oil and sprinkle salt over dough and knead as in Basic White Bread. Knead bread 5 to 10 minutes. Cut in half, shape, and place in greased pans. Let rise until nearly double and bake at 350° until done, about 1 hour and some minutes. If it begins to brown too quickly, reduce heat and bake longer. No glaze is needed, but you may oil the crust when baked to give shine and softer crust.

VARIATIONS

Experiments have shown that any bread enriched with the following formula can sustain life. Bleached flour in store bread will not. It is now possible to buy decent bread in the markets, but many people don't. Even bleached flour white bread will provide sufficient nutrition if you add 1 tablespoon soy flour, 1 tablespoon skim milk powder, and 1 teaspoon wheat germ to the bottom of each cup of flour called for before filling. This wheat bread recipe calls for about 6 cups flour, so you will need ⅓ cup soy flour, ⅓ cup milk powder, and 2 tablespoons wheat germ. The total amount of wheat flour is reduced to 5⅓ cups. Now you figure out the formula for Basic White Bread and give it a try. Oddly enough, the loaves even *taste* better as well as *being* better. Watch your oven temperature closely as the bread will tend to brown deeply.

Or, . . . replace the final 3 cups flour with any one or a blend of up to 3 of these various flours and grains: unbleached white flour, rolled oats, rye flour, cornmeal, roasted barley flour, cracked millet meal, etc. Have fun!

Basic Sourdough Bread

MASTER RECIPE

Starter 1
2 cups warm water

1 package yeast
2 cups unbleached flour
1 tablespoon sugar
    Mix well and let sit 2 days at room temperature, stirring occasionally.

Starter 2
2 cups warm potato water
2 cups unbleached flour
1 teaspoon salt
    Mix well and let sit 2 to 5 days until mixture bubbles well and has a distinct odor.

To Keep Sourdough: Each time you remove starter from bowl, say 2 cups, replenish with equal parts flour and water. Mix well and let sit overnight before removing more. Use once a week; or pour off some and replenish once a week. Keep under refrigeration in a tightly covered container, stirring occasionally.

This bread will not have a distinct sourdough flavor unless you develop a distinctive starter—but don't worry, it will taste like the finest French bread you've had since you were in Paris.

1 cup hot water
2 tablespoons margarine or butter
1 package yeast
3 tablespoons raw sugar or honey
1 to 1½ cups starter, room temperature
1 tablespoon salt
2 cups flour, unbleached
2 to 3 cups more flour

    Melt butter in water. Cool and add yeast. Stir in sugar. Add starter and salt. Beat in flour 1 cup at a time. Let rest 10 minutes. This is your sponge. Fold in additional flour until dough leaves sides of bowl. Turn out on floured surface and begin kneading. Add more flour as necessary to make a fairly stiff dough. Knead 15 to 20 minutes. No cheating. Place in a buttered bowl and let rise to double. Punch down and turn out on oiled surface. Let rest 15 to 30 minutes. Cut and shape into 1 or 2 loaves. Sprinkle baking sheet with cornmeal and place on baking sheet, well apart. Let rise to double. Make a long slash in center with a razor held almost flat, using a quick, clean motion. (As you get better, you can add more slashes.) Heat oven to 425°. Spray bread with lightly salted cold water. Use a plant or ironing sprayer. Place a pan on bottom rack of oven. Fill with boiling water. Close door and let oven fill with steam. Put in bread. Spray briefly 2 or 3 times more in next 15 minutes. Lower heat to 375° and bake until done, about 35 minutes more. You may glaze with egg if not browned to your liking after about 45 minutes, or just brush again with salted water when it comes out.

VARIATIONS

Cut dough into 12 equal pieces. Shape each as a small French bread. Bake as above, reducing time by 10 minutes or so.

Cut small pieces of dough and roll into thin pencils. Bake as above (you need not spray) and sprinkle with sea or coarse salt after brushing once with cold water. Bake about 10 minutes.

After kneading and resting dough, roll or pat out to about ½ inch thickness. Cut out 3-inch circles and set to rise (until doubled) on a surface well sprinkled with cornmeal. Bake on lightly oiled griddle over low heat for about 10 minutes on each side.

Beat together ½ cup milk, 2 eggs, and 1 teaspoon soda. Beat into risen sponge. Let sit 15 minutes. Bake on greased griddle. Makes very small hotcakes (2 tablespoons).

Mix together 1 cup starter, 2 cups water, and 2 to 3 cups unbleached white or whole wheat flour. Let sit overnight. Beat together 2 eggs, ½ cup milk, 2 tablespoons oil or melted shortening, 1 teaspoon soda, 1 large pinch salt, and 2 tablespoons raw or brown sugar. Beat into batter. Let sit and bake as above.
This loaf takes a total of about 9 hours to complete as there is a lot of rising time. You don't have to work hard or even watch it, just think about it from time to time and start it in the morning. This recipe will make a loaf that will give 24 people 2 slices each, so it's the perfect bread for a party—and a real showpiece!

RYE STARTER

Make a sourdough starter as in Basic Starter 1, using rye flour.

SPONGE

Mix together 1 cup starter, 2 cups rye flour, and ½ package yeast dissolved in ¼ cup warm water. Let rise *and fall.* (Takes about 2 hours.)

Add 2 cups whole wheat flour and ½ package yeast dissolved in 1½ cups warm milk. Blend well. Let rise and fall.

Add 2 cups white unbleached flour, 1 cup milk, 1 tablespoon salt, 3 tablespoons raw or brown sugar, 1 tablespoon dill, and 2 tablespoons caraway seeds. Optional and good—add 2 to 5 pounds minced onions and 1 teaspoon fresh pepper. Turn dough out on floured surface and let rest, covered, about 15 minutes.

Add about 2 cups more white flour. Knead it in carefully and sparingly. Form into 1 large oval and place on a baking sheet heavily sprinkled with cornmeal. Bake at 425° for 15 minutes. Reduce heat and bake at 350° until done, about another hour. If you don't trust your oven, just stay at 350° all the way. Oil the top when done.

Use all white unbleached flour with the rye and 5 onions. The loaf will be enormous and earthy looking, but not quite the perfect rye bread.

Quick Breads

CHOCOLATE COFFEE CAKE

½ cup semi-sweet chocolate pieces
¼ cup chopped nuts
1¼ cups granulated sugar
1 teaspoon cinnamon
2 cups sifted all-purpose flour
½ teaspoon baking powder
¼ teaspoon salt
1 cup sour cream
1 teaspoon baking soda
½ cup margarine or butter
2 eggs
½ teaspoon vanilla extract

Combine chocolate, nuts, ¼ cup sugar, and cinnamon. Set aside. Sift flour with baking powder and salt. Combine sour cream and baking soda. Cream margarine or butter with 1 cup sugar until light and fluffy. Add eggs, one at a time, beating well after each addition. Add vanilla. Gradually add flour mixture alternately with sour-cream mixture, beginning and ending with flour. Spoon one-half the batter into a greased 9-inch square pan. Top with one-half the chocolate nut mixture, carefully spreading with spatula to form a smooth layer. Repeat layers. Bake at 350° for about 30 to 35 minutes, or until cake just begins to pull away from sides of pan. Cool in pan and cut in squares. *Serves 9.*

CARROT CAKE

A spicy semi-sweet quick bread that is wonderfully moist and has great texture.

½ cup shortening
½ cup brown sugar
1 egg
1 teaspoon water
½ teaspoon salt
½ teaspoon nutmeg
½ teaspoon cinnamon
½ teaspoon baking soda
½ teaspoon baking powder
1¼ cups all-purpose flour
2 cups carrots, finely grated

Preheat oven to 350°. Cream together shortening and sugar. Beat egg and water together and add to sugar mixture. Sift dry ingredients together and add to sugar. Gradually stir in grated carrots. Lightly grease a ring pan and pour in the cake batter. Bake 30 to 40 minutes, or until top is firm. *Serves 8 or 9.*

PUMPKIN TEA BREAD

½ cup all-purpose flour
½ teaspoon salt
½ teaspoon baking soda
½ teaspoon baking powder
¼ teaspoon cinnamon

¼ teaspoon ginger
¼ teaspoon nutmeg
2 eggs
1 cup sugar
1 cup canned pumpkin, strained
½ cup melted margarine
½ cup chopped nuts

Sift flour, salt, baking soda, baking powder, cinnamon, ginger, and nutmeg together 3 times. Beat eggs until thick, adding sugar, gradually, as you beat. Whip in pumpkin, then melted margarine. Beat in dry ingredients, and mix well. Fold in nuts. Pour into 2 buttered and floured bread pans. Bake for 1 hour at 350°, or until a toothpick inserted in the center comes out clean. *Serves 8 or 9.*

COCONUT APPLE CAKE

2 cups sifted all-purpose flour
3 teaspoons double-acting baking powder
½ teaspoon salt
¼ cup margarine or butter
⅓ cup sugar
2 eggs
¾ cup milk
1⅓ cups (approximately) flaked coconut
¾ cup sugar
1½ teaspoons cinnamon
¼ teaspoon nutmeg
4 medium tart apples

Sift flour with baking powder and salt. Cream margarine or butter. Gradually blend in ⅓ cup sugar, creaming well after each addition. Add eggs, one at a time, beating well after each. Add flour mixture alternately with milk, beating after each addition until smooth. Set aside about ¼ cup coconut. Add remaining coconut to batter. Spread batter in 13 × 9-inch pan. Peel and core apples and cut into ¼-inch slices (makes about 3½ cups). Combine ¾ cup sugar, cinnamon, and nutmeg and mix with apple slices. Arrange mixture on batter in pan. Bake in 350° oven 50 minutes. Sprinkle reserved coconut over mixture in pan and continue to bake 10 minutes longer. *Serves 12 to 14.*

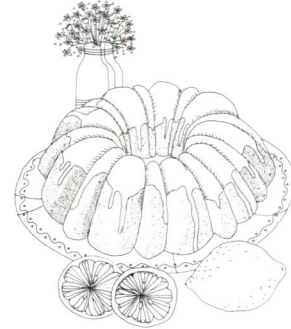

Cakes and Pies

Cake mixes are economical. Mixes for pound cake and angel food, for instance, are unsurpassable when you are budgeting. I have found that if you beat cake mixes by hand (but not angel food cake mix) rather than with the rotary electric beater, as suggested in cake mix recipes, the texture is closer to that of the from-scratch cakes. Beating the cake mixes makes them bake as fine as the least attractive of the ready-made cakes—so why do it?

There are a handful of cake, cookie, tart, and pie recipes it is fun to be able to say you've made yourself. If you bought them in a fancy bakery, they'd cost a fortune; but made at home, they're delicious and economical. It's also useful to know some delicious baked desserts that are low in calories. Included below are a few classic favorites you might like to make from scratch, along with a few calorie-savers.

LEMON CHIFFON CAKE

This cake has 96 calories per serving.

2¾ cups sifted cake flour
1 teaspoon salt

1 tablespoon baking powder
8 unbeaten egg yolks (⅔ cup)
¼ cup salad oil (corn oil is preferable)
2 tablespoons lemon juice, strained
2 teaspoons finely grated lemon rind
½ cup cold water
2 teaspoons vanilla
1 cup egg whites (7 or 8 eggs); or use equivalent in reconstituted powdered egg whites
1½ teaspoons cream of tartar
2 tablespoons liquid sugar substitute
⅛ teaspoon yellow food coloring

Take eggs out of refrigerator to ensure that they are at room temperature before using. Sift together flour, salt, and baking powder into small bowl and create a well in center of mixture. Add to it (in the center) egg yolks, oil, lemon juice, rind, water, and vanilla. With a wooden spoon, stir until smooth. In large bowl, beat egg whites until they are frothy. Add cream of tartar, sugar substitute, and food coloring. Beat at high speed until peaks are stiff and hold. Fold in batter gently until mixture is smooth. Pour immediately into ungreased, 10-inch tube pan. Bake in slow oven at about 300° for 40 minutes. Check to see if surface springs back when touched lightly before removing from oven. Invert baked cake on funnel or bottle until cool, so top of cake doesn't rest on surface. With spatula or knife loosen cake around sides and tube. Turn right side up, remove pan and serve. *Serves 12 to 14.*

GEORGIA CHOCOLATE POUND CAKE

A terrific cake to bake and freeze. It makes a superb last minute welcome home or surprise birthday cake.

3 cups cake flour
3 cups granulated sugar
1 cup cocoa
3 teaspoons baking powder
1 teaspoon salt
2 sticks margarine or butter, softened
1½ cups milk
3 teaspoons vanilla extract
3 eggs
½ cup milk or light cream
Quick Chocolate Icing

In the bowl of an electric mixer, sift together flour, sugar, cocoa, baking powder, and salt. Make a well in the center and add margarine or butter, milk, and vanilla. Beat mixture for 5 minutes. Add eggs, one at a time, and milk or light cream, beating mixture thoroughly after each addition. Turn batter into a well-oiled 10-inch tube pan and bake in a 325° oven for 1½ hours, or until cake tests as done. Cool cake on a wire rack and remove from pan. When cooled, cover with Quick Chocolate Icing. *Serves 8 to 10.*

QUICK CHOCOLATE ICING

1 cup semi-sweet chocolate bits
1 tablespoon honey or cane syrup
1 tablespoon margarine or butter

Cook ingredients over low heat until melted and well combined. Cool slightly and spread over cake.

EASY CHRISTMAS FRUITCAKE

You can save a great deal of money in the holiday budget by making your own fruitcake. Aging 3 to 4 weeks improves the flavor, so make it well before Christmas. If desired, add ¼ cup brandy or whiskey to the batter before baking.

½ cup sliced dates
½ cup seedless raisins
⅓ cup margarine or butter
¾ cup brown sugar, firmly packed
2 tablespoons dark molasses
¾ cup hot water
1 egg
1 8-ounce package prepared fruits and peels
1 cup chopped nuts
1½ cups sifted all-purpose flour
1 teaspoon powdered cinnamon
¼ teaspoon ground nutmeg
1 teaspoon baking soda
½ teaspoon baking powder
½ teaspoon salt

Combine dates, raisins, margarine or butter, brown sugar, molasses, and hot water in a saucepan. Boil gently for 3 minutes. Cool in a large mixing bowl. Beat in egg. Add fruits and peels and chopped nuts. Sift together dry ingredients and add gradually to fruit mixture, beating well after each addition. Line a loaf pan or small tube pan with greased waxed paper. Pour in mixture. Bake in 275° oven 2¼ hours. Remove from pan and cool thoroughly. Wrap securely in plastic wrap or aluminum foil. Store in clean air-tight container in cool place. *Serves 12 to 14.*

BLUEBERRY CAKE
WITH HARD SAUCE

A dessert to serve when you want to spoil your family or guests. In blueberry season, it's very economical.

½ cup margarine or butter
1 cup sugar
1 egg, well beaten
1 teaspoon salt

2 cups cake flour
4 teaspoons baking powder
1 cup milk
1½ cups blueberries
Hard Sauce

Cream margarine or butter and sugar. Add egg, and mix. Sift remaining dry ingredients. Reserve ¼ cup of mixture to dredge berries. Add dry ingredients alternately with milk, to butter-sugar-egg mixture. Fold in dredged berries and bake in a greased shallow pan in a 350° oven 35 to 45 minutes, or until a cake tester comes out dry. Serve hot with Hard Sauce. *Serves 4 to 6.*

HARD SAUCE

¼ cup margarine or butter, softened at room
    temperature
¾ cup granulated sugar or superfine sugar
½ teaspoon vanilla
⅛ teaspoon nutmeg

Cream margarine or butter and sugar with the back of a spoon until smooth. Add vanilla. Place in a smooth mound on a small dish and sprinkle with nutmeg.

CHRISTMAS GINGERBREAD COOKIES

Make your own Christmas-time cookies—and bake extra to give away. Decorate with *Thin Icing* (see below) and provide plenty of gay colored button candies, sprinkles, raisins, etc., so that young imaginations may roam in the decorating department. Make a small hole with a skewer in the top of each cookie, so when baked you can insert a thin ribbon through it and hang the decorated cookies on the Christmas tree.

½ cup shortening
½ cup sugar
½ cup unsulfured molasses
1 whole egg
2½ cups sifted all-purpose flour
½ teaspoon baking soda

1 teaspoon baking powder
1 tablespoon powdered ginger
1½ teaspoons powdered cloves
1½ teaspoons powdered cinnamon
¼ teaspoon powdered nutmeg

Preheat oven to 350°. Cream shortening, sugar, and molasses together. Add egg. Mix well. Sift together flour, baking soda, baking powder, and spices. Add to molasses mixture and mix well. Chill in refrigerator 1½ hours. Roll out ¼ inch thick on lightly floured board or pastry cloth. Cut with floured Santa Claus, Christmas tree, Christmas wreath, star, or gingerbread man cutters. Place on lightly greased cookie sheets and bake 10 to 12 minutes. The number of cookies depends on shapes selected—there should be a couple of dozen.

THIN ICING

1 cup confectioners' sugar
2 to 3 tablespoons milk or water
Food coloring (optional)

Sift sugar into a bowl. Gradually add milk or water, mixing to a smooth paste. If desired, divide icing into 3 bowls and tint contents of 1 with red food coloring, another with green, leaving the remainder white. The green, for instance, is just right for icing wreath cookies.

LOW-CALORIE NUTTY CHOCOLATE BROWNIES

There are 54 calories per brownie in this recipe—a classic to make yourself for diet reasons. If you leave out the nuts, you save 37 calories per brownie! To avoid the high cost of nuts (in calories and money) try browning oatmeal in a bit of margarine instead. Or mix into the batter ¾ cup of Country Morning cereal or Granola—a bit lower in calories than nuts.

⅓ cup margarine or butter
1 square (1 ounce) unsweetened chocolate
2 tablespoons liquid sugar substitute
2 teaspoons vanilla extract
2 eggs, well beaten

1 cup sifted cake flour
½ teaspoon baking soda
½ teaspoon salt
¾ cup chopped walnuts (optional)

Preheat oven to 325°. Over low heat, melt margarine or butter and chocolate in pan. Remove and add sugar substitute, vanilla, and beaten eggs. Stir, blending well. Add flour, baking soda, and salt, mixing until blended. Stir in nuts. Pour into square pan about 8 inches in diameter. Spread batter evenly in pan and bake for 20 minutes. Cut into squares.

Pies and Tarts

Pie fresh from the oven is a favorite dessert with most families, and easy on the budget when you make it yourself. The fast way to make a pie is to begin with a pie crust mix, but mixes are costly, so included here is a basic dry ingredient mixture you can make up ahead and measure whenever pie-making is in order.

Homemade Pie Crust

This makes mix enough for 10 double pie crusts. What we are doing here is mixing the dry ingredients ahead. When it's time to make a pie crust, measure out the dry ingredients, as described below, add shortening, then water, and the crust is ready. No floury mess to clean from the floor.

BASIC PIE CRUST MIXTURE (FOR 10 PIES)

20 cups all-purpose flour
5 teaspoons salt
7 tablespoons granulated sugar
5 teaspoons baking powder

In a very large bowl, place the sifter, add the ingredients, and sift thoroughly 3 times. Store in an air-tight container.

PIE CRUST

2 cups plus 2 teaspoons Basic Pie Crust Mixture
⅔ cup shortening
1 tablespoon butter
4 tablespoons ice water

Measure Basic Pie Crust Mixture into a large bowl and, using 2 knives, cut in shortening and butter until flour mixture is like coarse meal. Sprinkle ice water over mixture, and stir, pressing against the sides of the bowl, until a round ball has formed. If the ball remains floury and won't pick up the crumbs, add ½ tablespoon more of water. With your hands shape 2 flattened balls, and chill in the refrigerator 10 to 20 minutes. Roll half the chilled dough on a floured board with a floured rolling pin. Flip it one-quarter turn at each rolling until it is the size of your pie pan. If it sticks to the board, lift dough, and scatter a little more flour underneath. When ready, fold pastry twice (to quarter size), lift it into the pan, and unfold. Let rest 5 minutes, then pat it to fit the plate, and flute edges with a fork. If pie shell is to be used baked, preheat oven to 425°. Prick dough all over the bottom with a fork to keep it from bubbling as it heats, and bake for 15 to 20 minutes, or until golden brown. This recipe makes 2 pie crusts—1 for the bottom and 1 for the top. If you want only 1 pie crust, use half the ingredients listed.

APPLE–PEACH PIE

Apples in season are inexpensive and delicious. Use tart apples for pies. Couple apples with canned peaches, which are shown as an optional ingredient here, and you'll have one of the best apple pies you've ever tasted.

Pastry for a 2-crust 8-inch pie
6 closely packed cups peeled, cored apple slices or 5 cups apple slices and 1 cup closely packed, drained canned peach slices
½ cup light brown sugar, firmly packed
⅛ teaspoon salt
1 tablespoon cornstarch

¼ teaspoon cinnamon
⅛ teaspoon nutmeg
2 tablespoons butter
Cold milk

Preheat oven to 450°. Roll out half the pastry and line an 8-inch pie shell. Combine apple slices, or apple and peach slices, with sugar, mixed with salt, cornstarch, cinnamon, and nutmeg. Toss well, and scrape into pie shell. Dot with butter. Roll out the rest of the pastry, and cover apples. Crimp top and bottom edges together with fingers moistened in cold milk. Brush pastry top with cold milk, and make 6 small diagonal slashes in crust top to let out steam. Bake for 10 minutes at 450°, then lower heat to 350° and bake about 45 minutes. *Serves 7 to 9.*

CARROT PIE

The inexpensive carrot turns up here in a pie with a spicy flavor. You'd be amazed at just how good it is! Serve garnished with whipped cream, if desired.

1 pound carrots, scraped and cut into thick
    slices
1 cup boiling water
1 cup milk
⅛ teaspoon salt
½ teaspoon powdered cloves
1 teaspoon grated or finely chopped lemon
    rind
1 teaspoon cinnamon
1 teaspoon nutmeg
½ cup brown sugar
3 eggs, beaten
1 partially baked 8-inch pie shell

Preheat oven to 350°. Put sliced carrots in 1 cup boiling water, cover, and cook until barely tender when tested with a fork. Drain carrots and puree in a blender with milk. One at a time, stir in remaining ingredients, except pie shell, beating well after each addition. Pour into partially cooked pie shell and bake 35 minutes, or until top is set and lightly browned. *Serves 7 to 9.*

SOUR CHERRY PIE

This recipe is from my book, *The How to Grow and Cook It Book,* and it is one of my favorite pies. Fruit pies aren't costly if you make them during the fruit season. You can use less-than-perfect cherries for a pie.

Pastry for a 2-crust 8-inch pie
1 cup sugar
¼ teaspoon cinnamon
¼ teaspoon nutmeg
2 cups pitted, fresh sour cherries or drained,
    canned cherries
1 egg
Butter
Milk

Preheat oven to 425°. Roll out half the pastry and line an 8-inch pie shell. Combine sugar, cinnamon, and nutmeg. Toss pitted cherries in mixture. Beat egg until thick, then blend it into cherries. Turn into pie shell and dot with butter, about 1 tablespoon if you are counting calories or 2 tablespoons if you are not. Roll out the rest of the pastry, place it over cherries, crimp edges, moistening your fingers in milk, so the bottom and top pastries will stick together. Brush top of pastry shell with cold milk (it helps it to color well) and make 6 diagonal slashes in top crust to let out steam. Bake 30 to 40 minutes. *Serves 7 to 9.*

QUICK HONEY PUMPKIN PIE

1 envelope unflavored gelatin
¼ cup cold water
1½ cups cooked or canned pumpkin, drained
½ cup milk
¾ cup honey
½ teaspoon salt
½ teaspoon ground nutmeg
½ teaspoon powdered ginger
½ cup chopped walnuts (optional)
1 baked 9-inch pie shell

Soften gelatin in cold water. Combine all other ingredients except walnuts and pie shell, and heat over boiling water. Add softened gelatin and stir until gelatin is dissolved. Cool. Stir in walnuts and fill into pie shell. Chill until firm. *Serves 6 to 8.*

PUMPKIN PIE

Pastry for a 9-inch pie shell
2 eggs, slightly beaten
1 cup sugar
½ teaspoon salt
½ teaspoon powdered cinnamon
½ teaspoon ground nutmeg
½ teaspoon powdered ginger
¼ teaspoon powdered cloves
2 cups milk
2 cups cooked or canned pumpkin, well
*   drained*

Preheat oven to 450°. Line a 9-inch pie plate with pastry and flute the rim. Combine eggs, sugar, salt, and spices. Gradually stir in milk. Fold in pumpkin. Turn into unbaked pie shell and bake in 450° oven 15 minutes. Reduce heat to 350° and bake until a flat knife comes out clean when inserted into the center of the pie (about 25 to 30 minutes). *Serves 4 to 6.*

SWEET POTATO PIE

Rather like pumpkin pie, this delicious dessert is made from an inexpensive vegetable.

2 pounds sweet potatoes or yams
Water
4 eggs, well beaten
1 stick margarine or butter
¼ teaspoon salt
1/16 teaspoon nutmeg
1 teaspoon vanilla
1 to 1½ cups milk
1¼ cups sugar
1 unbaked 9-inch pie shell

Preheat oven to 350°. Boil unpeeled sweet potatoes until you can pierce them easily with a knife. Drain and cool. Peel potatoes and put them through a food mill or an electric blender, and then push them through a strainer. (For yams, the food mill isn't essential, since yams are less stringy.) Add eggs, margarine or butter, salt, nutmeg, and vanilla one at a time, beating after each addition. Beat at slow speed with an electric mixer or at moderate speed with a wooden spoon for about 2 minutes, or until well blended and smooth. Add ½ cup milk and blend. Then add sugar gradually, beating to blend. Stir in ½ to 1 cup more milk—enough to make a smooth, pourable batter, about the consistency of cake batter. Pour into pie shell, and bake about 45 minutes, or until the top is set and begins to brown. *Serves 4 to 6.*

STRAWBERRY TARTS

Can't afford fruit tarts on your diet? Make your own calorie-saver tarts using this basic recipe.

1 cup sifted flour
½ teaspoon salt
⅓ cup shortening
Cold water
1 quart strawberries, hulled
2 tablespoons liquid sugar substitute

Sift flour and salt, mixing well. Using 2 knives, cut in shortening. Sprinkle 1 tablespoon cold water over mixture. Mix with fork. Add more water until pastry sticks to fork in soft ball. Roll on lightly floured board until ⅛ inch thick. Press 8 pastry circles with inverted pastry pans and fit inside of shell pans. Trim edges. Prick pastry with fork and bake in 450° oven for 10 to 12 minutes. Cool slightly; remove from pans. Crush slightly 2 cups strawberries. Add sugar substitute and 3 tablespoons water. Simmer 5 minutes and cool, removing berries. Cook remaining liquid down to thicken. Place cooked strawberries in tart shells. Fill remaining cavity with whole berries. Spoon liquid over berries. *Makes 8 tarts.*

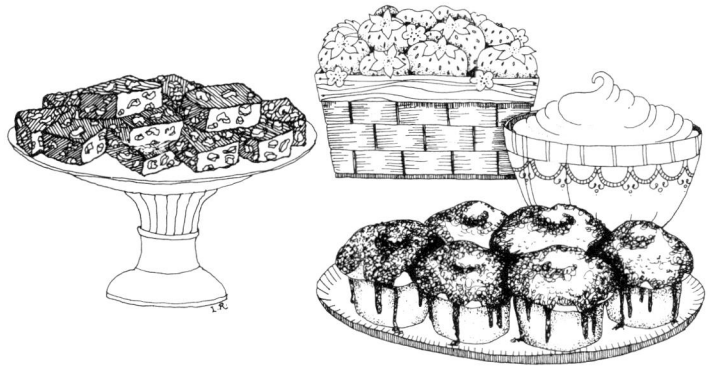

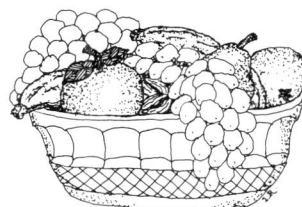

Chilled Desserts, Sauces, and Fruits

Although desserts today are a calorie luxury, they nonetheless add important nutrients to the balanced diet. And they do more—the sweets in desserts leave us with a "satisfied" feeling that can keep us from fatal snacking later, and from loading coffee and tea with extra sugar to meet our craving for sweets.

Use the desserts you serve to balance the meal budget in terms of dollars, and in terms of calories. A light, low-calorie meal, such as clear soup with a little meat and a salad, can afford a high-calorie dessert. By making the first half of dinner light in calories, you also make it light eating, leaving your family or guests hungry enough to really appreciate the sweet at the end. Nothing is more depressing than to make a smashing dessert and have everyone too full by the time it is served to appreciate the treat. When the main courses are heavy in calories, reverse the process and make the dessert low in calories by using egg whites and liquid sugar substitutes. Among the recipes that follow are many low in calories; these will give you some ideas on how to adapt the regular recipes here to lower calorie needs. Desserts made from scratch not only bring an extra dab of love to the dinner table, but they also bring an extra bit of cheer to the budget.

Chilled Desserts

You can make many frozen and chilled desserts from scratch without too much effort. All it takes is cream, a product nicer than the market ices. By using sugar substitute instead of real sugar, you cut the calorie count considerably. The sherbets are easy to make. Use the *Freezer Basic Citrus Sherbet* recipe as a guide to turn your favorite fruit flavors into icy sherbets.

Yogurt makes good ice cream, and when you make it from homemade yogurt the cost is minimal. Since it is made of milk instead of cream, it is lower in calories than other ice creams.

FREEZER PEACH WHIP

2½ cups heavy cream
1 cup sugar
1 cup canned peach slices or fresh peaches

Combine cream and sugar and add peaches. Pour into freezer trays and freeze. After 2 hours, remove from freezer and warm until ice crystals are gone. Return to freezer. Beat again after 2 more hours and freeze until hard. *Serves 6 to 8.*

FREEZER STRAWBERRY ICE CREAM

Substitute 1 pint pureed strawberries, fresh or frozen, for peaches in the recipe above, and proceed in the same manner. *Makes 1 quart.*

FREEZER DOUBLE CHOCOLATE ICE CREAM

4 squares unsweetened chocolate
2½ cups cream
1 cup sugar

Melt unsweetened chocolate and stir in ½ cup cream. Then mix with sugar and 2 more cups cream. Pour into freezer trays and freeze. After 2 hours, remove from freezer, and warm until ice crystals are gone. Return to freezer. Beat again after 2 more hours, and freeze until hard. *Makes 1 quart.*

FREEZER SMOOTH RAISIN ICE CREAM

1 cup chopped seedless raisins
¼ cup marshmallow cream
2½ cups cream
½ cup sugar

Combine raisins and marshmallow cream with cream. Add sugar and freeze as above. *Makes 1 quart.*

YOGURT AND FRUIT ICE CREAM

Apples should be cooked first with water, sugar, and cinnamon. For orange cream, use orange juice instead of milk.

2 cups fresh fruit, sliced
1½ cups Basic Homemade Yogurt
4 tablespoons honey
½ cup milk

Combine ingredients and blend in an electric blender until smooth. Pour mixture into a freezer tray and freeze for 4 or 5 hours. Stir several times while freezing to prevent crystalization. *Serves 6.*

FREEZER BASIC CITRUS SHERBET

Sherbet is a light and lively change from ice cream, and easier on the budget. Sherbet is also a terrific way to use frozen (or fresh) egg whites you've been saving. If you are using egg whites, thaw them before combining with other ingredients. A few drops of food coloring give any citrus sherbet more eye appeal. Use green for lime. One drop of red in lemon sherbet gives you pink lemonade ice. Or try red and yellow for a super orange sherbet. Another trick is to try a combination of citrus flavors—say, lemon and orange, or lemon and lime.

1 package unflavored gelatin
1½ cups sugar
2¼ cups water
1 tablespoon grated fruit rind (orange, lemon, lime, grapefruit)
1 6-ounce can frozen juice concentrate
1 cup milk
2 egg whites

Combine gelatin with 1¼ cups sugar. (If you use grapefruit increase the sugar to 1½ cups.) Stir in water and grated rind. Heat to boiling, stirring frequently. Lower heat and simmer 5 minutes. Off heat, stir in frozen juice and mix well. Pour through a sieve into a freezer tray. Cool fruit mixture for ½ hour, then stir in milk. Freeze about 4 hours, mixing occasionally with a spoon to keep large crystals from forming. Beat egg whites to the soft peak stage, gradually adding the remaining sugar. Beat frozen fruit mixture in a bowl with an electric mixer until smooth. Quickly fold in egg whites and spoon into large freezer container. Seal and freeze overnight. *Serves 6 to 8.*

Sauces for Ice Cream

Dress commercial ice creams with homemade sauces, and save. Commercial sauces are not nearly so good, and cost many times more.

Sauces you make yourself are great not only with ice cream, but also with leftover cakes and on plain vanilla yogurt.

NO-CALORIE RUM SAUCE

Real rum is very caloric (1½ ounces, 125 calories) so you had better resist substituting it for the rum flavoring we suggest.

1½ cups strong tea
1½ teaspoons liquid sugar substitute
1 teaspoon rum flavoring
2 teaspoons cornstarch

Combine ingredients in a small saucepan and stir over low heat until sauce thickens and clears. Chill before serving. *Makes 3 cups.*

LOW-CALORIE ORANGE SAUCE

1 cup orange juice
1 teaspoon cornstarch
½ teaspoon liquid sugar substitute (optional)
1 teaspoon grated orange rind

Combine ingredients in a small saucepan and stir over low heat until sauce thickens and clears. Chill before serving. *Makes 1 cup.*

STRAWBERRY SAUCE

This contains only 11 calories per tablespoon.

1 10-ounce package sweetened, frozen sliced strawberries, thawed
1 tablespoon lemon juice
1 teaspoon grated lemon rind
1 tablespoon cornstarch
¼ cup cold water

Combine first 3 ingredients and cook, stirring constantly, over low heat until mixture comes to a boil. Dissolve cornstarch in cold water, and, off heat, slowly stir into strawberry mixture. Return to low heat and cook until mixture returns to a boil. Chill and serve over *Meringue Shells. Makes 1½ cups.*

CHOCOLATE SAUCE

This contains about 20 calories per tablespoon.

⅔ cup water
¼ cup sugar
1 tablespoon cornstarch
⅓ cup cold water
3 tablespoons sifted cocoa
Pinch salt
½ teaspoon vanilla

Bring water and sugar to a boil. Dissolve cornstarch in cold water. Off heat, stir slowly into sugar mixture. Stir in cocoa. Return to heat and cook until mixture comes to a boil. Remove from heat and beat in salt and vanilla. Chill before serving. *Makes 1 cup.*

ALMOND BAR CHOCOLATE SAUCE

Here's a quick and easy, hot chocolate sauce that is hard to beat. But it does have calories.

4 milk chocolate bars with almonds (15¢ or 20¢ size)
¼ cup hot water

Melt chocolate bars in the top of a double boiler over hot, not boiling water. Add hot water, all at once, and stir to blend until smooth. *Makes ½ cup.*

Fruit Desserts

Fruit desserts that are classic—fruit cup, pears in wine—are among the nicest and easiest of desserts and provide that extra serving of fruit so important in the daily diet.

In season, fresh fruits are good buys, and you can take advantage of bargains to make your own canned products. Fresh fruit desserts out of season are costly, but you can work them into your budget by combining reasonably priced, available fresh fruits with canned fruits. Peaches and pears in cans are not costly, and can be combined with bananas, oranges, grapes, apple slices, or whatever is in season to create the fresh effect. In nearly all the recipes here, canned fruit can be substituted for fresh.

Don't overlook the bargain dried fruits. Dried apricots cooked into a compote following container directions are delicious alone or combined with sliced bananas, for instance. Dried figs, prunes, and raisins make good compotes, and make a fine dessert when topped with a dab of whipped cream or ice cream.

If the cooking liquid from a compote of fresh or dried fruit seems flavorless when the fruit is done, you can boil it down to intensify flavor, and/or add a tiny pinch salt, 1 tablespoon strained lemon juice, ½ teaspoon vanilla extract, perhaps a little more sugar. Or, before you start cooking fruit, add 1 tablespoon grated orange rind (grate, dry, and store rind from oranges and lemons, as it keeps for weeks when properly sealed in a herb bottle).

The recipe for basic *Poached Fresh Fruit* is a good approach to all seasonal fresh fruit bargains.

POACHED FRESH FRUIT

Poached fruit has been sadly neglected in this country. Europeans are more inclined to take advantage of this method of making desserts that are light, refreshing, and inexpensive. In addition, the syrup used for poaching may be strained after use, frozen and used again. For gala occasions, serve poached season fruit with the *Raspberry Sauce* below.

3 cups sugar
2 quarts water
4 sticks cinnamon
8 whole cloves
1 lemon, cut in quarters
6 pears—Anjou or Comice—not too ripe,
   or apples or peaches

In a large pan with a lid, dissolve sugar in water; slowly add cinnamon sticks, cloves, and lemon quarters. Cook in barely simmering water for ½ hour with lid on. Add pears. Poach gently until soft when pierced with a wood pick. Do not overcook. Chill before serving. *Serves 6.*

RASPBERRY SAUCE

1 12-ounce package frozen raspberries,
   thawed and drained
½ cup black currant preserves

Combine and run through a fine sieve. Chill before serving. *Serves 6.*

DRIED FRUIT COMPOTE

1 cup dried prunes
1 cup dried golden seedless raisins
1 cup dried apricots
4 cups water
Slivered rind of ¼ lemon
Sugar to taste (optional)

Place ingredients in a large kettle and cook on low until fruit is soft (1 to 2 hours). Chill before serving. *Serves 8.*

PEARS IN RED WINE

Leftover wine? Here's an exciting dessert to use it on.

4 firm, ripe pears
2 cups dry red wine
1 cup water
1 cup sugar
Small piece stick cinnamon
Rind of ½ lemon, cut in thin strips

Peel pears. Bring wine, water, sugar, cinnamon, and lemon rind to the boil and poach pears in mixture until they are tender, but not mushy, and still retain their shape. Remove pears. Simmer until syrup is reduced to half of its original quantity. Pour over pears. Serve warm or chill until ready to serve. *Serves 4.*

LOW-CALORIE PEACH WHIP

This has 100 calories per serving.

2 tablespoons cold water
1 tablespoon unflavored gelatin
1 egg, separated
½ pint plain yogurt

½ teaspoon liquid sugar substitute
Almond extract to taste
1 cup diced, fresh, or low-calorie canned
    peaches

In cold water, soften gelatin, then dissolve completely over hot water in a double boiler top. Beat egg yolk and add yogurt, sweetener, almond flavoring, and dissolved gelatin. Mix thoroughly. Chill mixture until it is almost set. Beat egg white until stiff. Fold in egg white and peaches. Pour into molds (or bowl) and chill until firmly set. *Serves 3.*

STUFFED APPLES

6 medium tart red apples
1 cup light brown sugar
¼ cup golden seedless raisins
1 tablespoon orange rind
¼ cup soft margarine
3 tablespoons orange juice concentrate
1 cup hot water

Wash, core, and stem apples, but don't peel them. Stand them in a buttered pan and stuff them with ⅔ cup brown sugar, raisins, and orange rind. Fill tops of core cavities with margarine and sprinkle remaining sugar over tops. Sprinkle orange juice concentrate over apples. Place pan in a large pan with 1 cup hot water in it. Bake at 350° for 1 hour. *Serves 6.*

ORANGE APPLESAUCE

4 to 5 medium tart apples, peeled, cored,
    and sliced
½ cup orange juice
½ cup sugar
1 tablespoon grated orange rind

Place ingredients in a kettle, and cook on low, stirring often, for 20 to 30 minutes.

STEWED RHUBARB

Nice with vanilla ice milk.

4 cups 2-inch pieces rhubarb
½ to ¾ cup sugar

½ cup water
2 tablespoons butter
½ teaspoon vanilla

Place rhubarb, sugar, and water in a kettle. Cover and cook 1 hour. Remove cover, turn off heat, and stir in butter and vanilla. Chill before serving. *Serves 6 to 8.*

STEWED RHUBARB
AND STRAWBERRIES

1 pound rhubarb
2 cups sugar
½ cup water
1 quart strawberries

Wash rhubarb thoroughly and cut into 1-inch pieces. Put into a saucepan with sugar and water and cook over low heat, covered, for 15 minutes. Meantime, hull and wash strawberries. At the end of 15 minutes, add them to rhubarb mixture and cook 5 minutes longer, covered. Test fruit for doneness. It should be soft, but not mushy. Remove from heat and place in a bowl. Chill thoroughly before serving. *Serves 8.*

MOCK AMBROSIA

The old-fashioned Southern favorite called Ambrosia is made with oranges and bananas, topped with sweetened whipped cream, flavored with bourbon or brandy. A simpler version gets down to basics—just fresh oranges, bananas, coconut, and sugar. You can add to it leftover bits of pineapple, slices of peaches, almost anything in the fresh fruit line the refrigerator offers. Add tag ends of liquors or liqueurs to the fruit—it's a great way to use them up. Top with a bit of leftover whipped cream or ice cream.

3 large fresh oranges
3 bananas
¼ cup confectioners' sugar
1½ cups shredded coconut

Peel oranges and bananas and cut into thin slices. Mix together sugar and coconut. Layer oranges and bananas and sugar–coconut mixture in a medium-size serving bowl, ending with a layer of coconut and sugar. Chill before serving. *Serves 6 to 8.*

LOW-CALORIE FRUIT CUP

A delicious fruit cup to make in late summer or fall when these fruits are reasonable.

2 grapefruits
½ pound red grapes
2 red apples

2 bananas
1 cup orange juice
3 tablespoons lemon juice, strained
Liquid sugar substitute to taste (optional)

Cut grapefruits in half and remove pulp sections carefully, eliminating all seeds and connecting tissue. Wash grapes, cut in half, and remove seeds. Wash apples, quarter, and remove core. Cut into chunks, leaving the skin on for color. Peel and slice bananas. Combine all fruits and add citrus juices and sugar substitute. Chill in refrigerator until ready to serve. *Serves 6.*

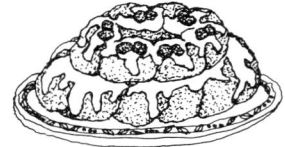

Yogurt, Puddings, and Cooked Desserts

Fabled Yogurt

Yogurt has about the same food value as whole milk but is less fattening, especially when it's made with skimmed or partly skimmed milk. It can be used in dessert or main course recipes much like sour cream. Yogurt has fewer calories than sour cream, and costs less. For many people, yogurt is tastier than milk, and even easier to digest.

As for the medicinal properties of yogurt, no one is quite sure. In the Middle East, where yogurt is a staple food, people believe it cures ulcers, hangovers, and food poisoning. Some scientists think yogurt bacteria cleans and detoxifies the digestive system. Many people use yogurt as a face cream or sunburn lotion.

For greater savings, make your own yogurt. The only real trick involved is heating at the right temperature. The *Basic Homemade Yogurt* recipe below explains how to make yogurt using conventional equipment. An easier and surer way, if you are going to go in for yogurt, is to buy a yogurt maker—a heating unit that keeps the ingredients at the exact temperature needed to make them set. Health food and department stores, and some hard-

ware, kitchen supply, and mail order firms sell yogurt makers at quite reasonable prices.

BASIC HOMEMADE YOGURT

1 quart milk, skim or whole
2 tablespoons milk powder
1 tablespoon yogurt or powdered culture

Combine fresh milk and milk powder in a saucepan. Scald just to 180° and remove from heat. Transfer to a bowl or glass container and allow to cool until 110°. Mix a little milk with the commercial yogurt or yogurt powder and blend until smooth. Stir into bowl of warm milk. (The yogurt can remain in bowl or be poured into slightly warmed individual cup containers.) Place bowl or container in a large kettle lined with a blanket, cover and set in a warm place. Allow to culture for about 12 hours, until the consistency is like thick cream. Do not jostle or move yogurt during this period. Chill before using.

You can keep making new yogurt with some of your old culture. If your yogurt batches start tasting too sweet, it's probably because the culture is being used too soon. Let it stand 2 or

187

3 days before making a new bowl. Yogurt takes a long time to spoil, especially plain yogurt. It usually gets more sour as it gets older. A good way to use sharper, aged yogurt is to drain it thoroughly overnight and use as a cheese spread. Add salt to this if you like, or chopped chives and nuts—whatever comes to mind.

VANILLA HONEY YOGURT

Add 1 cup nonfat powdered milk, 1 tablespoon honey, 1 teaspoon vanilla, and 2 cups milk in the *Basic Homemade Yogurt* recipe. Blender together, combine with balance of ingredients in basic recipe, and proceed with recipe.

ORANGE YOGURT

Before turning completed yogurt mixture into bowl or glasses for setting, add 1 tablespoon per portion of orange marmalade to the bottom of container or containers.

FRESH FRUIT YOGURT

Prepare ½ cup sugared or otherwise sweetened very ripe, peeled, sliced fruit for each yogurt portion you are making, and place it in the bottom of container or containers before adding yogurt.

BLUEBERRY, CURRANT, RASPBERRY YOGURT

Add 1 tablespoon per portion of fruit jam to the bottom of container or containers for the yogurt before you pour in yogurt mixture.

YOGURT APPLE PANCAKES

Serve with a light syrup, or brush with melted margarine and sprinkle with powdered sugar.

⅔ cup drained yogurt
⅔ cup milk
2 eggs, well beaten
1½ cups sifted all-purpose flour

¾ teaspoon salt
2 tablespoons sugar
1 teaspoon baking powder
½ teaspoon baking soda
½ teaspoon cinnamon
1 cup tart apples, peeled and grated
¼ cup melted margarine

Thoroughly mix yogurt and milk with beaten eggs. Sift dry ingredients and add to above mixture. Add grated apple and melted margarine. Drop batter on heated griddle in about 4-inch circles. Bake until bubbles appear on surface. Turn and bake other side until golden brown. *Serves 4.*

TVOROZHNIKI

A cheesy dessert beloved of Russians—it begins with cottage cheese. Use a low-calorie cottage cheese if you wish to save calories.

1 pound cottage cheese
2 eggs
Flour, as needed
Juice of 1 lemon
Salt and freshly ground pepper
¼ cup (approximately) margarine or butter
Sour cream
Sugar to taste

Rub cheese through a fine sieve. Add eggs and enough flour to hold mixture together. Add lemon juice, and salt and pepper to taste. Shape on a floured board into small round patties about 3 inches in diameter. Fry in heated margarine or butter until brown on both sides, adding more if needed. Serve sour cream on the side and sugar to taste. *Serves 4.*

Puddings and Cooked Desserts

Among the best buys in homemade desserts are the puddings. Made from skimmed milk, the calorie count is way down, especially if you sweeten them with a liquid sugar substitute. Rice puddings and Indian pudding are among the classical desserts of this sort, and take very little effort to make. Skip the starch for the main course when offering such rich desserts, and the overall calorie count of the meal won't be bad. Plum pudding is an exception—you can't save calories here, but you can save dollars by making your own for state occasions.

COCONUT MILK PUDDING

This is an Indian dessert that relies on milk and is economical and good. Serve with your favorite cookies or fresh berries or plain. This pudding may be prepared in advance and kept in the refrigerator.

2 heaping tablespoons cornstarch
2 heaping tablespoons rice flour (4 heaping tablespoons cornstarch may be used instead)
½ cup cold water
2 quarts milk
1 cup sugar
4 ounces shredded coconut
1/16 teaspoon salt

Place cornstarch and rice flour in a bowl, add ½ cup cold water, stir, and set aside. Place milk in a saucepan, add sugar, coconut, and salt. Bring to a boil over medium heat. Pour cornstarch mixture in slowly, stirring constantly. Cook about 30 minutes, stirring all the time. Simmer and stir occasionally until mixture thickens to the consistency of a thick pudding (about 15 minutes). Remove from heat, pour into separate serving bowls for individual helpings or into 1 serving dish. Brown surface under the broiler if desired. In that case, a flameproof dish should be used. Allow to cool for about 2 to 3 hours. *Serves 8 to 10.*

COUSIN CLARA'S RICE PUDDING

¼ cup long grain rice
½ cup sugar
½ teaspoon vanilla
¼ teaspoon salt
1 quart milk
2 sticks cinnamon
1 teaspoon butter
Raisins (optional)

Combine ingredients in a baking dish and bake in a 350° oven 3 hours, stirring several times in the first hour and being careful not to break the crust any more than necessary. Raisins may be added if desired. Remove cinnamon sticks before serving. This dessert may be served hot, warm, or chilled. *Serves 6.*

RICE PUDDING

1 cup raw converted rice
2½ cups milk
⅔ cup granulated sugar
½ cup golden seedless raisins
½ teaspoon salt
½ teaspoon nutmeg
Rind of half a lemon, slivered
½ teaspoon vanilla

Place ingredients in a casserole, cover, and stir once. Cook on low for 1 to 2 hours. *Serves 6.*

INDIAN PUDDING

3½ cups cold milk
⅓ cup yellow cornmeal
2 eggs
¼ cup dark molasses
½ cup light brown sugar, firmly packed
½ teaspoon salt
½ teaspoon ground ginger
1 teaspoon ground cinnamon
½ teaspoon nutmeg
4 tablespoons butter
¾ cup golden seedless raisins
1 cup hot water
½ pint light cream (optional)

Over medium heat in a large saucepan heat 3 cups milk. Combine ½ cup cold milk with cornmeal and turn into saucepan. Stir continuously until mixture begins to thicken. Lower heat and stir 20 minutes more. Beat eggs in a small bowl and stir in molasses, sugar, salt, ginger, nutmeg, and cinnamon. Cut butter into cornmeal mixture and stir in raisins. Add egg mixture and whip briskly, then pour into a buttered 2-quart mold. Pour 1 cup hot water into bottom of a large pan, set mold in pan, then set both in a 325° oven. Bake 1½ to 2 hours. Serve warm with cream. *Serves 8.*

MOCK CRÈME BRÛLÉE

A pleasant substitute when you have a yen for crème brûlée but no time to make it.

2 4-ounce packages vanilla pudding and
   pie filling mix
2 cups milk
2 cups half-and-half
½ cup chopped pecans
½ cup brown sugar, firmly packed

Cook pudding and pie filling mix as directed on package using milk and half-and-half. Cool slightly. Pour into 1½-quart baking dish. Sprinkle pecans and brown sugar evenly over top. Chill thoroughly. Just before serving, place on broiler rack 5 inches from heat source for 4 to 5 minutes to allow sugar to melt and become bubbly. *Serves 8.*

MERINGUE KISSES

Meringue is a boon to budgeteers saving on calories. The kisses have 28 calories each; the shells, 70. Fill the shells with low-calorie ice milk and top with one of the low-calorie sauces in this book.

¼ teaspoon cream of tartar
3 egg whites, at room temperature
½ cup plus 1 tablespoon sugar

Sprinkle cream of tartar over egg whites and beat with an electric mixer for about 10 seconds at high speed. Start adding sugar, gradually, and continue beating until whites are very stiff and glossy. Drop meringue by heaping teaspoons onto a brown paper-covered cookie sheet bringing them to a peak in the center like chocolate kisses. Leave a little space between each, as meringue expands during baking. Bake in a 275° oven for 40 to 45 minutes. Turn off heat and leave in oven to cool completely. *Serves 8 to 10.*

MERINGUE SHELLS

Use about ⅓ cup *Meringue Kisses* batter for each shell. Drop onto brown paper-covered cookie sheet and hollow centers, building up around the edges. Bake in a 275° oven for 50 to 60 minutes. Turn off heat and leave in oven to cool completely. *Makes 7 shells.*

TOASTED ALMOND PARFAIT

This is easy to prepare and can be made whenever ice cream, nuts, and syrup are obtainable. For an alternate method, honey may be substituted for the maple syrup.

1 6-ounce package almonds, unskinned
¾ cup (or more) maple syrup
2 pints vanilla ice cream, softened, or ice milk
Whipped cream, or low-calorie topping

Preheat oven to 400°. Spread almonds on a baking sheet and toast them in oven, turning occasionally until they are a dark brown. Chop them very fine or put through a food chopper. Mix almonds with maple syrup to make a thin paste, adding more maple syrup if it seems too thick. Spoon a generous tablespoon of almond paste into the bottoms of 6 to 8 parfait or wine glasses. Cover it with a thick layer of ice cream. Continue in this manner, alternating almond paste with ice cream until glasses are nearly filled. Cover parfaits with plastic wrap and freeze until they are hard. Remove them from freezer about 30 minutes before serving and put in refrigerator. Top with whipped cream. *Serves 6 to 8.*

APPLE BROWN BETTY

This is one of the most cockle-warming desserts you can serve on a cold day, just as your great-grandmother did years ago.

2 cups soft bread crumbs
3 cups peeled, sliced apples
⅔ cup brown sugar
¼ cup water
¼ teaspoon cinnamon

¼ *teaspoon nutmeg*
2 tablespoons melted margarine
Hard Sauce

Cover bottom of buttered baking dish with ⅓ of the bread crumbs. Cover with half of the apples, sugar, water, and spices. Cover with another ⅓ of the crumbs and add the remainder of the fruit, sugar, water, and spices. Mix the rest of the bread crumbs with the margarine and sprinkle over the top of the pudding. Bake in 375° oven 1 hour. Serve with Hard Sauce. *Serves 6.*

Party Appetizers, Exotic Main Dishes, Desserts

Budget Canapés

When you invite friends to stop in for a long cool drink in summer, or if you offer something to drink before dinner, you will want to provide simple, but delicious tidbits as an accompaniment. It's nice, however simple the party, to have at least one cold and one hot canapé; though if you are short of either time or wherewithal, your guests will be happy with either one or the other.

One of the most popular canapés you can possibly serve, from the point of view of appearance, lack of calories, and general acceptability, is a beautifully arranged plate of raw vegetables with a small bowl of seasoned salt to dip them into.

Carrot Sticks: Peel, quarter, and put into ice water. Store in refrigerator to chill before serving.

Cauliflower: Break away small florets, soak in ice water, and drain well before serving.

Celery Sticks: Treat like carrot sticks (see above).

Cucumber Sticks or Rounds: If the cucumbers are waxed, peel them. Cut into thin sticks or rounds and chill in a plastic bag, before arranging.

Green and/or Red Pepper Sticks: Seed, cut into sticks, and refrigerate, but do not put into ice water.

Plum or Cherry Tomatoes: Wash and dry on paper towels. If they have stems, leave them on for easy handling.

Radishes: Scrub thoroughly. Trim leaves, but leave stems on. Crisp in the refrigerator in ice water. Drain on paper towels before arranging.

Sunchokes: These used to be called Jerusalem artichokes. Peel and cut into sticks. Place in ice water in the refrigerator until ready to arrange. Dry well on paper towels. They taste not unlike Chinese water chestnuts.

This collection gives you a good variety of color. But don't forget that you can eat raw any vegetable you ever heard of—and probably more—so use your own artistic eye and palate in choosing what you'll serve.

GUACAMOLE DIP

This is one of the special dips. Offer it with anything from corn chips to celery sticks. The avocado must be ripe.

1 ripe avocado
3 tablespoons mayonnaise
½ teaspoon prepared mustard
Salt to taste
Garlic powder to taste
1 teaspoon (or more to taste) chili powder

Cut avocado and remove pit. Scoop out meat with a spoon. Mash with a fork until there are no lumps. Mix with other ingredients. If not to be used at once, seal bowl very well with plastic wrap and store in refrigerator. *Serves 6 to 8.*

ONION SOUP DIP

This classic instant dip can be made in about 20 seconds using a blender. It tastes like something much more elaborate.

1 pint cultured sour cream
1 package onion soup mix

Place both ingredients in a blender container and blend at high speed. Or mix thoroughly in a bowl until soup mix has dissolved. Chill at least an hour before serving. *Serves 10 to 12.*

DILL DIP

½ cup sour cream or drained yogurt
½ cup mayonnaise
1 or 2 tablespoons chopped chives or scallions
1 tablespoon chopped parsley
3 teaspoons dried dillweed
Salt to taste
Pepper to taste

Mix all ingredients, except salt and pepper. Taste for seasoning and correct with salt and pepper if you wish. Chill for at least 1 hour before serving. *Serves 6 to 8.*

BLUE CHEESE DIP

1 clove garlic, peeled
1 cup mayonnaise
2 ounces blue cheese, at room temperature
6 ounces cream cheese, at room temperature
2 drops Tabasco sauce, at room temperature

Crush garlic until very fine. Add mayonnaise and blend. Work in cheeses, beating with a wooden spoon. Or use medium speed on the electric beater. Season with Tabasco and chill. *Serves 8 to 10.*

HUNGARIAN DIP

1 cup creamed cottage cheese, at room
    temperature
1 8-ounce package cream cheese, at room
    temperature
½ cup sour cream
1 tablespoon prepared mustard
1 tablespoon caraway seed
2 tablespoons capers
Freshly ground pepper to taste
1 ¾-ounce package onion soup mix
2 teaspoons hot paprika
¼ cup minced parsley
1 tablespoon chopped pimiento
Potato chips

Mix cheeses with sour cream to blend well. Add all other ingredients except pimiento and chips and blend well. Refrigerate. When ready to serve, mound on a plate and decorate with pieces of pimiento. Serve with potato chips to scoop it up. *Serves 8 to 10.*

LOW-CALORIE ITALIAN MERINGUE CANAPÉS

These contain about 15 calories each.

3 egg whites, at room temperature
1 tablespoon anchovy paste
⅓ cup grated Parmesan cheese
¼ teaspoon grated nutmeg

Beat egg whites until stiff, glossy peaks are formed. Fold in anchovy paste, cheese, and nutmeg. Drop by the teaspoon onto a lightly oiled baking sheet. Bake for 20 or 30 minutes in a 300° oven until lightly browned. Remove from baking sheet and serve hot. Or turn off heat and allow to cool completely in oven. Store in a tightly covered container. *Makes 36.*

CHICKEN STUFFED CRÊPES

These delicious, thin pancakes, stuffed with chopped chicken, turkey, or most any meat left-over, moistened with a bit of gravy, and seasoned with salt, pepper, and herbs make a show-stopping canapé. These may be made ahead and reheated when ready to use.

4 eggs
2 cups milk
½ teaspoon salt
2 cups all-purpose flour
¼ cup melted margarine
3 cups ground cooked chicken, seasoned (see above)

Beat eggs well. Add milk and mix well. Add salt and flour and beat until smooth. Add margarine and beat again. The consistency of the batter should be that of heavy cream. If it is too thick, add a bit more milk. Butter a 6- to 7-inch skillet or crêpe pan lightly and heat to smoking. Pour in about 3 tablespoons batter and tilt pan so that entire bottom is covered. Cook until lightly brown (about 1 minute), turn and cook other side for about ½ minute. That side will be spotty and is usually used for the inside of a filled crêpe. Arrange a long, thin ridge of stuffing down the left side, roll up, and keep warm. *Serves 5.*

PÂTÉ MAISON MARCEL

This is my father's recipe from the *Take-It-Along Cookbook*, adapted to use fat drippings from a pork roast. Instead of 2 cups cooked pork roast, you can start from scratch and use 1 pound pork shoulder.

1 pound chicken legs
2 to 3 cups cooked fatty meat from pork plus meaty bones

1¾ teaspoons salt
½ teaspoon pepper
1 bay leaf
1 teaspoon ground thyme
⅛ teaspoon ground allspice
1 teaspoon ground savory
1 small onion, peeled and stuck with 6 whole cloves
2 cups cold water
¾ pound chicken livers
1 cup pork roast drippings and fat
3 small cloves garlic, peeled and crushed
½ bunch fresh parsley, minced fine
Salt and pepper as needed

In a large kettle, combine chicken legs, pork, salt, pepper, herbs, spices, and cold water. Over medium heat, bring these to a rapid boil, then cover tightly, reduce heat, and simmer 2 hours. Do not add more water. Remove meat, reserving liquid. Pick meat and meaty fat from bones and chop fine. Place chicken livers in cooking liquid, and simmer 10 minutes over low heat. Remove and chop livers fine. Discard bay leaf and onion. Add the pork fat and drippings to cooking liquid and boil rapidly for 10 minutes. Put meat and liver through an electric blender 1 cup at a time, adding to each batch a little of the fatty cooking liquid. Turn meats into a large bowl and mix well with garlic and parsley. Taste, and add salt and pepper as needed. Scoop into a 1-quart mold, or into several smaller molds, and chill overnight before serving. *Serves 20 to 30 as a canapé spread; serves 16 to 24 as a first course.*

CHOPPED CHICKEN LIVER

1 large minced onion
2 to 6 tablespoons chicken fat or butter
1 pound fresh chicken liver
1 tablespoon water
2 hard-boiled eggs
Salt and pepper to taste

Sauté onion in chicken fat or butter until transparent but not browned. Add liver and water, and cook over medium heat until liver is no longer red inside. Cool. Chop liver and eggs finely with a sharp knife. Add whatever cooking liquid may be left and enough chicken fat or butter to moisten. Mash with a fork and season with salt and pepper to taste. Use as a sandwich spread or serve with crackers for hors d'oeuvres. *Serves 4.*

POTTED SHRIMP

Fresh tiny shrimp usually are very inexpensive. Throw these into boiling salted water, flavored with 1 bay leaf, ½ onion, and a pinch of thyme. When they turn pink—4 to 5 minutes—turn off the heat, cool the cooking liquid with ice cubes, and peel the shrimp.

1 pound very small shrimp, cooked
2 sticks butter, melted
Cayenne pepper to taste
½ teaspoon mace
1 teaspoon freshly grated nutmeg

Blender shrimp or put through a food mill with butter. Add seasonings. Cook 2 to 3 minutes over low heat. Pour into a couple of individual soufflé dishes or other containers of your choice and refrigerate to chill well. Remove from refrigerator ½ hour before serving so that it will be easy to spread. *Serves 10 to 12.*

CHEESE LOAF

This has 200 calories per loaf.

½ pound farmer cheese
Caraway seeds or sliced raw onions

Shape cheese into a loaf. Cut loaf in half. Line with caraway seeds or sliced raw onions and wrap in several layers cheesecloth. Place in an uncovered dish and set in a warm spot for about a week. Unwrap and serve in thin slices. Any left over should be stored in refrigerator. *Serves 6 to 8.*

BACON CRISPS

8 slices bacon, at room temperature
16 "Club" crackers

Cut bacon slices in half, crosswise. Wrap a piece of bacon around each cracker. Place on a rack in a baking pan and bake in 250° oven until bacon is crisp and crackers lightly brown (about 1 hour). *Serves 4 to 6.*

MARINATED CELERY APPETIZER

1 bunch celery
2 cups beef broth
1 cup olive oil
2 tablespoons red wine vinegar
1 clove garlic, mashed
Salt and pepper to taste

Trim celery and separate into ribs. Heat broth to boiling in a large skillet. Add celery ribs, reduce heat, and simmer 10 minutes, or until celery is barely tender. Drain and cool. Put celery in a lidded dish. Combine oil, vinegar, salt, and pepper and mix well. Pour over celery, cover, and marinate at least 12 hours. *Serves 6.*

PICKLED MUSHROOMS

About 125 calories per quart. Great to pass around at a party; or serve as a relish along with dinner. Choose tiny mushrooms to make this.

1 pound fresh small mushrooms
1¼ cups cider vinegar
⅓ cup water
1 tablespoon instant minced onion
1½ teaspoons salt
8 peppercorns or ½ teaspoon freshly ground
    black pepper
2 bay leaves
8 celery leaves
3 sprigs parsley

Rinse, pat dry, and trim stem ends of mushrooms. Place mushrooms in a bowl. In a small saucepan, combine remaining ingredients. Bring to a boil, reduce heat, and simmer 5 minutes. Pour hot marinade over mushrooms and cool. Spoon mushrooms and marinade into a 1-quart jar with a tight cover.

Refrigerate at least 24 hours before serving. *Serves 12 to 14.*

OVEN TOAST

If you are stuck at the last minute for an appetizer, you can top chunks of pimiento, sardines, or dabs of leftover meat loaf with most anything and have an elegant canapé.

8 slices white bread
½ cup softened margarine or butter
Topping (see above)

Cut crusts from bread. Butter each slice generously on 1 side only. Cut across into triangles. Place, buttered side up, on a shallow tin and bake in 250° oven about 1 hour, or until golden brown. Dab with topping just before serving. *Serves 6.*

CHEESY CUCUMBER SLICES

The cheese mixture in this recipe keeps for weeks in the refrigerator and is delicious on crackers.

1 3-ounce package cream cheese
¼ pound blue cheese, at room temperature
2 tablespoons sour cream
Dash dry mustard
Salt to taste
1 tablespoon domestic brandy
1 large cucumber, sliced in ¼-inch rounds
Paprika

Mix cheeses with a fork until all lumps are removed (or put blue cheese through a sieve). Add sour cream and mix well. Add mustard, salt, and brandy, and mix to blend well. If cucumber is waxed, peel it. Spread cheese mixture liberally on the slices. Sprinkle with paprika. *Serves 8 to 10.*

Exotic Main Dishes

The German, Scandinavian, British, French, Italian, and Spanish recipes in earlier chapters will be familiar to most of your guests. Many are terrific party dishes. But the best way to thrill dinner guests without breaking the budget is to serve meals from countries whose food your guests are not familiar with. A large proportion of the main dish and vegetable recipes that follow in this section are in the "exotic" category. Only a handful of recipes —those particularly suited to entertaining a crowd for pennies—are from Europe.

Chinese, Indian, and Caribbean cooking, along with Greek and Near Eastern dishes, is truly low cost, though the ingredients often seem to belong in the high-cost category. One reason the overall costs are low is that only a small amount of expensive meat or fish is used. For example, the fried shrimp recipe serves four or more, depending on how many other dishes are offered at the meal. Yet only ½ pound shrimp is used to make the entire dish. Chinese and Indian cuisines rely heavily on vegetables as stretchers, and if you've eaten in a good Chinese or Indian restaurant, you'll agree the food is excellent.

Invest in a Wok

If you take an interest in Chinese, or any Eastern cooking, you will find a wok handy. A wok is a wide, shallow metal saucepan, with handles on either side—all curves and no angles. It is used to "stir-fry"—a way of cooking that is the secret of those crispy vegetables of Oriental dishes. A wok can cost between $5 and $15, in sizes 12 to 14 inches wide. It comes equipped with a perforated ring which is set on the top of the stove burner, with the wok resting on top of it.

You can stir-fry in a large, heavy skillet perfectly well, and also in a big electric fry pan of the circular type.

The stir-fry method is simple to learn. You add a little oil to the hot wok, swirl it around to coat the wok interior, add the recipe ingredients one at a time, stirring all the while. The very high heat of the wok quickly sears and cooks—and will burn—if you don't keep the pieces moving. Ingredients are added in a specific sequence: slow-to-cook ingredients go in first, since they will be cooking longest, while quick-to-cook ingredients go last, since they will have to come out soonest.

All this happens very quickly, a matter of 3 to 10 minutes for most wok recipes. Once you start the cooking, you can't stop stirring until the dish is done. So all the measuring and cutting and preparing for an Oriental dish must be done before the cooking starts. Line ingredients up in the order in which they will go into the wok, and set them close to the stove, including flavorings such as salt and soy sauce, and binding sauces, such as cornstarch and water.

Stir-fry foods are generally at their best a minute or two after the cooking ends, just time to get them to the table and served. They must, therefore, be served as soon as they are done. These foods are high in nutrition, as the flash-cooking does not destroy vitamins in vegetables.

Substitute for Missing Ingredients in Exotic Meals

If you are going to go in for exotic cooking, you will have to invest in the condiments of the countries whose cooking interests you. You can't cook Eastern dishes without soy sauce, ginger, and some other special condiments. Bean sprouts and water chestnuts are two other ingredients often called for in Oriental dishes; while these are important, you can get away with substitutes on occasion. Water chestnuts are almost flavorless, and are added for texture more than for taste. You can substitute diced celery, winter radishes, or peeled, young turnips if you don't have water chestnuts on hand. Or even thinly sliced pieces from the hard inner core of a cabbage. Lobster can be replaced by shrimp, iceberg lettuce or winter cabbage can replace Chinese cabbage, and so on. The flavor of a dish in which many substitutions have been made obviously won't be exactly as it would be if you had included the original ingredients, but it will still be good—and better than no dish or a dish interrupted by a trip to the grocery store.

Building a Larder for Exotic Cooking

Once you have cooked half a dozen dishes from one country—China or Mexico, for instance—you will have bought the major condiments basic to that kind of cooking. Although in the beginning it may seem you have to invest in a lot of new spices every time you try a dish from a particular country, in fairly short order, you'll have all the main spices already in your kitchen. The more spices and condiments you have, the more cuisines from other lands you can experiment with without purchasing new condiments. And the condiments can be used to liven-up even your day-to-day, American dishes.

Planning Exotic Meals

The easiest way to learn how exotic meals are served in their lands of origin is to go to a restaurant specializing in such foods. In the Orient and in some areas of the Near East, courses aren't served in sequence, but rather are placed on the table all together. However, most Western hostesses adapt exotic foods to their own native serving habits, and offer salty appetizers with drinks before dinner, soup as a first course, and sweets last.

In planning exotic meals, you can pretty well mix and match recipes from related regions without confusing anyone's palate. Chinese, Japanese, Indian, and Polynesian dishes go well together, since all tend to mix sweet and sour and hot and cool dishes together. Most foods from any given Caribbean country will go well with foods from another Caribbean country.

The handful of recipes here are just a sampling of popular dishes from exotic lands. Try a few, and if you find a style of cooking that especially appeals to your family, buy a cookbook with a large collection of recipes from that land. There are many good books on the market with recipes adapted to ingredients available in North America.

Far East and Polynesian Recipes

BEAN CURD SOUP

Bean curd, or *tofu*, can be bought in Oriental food stores. Made from soybeans, it is a protein-rich meat substitute. Although light, this simple soup is very nourishing.

4 cups chicken broth or bouillon
2 cups diced bean curd
2 eggs, lightly beaten
¼ cup scallions, chopped

Heat chicken broth to the boiling point and add diced bean curd. Reduce heat and simmer 5 minutes. Pour eggs in, in a thin stream, stirring vigorously until you see eggs start to cook in the hot liquid. At once, add chopped scallions and cook another minute or so. Remove from heat and serve immediately. *Makes 4 cups.*

BOULA SOUP

1 10-ounce can condensed green pea soup
1 10-ounce can green turtle soup
1 tablespoon dry sherry
¼ cup cream, whipped with a dash salt

Mix soups with sherry. Heat well, but do not boil. Pour into 4 flameproof onion soup pots and cover with a thin film of whipped cream. Brown lightly under broiler. *Serves 4.*

HAWAIIAN SHORT RIBS

Short ribs are the trim ends from a rib roast. They often are sold at a good price. Or ask the butcher to trim off the rib ends from the next rib roast you buy—then you'll get two meals for the price of one.

3 pounds beef short ribs
2 tablespoons shortening
1 onion, thinly sliced
1 teaspoon ground ginger
2 teaspoons dry mustard
2 tablespoons granulated sugar
1 teaspoon salt
¼ teaspoon pepper
2 cloves garlic, finely chopped
2 tablespoons chopped parsley
2 tablespoons soy sauce
2 tablespoons white vinegar
½ cup water

Trim away any excessive fat from ribs and cut them into serving pieces. Place a large deep skillet, or a Dutch oven, over medium-high heat, add shortening, and sauté onion lightly. Remove. Brown ribs on all sides in remaining shortening. Combine remaining ingredients and pour over ribs. Add onion slices. Scrape up the pan juices. Cover skillet, or Dutch oven, reduce heat, and cook 2 to 3 hours. Add a little more water if the ribs dry out. *Serves 4.*

CHINESE BEEF AND ONIONS

Cuts of round, top or bottom, can be tough. Slice them into shoestring strips, and stir-fry the Chinese way, either with these ingredients or flavorings of your own choice. It's the quick cooking of the thin strips that makes a fryable cut of round.

¼ cup oil
4 large onions, cut into rings
2 tablespoons soy sauce
½ teaspoon sugar
2 teaspoons sherry
2 teaspoons cornstarch
½ pound top round, sliced into 1×3½-inch strips

Heat 2 tablespoons oil in frying pan. Add onions and fry 4 to 5 minutes, stirring often. Add 1 tablespoon soy sauce, sugar, and 1 teaspoon sherry. Cook 2 minutes more. Place in bowl. Keep warm. Mix cornstarch and remaining soy sauce and sherry. Dredge beef in mixture. Heat remaining oil in the same pan, add beef, and cook until done (about 1 minute). Add onion mixture, heat well, and serve. *Serves 4.*

SCALLOPS STIR-FRIED

Most sea foods are low in calories. This recipe makes a fine Lenten dish as well as an easy diet staple.

2 tablespoons oil
2 cups small raw scallops
½ pound mushrooms
1 scallion or green onion
1 teaspoon fresh minced ginger root or ½ teaspoon ground ginger
2 tablespoons soy sauce
1 teaspoon salt
1 teaspoon sugar

Measure oil. If scallops are large, cut in half or quarters, to the size of small bay scallops. Wipe mushrooms and slice into t-shaped pieces ⅛ inch thick. Cut scallion into 1-inch pieces. Prepare and measure other ingredients and set everything by the range in the order listed. Bring wok or fry pan to almost smoking hot. Swirl in oil, count to 20. Add scallops and stir-fry 5 minutes. Add mushrooms, scallion, ginger, soy sauce, salt, and sugar. Stir-fry 2 minutes more and serve at once. *Serves 4.*

TEMPURA SAUCE

The Japanese use a sweet saké called mirin, sometimes obtainable in North America.

1 cup soy sauce
½ cup sweet white wine or sake
1 clove garlic, crushed
1-inch fresh ginger, crushed
4 slices carrot
4 slices onion

Bring ingredients to a boil. Reduce heat and cook at a low simmer for about 1 hour. Strain. *Makes about 1½ cups.*

FISH FILETS TEMPURA

22 ounces flounder filets, fresh or frozen, defrosted
1 cup all-purpose flour
1 cup water
1 egg
1 teaspoon salt
Peanut or vegetable oil for frying
Tempura Sauce

Cut fish into pieces about 2×3 inches. Mix flour, water, egg, and salt together lightly. Batter should be lumpy, like popover batter. Allow batter to rest 20 minutes. Dip pieces of fish into batter and fry, a few at a time, in 375° oil until pale golden and crisp—1 or 2 minutes. Offer with Tempura Sauce on the side. *Serves 3 or 4.*

FRIED SHRIMP WITH CHINESE VEGETABLES

You can make this recipe easier and lower in calories by cutting the shrimp into ½-inch chunks and adding them to the flash cooking vegetables along with the mushrooms instead of coating them in batter for deep frying.

½ pound cleaned shrimp
½ egg white, slightly beaten
2 tablespoons all-purpose flour
¼ pound Chinese cabbage
1 ounce canned bamboo shoots
8 water chestnuts
½ cup fresh mushrooms
½ ripe, red bell pepper or ¼ cup canned pimiento
12 snow pea pods or Italian green beans
3 cups plus 2 tablespoons vegetable oil
1 clove garlic, peeled
1 teaspoon cornstarch mixed with 3 tablespoons water
1 teaspoon salt
1 teaspoon sugar
1 tablespoon soy sauce
1 tablespoon dry sherry

Split shrimp down the back but do not cut in half. Mix egg white and flour to make a batter. Cut Chinese cabbage into diagonal strips, ¼ inch wide. Slice bamboo shoots and water chestnuts into ⅛-inch-thick rounds. Clean mushrooms and cut into t-shaped pieces, ⅛ inch thick. Cut seeded pepper, or the canned pimiento, into ⅛-inch-thick strips. Set all ingredients, in the order listed above, by the range. Heat 3 cups oil to 360° in a deep kettle. Dip shrimp into batter and fry until pale gold, about 2 minutes. Drain and keep warm. Heat wok, or a large frying pan, close to smoking hot. Swirl in 2 tablespoons oil. Slice garlic into oil and stir-fry ½ minute. Discard garlic. Quickly add cabbage, stir twice; add bamboo shoots and chestnuts. Stir-fry 30 seconds. Add mushrooms, pepper, and snow peas, and stir-fry until peas become a deeper green, 2 or 3 minutes. (If using pimiento instead of peppers, mix these gently into the vegetables when ready to serve, as the pimientos are already cooked.) When peas are bright green, add shrimp, cornstarch mixed with water, salt, sugar, soy sauce, and sherry. Stir and mix until juices have thickened and vegetables are glazed. Serve at once. *Serves 4.*

RUMAKI

This is from Polynesia.

1 pound chicken livers
Onion powder
1 7-ounce can water chestnuts, drained
4 to 5 slices bacon
1 cup soy sauce
1 teaspoon curry powder
½ teaspoon ground ginger
¼ teaspoon ground cinnamon
2 tablespoons dry sherry
1 clove garlic, crushed

Slice livers in half. If this leaves any very large pieces, cut them in two. Sprinkle with onion powder. Cut water chestnuts into 3 slices each. Place a slice of water chestnut on a piece of liver and fold the liver over. Pierce with a toothpick so that it goes through center of water chestnut and through second half of liver. Cut each slice of bacon in half lengthwise, then crosswise. Wrap a piece of bacon around each liver, securing it well on a toothpick. Mix remaining ingredients well and pour over prepared livers. Let stand at room temperature for a couple of hours, turning occasionally to be sure that all rumaki are well soaked with the marinade. Place rumaki in a

pan and broil about 5 inches from heat, turning once, until brown on both sides (about 10 minutes). *Serves 8 to 10.*

INDONESIAN FRIED RICE

If shrimp and crabmeat seem anything but budget foods to you, you can eliminate them. But the quantities required, as in most Oriental recipes, are very small, so they won't cost much.

4 eggs
4 tablespoons vegetable oil
1 medium onion, sliced paper thin
2 small onions, minced
½ clove garlic, crushed
⅓ cup minced raw pork
⅓ cup cooked, shelled shrimp
1½ tablespoons soy sauce
2 tablespoons peanut butter
Salt and freshly ground pepper to taste
1 small bay leaf, crushed
½ teaspoon ground cumin seed
1 teaspoon ground coriander
1/16 teaspoon mace
1½ cups cold cooked rice
⅓ cup crab meat
¼ cup finely chopped celery
1½ cups thinly sliced hot red peppers (optional)

Beat eggs. Heat a small skillet and grease with a few drops oil. Put 2 tablespoons beaten egg into skillet and tip to spread thinly over bottom of pan. Cook over moderate heat until light brown underneath. Repeat process 4 times. Roll each omelet and cut it into ⅛-inch strips. Reserve for garnish. Add 1 tablespoon oil to skillet and heat. Pour in remaining beaten egg and make 1 thicker omelet. Cut this into ½-inch squares. Fry sliced onion in 1 tablespoon oil until golden. Remove the onion. Drain and reserve for garnish. Fry minced onions and garlic in 1 tablespoon oil for 2 minutes. Add minced pork and cook, stirring, until pork is done (2 to 3 minutes). Add shrimp and omelet strips. Blend soy sauce with peanut butter, salt, pepper, and other seasonings. Add to pork and shrimp mixture. Stir until mixed. Add rice, crab meat, and celery, and mix well. Cook over low heat 10 minutes longer. Garnish with sliced omelet, fried onion, and hot red peppers (for color) if desired. *Serves 4.*

CHINESE FRIED RICE

In various areas of China, other ingredients are added to fried rice. If you have leftover pork, shrimp, chicken, or beef, cut up well and add any or all to the fried rice to make it a main course in itself. Leftover cooked green peas are also a pretty addition.

4 eggs
2 teaspoons dry white wine
1 small stalk scallion, minced
2 tablespoons vegetable oil
4 cups cold cooked rice
Salt to taste

Beat eggs with a fork. Add white wine and scallion. Heat oil and fry rice in it, stirring constantly, for 5 minutes. Add egg mixture. Stir constantly for another 5 minutes. Add salt and mix well. *Serves 4 to 6.*

BEEF FRIED RICE

3 tablespoons vegetable oil
2 eggs, lightly beaten
3 cups cold boiled rice
½ teaspoon salt
2 tablespoons soy sauce
2 ounces cooked beef, finely chopped or shredded
1 scallion, finely chopped

Heat 1 tablespoon oil in a large skillet. Pour in beaten eggs and allow them to set as for an omelet, for about 20 seconds. Lift up the edges with a fork to let uncooked egg run onto pan. When egg-pancake is completely done, but not browned, turn it out of pan. Allow it to cool slightly and cut it into thin strips. Now add 2 tablespoons oil to the pan and heat. Put in rice and heat for about 2 minutes, stirring con-

stantly, until all the rice is covered with oil. Rice should not brown. Add salt, soy sauce, and beef shreds, and continue stirring for about 30 seconds. Put in egg strips and chopped scallion, and stir until eggs are warm. Remove from heat and serve immediately. *Serves 4.*

CHOW MEIN

This is a simplified version of the Chinese dish. It uses up any leftover bits of cold cuts, bacon, or vegetables. Vermicelli or thin linguine cook very quickly. Start them cooking while you plan your list of ingredients. Use your imagination, but remember that to give it the particular Chinese flavor you must include the mung beans, soy sauce, and garlic flakes. You can also add small bits of ginger and a little ginger syrup to spice it up. Substitute rice for pasta, and you've made Chow Fan.

3 cups cooked vermicelli or other pasta (see above)
Water to cook vermicelli
1 medium onion, sliced, slices cut in half
1 cup finely diced meat
2 rashers bacon, crumbled
2 tablespoons oil
1½ cups mung beans
1 cup mixed vegetables
½ cup finely sliced celery (raw)
½ cup nuts (preferably almonds)
1 cup bamboo shoots (optional)
3 tablespoons soy sauce
2 teaspoons garlic flakes (dried)
Salt and pepper to taste
1 tablespoon finely diced ginger (optional)

While vermicelli is cooking, place all other ingredients except last 4 in a large skillet and sauté lightly. When vermicelli is cooked (al dente), lift out of water and add to skillet with last 4 ingredients, bring heat to high, and stir briskly for 3 minutes. *Serves 4.*

CHINESE CABBAGE

This is an inexpensive and delicious vegetable side dish for Oriental meals.

1 large Chinese cabbage
2 to 3 tablespoons oil or chicken fat
½ cup water
½ teaspoon sugar
½ teaspoon salt
½ tablespoon cornstarch
1 tablespoon water

Discard outer leaves of cabbage, wash and cut into 2- to 2½-inch pieces. Heat oil in frying pan. Add cabbage and stir until wilted. When wilted add ½ cup water. Cover and cook on low heat until tender (7 to 8 minutes). Add sugar and salt. Mix cornstarch with 1 tablespoon water. Add to cabbage and stir. When sauce clears and thickens, serve immediately. *Serves 4.*

CELERY WITH MUSHROOMS

This is economical only when mushrooms are reasonable, but it is a wonderful vegetable dish even with Western foods—and fast. If not dieting, double the oil.

1 tablespoon oil
½ pound fresh mushrooms
2 tablespoons soy sauce
½ teaspoon salt
1 teaspoon sugar
1 medium bunch celery

Measure oil. Wipe mushrooms and cut into t-shaped pieces, ¼ inch thick. Measure soy sauce, salt, and sugar. Remove celery leaves, wash stems. Cut stems into 1-inch arrow-shaped chunks across line of ribbing. Assemble all ingredients by the range in order listed. Heat fry pan to almost smoking hot, swirl in oil, count to 20, add mushroom slices, stir-fry 1 minute. Add soy sauce, salt, and sugar, and mix well. Add celery and stir-fry 3 to 4 minutes, or until celery is crunchy but tender and still shows traces of bright green. Keep warm until ready to serve. *Serves 4.*

CHICKEN, MUSHROOMS, AND SNOW PEAS

Once the ingredients have been cut up and prepared, this dish is ready in 20 minutes.

2 tablespoons oil
2 pounds chicken thighs
1 tablespoon soy sauce
5 slices fresh ginger root ¼ inch thick or 2 teaspoons ground ginger
1 teaspoon salt
2 cups plus 3 tablespoons water
15 dried Chinese mushrooms, or use fresh mushrooms
2 scallions
8 water chestnuts
1 package frozen snow peas or Italian beans
¼ teaspoon pepper
½ teaspoon sugar
1 tablespoon oyster sauce (optional)
2 tablespoons cornstarch

Measure oil. Chop chicken thighs into thirds, remove bone, rinse away broken bits of bone, toss in soy sauce. Slice ginger. Measure salt. Boil 2 cups water, cover dried mushrooms, and cook 20 minutes. (If using fresh, cut into t-shaped ¼-inch-thick slices and do not soak.) Drain dried mushrooms, reserving liquid. Chop scallions into 1-inch lengths. Rinse water chestnuts and drain. Thaw frozen snow peas. Measure remaining ingredients, and mix cornstarch with 3 tablespoons water. Place prepared ingredients by the range. Bring wok or fry pan to almost smoking hot. Swirl in oil, count to 20, add chicken pieces and stir-fry 2 minutes. Add ginger and salt, stir-fry 1 minute. Add mushroom liquid (or plain water if you are using fresh mushrooms), mushrooms, scallions, water chestnuts, snow peas, pepper, and sugar. Cover, simmer 10 minutes, or until chicken is tender. Stir in oyster sauce and bring to a simmer. Pour cornstarch mixture down the side of the wok, and stir with vegetables until sauce thickens and clears. Serve. *Serves 4.*

VEGETABLE MIX

The pork in this recipe is a flavoring rather than a main ingredient. Next time you have a pork roast, reserve ¼ cup of lean meat and freeze to make this vegetable mix.

2 tablespoons oil
¼ cup lean pork shreds, cooked or raw
½ cup Chinese cabbage, shredded
¼ cup celery in ½-inch-thick rounds
1 green pepper, shredded
3 scallions, minced
½ cup bean sprouts
1 cup beef stock or bouillon
½ teaspoon salt
2 tablespoons soy sauce
1 tablespoon cornstarch
3 tablespoons water

Prepare ingredients, mixing cornstarch with water, and set by the range in the order listed. Heat wok or fry pan to almost smoking hot, swirl in oil, count to 30, add pork shreds, and stir-fry ½ minute. Add cabbage, stir-fry ½ minute; add celery, stir-fry ½ minute. Add pepper and scallions and stir-fry ½ minute. Add bean sprouts, stir-fry 3 minutes more. Push ingredients to the side and pour beef stock or bouillon into wok. Season with salt and soy sauce, and bring to simmer. Add cornstarch mixture and stir until sauce thickens and clears. Mix with vegetables and serve at once. *Serves 4.*

EGGS FOO YONG

A Chinese chow mein omelet especially apropos for Sunday brunch. Pass Chinese noodles.

1 cup bean sprouts
½ cup thinly sliced scallions
½ cup thinly sliced celery
1 tablespoon finely chopped green pepper or
    parsley
Salad oil
6 eggs
1 teaspoon soy sauce

Sauté bean sprouts, scallions, celery, and green pepper or parsley in 2 tablespoons salad oil for 3 minutes; cool. Beat eggs with soy sauce. Stir in sautéed vegetables. Heat 2 tablespoons oil in a large skillet. Spoon egg and vegetable mixture into hot oil as if you were making 5-inch pancakes. Cook until light brown on each side, turning with pancake

turner. Serve with additional soy sauce. *Serves 4.*

CHINESE SPARERIBS

4 pounds spareribs
½ cup soy sauce
½ cup dry sherry
½ cup water
4 tablespoons dark brown sugar
2 cloves garlic, peeled and crushed

Arrange spareribs in a large roasting pan. Combine remaining ingredients and mix well. Pour over ribs. Cover pan with foil and bake in a 350° oven 45 minutes, turning ribs a couple of times and basting with sauce. Remove ribs from oven, pour off accumulated juices to use as a basting sauce, and arrange ribs in a single layer in a clean, shallow baking dish. Refrigerate until near meal time. About 1 hour before you want to serve them, remove from refrigerator and preheat oven to 350°. Return ribs to oven, uncovered, to bake for another 45 to 50 minutes. Turn them once or twice and baste until they are brown, crispy, and tender. *Serves 6.*

BEEF SHREDS WITH ONION

A delicious way to handle inexpensive beef cuts. Serve with another Chinese dish that includes lots of vegetables and you will have a meal for 4.

1 pound flank steak or other lean beef
1 teaspoon baking soda
2 tablespoons soy sauce
1 tablespoon cornstarch
3 tablespoons oil
½ teaspoon salt
1 medium onion, chopped
⅛ teaspoon pepper

Slice beef across the grain into strips 2 inches long by 1 inch wide by ¼ inch thick. In a medium bowl, toss beef with baking soda and let stand 15 minutes. Mix soy sauce and cornstarch; toss beef with this mixture, and let stand 10 minutes more. Set marinated beef with all other ingredients, prepared and measured, by the range, along with a slotted spoon and a small bowl. Heat wok or fry pan to almost smoking hot, swirl in 1 tablespoon oil, add salt, count to 30, add onion, and stir-fry 2 minutes. Remove onion to bowl with slotted spoon. Add 2 tablespoons oil, count to 30, add meat, sprinkle on pepper, and stir-fry until meat is gray (2 to 3 minutes). Return onion to wok and mix well with beef. Serve at once. *Serves 4.*

INDIAN SPICED SPINACH LEAVES

This makes an interesting appetizer, or can be served as one of several dishes at an Oriental meal. Choose thick, mature spinach leaves and wash very thoroughly.

1 pound fresh spinach
1 cup all-purpose flour
1 cup milk
1 teaspoon salt
1 teaspoon crushed red pepper
6 coriander seeds, crushed

Wash spinach, discard stems, and drain well. Beat flour, milk, salt, and spices together thoroughly. Let batter rest 20 minutes. Dip spinach leaves into batter and fry in 400° deep fat until golden brown, turning once. Drain on absorbent paper. *Serves 6 to 8.*

INDIAN PILAU

5 whole cloves
5 whole cardamom seeds, cracked
¼ teaspoon whole black pepper
¼ teaspoon whole cumin seeds
2 bay leaves
2 2-inch sticks cinnamon
1 cup long-grain rice
4 tablespoons margarine or butter
2 cups boiling chicken bouillon
1 teaspoon salt

Tie spices in a cheesecloth bag. Sauté with rice in margarine or butter 3 minutes. Add chicken bouillon and salt. Cover and cook, without stirring, until rice is tender and has

absorbed bouillon (about 20 minutes). Remove spices and toss rice lightly before serving. *Serves 6.*

Greek and Near Eastern Specialties

DOLMAS

These are stuffed grape leaves. They freeze well.

1½ cups water
1 cup raw brown rice
2 12-ounce jars canned grape leaves
1 cup olive oil
1 tablespoon margarine or butter
4 medium onions, finely chopped
1 teaspoon salt
3 cups chopped cooked meat
3 large bunches scallions, chopped,
    including greens
3 tablespoons shelled pine nuts or cashews
1 cup chopped fresh dill
½ cup chopped fresh mint
½ cup chopped fresh oregano
½ cup chopped fresh parsley
2½ cups boiling water
Salt and freshly ground pepper to taste
Juice of 2 large lemons, strained
3 bouillon cubes, chicken or beef
1 cup tomato juice, fresh or canned

Bring 1½ cups water to the boil. Add rice, reduce heat to low, cover and simmer 20 minutes. Drain. Soak canned grape leaves in hot water 10 to 20 minutes. Meanwhile, heat half the oil and the margarine or butter in a large skillet and cook onions over very low heat with 1 teaspoon salt, stirring occasionally, until transparent. Remove from heat. Add rice, meat, scallions, nuts, herbs, and ½ cup boiling water. Mix. Add salt and pepper to taste and half the lemon juice. Return to heat and cook until liquid is absorbed. Separate grape leaves completely and remove stems. Place each leaf with the shiny side down on a flat surface. Place a teaspoon to a tablespoon of filling on each leaf (the canned ones vary greatly in size). Starting at the stem end fold over and fold in sides, rolling tightly toward the point. Place stuffed leaves in layers in a large kettle. Add remaining half cup oil, half the lemon juice, remaining boiling water, and bouillon cubes. Weigh down dolmas with a heavy plate to prevent filling from bursting leaves when rice expands, and boil 5 minutes over high heat. Cover, lower heat, and simmer 20 minutes. Add tomato juice and simmer 25 minutes longer, or until all the liquid has been absorbed and rice is tender. *Serves 12 to 16.*

MOUSSAKA

4 small eggplants
1½ teaspoons salt
1½ tablespoons oil
3 tablespoons margarine
1½ pounds ground lamb or beef
2 onions, chopped
⅛ teaspoon pepper
¼ teaspoon cinnamon
4 tomatoes, peeled, seeded, and chopped
3 tablespoons chopped parsley
2 to 3 tablespoons white wine
6 tablespoons dry bread crumbs
6 tablespoons grated Parmesan cheese
3 egg yolks
2 cups hot Béchamel Sauce

Dip eggplants into boiling water, and cut into slices. Sprinkle with 1 teaspoon salt and rest under a heavy weight 15 minutes. Wash off salt and drain. Heat oil in a skillet. Add eggplant slices and fry until lightly browned on both sides. Remove and drain on paper towels. Heat margarine in a frying pan and brown meat. Add onions and fry until soft and golden. Season with remaining salt, pepper, and cinnamon. Add tomatoes, parsley, and wine. Bring to a boil and simmer 20 minutes. Make 2 layers—bread crumbs, meat, eggplant, and cheese—in a baking dish. Reserve ⅓ of the bread crumbs and cheese. Beat egg yolks. Beat in a few tablespoons of hot Béchamel Sauce and pour back into sauce. Pour sauce over the dish, sprinkle with remaining cheese and

bread crumbs, and bake in a preheated 350° oven 45 minutes. *Serves 6 to 8.*

KURU KOFTE

Excellent with hot French fries and a green salad.

1 pound lean beef, ground twice
1 large onion, grated
2 slices stale white bread (soaked in water and squeezed dry)
2 eggs, slightly beaten
2 tablespoons chopped parsley
1 teaspoon salt
⅛ teaspoon pepper
1 tablespoon all-purpose flour
2 tablespoons shortening

Combine ground beef, onion, bread, eggs, parsley, salt, and pepper in a bowl. Knead well for 10 minutes. Wet palms with warm water and shape meat into round rolls about 3 inches long, like thick fingers. Roll in flour. Place shortening in frying pan and heat. Brown meat fingers evenly on all sides over medium heat. Serve hot. *Serves 6.*

European Recipes

CHICKEN AND SAUSAGE IN WHITE WINE

The Italian sausage used in this dish (cervelat) is cheese flavored and is usually available at Italian butcher or pork stores and in many Italian delicatessen stores.

½ ounce dried mushrooms
2 tablespoons vegetable oil
2 tablespoons margarine
1 clove garlic, peeled
1 3-pound broiler-fryer, cut into frying pieces
½ pound cervelat
1 teaspoon salt
⅛ teaspoon pepper
1½ cups white wine

Soak dried mushrooms according to package directions. Heat vegetable oil and margarine in large skillet. Add mushrooms and garlic and sauté. When garlic is golden, remove and discard it. Place chicken and cervelat in skillet. Add salt and pepper. Brown chicken and sausage on all sides. Add wine. Cook, covered, for 10 minutes. Remove cover and cook for another 10 minutes. Serve on a platter with cervelat placed around chicken. *Serves 4.*

BLANQUETTE OF CHICKEN

This is the recipe used to cook the casserole shown on the cover of this book. It can be made with cut-up chicken of almost any kind, including boiling fowl. The original recipe is a French gourmet dish called Blanquette de Veau—but veal being the price it is, I find myself making the chicken version more often than the veal version. To make the cover recipe, we did not use mushrooms, which appear here as an optional ingredient. They are always included in a real blanquette, whether of veal or chicken.

2 to 3 pounds chicken, cut up
4 whole cloves
1 small onion, peeled
1 quart boiling water
5 carrots, scraped and quartered
1 bay leaf
⅛ teaspoon dried thyme
2 sprigs parsley
½ cup diced celery
4 peppercorns
1 tablespoon salt
¼ cup plus 2 tablespoons margarine or butter
15 (1 pound) small white onions, peeled
1 pound small mushrooms (optional)
¼ cup all-purpose flour
3 cups chicken stock (cooking liquid)
2 egg yolks
2 tablespoons lemon juice, strained
3 tablespoons finely minced fresh parsley

In a large kettle, simmer chicken with cloves pressed into onion, 1 quart boiling water, carrots, bay leaf, thyme, parsley sprigs, celery, peppercorns, and salt for 1 hour, or until tender. Drain and reserve stock. There should be about 3½ cups. Discard onion, bay leaf, and peppercorns. When chicken has cooled enough to handle, cut into pieces, 1½ to 2 inches long. While chicken cooks, melt ¼ cup margarine or butter in a medium saucepan, and add peeled onions. Cover tightly, and simmer until soft, about 15 to 20 minutes. Set aside in the serving casserole or bowl. Add mushrooms, stemmed and wiped clean, to butter in which onions cooked, and sauté over medium high heat for 10 to 15 minutes, until cooked enough so the liquid is done. Salt lightly, and spread into the serving casserole. When chicken is cooked and cut up, melt 2 tablespoons margarine or butter in onion saucepan, over very low heat. Stir in flour, then stir ½ cup chicken stock into flour rapidly to keep sauce smooth. Add remaining 2½ cups chicken stock, stir, and let simmer over low heat while you beat yolks and lemon juice together just enough to combine them well. Dip ¼ cup sauce from saucepan, and stir it quickly into yolk and lemon mixture, then pour this slowly back into the simmering sauce. Simmer another 3 to 5 minutes, then add the chicken pieces, carrots, and celery to the serving casserole. Reheat in 325° oven just before serving. *Serves 6 to 8.*

BEEF BLINTZES

1 tablespoon chicken fat
2 tablespoons chopped onions
2 tablespoons chopped celery
1 teaspoon salt
⅛ teaspoon pepper
4 eggs, beaten
½ cup beef bouillon
1½ pounds chuck steak (ground)
1½ cups potato starch
½ teaspoon salt
¾ cup orange juice
1 tablespoon chicken fat

Heat chicken fat in fry pan and sauté onions and celery until golden, and remove. Add salt and pepper to 1 egg and stir into bouillon. Add this to steak, with onions and celery. Into 3 eggs, blend potato starch and salt. Add orange juice and stir until it becomes a thin batter.

With chicken fat, grease an 8-inch fry pan. Place over medium heat and pour in ¼ cup batter. Spread batter evenly over pan. When lightly browned on bottom, remove to a paper towel. Place 2 heaping tablespoons meat filling on top of cooked side, roll up, tuck ends in. When all are done, melt more chicken fat in a very big skillet. When sizzling, add the blintzes and brown all sides. If necessary, add more chicken fat. *Serves 4 or 5.*

SAUCISSON EN BRIOCHE

A gala dish to serve for a very special occasion, this is made in two steps. The brioche rests overnight in the refrigerator.

1 package dry yeast
2 tablespoons warm milk
1½ cups flour
1 teaspoon sugar
½ teaspoon salt
2 eggs
1 stick margarine, softened
Cold water
1 large garlic sausage
2 tablespoons milk
1 tablespoon egg yolk

Sprinkle package of dry yeast over 2 tablespoons warm milk to soften. In a bowl, sift together flour, sugar, and salt; make a well in center. Break in 2 eggs, add softened yeast, and knead paste to make a smooth mixture. With hands, beat in stick of softened margarine until dough is thoroughly mixed. Shape soft dough into a ball and place in a bowl sprinkled with flour. Cut a deep crosswise incision across the top, cover bowl with a towel, and let dough rise in a warm place until it doubles in bulk. Punch dough down, cover it again, and let it chill overnight.

Preheat oven to 375°. Place sausage in a pan in which it can lie flat. Cover with cold water and cook over low heat, with water scarcely moving for 45 to 60 minutes. Remove sausage from water and when it is cool enough to be handled comfortably, carefully remove skin. Turn brioche dough out onto a floured board and roll it into a rectangle about ¼ inch thick.

Work swiftly while dough is still cool from the chilling. Place barely warm sausage in center of dough and gather dough around it without stretching. With fingers moistened in cold water, pinch edges of dough together lightly. If desired, press little cutouts of dough on top for decoration, and place roll on a lightly buttered baking sheet. Brush top and sides with milk mixed with egg yolk. Bake roll in a 375° oven 35 to 45 minutes, or until brioche is a golden brown. Let roll stand for about 5 minutes before serving. *Serves 6.*

Latin American Recipes

BLACK BEAN SOUP

1 cup black beans
4 cups cold water
1 tablespoon margarine
1 small onion, sliced
1 stalk celery, chopped
¼ teaspoon salt
Dash dry mustard
Dash cayenne pepper
3 tablespoons dry sherry
1 hard-boiled egg, sliced
1 lemon, thinly sliced

Soak beans overnight in water to cover. Drain and add cold water. Melt margarine and in it sauté onion and celery over low heat until soft but not brown. Add to beans and simmer (covered) 3 hours, adding more water if soup gets too thick (it should not be runny). Put soup through a sieve or whirl it in blender. Add seasonings and sherry. Reheat, stirring constantly, but do not boil. Serve garnished with slices of hard-boiled egg and lemon. *Serves 4 to 6.*

SERVICHE

From Peru, this is unusual and good; a South American way with raw fish. Sashimi is the Japanese version.

2 pounds frozen flounder or other fish filets,
    defrosted
Juice of 3 large limes

3 *medium onions, sliced very thin*
Salt and freshly ground pepper to taste

Lay filets out side by side and sprinkle lime juice over them, removing seeds. Let stand in refrigerator at least 8 hours, or until fish is completely "cooked" by lime juice. Sprinkle onion slices over all. Add salt and freshly ground pepper to taste. Serve as a first course. *Serves 6 to 8.*

SANCOCHO DE FRIJOLES (BEAN STEW), DOMINICAN REPUBLIC STYLE

Nice with crusty bread and a mixed green salad.

2 cups red kidney or California pink beans
1 pound lean boneless pork, cut into 1-inch cubes
3 quarts water
2 ounces salt pork, diced, or 3 slices bacon, chopped
2 medium onions, finely chopped
2 cloves garlic, minced
1 green bell pepper, seeded and chopped
½ pound garlic sausage, skinned and cubed
2 medium tomatoes, peeled and chopped
1 bay leaf
¼ teaspoon oregano
1 tablespoon parsley, chopped
Salt and pepper to taste
1 pound sweet potatoes, peeled and sliced
1 pound potatoes, peeled and sliced
2 ripe plantains, or 3 slightly underripe bananas, peeled and cut into ½-inch slices
2 tablespoons tomato paste
2 tablespoons white vinegar

Wash beans and put them into a large soup kettle. Add pork and water, cover and simmer gently for 1½ hours. Meanwhile fry out salt pork or bacon in a heavy skillet until it has given up all its fat. Add onions, garlic, and green pepper, and sauté until onions are tender but not browned. Add garlic sausage, tomatoes, bay leaf, oregano, and parsley and cook, stirring frequently, until well blended, about 5 minutes. Season to taste with salt and

pepper and add to beans with sweet potatoes, potatoes, and plantains and cook, partially covered, stirring occasionally, until all ingredients are tender, about 30 minutes. Stir in tomato paste mixed with vinegar, and cook for a minute or so longer. The beans should be tender, but still whole, and sauce thick and creamy. *Serves 6 to 8.*

RICE AND BEANS, PUERTO RICAN STYLE

3 pounds (6 slices) pork, cut off end of loin, and boned
2 tablespoons margarine or butter
1 large onion, peeled and coarsely chopped
1 bay leaf
½ teaspoon thyme
1 teaspoon salt
⅛ teaspoon pepper
3 8-ounce cans tomato sauce
1 tablespoon tomato paste
1 cup water
Grated rind of 1 lemon
3 20-ounce cans kidney beans
4 cups cooked white rice

Cut each slice of pork into 3 equal pieces and cut off any surplus fat. Heat margarine or butter in a large, heavy skillet. Sauté meat, a few pieces at a time, until lightly browned on both sides. As meat browns, lift to a heavy 4- to 5-quart ovenproof casserole that has a cover. Add onion, bay leaf, thyme, salt, pepper, tomato sauce, tomato paste, and 1 cup water. Place over a moderate heat and bring to a boil. Add lemon rind and beans with all their liquid. Mix together carefully with 2 spoons. Bring to a boil again. Cover and place in a preheated 325° oven for 1 hour, or until meat is tender when pierced with a fork. Serve with hot, cooked rice. *Serves 8.*

GARBANZO PATTIES

2 cups canned garbanzos, drained and rinsed
4 pieces stale whole wheat bread
1 large onion, finely chopped
¼ cup water

¼ cup milk
2 cloves garlic, mashed
1 teaspoon salt
½ teaspoon pepper

Preheat oven to 350°. Blend beans, bread, water, and milk in a blender until smooth, or run beans and bread through a grinder. Mix with other ingredients in a bowl. Shape mixture into 8 to 10 patties. Arrange patties in a large, shallow, well-oiled baking dish. Bake in preheated oven 30 minutes, or until lightly browned. *Serves 4.*

EMPANADAS

A popular dish from Chile.

½ pound ground lean beef
2 onions, chopped
1 teaspoon crushed red pepper
½ teaspoon ground cumin
3 tablespoons butter, margarine, or bacon fat
Pastry for a 2-crust pie
2 hard-boiled eggs, coarsely chopped
½ cup sliced ripe olives
½ cup chopped white raisins
1 egg, beaten
Coarse salt

Fry meat, onions, red pepper, and cumin in fat, stirring with a fork, until meat loses its color. Prepare pastry and roll it out ⅛ inch thick. Cut into rounds with a cutter 3 inches in diameter. Place a little meat mixture, a bit of hard-boiled egg, 1 or 2 olive slices, and a bit of chopped raisin on each round and fold over, pressing tightly on the edges with a wet fork to decorate and hold them together. Place on a lightly greased cookie sheet or sheets and refrigerate until 15 minutes before you want to serve them. Brush with beaten egg, sprinkle with salt, and bake in 425° oven 15 minutes, or until nicely brown. *Serves 6 to 8.*

Desserts

PLUM PUDDING AND SAUCE

A traditional Christmas dinner dessert. You can save dollars by making your own. Make it

a week or two in advance. It keeps well—gets better, in fact. A great gift for the holidays.

1 teaspoon cinnamon
1 teaspoon nutmeg
1 teaspoon powdered cloves
1 cup all-purpose flour
1 teaspoon salt
1 cup seeded raisins
⅓ cup whole seedless raisins
1 cup currants
1 cup chopped citron
1 cup chopped suet
1 cup molasses
1 cup sugar
3 eggs, well beaten
2 cups bread crumbs
1 teaspoon baking soda
1 cup milk
½ cup brandy, warmed
Foamy Sauce

Add spices to flour and salt and mix thoroughly with fruit. Mix suet, molasses, sugar, and eggs with bread crumbs. Dissolve baking soda in milk and add to mixture. Last, stir in fruit and flour. Place in a 2-quart pudding mold, cover mold, and steam over or in simmering water for 4 hours, adding more water as necessary. Cool in mold and refrigerate until ready to serve. Before serving, steam at least 1 hour to reheat well. When ready to serve, unmold and put a piece of holly in center. Pour ½ cup warmed brandy over and ignite. Bear to the table flaming. Serve with Foamy Sauce. *Serves 10 to 12.*

FOAMY SAUCE

3 egg yolks
½ cup powdered sugar
Dash salt
¼ cup domestic brandy
3 egg whites

Beat egg yolks with sugar and salt over hot water until thick and lemon colored. Add brandy. Beat egg whites stiff. Fold into original mixture and serve at once. *Makes enough to go with plum pudding.*

QUICK CHERRIES JUBILEE

This just takes minutes, doesn't cost much, and the flames make a fancy finale to a party meal.

1 20-ounce can pitted Bing cherries
¼ cup brandy
1 quart vanilla ice cream

Heat cherries in their juice. Heat brandy separately. When ready to serve, place a ball of ice cream in each of 6 individual dishes. Take ingredients to table, and at once pour warm brandy over cherries and ignite. Spoon cherries and juice, still flaming, over ice cream. *Serves 6.*

POTS DE CRÈME

This marvelous French dessert is easier to make than you might think. And, of course, it tastes out of this world. It should—it is loaded with calories.

1 cup heavy cream
3 egg yolks
¹/₁₆ teaspoon salt
2 tablespoons sugar
1 6-ounce package semi-sweet chocolate
  morsels
1 tablespoon strong coffee
1 teaspoon vanilla extract

Combine cream, egg yolks, salt, and sugar in a saucepan and mix until thoroughly blended. Place over a very low heat, stirring constantly, until mixture begins to thicken. This will take about 3 minutes. Remove from heat and stir in chocolate morsels, coffee, and vanilla. Continue stirring until smooth. Pour into little custard cups. Chill covered, before serving. *Serves 6.*

COEUR À LA CRÈME

Traditionally, this is made in a heart-shaped wicker basket. You will find one in a kitchen equipment shop. Or line a shallow colander with cheesecloth, and use that instead.

1 pound creamed cottage cheese
1 tablespoon sugar
¹/₁₆ teaspoon salt
1 cup heavy cream
1 pint fresh strawberries or raspberries,
  lightly sweetened

Beat cheese, sugar, and salt with a rotary beater until smooth. Gradually add cream, still beating. Line a heart-shaped basket (see above) with cheesecloth and put mixture into basket. Stand on a plate in refrigerator to drain overnight. Unmold, remove cheesecloth, and serve surrounded by whole strawberries or raspberries. *Serves 6.*

LEMON MELTING MOMENTS

4 cups heavy cream
1 cup lemon juice
1 can sweetened condensed milk
1 cup sugar
Grated lemon rind

Mix cream, lemon juice, and condensed milk in a large bowl and chill several hours. Stir in sugar and whip until thick. Turn into a serving dish or into individual dishes and refrigerate, covered, until firm, about 2 hours. Sprinkle with lemon rind. *Serves 12 to 14.*

SWEET POTATO CAKE, HAITIAN STYLE

This is a cross between a pudding and a cake. Served with rum-flavored whipped cream, it makes an elegant but inexpensive dessert.

2 pounds sweet potatoes
Boiling salted water to cover
1 large ripe banana
4 tablespoons unsalted margarine, melted and
  cooled
3 eggs, well beaten
1 cup sugar
1 cup evaporated milk
¼ cup raisins
½ cup molasses
¼ teaspoon grated nutmeg

¼ teaspoon ground cinnamon
½ teaspoon vanilla
1 pint whipped cream, flavored with 2 tablespoons rum

Peel and slice sweet potatoes and cook in boiling salted water to cover until tender, about 25 minutes. Drain thoroughly, and mash. Peel and mash banana and add to sweet potatoes. Add other ingredients, mixing thoroughly. Pour into a 9 × 5 × 3-inch loaf pan and bake in center of a 350° oven 1½ hours, or until a cake tester comes out clean. Dollop with whipped cream as you serve. *Serves 6 to 8.*

LOW-CALORIE BABA AU RHUM

This is a variation on the bread theme—and one of the nicest French desserts. It is inexpensive; made with liquid sugar substitute, it has only 85 calories per baba. Refrigerate babas overnight before baking the following day.

2 packages active dry yeast
⅓ cup warm water
½ teaspoon liquid sugar substitute
2 cups sifted all-purpose flour
3 eggs, beaten
1 tablespoon grated lemon peel
2 tablespoons melted margarine or butter
½ teaspoon salt
No-Calorie Rum Sauce

Dissolve yeast in warm water, stirring constantly. Add sugar substitute. Combine ½ cup flour with yeast mixture. Cover, letting rise in a warm place until mixture has doubled in bulk. Add eggs, remaining flour, melted margarine or butter, and salt. Beat briskly for about 5 minutes. Fill 12 greased cavities of a muffin pan with mixture. Cover and permit to rise until doubled in bulk, in refrigerator overnight. Bake in a 350° oven 25 minutes. Remove and cool, pricking muffin bottoms with fork. Place in a deep dish and cover with No-

Calorie Rum Sauce. Keep spooning sauce over babas until they are saturated. *Serves 12.*

CHOCOLATE SOUFFLÉ

If desired, garnish soufflé with additional whipped cream and chocolate curls.

2 envelopes unflavored gelatin
2 cups milk
1 cup granulated sugar
¼ teaspoon salt
4 eggs, separated
1 12-ounce package or 2 6-ounce packages (2
  cups) semi-sweet chocolate pieces
1 teaspoon vanilla
2 cups heavy cream, whipped

Sprinkle gelatin over milk in 2½-quart saucepan to soften. Add ½ cup sugar, salt, egg yolks, and chocolate pieces; stir until thoroughly mixed. Place over low heat; stir constantly until gelatin is dissolved and chocolate melted, 6 to 8 minutes. Remove from heat; beat with rotary beater until chocolate is blended. Stir in vanilla. Chill, stirring occasionally, until mixture mounds slightly when dropped from spoon (about 20 minutes in refrigerator). Beat egg whites until stiff but not dry; gradually add remaining ½ cup sugar and beat until very stiff. Fold into chocolate mixture. Fold in whipped cream. Turn into 2-quart soufflé dish with a 2-inch collar (see general directions for making soufflés). Chill until firm. Remove collar. *Serves 10 to 12.*

CHOCOLATE BREAK POUFS

A happy combination of two of America's favorite treats—chocolate and crullers! Great for skating or ski parties.

3½ cups sifted all-purpose flour
2 teaspoons baking powder
1 teaspoon baking soda
1 teaspoon cinnamon
1 teaspoon salt
2 eggs, well beaten
3 tablespoons soft shortening
1¼ cups sugar

*2 squares unsweetened chocolate, melted, or
    2 envelopes (1 ounce each) no-melt choco-
    late*
¾ cup buttermilk
2 teaspoons vanilla extract
3 cups fresh vegetable oil
Confectioners' sugar (optional)

Mix and sift first 5 ingredients. Set aside. Beat eggs well, then beat in shortening, sugar, chocolate, buttermilk, and vanilla. Add flour mixture all at once, beating just until smooth. Dough will be soft. Chill for 2 or 3 hours. Work with about ¼ the dough at a time, refrigerating the rest. Roll dough ½ inch thick on lightly floured surface. Cut with floured 1-inch round cookie cutter. Fry a few poufs at a time in oil (about 1½ inches deep in skillet), heated to 375°, about 3 minutes. The poufs will turn themselves when underside is done. Remove with slotted spoon and hold over skillet to drain. Place on paper towels to finish draining. Dust with confectioners' sugar, if desired. *Serves 8 to 10.*

CHOCOLATE FONDUE

Here's something really unique for your fondue pot! Use for dipping fresh strawberries, apple slices, banana slices, seedless grapes, dried apricots.

3 squares unsweetened chocolate
½ cup light cream
¾ cup sugar
3 tablespoons margarine
⅛ teaspoon salt
¾ teaspoon vanilla extract
Fruit (see above)

Combine chocolate and cream in a saucepan. Over a low heat, stir constantly until mixture is smooth and well blended. Add sugar, margarine, and salt. Continue cooking and stirring for 3 to 5 minutes, or until slightly thickened. Remove from heat and add vanilla. Keep mixture warm in a fondue pot or chafing dish. Everyone serves themselves by dipping pieces of fruit into the chocolate mixture with fondue forks. *Serves 4.*

Drinks, Hot and Cold

With or without alcohol, drinks play a role in our social lives. The collection of drink recipes here includes every type of beverage from a group of coffee drinks through nonalcoholic diet punches, to a handful of drinking-man's drinks from some of the well-known colleges.

You needn't follow drink recipes to the letter. There are many substitutions possible. Lemon and lime are almost interchangeable. Also, 7up and ginger ale. Bourbon and Scotch can sometimes substitute for each other, and almost any dry white wine can be used instead of almost any other dry white wine. You can lower drink costs in many ways, but especially by making your own basic ingredients—for example, consommé, chocolate milk, and yogurt.

Liquor for mixed drinks and punches need not be the finest brands for the end product to taste good. Since other flavorings will be included, it is customary to buy moderate- to low-priced alcohols for punches and grogs.

After-Dinner Coffees

CAFÉ FILTRE

This is the coffee drink used in France to top off fine meals. To make it, you need a filter coffee maker and dark-roasted coffee that is finely ground. Serve with a lemon peel. For each cup you will need:

2 tablespoons filter coffee
¾ cup water

Pour freshly boiling water over coffee and, when dripping process is completed, serve at once. *Serves 1.*

ESPRESSO COFFEE

This requires an espresso machine and is not just another version of *Café Filtre*, the French product. Espresso coffee is Italian. Each espresso machine has its own method of working, so follow the directions on yours to the letter. Serve coffee with a twist of lemon peel.

COFFEE CAPPUCCINO

This is a delectable concoction if you like the taste of strong coffee, but to make it you must have an espresso machine. Make it by combining equal parts of espresso coffee, hot whole milk, a dash of nutmeg, and a bit of cinnamon. The milk, when heated, froths a little, and gives the coffee its creamy surface. You can add sugar to taste.

IRISH COFFEE

Irish coffee is made from strong after-dinner coffee, which can be prepared in your regular coffee-making fashion. You will also need, for each cup of Irish coffee:

1 cup strong hot coffee
1 jigger Irish whiskey
1 teaspoon sugar
Chilled whipped cream, unsweetened

Warm whiskey and sugar together in a small saucepan and pour into coffee cups or thick goblets. Fill cups or goblets to within 1 inch of the top with hot coffee. Float whipped cream to fill the cup on top of the coffee. *Serves 1.*

COFFEE MONK

This is a modified, but more elegant, version of a *Cappuccino.*

1 tablespoon cognac
1 teaspoon brown sugar
1 cup boiling hot very strong coffee
1 or 2 tablespoons whipped cream, flavored
    with 1 drop vanilla extract
1 teaspoon dry cocoa

Blend cognac and sugar in a coffee cup until all sugar is dissolved. Pour in hot coffee, stir briskly for a few seconds to mix. Carefully ladle 1 or 2 tablespoons stiffly whipped cream flavored with vanilla extract on top of coffee and sprinkle with dry cocoa. Do not use a teaspoon to stir coffee. It should be sipped so that one gets the taste of the cognac-flavored coffee, the texture of the cream against the lips, and the smell of the cocoa in one's nose. *Serves 1.*

Cold Drinks

THE SLIM 'N TRIM

This contains only 15 calories per serving.

2 10½-ounce cans consommé
1 14-ounce bottle clam juice
1 tablespoon prepared horseradish (or to
    taste)
Juice of ½ lime
Salt and freshly ground black pepper to taste
Lime wedges (garnish)

Combine all ingredients except lime wedges, in a cocktail shaker. Shake vigorously and chill well before serving. *Serves 8.*

LIME–TEA PUNCH

With this punch you can serve sweet items like cookies or cake, little sandwiches, salted nuts, and olives.

4 tea bags
1 cup boiling water
1 cup light corn syrup
4 cups ice water
1 cup chilled lime juice
1 quart ginger ale

Steep tea bags in boiling water for 5 to 7 minutes. Remove tea bags and discard. Add corn syrup to tea and mix well. Add ice water and lime juice. Just before serving pour over ice in punch bowl and add ginger ale. Garnish with lime slices. *Serves 10 to 12.*

PEPPERMINT CHOCOLATE MILK

Top with whipped cream and garnish with additional crushed candy or use peppermint sticks as stirrers.

1 quart chocolate milk or chocolate dairy
    drink
½ cup crushed peppermint candy

Combine chocolate milk and crushed candy; heat just to simmering stage, stirring occasionally until candy dissolves. Pour into serving cups. *Serves 4.*

YOGURT SHAKE

You can use dried fruits such as raisins or apricots, and even nuts if you like, instead of fresh fruit; or use canned fruit salad. A blender is essential for this one.

1 cup plain yogurt
1 cup milk
¼ cup crushed ice
2 tablespoons honey
¾ cup sliced fresh fruit

Mix ingredients at medium speed in a blender for 2 minutes. *Serves 2 to 4.*

APRICOT PUNCH

Serve with the same foods as suggested for the *Lime–Tea Punch,* with the possible addition of stuffed dates and/or stuffed prunes. Or use artificial flavor syrups.

1 pound dried apricots
1 cup honey
2 cups orange juice
2 cups lemon juice
2 cups apple juice
2 quarts club soda

Soak apricots in hot water for 2 hours. Simmer, covered, until soft (15 to 20 minutes). Drain and press through a sieve. Add honey and mix well. Add fruit juices and chill. When ready to serve, pour mixture over ice in a punch bowl and add club soda. Garnish with orange and lemon slices. *Serves 14 to 16.*

APPLE CIDER NOG

2 eggs, beaten
½ cup granulated sugar
1 cup apple juice or cider
¼ teaspoon salt
¼ teaspoon cinnamon
⅛ teaspoon nutmeg
3 cups milk, scalded
½ cup heavy cream, whipped

Combine eggs, sugar, cider, salt, and spices. Add scalded milk gradually. Heat, stirring constantly. May be served hot or chilled. Pour into mugs and top with whipped cream. *Makes about 4½ cups, or 6 servings.*

Punches and Drinks with Wine or Alcohol

EGGNOG

This is a costly drink but much better than the commercial eggnog. You can shave the cost a little by using rum flavoring to taste, instead of rum. Serve this with thinly sliced fruitcake, salted nuts, spiced nuts, paper-thin Swedish bread, and thin white-meat-of-chicken sandwiches.

¼ cup granulated sugar
8 eggs, separated
1 fifth bourbon
1 cup light rum
2 cups milk
2 cups heavy cream
1/16 teaspoon nutmeg

Beat sugar into egg yolks. Add bourbon, rum, and milk. Beat cream until it holds its shape, and fold into sugar and egg yoke mixture. Beat egg whites stiff and fold in. Chill well. To keep cold when serving, place bowl in a larger bowl containing crushed ice. Sprinkle with freshly grated nutmeg. *Makes about 24 punch cups full.*

WASSAIL BOWL

For years this has been served in England on Christmas Eve. The name comes from the Anglo-Saxon *wes hal* ("Be of Good Health"). With this, serve an assortment of cheeses with crackers, potted shrimp, and a sizable assortment of crisp raw vegetables with seasoned salt to dip them into. Or go really British and serve tiny mince pies, sprinkled with icing sugar.

2 cups water
4 cups sugar
1 teaspoon freshly ground nutmeg
2 teaspoons powdered ginger
6 whole cloves
6 whole allspice berries
1 stick cinnamon
4 cardamom seeds

4 bottles sherry or Madeira
12 eggs, separated

Put water, sugar, and spices into a large saucepan and bring to a boil. Reduce heat and simmer 10 minutes. Add wine and keep warm. Beat egg yolks and whites separately and fold together. Strain some of the original mixture over eggs and mix well. Strain remainder of original mixture and bring it to a boil. Pour over egg mixture in a punch bowl. If desired, garnish with small baked apples and add 1 cup warmed brandy, mixing well. *Makes about 30 punch cups full.*

MULLED WINE

Serve this with wine cheese sticks, mushrooms marinated in white wine, hot buttered Triscuits, or tiny baking powder biscuits filled with deviled ham. Also great with cinnamon toast.

4 cups water
2 cups granulated sugar
8 cloves
2 sticks cinnamon
½ teaspoon nutmeg
2 bottles port or claret
Slices orange and lemon

Boil water with sugar and spices for 10 minutes. Strain, and add wine. Heat well but do not boil. Serve in heatproof cups with a slice of orange or lemon in each. *Serves 16.*

MAYWINE

Maywine is sold in wine shops quite inexpensively in spring. But you can make your own special brew if you have fresh woodruff, a herb that grows easily in shady corners of the garden.

1 handful fresh woodruff
1 bottle Rhine, Moselle, Alsatian, Chilean,
*   or California dry white wine*
1 teaspoon granulated sugar
2 tablespoons wine
Strawberries (optional)

If you have fresh woodruff, put it in a bowl and pour wine over it. Warm sugar and 2 tablespoons wine until sugar melts and stir into bowl. Let steep 2 hours. Remove greenery and add an ice block or a handful of cubes. Serve with 1 berry in each cup, if you like. *Serves 4 to 6.*

SANGRIA (for summer)

This is traditionally served before a paella dinner, during the dinner, with fruits strained out, or as a party drink. It's a light, pleasant Spanish drink.

Some inexpensive wines you might use are white Rioja from Spain; white Graves from Bordeaux; white Beaujolais from Burgundy; Undurraga or Concha y Toro white from Chile; Rizling from Yugoslavia; Liebfraumilch from Germany; rosé or red from Portugal; a Lake Country white from New York State or a Mt. White or Pinot Blanc from California. It is also often made with any cheap red wine.

1 bottle wine
Juice of 2 oranges, strained, and a long strip
*   of rind*
Juice of 2 lemons, strained, and a long strip
*   of rind*
Strips of rind of 1 small cucumber
½ cup granulated sugar
3 ounces brandy or rum
1 pint club soda

Mix all but the soda in a large pitcher. Marinate an hour or more. Add soda and ice when ready to serve. Do not make more than you think will be used up. It is far better drunk fresh. *Serves 6 to 8.*

FARMER'S BISHOP

The name dates from the 17th century. Great for a chilly night, as this drink is served hot. If you have a big metal punch bowl with a heating unit (such as Sterno or alcohol) underneath, you're really in business. If not, you'll have to make this in a big kitchen pot and serve from there. Instead of Apple Jack, you can use apple brandy.

4 oranges, stuck with cloves
1 fifth Apple Jack
½ gallon apple cider or juice
3 cinnamon sticks

Put oranges in oven at 400° for ½ hour, or until they begin to brown and ooze. Meanwhile, set the bottom ¾ of the Apple Jack bottle (opened) in hot water and heat. Pour cider into another pot and heat (don't boil). When ready to serve, pour Apple Jack over oranges and light. The liquor will burn with a lovely blue flame. Don't let it burn more than 1 or 2 minutes, extracting the orange oil and clove taste from the oranges. Immediately douse with cider. Serve in punch cups with a cinnamon stick as a stirrer or dust the top with ground cinnamon. *Serves 15.*

COFFEE–VANILLA LIQUEUR

Liqueurs are elegant accompaniments to after-dinner coffee. They are also expensive. But you can make a delicious one yourself. This also makes a fine Christmas gift, poured into a little decanter sealed with wax to prevent the stopper from falling out. The liqueur can also be made with instant decaffeinated coffee.

1½ cups brown sugar, firmly packed
1 cup granulated sugar
2 cups water
1 cup instant coffee powder
3 cups vodka
½ vanilla bean, split, or 2 tablespoons pure
*   vanilla extract*

Combine sugar with water. Bring to a boil and boil for 5 minutes. Gradually stir in coffee, using a wire whisk. Cool. Pour into a jar or jug. Add vodka and vanilla. Mix thoroughly. Cover and let stand at least 2 weeks. Remove the vanilla bean. *Makes about 5 cups.*

BRIDESMAID'S BOWL

This is a recipe from Germany, and as the name indicates it is ideal for a bridal shower or even served before a bridal breakfast. Peaches

or any other pale fruit can be substituted for the strawberries.

2 bottles white wine (inexpensive, dry)
2 pints club soda
1 small can fruit salad with light syrup
1 cup quartered strawberries
Ice cubes

Mix ingredients in a large punch bowl, stirring as little as possible. Light in alcohol, this is a drink children can join in. Serve in small glasses. *Serves 8 to 10.*

FROM PRINCETON: POISONED IVY

1 ounce saké
3 ounces vodka
Tips of ivy sprigs (optional)

Combine saké and vodka, and serve over ice. Decorate with sprigs of ivy if you wish. *Serves 1.*

FROM HARVARD: THE CRIMSON PIRATE

1 ounce saké
1 ounce Scotch
1 ounce cherry brandy
3 ounces orange juice

Stir together and serve over ice. *Serves 1.*

FROM YALE: THE SAKÉ MORY

1½ ounces orange juice
¾ ounce lemon juice
½ ounce lime juice
3 ounces saké
1 ounce light Puerto Rican rum
¼ ounce Curaçao
Maraschino cherries

Place ingredients in a cocktail shaker with crushed ice, shake well, and strain into cocktail glasses. Garnish each drink with a maraschino cherry. *Serves 2 or 3.*

FROM DARTMOUTH:
THE SNOWBALL

Shaved ice or clean snow
3 ounces saké
1 ounce maple syrup
1 ounce lemon juice

Pack a snowball of crushed ice and force into a stemmed glass with a large bowl. Combine remaining ingredients and pour over ice. Serve with a short drinking straw. *Serves 1.*

THE W.C.T.U. BREW

Freeze water into a block in a small saucepan before you start this.

2 large cans Hawaiian Punch chilled
1 large can orange juice, chilled
1 large can lemonade, chilled
Ice
1 quart lemon or orange ice or sherbet
1 quart club soda

Into a large punch bowl, pour all the juices and let marinate for 1 hour. The last 20 minutes, add a block of ice. When the guests arrive, put in sherbet to melt. Remove ice, and at the last minute add soda. Don't stir too much or you'll lose the bubbles. *Serves 25.*

MISCH HOUSE PUNCH

For a delicious variation, substitute a bottle of rum for the bourbon. Then it becomes the original "Fish House" punch. Freeze a medium saucepan of ice before you start making this.

1½ cups granulated sugar
3 cups lemon juice
1½ quarts cold water
1 quart bourbon
1 quart brandy
1 cup peach brandy (optional)
Ice

In a large bowl, dissolve sugar in lemon juice. Add water, whiskey, and brandy or brandies. Let stand for 3 or 4 hours. Before serving, put in a block of ice. *Serves 20 to 25.*

Index

A

Acorn squash, stuffed, 89
Aioli sauce, 70, 102
Alcohol, drinks with, 218–221; *see also* Wine, drinks with
    coffee-vanilla liqueur, 220
    Crimson Pirate, 220
    eggnog, 218
    Farmer's Bishop, 219–220
    Misch House Punch, 221
    Poisoned Ivy, 220
    Saké Mory, 220
    Sangria, 219
Almond bar chocolate sauce, 183
Almond parfait, 190
Ambrosia, mock, 185–186
Appetizers. *See* Canapés
Apple
    brown Betty, 190–191
    cake, coconut (quick bread), 171
    cider, hot, 218
    and ham sandwich, 153
    pie, with peaches, 175–176
    salad, with cottage cheese, 107
    salad, with ham, 107
    salad, with salmon, in lime dressing, 107
    salad, Waldorf, 107
    stuffed, 185
    stuffing, for turkey, 56

Applesauce
    ham loaf, 155–156
    meat loaf, 27
    orange, 185
Apricot punch, 218
Apricots, chicken with, 51–52
Aspics, 92–94
    about, 92
    meat-flavored, vegetables in, 93
    stock for, 92–93
    tomato, deviled eggs in, 142
    tomato, in gelatin aspic, 93
    veal loaf in, 31
    vegetable ring, jellied raw, 93–94
Au Gratin. *See* Gratinées

B

Baba au Rhum, low-calorie, 214
Bacon
    and cheese toasts, 156
    crisps, 198
    omelet, 145
Baked beans, 117
Baked bean sandwiches, 154
Baked fish recipes, 77–79
Baked goods, 159–177; *see also* Breads, Cakes, Pies, Quick Breads
    about, 159
    freezing, 10–11, 12

223

Baking powder, 163
Baking soda, 163
Barley flour, 160
Barley soup, beef and, 134–135
Bean curd soup, 201
BEANS
    baked, 117
    baked bean sandwiches, 154
    black bean soup, 210
    black-eyed chicken, 117–118
    California beef-and-bean pot, 118
    casserole, mixed bean, 117
    chili, 116
    chili con carne, 25, 116
    dried, about, 115–116
    franks with, 118
    garbanzo patties, 211–212
    green, dilled, salad, 84
    kidney bean soup, 135
    lentil loaf with cheese sauce, 119
    lentil soups, 135
    rice with, Puerto Rican style, 211
    salad, three bean, 110
    stew, Dominican Republic style, 211
    tomato bean rarebit, quick, 118
Béchamel Sauce, 91
BEEF, 17–23; *see also* GROUND BEEF
    about, 17–18
    basic cuts, 19
    Berne, 22
    blintzes, 209–210
    boiled, with sauerkraut, 18–19
    bouillon, 134
    California beef-and-bean pot, 118
    casserole, with corn, Jamaica-style, 20
    Chinese, with onions, 201
    cold, in Rémoulade sauce, 23
    cooked in beer, 18
    cooking methods for different cuts, 18
    corned beef rolls, 153
    with fried rice, 204
    with ham leftovers, 21
    Hawaiian short ribs, 201
    leftover, Crêpes Maroth, 29
    leftover, German Beef Roulade, 23
    liver, baked, French style, 61
    liver, hash, 62
    liver, Italian style, 61–62
    liver, with kidneys in red wine, 63
    liver, with onion butter, 61
    liver, Reformé, 61
    oxtails in wine sauce, 22–23
    roast, Charlene's chuck, 21–22
    roast, how to cook, 18
    roast, how to stretch, 17–18
    roast, rump, in foil, 21
    soup, with barley, 134–135
    steak, flank, broiled, 20
    steak, with peppers, 21
    steak, round, London Broil, 21
    steak, round, Swiss, 20–21
    stew, braised beef, 22
    stew, Carbonade Flamande, 18
    stew, with lamb kidney, 64
    stew, with red wine, 20
Beer, beef cooked in, 18
Beet relish, 83–84
Black-eyed chicken, 117–118
Blanching fresh produce for freezing, 9
Blanquette of chicken, 209
Blintzes, beef, 209–210
Blueberry cake with hard sauce, 173–174
Blueberry yogurt, 188
Blue cheese dip, 196
Blue cheese dressing, 102
Boiled beef with sauerkraut, 18–19
Borscht, cabbage, 138
Bouillon, 134
Boula soup, 201
Brains, 64–66
    about, 64
    au Beurre Noir, 65–66
    vinaigrette, 65
Braising beef, 19, 22
Bran, flakes and meal, 161
BREADS, 159–171; *see also* Quick breads
    basic ingredients, 159–164
    buying, 7
    coffee cake, simple, 165
    cottage herb, 166
    flavorings used in, 163–164
    flours used in, 159–160
    grains, meals and seeds used in, 160–161
    leavening used in, 162–163
    liquids used in, 161
    onion buns, 164–165
    pizza, homemade, 165–166
    pretzels, soft, 165
    rolls, cloverleaf, 165
    rolls, stuffed, 166
    shortening used in, 162
    sourdough, 169–170
    spaghetti-dinner, 166
    sticky buns, 165
    sweet, 167–168
    sweeteners used in, 161–162

wheat, 168–169
white, basic, 164
white, basic rich, 166
Breast of veal, stuffed, 31
Brewer's yeast, 163
Bridesmaid's bowl, 220
Brioche, Saucisson en, 210
Broccoli soufflé, 144
Broiling
fish, 74–75
steak, 20, 21
Brown Betty, apple, 190–191
Brownies, low-calorie nutty chocolate, 174–175
Brown sauce, fish with, 76–77
Brussels sprouts, grouse and, 58
Buckwheat flour, 160
Buckwheat groats, 161
Budget, food, 6–7
Buns
onion, 164–165
sticky, 165
Butter
for breadmaking, 162
freezing, 11, 12
onion, for liver, 61
Buttermilk, 161

C

Cabbage
about, 84
à la Milan, 96
Borscht, 138
browned, and noodles, 96
Chinese, 204–205
frankfurter jubilee, 43
pig's knuckles and, 41–42
red, spiced, 85
soup, 138
stuffed, 95–96
Caesar salad, 110
Café Filtre, 216
CAKES, 172–175
about, 172
blueberry, 173–174
carrot (quick bread), 171
coconut apple (quick bread), 171
coffee, chocolate, 170–171
coffee, simple, 165
fruitcake, Christmas, easy, 173
Georgia chocolate pound, 173
icing, chocolate, 173

icing, thin, 174
lemon chiffon, 172–173
mixes, 172
sweet potato, Haitian style, 213–214
California beef-and-bean pot, 118
Calories, 2; see also Low-calorie recipes
Calves brains, 65–66
Canadian supper pie, 99
CANAPÉS, 195–199
about, 195
bacon crisps, 198
celery, marinated, 198
cheese loaf, 198
cheesy cucumber slices, 199
chopped chicken livers, 197–198
crêpes, chicken stuffed, 197
dips for, 196
Italian meringue, low-calorie, 196–197
mushrooms, pickled, 198
oven toast, 199
Pâté Maison Marcel, 197
raw vegetables and dips, 195–196
shrimp, potted, 198
Candied carrots, 86
Candied fruits, 163
Canning, 7–8, 11
Caraway seeds, 161
Carbohydrates, 3
Carbonade Flamande, 18
Carbonara, Spaghetti alla, 126
Carob flour, 160
Carrots
cake (quick bread), 171
candied, 86
celery and, 87
coleslaw with, 111
cooked in bouillon, 85
in cream, 86
in garlic sauce, 85
lemon, 85–86
orange, 86
pie, 176
-potato fritters, 86
-potato soup, 137
with rice (Plaki), 96
sticks, 195
CASSEROLES; see also Stews
bean mixed, 117
beef and corn, Jamaica-style, 20
cabbage à la Milan, 96
cabbage, and noodles, 96
cabbage, stuffed, 95–96
Canadian supper pie, 99

carrot Plaki, 96
chicken, with egg noodles, 53
chicken liver, with rice, 61
egg, ham and potato, 141
eggplant Parmesan, 97–98
eggplant, stuffed, 97
eggplant, Woods Hole, 97
frankfurter, red and green, 43
ham and potato, 44
ham and vegetable, 45
lamb chop, gourmet, 34–35
lamb chop, New Zealand style, 34
lasagne and cheese, 129
lasagne and chicken, 129
Ratatouille, 99
rice, with chicken, 121
rice, with tuna, 121
Tetrazzini, 127–128
turkey, 48
veal and chicken, 33
veal and vegetable, 32
vegetable, 92, 95–99
vegetable and egg dinner, 98
vegetable loaf, mixed, 98–99
Cauliflower, raw, as canapé, 195
Celery
about, 84
with carrots, 87
cream sauce, 91
marinated, 198
with mushrooms, stir-fried, 205
"noodles," 24
soup, cream, 137
sticks, 195
super simple simmered, 86
Cereals, buying, 7
Charlene's chuck roast, 21–22
CHEESE; see also Cottage cheese, Cream cheese
about, 149–150
American, pudding, 151
in breadmaking, 164
chicken cheese melts, 151
cucumber slices, cheesy, 199
dessert, soft, 149–150
fondue, 150–151
freezing, 11
for grating, 150
lasagne casserole, 129
loaf, as canapé, 198
macaroni and, à la Bauserman, 127
macaroni and, from scratch, 151
omelet, 145

salad for dieters, frozen, 111
sandwiches, with ham, 152–153
sauce, 119
soufflé, basic, 143–144
soup, 139
storing, 150
Welsh Rarebit, 150
Chef's salads I and II, 108
Cherries jubilee, quick, 213
Cherry pie, sour, 176
CHICKEN, 46–56
about, 46–47
à la King, 54
and sausage in white wine, 208
baked, with apricots, 51–52
baked, with onion and spices, 53
baked, with sour cream, 51
black-eyed, 117
Blanquette of, 209
bouillon, 134
casserole, egg noodle, 53–54
casserole, lasagne, 129
casserole, with rice, 121
casserole, with veal, 33
Charlotte, with chopped clams, 49
cheese melts, 151
Chinese, with mushrooms and snow peas, 205
Cordon Bleu, 55
corn crisped, 50
crêpes, for canapes, 197
curried, mousse, 55–56
curried, sandwiches, 153
custard, 54
cutting up whole, 46
Divan, 54
with eggplant, 52–53
freezing, 8, 12, 46–47
fricassée, 50
fried, spring, 53
giblet gravy, 48–49
glazed, 59
gumbo, New Orleans, 56
lemony herbed thighs, 52
liver casserole, with rice, 61
liver, chopped, 197–198
liver omelet, 146
livers, Rumaki, 203
with Olive Condite, 49–50
Pilau, and rice, St. Lucia style, 50
pudding, Southern, 49
roast, basic, 48
roast, French baked, 48

roll, homemade, 51
salad, 108
salad, with orange, 105
sandwich, Croque Madame, 152
sandwich, open-face, 153
sausage and, in white wine, 208
soufflé, 144
stewing, 55–56
Tetrazzini casserole, 127–128
Tetrazzini, economy style, 50
wings, Marcel, 52
Chiffonade salad, 111
Chiffon cake, lemon, 172–173
Chili beans, 116
Chili con carne, 116
from scratch, 25
Chinese cooking, about, 199–200; see also Far
East recipes
Chocolate
break poufs, 214–215
brownies, low-calorie, 174
coffee cake, 170–171
fondue, 215
ice cream, 182
icing, quick, 173
pound cake, Georgia, 173
sauces, 183
soufflé, 214
Chops. See Lamb, Pork
Chow Mein, 204
Christmas fruitcake, easy, 173
Christmas gingerbread cookies, 174
Chutney, deviled ham and, 152
Cider, hot apple, 218
Citron, 163
Clams
chicken Charlotte, 49
and cream cheese sandwiches, 154–155
white clam sauce, 127
Cloverleaf rolls, 165
Cocktail sauce, 104
Coconut apple cake, 171
Coconut milk pudding, 189
Cod filets, baked, 77
Coeur à la Crème, 213
Coffees, after-dinner, 216–217
Café Filtre, 216
Cappuccino, 216
coffee monk, 217
Expresso, 216
Irish, 217
Coffee-vanilla liqueur, 220

Coffee cake, chocolate (quick bread), 170–171
Coffee cake, simple, 165
Coleslaw, with carrots, 111
Coleslaw, diet, 111
Collard green omelet, 145–146
Cookies
chocolate brownies, low-calorie, 174
Christmas gingerbread, 174
Cordon Bleu, chicken, 55
Corned beef rolls, 153
Corn fritters, 87
Cornmeal
about, 120, 160
Indian pudding, 189
with okra, Barbados style, 122
Polenta, 122–123
Corn pudding, 94–95
Cottage cheese
bread made with, 166
dessert (Tvorozhniki), 188
salad, with apple, 107
salad, with fruit, 106
salad, with vegetables, 110–111
Crabmeat, shrimp and, 79–80
Cracked wheat, 161
Cranberry tuna salad, 106
Cream; see also Sour cream
in breads, 161
Coeur à la Crème, 213
freezing whipped, 11, 12
Pots de Crème, 213
Cream cheese, French dressing with, 102
Cream sauces, 91
Crème Brulée, mock, 190
Creole fish, 79
Crêpes, chicken stuffed, 197
Crêpes, Maroth, 29
Croaker chowder, quick, 139
Crockery cooking, 13, 134
Croquettes, rice, 122
Cucumbers
cheesy slices, 199
lamb stew, Aruba style, 37–38
raw, with dip, 195
sandwiches, 154
stuffed, 87
Cumin seeds, 161
Currant yogurt, 188
Curry
chicken mousse, 55–56
chicken sandwiches, 153
lamb, cooked, 36

lamb, from scratch, 35–36
pork, 44
rice, cold, with peas, 120
soup, quick, 138
veal, 33
Custard, chicken, 54

D

Dairy foods
amounts to buy, 5
freezing, 11
Daisy ham, delicious, 44
Deep fried fish, 73–74
DESSERTS, 181–191, 212–215; *see also* Cakes, Pies
about, 181
ambrosia, mock, 185–186
apple brown Betty, 190–191
apples, stuffed, 185
Baba au Rhum, low-calorie, 214
cheese (Tvorozhniki), 188
cherries jubilee, quick, 213
chilled, 181–182
chocolate break poufs, 214–215
chocolate fondue, 215
chocolate ice cream, 182
chocolate soufflé, 214
coconut milk pudding, 189
Coeur à la Crème, 213
cooked, 188–191
Crème Brulée, mock, 190
dried fruit compote, 184
frozen, storage time for, 12
fruit, 183–186
fruit cup, low-calorie, 186
Indian pudding, 189–190
lemon melting moments, 213
meringue kisses, 190
meringue shells, 190
orange applesauce, 185
party, 212–215
peach whip, 181, 184
pears in red wine, 184
plum pudding, 212
poached fresh fruit, 184
Pots de Crème, 213
puddings, 188–189
raisin ice cream, 182
rhubarb, stewed, 185
rice puddings, 189
strawberry ice cream, 182
toasted almond parfait, 190

yogurt apple pancakes, 188
yogurt and fruit ice cream, 182
yogurt, homemade, 187–188
Deviled eggs
Risotto, 142
sandwiches, 154
in tomato aspic, 142
Deviled ham sandwiches, 152
Deviled lamb kidneys, 63–64
Diet foods. *See* Low-calorie recipes
Dill dip, 196
Dilled green bean salad, 84
Dill sauce for lamb, 38
Dill seeds, 161
Dips for canapés, 196
Divan, chicken, 54
Dolmas (stuffed grape leaves), 207–208
Doughnuts, 168
Dressing, salad, 100–104
about, 101–102
Aioli, 102
blue cheese, 102
French, with cream cheese, 102
French, oil and vinegar, 101
green goddess, 102
honey, for fruit salads, 102
horseradish, 104
Italian, 101
lime, 107
mayonnaise, 103
mayonnaise, Chantilly, for fruit salads, 102
mayonnaise, fresh, 101–102
mayonnaise, herb, 102
mayonnaise, orange, for fruit salads, 103
Russian, 102
sour cream, 103
Thousand Island, 103
yogurt-garlic, 103
Dressing, for goose, 57–58
Dried beans, about, 115–116
Dried fruits, 163, 184
Drinks, cold, 217–221
about, 216
apricot punch, 218
bridesmaid's bowl, 220
Crimson Pirate, 220
eggnog, 218
lime-tea punch, 217
Maywine, 219
Misch House Punch, 221
Poisoned Ivy, 220
Saké Mory, 220
sangria, 219

slim 'n trim, 217
Snowball, 221
W. C. T. U. Brew, 221
yogurt shake, 217–218
Drinks, hot; *see also* Coffees, after dinner
Farmer's Bishop, 219–220
hot apple cider nog, 218
mulled wine, 219
peppermint chocolate milk, 217
Wassail bowl, 218–219
Duckling, about, 47
Duckling, roast, 58

E

EGGS AND EGG DISHES, 140–148
about, 140
baked, Parmentier, 147
in breadmaking, 163
buying, 7, 140
en Cocotte with tuna, 147
deviled, Risotto, 142
deviled, in tomato aspic, 142
Foo Yong, 206
freezing, 11, 12
hard-boiled, Grimes Cove, 141
hard-boiled, ham and potato casserole, 141
hard-boiled, Hongrois, 142–143
omelets, 144–146
and parsley ring, 140–141
poached, and tongue salad, 109
quiches, 98, 141–142
salad, savory, 105
sandwiches, with bacon, 154
sandwiches, deviled, 154
scrambled, Marvin Gardens, 147
scrambled, Pipérade, 147
soufflés, 92, 94–95, 143–144
spinach Frittata, 146–147
substitutes for, 163
vegetable dinner, 98
Eggnog, 218
Eggplant
casserole, Woods Hole, 97
chicken and, 52–53
Moussaka, 208
Parmesan, 97–98
stuffed, Entrée, 97
Empanadas, 212
Espresso coffee, 216
European recipes, 208–210
beef blintzes, 209–210

Blanquette of chicken, 209
chicken and sausage in white wine, 208
Saucisson en Brioche, 210
Extracts, flavor, 163

F

FAR EAST AND POLYNESIAN RECIPES, 201–207
about, 199–200
bean curd soup, 201
beef fried rice, 204
beef shreds with onion, 206
Boula soup, 201
celery with mushrooms, 205
chicken, mushrooms and snow peas, 205
Chinese beef and onions, 201
Chinese cabbage, 204–205
Chinese fried rice, 204
Chinese spareribs, 206
Chow Mein, 204
Eggs Foo Yong, 206
fish filets Tempura, 202
fried shrimp with Chinese vegetables, 202–203
Hawaiian short ribs, 201
Indian Pilau, 207
Indian spiced spinach leaves, 207
Indonesian fried rice, 203
Rumaki, 203
scallops, stir-fried, 202
Tempura sauce, 202
vegetable mix, 205–206
Farmer's Bishop, 219–220
Fats, foods high in, 3
Fennel seeds, 161
FISH, 69–80
about, 69–71
Aioli sauce, 70
amounts to buy, 5, 69–70
baked, 77–79
Bonne Femme, 76
braised in soy sauce, 72–73
broiled, 74–75
with brown sauce, 76–77
Chinese style, sautéed, 72
and chips, 73
cod filets, baked, 77
cooking methods, 71–72, 73, 74, 75, 77
Creole, 79
deep fried, 73–74
Duglère, 76
filet Meunière, 72
filets tempura, 202

Florentine style, baked, 78
freezing, 8, 10, 12
fried, with garlic and herbs, 72
haddock filets, baked, 77
homestyle, broiled, 75
leftovers, 70, 80
Mexican parsleyed, 77
Norwegian fish balls, 76
Orly, 73–74
pan fried, 71–73
with paprika sauce, 76
poached, 75–77
Porgy à la Taj, 74
salmon steaks, broiled, 75
salmon steaks, sautéed, 73
sauces for, 70–71
sautéed, 71–73
scallops stir-fried, 202
sea bass filets, baked, 77
Serviche, 210
shellfish Jambolaya, 79
shrimp and crabmeat deluxe, 79
shrimp, fried, with Chinese vegetables, 202–203
stuffed tomatoes Neptune, 80
with tomatoes and sausage, 74
Viking style, baked, 78
whiting, baked stuffed, 78
Flank steak, broiled, 20
Flank steak, peppers and, 21
Flour, types of, 159–160
Fondue, cheese, 150–151
Fondue, chocolate, 215
Food groups, basic, 2–3
Fowl, about, 47
boiled, 55
glazed, 59
Frankfurters
beans and franks, 118
jubilee, with cabbage, 43
red and green casserole for a crowd, 43
Freezing
baked goods, 10–11
dairy products, 11
fish, 8–10
fruits, 8, 9
meats, 8, 10
poultry, 8, 10
vegetables, 7–8, 9
storage time for frozen foods, 12
tips, 11
French dressings, 101, 102

French fries, homemade, 89
Fried rice
beef, 204
Chinese, 204
Indonesian, 203–204
Fritters, carrot-potato, 86
Fritters, corn, 87
Frozen desserts, 181–182
Fruit
amounts to buy, 5
canning, 7
dried, for breadmaking, 163, 184
for flavoring bread, 163
freezing, 8, 9, 12
Fruitcake, easy Christmas, 173
FRUIT DESSERTS, 183–186
about, 183–184
ambrosia, mock, 185
apples, stuffed, 185
dried fruit compote, 184
fruit cup, low-calorie, 186
orange applesauce, 185
peach whip, freezer, 181
peach whip, low-calorie, 184
pears in red wine, 184
poached fresh fruit, 184
rhubarb, stewed, 185
Fruit ice cream, yogurt and, 182
FRUIT SALADS, 104–107
about, 104–105
apple-salmon, 107
cottage cheese and apple, 107
cottage cheese and fruit, 106
cranberry tuna, 106
fresh fruit salad luncheon, 105
ham and apple, 107
honey dressing for, 103
Hungarian, 107
mayonnaise Chantilly dressing, 102
orange-chicken, 105
orange mayonnaise, 103
Waldorf, 107
winter, with tangerines, 106
Fruit yogurt, 188

G

Game birds, about, 47
Garbanzo patties, 211–212
Garlic sauce, carrots in, 85
Garlic, spaghetti with, 129

Giblet gravy, 48–49
Giblets, goose, 57
Gingerbread cookies, Christmas, 174
Glazes for sweet breads, 167, 168
Goose
    about, 47
    dressing for, 57–58
    roast, 57
    Salmi of, made from leftovers, 58
Grains and meals, 160–161
Grapes, frosted, 105
Gratinées
    about, 92
    potatoes, 95
    pumpkin, 95
    scalloped vegetables, 95
Gravy, chicken giblet, 48–49
Greek and Near Eastern recipes, 207–208
    Dolmas, 207
    Kuru Kofte, 208
    Moussaka, 208
Green Goddess dressing, 102
Grits, 161
GROUND BEEF, 23–29
    about, 23–24
    beef loaf Wellington, 27–28
    cabbage à la Milan, 96
    chili con carne, 25, 116
    chopped beef loaf, 26
    Crêpes Maroth, 29
    Empanadas, 212
    ham rolls and, 24–25
    Hopping John, skillet, 25
    Kuru Kofte, 208
    meatballs and celery "noodles," 24
    meatball stew, 24
    meat loaf, applesauce, 27
    meat loaf, fancy, 26
    meat loaf, no-bake easy, 25
    meat loaf, party, 28
    meat loaf, pickle, 27
    meat loaf, pizza, 27
    meat loaf, skillet, 26
    Moussaka, 208
    spaghetti sauce, classic, 126
    stuffed cabbage, 95–96
    stuffed peppers, 28
Ground lamb loaf, 38
Ground veal loaf, 33
Grouse and sprouts, 58–59
Guacamole dip, 196
Gumbo, chicken, New Orleans, 56

H

Haddock filets, baked, 77
HAM
    about, 44
    apple salad, 107
    bean casserole, 117
    beef with, 21
    Canadian supper pie, 99
    casserole, with vegetables, 45
    creamed luncheon meat, 45
    delicious Daisy, 44
    egg and potato casserole, 141
    hocks, Creole-style soup, 136
    loaf, with applesauce, 155
    omelet, 146
    potato casserole, 44
    quiche, 141–142
    rolls, with ground beef, 24
    Russian salad, 109–110
    sandwiches, with apple, 153
    sandwiches, with cheese, 152
    sandwiches, with chutney, 152
    sandwiches, Croque Monsieur, 152
    sandwiches, Sebastian, 152
    veal shoulder stuffed with, 32
Hard sauce, 174
Hash, beef liver, 62
Hashed brown potatoes, 89
Hawaiian delight sauce, 104
Hawaiian short ribs, 201
Headcheese from leftover pork, 43
Heart, 67–68
    about, 67
    Chasseur, 68
    chicken-fried, 68
    steamed, 68
    stuffed, 67–68
Herbs
    bouquet, 18
    bread, with cottage cheese, 166
    in breadmaking, 164
    chicken thighs, lemony, 52
    mayonnaise, 102
    stuffed pork chops, 40–41
    yogurt sauce, 70–71
Hero sandwiches, 153
Honey
    in breadmaking, 161
    dressing for fruit salads, 103
    pumpkin pie, quick, 176
    yogurt, vanilla, 188

Hongrois, eggs, 142
Hopping John, skillet, 25
Hors d'Oeuvres. *See* Canapés
Horseradish dressing, 104
Hot dogs. *See* Frankfurters
Hungarian dip, 196
Hungarian salad, 107
Hunter's turkey, 56–57

I

Ice cream, freezer
    citrus sherbert, 182
    double chocolate, 182
    raisin, smooth, 182
    sauces for, 182–183
    strawberry, 182
    yogurt and fruit, 182
Icing, chocolate, quick, 173
Icing, thin, 174
Indian Pilau, 207
Indian pudding, 189–190
Indian spiced spinach leaves, 207
Indonesian fried rice, 203
Irish coffee, 217
Italian dressing, 101
Italian meringue canapés, 196

J

Jambalaya, shellfish, 79
Jellying, 11

K

Kidney bean soup, 135
Kidneys, 62–64
    about, 62–63
    lamb, with beef, 64
    lamb, deviled, 63–64
    sautéed, with mustard sauce, 63
    veal, with liver, in red wine, 63
Kuru Kofte, 208

L

Labels, food
    ground beef, 23–24
    nutrition information on, 1–3

LAMB AND MUTTON, 33–38
    about, 33–34
    breast, Pôt à Tout Faire, 35
    casserole, Gourmet, 34–35
    casserole, New Zealand style, 34
    chops, Reformé, 35
    chops, Risotto skillet, 36
    curry, of cooked lamb, 36
    curry, from scratch, 35–36
    cuts, basic, 34
    with dill, 38
    kidney, deviled, 63–64
    kidney, with mustard sauce, 63
    kidney, stew, with beef, 64
    loaf, 38
    Scotch broth, 138
    shanks, braised, 36–37
    shanks, in tomato sauce, 37
    stew, with cucumbers, Aruba style, 37–38
    strips with lima beans, Oriental style, 37
    yogurt marinade for, 34
Lard, 162
Lasagne
    and cheese casserole, 129
    and chicken casserole, 129
    Milanese, 129
Latin American recipes, 210–212
    bean stew (Sancocho de Frijoles), 211
    black bean soup, 210
    Empanadas, 212
    garbanzo patties, 211–212
    rice and beans, 211
    Serviche, 210–211
Leavenings in breadmaking, 162
Lecso, omelet (Hungarian), 146
Lemon
    carrots, 85–86
    chiffon cake, 172–173
    herbed chicken thighs, 52
    sauce, for veal, 33
    sugar glaze, 168
Lentil loaf, with cheese sauce, 119
Lentil soups, 135
Lima beans, lamb with, Oriental style, 37
Lime-tea punch, 217
Linguine and white clam sauce, 127
Liver, 60–62
    about, 60
    beef, baked, French style, 61
    beef, hash, 62
    beef, Italian style, 61–62
    beef, with kidneys in red wine, 63
    chicken, casserole, with rice, 61

chicken, chopped, 197–198
chicken, omelet, 146
with onion butter, 61
Pâté, Ardennais, 62
Reformé, 61
Lobster sauce, red, 71
London broil, 21
Low-calorie recipes
Baba au Rhum, 214
brownies, nutty chocolate, 174
drink, 217
fruit cup, 186
Italian meringue canapés, 196
orange sauce, 183
peach whip, 184–185
salads, 110–111
sandwiches, open-faced, 153
Thousand Island dressing, 103
Luncheon meat
Canadian supper pie, 99
creamed, 45
Vienna supper loaf, 155

M

Macaroni and cheese à la Bauserman, 127
Macaroni and cheese from scratch, 151
Main dishes, storage time for frozen, 12
Marinara sauce, 126
Marinated pork chops, 41
Marketing, 4–5
Mayonnaise
Chantilly, for fruit, 102
dressing, 103
fresh, 101–102
herb, 102
orange, for fruit, 103
Maywine, 219
Meat; *see also* Beef, Ground Beef, Ham, Lamb,
Pork, Variety Meats, Veal
buying, 5, 6, 17
freezing, 8, 10, 12
nutrients in, 2, 3
stretching, 17
Meatballs, 24
Meat loaf
applesauce, 27
chopped beef, 26
fancy, 26
lamb, 38
no-bake easy, 25–26
party, 28

pickle, 27
pizza, 27
plain, 26
skillet, 26
veal, 31, 32
Wellington, 27
Meringue canapés, Italian, 196
Meringue kisses, 190
Meringue shells, 190
Mexican parsleyed fish, 77
Microwave cooking, 13
Milk
in breadmaking, 161
buying, 7
freezing, 11, 12
peppermint chocolate, 217
Millet, 160
Minestrone Milanese, 138–139
Misch House Punch, 221
Molasses, in bread, 162
Moussaka, 208
Mousse, curried chicken, 55
Mushrooms
luncheon meat and, 45
omelet, 146
pickled, 198
stir-fried, with celery, 205
stir-fried, with chicken, 205
Mustard sauce, for kidneys, 63
Mutton, about, 34

N

Neapolitan tomato sauce, 128
Niçoise, Salade, 109
Noodle casserole, with chicken, 53–54
Noodle ring, zucchini in, 128–129
Norwegian fish balls in sauce, 76
Nutrition, basic facts of, 1–3
Nuts, in breadmaking, 163

O

Oatmeal, 160
Oats, rolled, 160
Oils, vegetable, 162
Okra, cornmeal with, Barbados style, 122
Olive Condite, chicken with, 49–50
Olive oil, 162
Omelets, 144–146
about, 144–145

bacon, 145
cheese, 145
chicken liver, 146
Chinese (Eggs Foo Yong), 206
collard green, 145–146
filled, 145
folded, 145
ham, 146
Lecso (Hungarian), 146
mushroom, 146
Nulljails, 146
onion, 146
pluperfect, 144–145
rolled, 145
spinach, 145–146
spinach, Frittata, 146–147
Onion
buns, professional, 164
butter, liver with, 61
chicken baked with, 53
creamed, canned, 84
creamed, fresh, 87–88
dip, 196
omelet, 146
quiche, 98
Orange
applesauce, 185
carrots, 86
-chicken fruit salad, 105
sauce, for ice cream, 183
yam-stuffed, 90
yogurt, 188
Oxtails in wine sauce, 22–23

P

Pancakes, yogurt apple (dessert), 188
Pan fried fish recipes, 71–73
Paprika sauce, for fish, 76
Paprika, veal, 30–31
Parfait, toasted almond, 190
Parsley, fried, 74
Parsley ring, with eggs, 140
Parsnip cakes, 88
Parsnips, fried sticks, 88
Pasta, 124–130; *see also* individual names
about, 124–126
cooking, 124–125
Pastry, beef loaf Wellington, 28
Pastry, dessert pie, 175
Pâté, liver, Ardennais, 62
Pâté Maison Marcel, 197

Peach pie, with apples, 175
Peach whip, 181, 184–185
Pears in red wine, 184
Peas
cold curried rice with, 120
creamed ham and, 45
snow peas, 205
soup, 135–136
Peppermint chocolate milk, 217
Peppers, green
and steak, 21
sticks, 195
stuffed, 28
stuffed with sausage, 42
Pheasant, 58
Pickle meat loaf, 27
Pies, 175–177
about, 175
apple-peach, 175–176
basic pie crust, 175
carrot, 176
pumpkin, 177
pumpkin, quick honey, 176
sour cherry, 176
sweet potato, 177
Pig's knuckles and cabbage, 41
Pilaf, rice, 120
Pilau
chicken and rice, 50
Indian, 207
turkey, 57
Pizza, homemade, 165–166
Pizza meat loaf, 27
Plum pudding, 212
Poached fish recipes, 75–77
Polenta, 122–123
Pollock filets, for Norwegian fish balls, 76
Polynesian recipes. *See* Far East and Polynesian
Recipes
Popover surprise, 156
Poppy seeds, 161
Porgy à la Taj, 74
PORK, 39–44; *see also* Frankfurters, Ham, Sausages
about, 39
basic cuts of, 40
chops, braised, 41
chops, herb-stuffed, 40–41
chops, marinated, 41
chops, roast, 40
curry, 44
headcheese from leftover pork, 43
Hungarian salad, 107
Oriental style, sliced, 41

Pâté Maison Marcel, 197
pig's knuckles and cabbage, 41
spareribs, barbecued, 42
spareribs, Chinese, 206
spareribs and sauerkraut, 42
with vegetable mix, Chinese, 205
Potatoes; *see also* Sweet potato
about, 84–85
au gratin, 95
casserole, with ham, 44
egg-crowned (Eggs Parmentier), 147–148
flour, 160
French fries, homemade, 89
fritters, with carrots, 86
hashed brown, 89
salad, 109
soups, 137
stuffed, 88
water, for breads, 161
Pots de Crème, 213
Poultry; *see also* Chicken, Duckling, Fowl, Goose,
Grouse, Turkey
about, 46–48
amounts to buy, 5
freezing, 8, 10, 12, 46–47
Pound cake, Georgia chocolate, 173
Preserving, 11
Pressure cooking, 13
Pretzels, soft, 165
Proteins, foods high in, 2–3
Puddings, dessert, 188–189
about, 188
coconut milk, 189
Indian, 189
plum, with sauce, 212
rice, 189
rice, Cousin Clara's, 189
Puddings, main course
American cheese, 151
corn, 94–95
Southern chicken, 49
Pumpkin
au gratin, 95
pie, 177
pie, quick honey, 176–177
tea bread, 171
Punch
apricot, 218
bridesmaid's bowl, 220
eggnog, 218
lime-tea, 217
Misch House, 221
mulled wine, 219

Wassail bowl, 218–219
W. C. T. U. brew, 221

Q

Quiche, ham, 141–142
Quiche, onion, 98
Quick breads, 170–171
about, 159
carrot cake, 171
chocolate coffee cake, 170–171
coconut apple cake, 171
pumpkin tea bread, 171

R

Radishes, raw, for canapés, 195
Raisin ice cream, 182
Rarebit
tomato bean, quick, 118
Welsh, 150
Raspberry sauce, for fruit dessert, 184
Raspberry yogurt, 188
Ratatouille, 99
Ravigote sauce, 104
Recommended Daily Allowances (RDA), 2, 3
Relish, canned beet, 83–84
Rhubarb, stewed, 185
RICE, 120–122; *see also* Fried rice, Risotto
and beans, Puerto Rican style, 211
casserole, with chicken, 121
casserole, with chicken livers, 61
casserole, with tuna, 121
chicken and, St. Lucia style, 50
cold curried, with peas, 120
croquettes, 122
flour, 160
green quick, 122
Pilaf, 120
puddings, 189
salad, 108–109
salad, hearty, 122
with tomatoes, 121
Rigatoni "Tutto Giardino," 126–127
Risotto
deviled eggs, 142
skillet, lamb chop, 36
with vegetables, 121–122
Roast beef
Charlene's chuck roast, 21

cooking, 18
in foil, 21
how to stretch, 17–18
leftover, Crépes Maroth, 29
leftover, German Beef Roulade, 23
Roast chicken, 48
Roast duckling, 58
Roast goose, 57
Rolls, cloverleaf, 165
Rolls, stuffed, 166
Rumaki, 203
Rum sauce, no calorie, 183
Russian dressing, 102
Russian salad, 109–110
Rye flour, 160, 170
Rye meal, 161

S

Saké, drinks with, 220–221
SALADS, 100–111; *see also* Dressing, salad; Fruit
    salads
    about, 100
    bean, 110
    Caesar, 110
    Chef's, 108
    chicken, 108
    Chiffonade, 111
    coleslaw with carrots, 111
    cottage cheese and vegetable, 110
    dilled canned green bean, 84
    egg, savory, 105
    everything, 108
    frozen cheese, for dieters, 111
    green, 110–111
    meat and fish, 108–109
    Niçoise, 109
    poached eggs and tongue, 109
    potato, 109
    red and green, 111
    rice, 108, 122
    Russian, 109–110
    three bean, 110
    vegetable, 110–111
Salmi of goose made from leftovers, 58
Salmon
    salad, with apples and lime dressing, 107
    steaks, broiled, 75
    steaks, sautéed, 73
Salt in breadmaking, 163
SANDWICHES, 151–155
    about, 151–152

apple and ham, 153
baked bean, 154
clam and cream cheese, 154
corned beef rolls, 153
Croque Madame, with chicken, 152
Croque Monsieur, with ham, 152
cucumber, 154
curried chicken, 153
deviled egg, 154
deviled ham, 152
egg and bacon, 154
freezing, 12, 151
ham and cheese on rye, 152
hero, 153
open-face, for dieters, 153
Sebastian, with ham, 152
tongue, 153
tuna and water chestnut, 154
Sangria, 219
SAUCES
    Aioli, for fish, 70
    Béchamel, 91
    for beef and corn casserole, 20
    brown, fish with, 76–77
    celery cream, 91
    cheese, 119
    cheese soufflé base, 143
    chili con carne, 116–117
    clam, white, 127
    cocktail, 104
    for Crêpes Maroth, 29
    dill, for lamb, 38
    for fish, 70–71
    green yogurt, for fish, 75
    hard, 174
    Hawaiian delight, 104
    herb yogurt, for fish, 70–71
    for ice cream, 182–183
    lemon, for veal, 33
    lobster, red, 71
    Marinara, for spaghetti, 126
    meat, for spaghetti, 126
    mustard, for kidneys, 63
    paprika, for fish, 76
    for pasta, about, 125–126
    for pizza, 166
    raspberry, 184
    Ravigote, 104
    Rémoulade, cold beef in, 23
    rum, no-calorie, 183
    sherry, for sweetbreads, 66
    Spanish, 140–141
    Tartare, 104

Tempera, 202
 tomato, Neapolitan, 128
 for vegetables, 91
 white, medium, 66
 yogurt marinade for lamb, 34
Saucisson en Brioche, 210
Sauerkraut, boiled beef with, 18
Sauerkraut, spareribs and, 42
Sausage
 chicken and, in white wine, 208
 fish and tomatoes with, 74
 peppers stuffed with, 42
 Saucisson en Brioche, 210
Sautéed fish recipes, 71–73
Scallops stir-fried, 202
Scotch broth, 138
Sea bass filets, baked, 77–78
Seafood. *See* Fish
Sea salt, 163
Sebastian sandwich, 152
Seeds used in baking, 161
Serviche, 210
Sesame oil, 162
Sesame seeds, 161
Shellfish. *See* Fish
Sherbet, citrus, 182
Sherry sauce, sweetbreads in, 66
Shortening for breadmaking, 162
Shrimp
 and crabmeat, 79–80
 fried, with Chinese vegetables, 202–203
 potted, 198
Snack foods, 155–156
 about, 155
 applesauce ham loaf, 155
 bacon and cheese toasts, 156
 popover surprise, 156
 surprise loaf, 156
 Swiss supper loaf, 155
 Vienna supper loaf, 155
Snow peas, with chicken, 205
Soufflés, 94–95, 143–144
 about, 92, 143
 basic cheese, 143–144
 beet, 94
 broccoli, 144
 chicken, 144
 chocolate, 214
 corn pudding, 94–95
 shrimp, 144
 spinach, 144
 vegetable, 94
 yam, 144

SOUP, 133–139
 about, 133–134
 bean curd, 201
 beef and barley, 134–135
 black bean, 210
 bouillon, 134
 Boula, 201
 cabbage, 138
 carrot-potato, 137
 cheese, 139
 clear-the-fridge, 136
 cream of celery, 137
 croaker chowder, quick, 139
 ham hock, Creole style, 136
 kidney bean, 135
 lentil, Italian style, 135
 lentil, use-it-all-up, 135
 Minestrone Milanese, 138–139
 potato, 137
 Scotch broth, 138
 split pea, 135–136
 vegetable base for, 133
 Vichyssoise, 136–137
Sour cherry pie, 176
Sour cream
 in breadmaking, 161
 chicken baked with, 51
 dressing, 103
 fish with, Russian style, 74
 veal and, 32
Sourdough, 163
 bread, 169–170
 starters, 169, 170
Soy extenders, 24
Soy flour, 160
Soy milk, 161
Spaghetti
 alla Carbonara, 126
 classic, in meat sauce, 126
 cooking, 125
 -dinner bread, 166
 with garlic, 129–130
 with Marinara sauce, 126
Spanish sauce, 140–141
Spareribs
 barbecued, 42
 Chinese, 206
 and sauerkraut, 42
Spices, ground, 164
Spinach
 Frittata, 146–147
 leaves, Indian spiced, 207
 omelet, 146–147

soufflé, 144
Split pea soup, 135–136
Squash, acorn, stuffed, 89
Steak. *See* Beef, Salmon
Stews
    bean, Dominican Republic style, 211
    beef, Carbonade Flamande, 18
    beef and kidney, 64
    beef in red wine, 20
    chicken, 55–56
    lamb and cucumber, Aruba style, 37–38
    meatball, 24
    turkey, 56
    veal, 30
Stir-frying, 199–200
Stock, all-purpose, 92–93
Stock, aspic, 92–93
Strawberry
    ice cream, 182
    rhubarb and, 185
    sauce for ice cream, 183
    tarts, 177
Stuffing for goose, 57–58
Sugar, confectioners', for glazing, 162
Sugar, raw, 162
Sugar, substitutes for, 162
Sugar syrups for freezing fruit, 8
Sunchokes, 195
Sunflower seeds, 161
Surprise loaf, 156
Sweetbreads, 64–67
    about, 64–65
    à la Maid of Honor, 67
    braised, 66
    in sherry sauce, 66
    Virginia, 66–67
Sweet potato cake, Haitian style, 213
Sweet potato pie, 177
Sweet potato puffs, 88
Swiss steak, braised, 20–21
Swiss supper loaf, 155
Syrups, for breadmaking, 162
Syrups, for freezing fruit, 8

T

Tartare sauce, 104
Tart, strawberry, 177
Tempura sauce, 202
Tetrazzini casserole, 127–128
Tetrazzini, chicken, 50–51
Textured vegetable protein, 24

Thousand Island dressing, 103
Tomatoes
    aspic, deviled eggs in, 142
    broiled, 90
    cherry or plum, 195
    fish and sausage with, 74–75
    in gelatin aspic, 93
    rarebit, with beans, 118
    rice with, 121
    sautéed, 90
    stuffed, Neptune, 80
Tongue
    Chef's Salad I, 108
    salad, with poached eggs, 109
    sandwiches, 153
Tuna
    casserole, with rice, 121
    eggs en Cocotte with, 147
    salad, with cranberries, 106
    sandwiches, with water chestnuts, 154
Turkey, 56–57
    about, 47
    apple-stuffed, 56
    casseroles, 48
    hash, St. Germain, 47
    Hunter's, 56–57
    leftovers, 47–48, 57
    pieces, 56–57
    Pilau of, 57
    stew, Dominican Republic style, 56
Turnips, mashed, 90
Tvorozhniki, 188

V

Vanilla honey yogurt, 188
Variety meats, 7, 60–68
    about, 60
    brains, 64–66
    heart, 67–68
    kidneys, 62–64
    liver, 60–62
    sweetbreads, 64–67
VEAL, 30–33
    about, 30
    breast, stuffed, 31
    casserole, with chicken, 33
    casserole, with vegetables, 32
    curry, 33
    kidney, about, 62–63
    kidney, with liver in red wine, 63
    kidney, with mustard sauce, 63

in lemon sauce, 33
loaf, in aspic, 31
loaf, with ground veal, 32
meat loaf, 32–33
paprika, 30–31
salad, Hungarian, 107
shoulder, stuffed with ham, 32
sour cream with, 32
stew, 30
VEGETABLES, 83–99, 115–119; *see also* individual
names
about, 83, 84–85, 115–116
amounts to buy, 5–6
aspics, 92–94
in breadmaking, 163
Canadian supper pie, 99
canned, recipes for, 83–84
canning fresh, 7–8
casseroles, 95–99
dried, 115–119
egg dinner with, 98
freezing, 7–8, 9, 12
fresh, about, 84–85
fresh, recipes for, 85–90
gratinées, 92, 95
jellied raw, 93–94
leftover, 84
main one-dish dinner recipes, 92–99
Ratatouille, 99
raw, as canapé, with dip, 195
Risotto with, 121–122
salads, 110–111
sauces for, 91
scalloped, au Gratin, 95
soup base, 133
soufflés, 94–95
Vichyssoise, 136–137
Vienna supper loaf, 155
Vinaigrette, brains, 65
Vitamins, 2–3

W

Waldorf salad, 107
Wassail bowl, 218–219
Welsh rarebit, 150

Wheat
berries, 160
bread, basic, 168–169
cracked, 161
flour, 159–160
germ, 160–161
whole, 160
White sauce, medium, 66
Whiting, baked stuffed, 78
Whole wheat flour, 160
Wine, drinks with
bridesmaid's bowl, 220
Maywine, 219
mulled wine, 218
sangria, 219
Snowball, 221
Wassail bowl, 218–219
Wine, recipes with
beef in red wine, 20
chicken and sausage in white wine, 208–209
liver and kidneys in red wine, 63
oxtails in wine sauce, 22–23
pears in red wine, 184
Woks, about, 199–200

Y

Yam soufflé, 144
Yam-stuffed oranges, 90
Yeast, in breadmaking, 162
Yeast, Brewer's, 163
Yogurt, 187–188
about, 187
apple pancakes, 188
homemade, 187–188
ice cream, with fruit, 182
marinade for lamb, 34
salad dressing, with garlic, 103
sauces, 70–71, 75
shake, 217–218

Z

Zucchini in noodle ring, 128